D1623853

(Continued from front flap)
one another and to the theory of social behaviorism as a whole. The essays, many of which were written expressly for this volume, include these valuable contributions to social behavioristic thought: the fullest available summary and critical review of the ideal type; a highly critical essay on Talcott Parsons, tracing the basic shift in his thinking from social behaviorism to macrofunctionalism; the only complete review available of the theory of the city; an absorbing comparative study of national character, with particular reference to Germans and Americans; essays on the sociology of culture that outline a complete social behavioristic approach to the sociology of art; and a pioneering study of social disorganization that redraws the distinction between normative and empirical social theory, while illustrating the value of separating the problems of pure and applied sociology.

Written in the individualistic tradition that has inspired some of the greatest social theorists from Tarde and Giddings to Weber and Veblen, this work is a stimulating challenge to use the insights of social behaviorism to broaden our understanding of society.

About the Author
Don Martindale is Professor of Sociology at the University of Minnesota. His many published works include *American Social Structure*, *American Society*, *The Nature and Types of Sociological Theory*, and *Social Life and Cultural Change*. In addition, he is co-translator and co-editor of four of Max Weber's leading works.

COMMUNITY, CHARACTER
and CIVILIZATION

DON MARTINDALE

COMMUNITY,
CHARACTER
AND CIVILIZATION

STUDIES IN SOCIAL BEHAVIORISM

ST. JOSEPH SEMINARY COLLEGE
LIBRARY

THE FREE PRESS OF GLENCOE
Collier-Macmillan Limited, London

COPYRIGHT © 1963 BY THE FREE PRESS OF GLENCOE
A DIVISION OF THE MACMILLAN COMPANY

PRINTED IN THE UNITED STATES OF AMERICA

All rights in this book are reserved. No part of this book may
be used or reproduced in any manner whatsoever without written
permission except in the case of brief quotations embodied in
critical articles and reviews.

For information, address:
The Free Press of Glencoe
A Division of The Macmillan Company
The Crowell-Collier Publishing Company
60 Fifth Avenue, New York 11

Designed by SIDNEY SOLOMON

Library of Congress Catalog Card Number: 63–13540

Collier-Macmillan Canada, Ltd., Toronto, Ontario

for Louise P. Olsen

PREFACE

The present essays, some of which have never before been published, were written during the period from 1947 to 1962. They represent, thus, a sampling of a development of ideas over a period of fifteen years. The point of view central to them I have come to designate as Social Behaviorism, though it is present in the earlier essay more by implication than by self-conscious intention. My shift toward this position had already begun while I was a graduate student in the Department of Sociology at the University of Wisconsin. In those days I could never feel at ease with the curious combination of Positivistic Organicism and Formalism which was then being presented for the solution of all sociological problems.

In contrast to those views, which seemed to create more problems than solutions, the writings of George Herbert Mead and Charles H. Cooley, of Gabriel Tarde and F. Stuart Chapin, and above all, of John R. Commons, Thorstein Veblen, and the incomparable Max Weber, all of which I had begun to examine at this time, provided a flexible body of ideas which permitted one to include individuals and large-scale social structures in a single perspective. However, at the time I was not at all convinced that these various thinkers represented parallel explorations of the same general category. This became clear only in retrospect and on the basis of further analysis.

To pretend that the present collection of studies represents a fully developed form of Social Behaviorism, which was from the beginning complete and unified, would be to distort the facts most radically. The studies are a record of the attempt not only to understand various areas of social life but also to achieve clarification of ideas in the process.

For this reason the impulse to revise the essays for the present publication has been resisted. It would not be difficult to eliminate the evidences of change of tactics and repair the breaks and discontinuities that occur in the ideas contained in the essays, but this would be to impose a unity upon them that they did not possess in the first instance. As they stand, they are a record of change and, I hope, of growth. To impose an artificial unity upon them now, by neat additions and deletions from the standpoint of the present, would seem to me, somewhat, as a kind of rewriting of history in the manner of Winston Smith for the Ministry of Truth in Orwell's *1984*.

The previously published essays, in the order of their appearance in this volume, are "Sociological Theory and the Ideal Type" in *Symposium on Sociological Theory* edited by Llewellyn Gross (New York: Harper & Row, 1959), pp. 57–91; "Talcott Parsons' Theoretical Metamorphosis from Social Behaviorism to Macrofunctionalism" in *The Alpha Kappa Deltan*, Volume XXIX, Winter, 1959, Number 1, pp. 38–46; "The Variety of the Human Family" in *Family, Marriage, and Parenthood* edited by Howard Becker and Reuben Hill, copyright © 1955, (Boston: D. C. Heath & Co., 1955), pp. 50–83; "The Theory of the City," Preface to Max Weber, *The City*, translated and edited by Don Martindale and Gertrud Neuwirth (New York: The Free Press of Glencoe, 1958), pp. 9–62, and W. Heinemann Ltd., London; "Max Weber's Sociology of Music" with Johannes Riedel, Introduction to Max Weber, *The Rational and Social Foundations of Music*, translated and edited by Don Martindale, Johannes Riedel, and Gertrud Neuwirth, copyright © 1958, (Carbondale: Southern Illinois University Press, 1958), pp. xi–lii; "Sociology and Aesthetics" in *Arts in Society* (Madison, Wisconsin, University of Wisconsin Extension Division, Winter Issue, January, 1958), pp. 53–68; and "Social Disorganization: The Conflict of Normative and Empirical Approaches" in *Modern Sociological Theory*, edited by Howard Becker and Alvin Boskoff (New York: Holt, Rinehart and Winston, 1957), pp. 340–367.

The idea for the present volume of essays came from various students and friends who have, from time to time, urged that a collection be made. Credit for the present project must be given to Alex Simirenko of the University of Nevada who supplied the outline of the various publications, explored the possibility of such a volume with the publisher, and gave unstintingly of his time and energy in carrying through the editorial work.

Other students in the field of sociology who have urged the publication of such a collection and to whom thanks are due for their interest and encouragement include Ronald Althouse, Noel Iverson, Balwant Nevaskar, Robert Stebbins, Thomas Philbrook, Roger Krohn, Warren Hagstrom, Alvin Boderman, Perry Jacobson, C. Dale Johnson, Leonard Weller, Mary Adams, Santosh Nandy and Nicos Mouratides. Few men have been so fortunate in possessing such a rich circle of able students and colleagues. In their imagination, their wit, their love of letters, the intellectual life runs fresh as a mountain stream, sometimes racing over the rapids and leaping over sunlit waterfalls, sometimes plunging into deep pools, only to emerge and go gaily on once again. Surely I am justified in anticipating great things from them in the future.

For her work on the manuscripts in all their various stages, I am deeply obligated to Edith Martindale. And finally, I am indebted to Louise P. Olsen for her conscientious labor not only on this project but also on many previous ones. It is in appreciation of an honest critic and a good friend that the volume is dedicated to her.

DON MARTINDALE

CONTENTS

PART FIVE *Studies in the Sociology of Culture*

PART SIX *Pure and Applied Sociology*

PART ONE

INTRODUCTION

1

SOCIAL BEHAVIORISM:

ITS NATURE

AND PLACE

IN SOCIOLOGICAL

THEORY

MAN IS NOT BORN SOCIAL; HE IS MADE social by members of the society in which he is reared. At a fairly early age he ordinarily becomes an eager participant in the process of creating a self acceptable to his associates. In the beginning the human individual is socially nothing *in fact*, but almost anything *in potential*. In endlessly varied ways the individual is committed to his times. Walter Bagehot formulates this as follows:

"Men are formed, indeed, on no ideal type. Human nature has tendencies too various and circumstances too complex. All men's characters have sides and aspects not to be comprehended in a single definition." Training and what he calls in the present work the "cake of custom" solidify this flexibility: "Take the soft mind of the boy and (strong and exceptional aptitudes excepted) you make him merchant, barrister, butcher, baker, surgeon, or apothecary. But once make him an apothecary and he will never afterwards bake wholesome bread; and make him a butcher, and he will kill too extensively even for a surgeon. . . ." From this pleasant exaggeration Bagehot argues that just as acquired habit makes the professional man, so it makes the sober citizen of a particular state. Upon this miracle rest the stability and the comfort of good government; gently drilled by habit, everybody knows what to do and, as we say, "behaves."[1]

From the commitment of human plasticity in relatively inelastic forms, Bagehot draws various ironic conclusions concerning social stability in the face of the potential of the human individual for variation. The source of the English government's strength is attributed to the stupidity of the population, including the majority of the people elected to the House of Commons. The resigned lethargy of the majority under the pressure of custom permits a few thinking individuals to direct the course of the " 'best' English people" who "keep their minds in a state of decorous dullness."

"If everybody does what he thinks is right," says Bagehot, "there will be 657 amendments to every motion, and none of them will be carried or the motion either." The irrelevant feelings of party interest must be aroused and used to push forward the real and complex enterprises of state. "There never was an election without a party. You cannot get a child into an asylum without a combination. At such places you see, Vote for Orphan A upon a placard and Vote for Orphan B (also an Idiot!!!) upon a banner, and the party of each is busy about its placard and banner."[2]

The colleges and universities, in Bagehot's opinion, are museums of archaic knowledge and taste.

The academies are asylums of the ideas and tastes of the last age. "By the time," I have heard a most eminent man of science observe, "by the time a man of science attains eminence on any subject, he becomes a nuisance upon it, because he is sure to retain errors which were in vogue when he was young, but which the new race have refuted." These are the sorts of ideas which find their home in academies, and out of their dignified windows pooh-pooh new things.[3]

Hence, our colleges and universities are largely sealed off from the explosive force of new ideas.

In these formulations Bagehot manages to state with special poignancy the fundamental problems of sociology. A social order persists in the face of the plasticity of individuals who are quite able to transform it. Unless we are willing to attribute the condition of the social order to "historical accident"—which is to circumvent scientific explanation —a task for sociology has been posed: to account for the rise of society in the first place. Moreover, even if we avoid the problem of origins, we still must deal with the question of social change and either invoke "historical accident" to explain how societies change or look for scientific explanations of the factors involved.

These are the ultimate problems of sociology: how social forms and structures are established and transformed, how they operate, and how they maintain their continuities.

PRE-SCIENTIFIC
EXPLANATIONS
OF SOCIETY

If it is true that a social order merely represents a complex of collective habits (Bagehot's "cake of custom") which must be learned and maintained from case to case, this would apply as well to societies other than our own. The collective habits of pre-modern societies were also subject to disruption, and just as there are an alert and vigilant few ready to innovate in the present, there were innovators in the past.

All societies have had some persons who attempted to understand and consciously account for the scheme of social life. The attempt to account for society scientifically has become a general phenomenon only in the last hundred years or so. In pre-scientific societies the key intellectuals accounted for social phenomena as best they could in the terms available to them, which placed their social thought in non-scientific contexts.

Even in pre-literate society, Paul Radin maintains, "there exists the same distribution of temperament and ability as among us." And while "thinkers . . . are not, and can not be, isolated from life among primitive peoples in the same way as this has repeatedly been done among us," like modern intellectuals they have attempted to account for their own culture.[4] The primitive thinker, Radin believes, is pre-eminently a practical man who does not ask for rain from a cloudless sky during the dry season nor for security against capsizing in a canoe when setting out during a storm. The religions and magical formulas that seem all important to external spectators are simply aids to the attainment of his goals. For example, a war party among the Winnebago Indians is organized as follows.

In a dream communication from the spirits he [the leader of the party] ascertains the necessary number of moccasins and the necessary amounts of food to be consumed on the expedition; he is told how many men he is to take along and how many of the enemy he is to kill. His divine certificate is then closely scrutinized by experienced elders and if it is accepted, then in the ceremony preparatory to his actually starting out he pre-visions his enemy. He destroys his courage, deprives him of his power of running, paralyzes his actions, and blunts his weapons. Thus protected and his enemy correspondingly weakened and constrained, he proceeds to the attack.[5]

Much of the primitive's knowledge of his social reality and his explanation of it comes to form the core of his mythology.

Social reality is to him something unique and definitely distinct from the individual and no more emanates from him than does the external world. It is coexistent with the individual, both constraining and in its turn being constrained by him.[6]

Working principles of behavior from the primitive's conception of his social world are formulated in his proverbial lore. This may be illustrated by some Maori proverbs.

1. Though the grub may be a little thing, it can cause the big tree to fall.
2. A spear shaft may be parried, but not a shaft of speech.
3. The weaving of a garment may be traced, but the thoughts of man cannot.
4. Son up and doing, prosperous man; son sitting, hungry man.
5. Did you come from the village of the liar?
6. The offspring of rashness die easily.
7. The women shall be as a cliff for the men to flee over.
8. Great is the majority of the dead.
9. The home is permanent, the man flits.
10. Outwardly eating together; inwardly tearing to pieces.
14. Well done, the hand that roots up weeds!
15. A chief dies; another takes his place.
26. Great is your going forth to war, small your return.[7]

Proverbs such as these, Radin argues, indicate that one cannot reduce the primitive's view of life to some group activity vaguely in accord with the folkways. The proverbs illustrate "the personal envisaging of life by those individuals who in any group are concerned with and interested in formulating their attitude toward God, toward man, and toward society."[8]

The sage among the elders and the medicine man or wizard formulate the primitive people's views of society and transmit them in the form of myths on the one hand and working formulas or proverbs on the other. In more complex societies, where specialized religious institutions have arisen, the task of accounting for the society in which these institutions operate has fallen to the priests who have emerged as dominant intellectuals. St. Augustine's *City of God* may illustrate the priestly interpretation of society.

One of the predominant facts of the Western world in the first centuries of our era was the decline of the Roman world's civic society. As it slowly crumbled into ruins, despite all efforts to stay the process, there was an upsurge of oriental religions. Among them, Christianity arose to such a preponderant position that Constantine eventually reversed the imperial policy of sporadic persecution of the Christian sects and made Christianity the official faith of Rome. It seemed to the Emperor that Christianity was what the state itself most needed. For this religion was one of the few institutions thriving in a declining world.

However, it was evident to intelligent Christians and pagans alike that the decay of the Roman social system could not be halted. Eventually, after eleven hundred years of supremacy, Rome itself was taken and sacked by Alaric the Goth in A.D. 410. This was a shock to Christian and pagan alike.

St. Augustine, who was a participant in the decline of Rome and the rise of Christianity, conceptually separated the fortunes of these two configurations which Constantine had joined.

There is a city of God, and its Founder has inspired us with a love which makes us covet its citizenship. To this founder of the holy city the citizens of the earthly city prefer their own gods.[9]

The pursuit of false gods by members of the earthly city is only a continuation of the process, with roots in the beginning of the world, which leads step by step to destruction of earthly things. The decline of the secular world is accepted as a fact and woven into St. Augustine's explanations.

The past of mankind and its future, spiritual and secular, all are brought together into a single formulation by St. Augustine in his "endeavour to treat of the origin, and progress and deserved destinies of the two cities (the earthly and heavenly, to wit), which, as we said, are in this present world commingled, and as it were, entangled together." [10] The foundation of these two cities, St. Augustine argued, was originally laid in differences that arose among the angels.

God . . . created the universal cosmos, created all the animals, souls as well as bodies. Among the terrestrial animals man was made by Him in His own image and . . . was made one individual, though he was not left solitary. For there is nothing so social by nature, so unsocial by its corruption, as this race. And human nature has nothing more appropriate, either for the prevention of discord, or for the healing of it, where it exists, than the remembrance of that first parent of us all, whom God was pleased to create alone, that all men might be derived from one.[11]

However, God did not make man so much like the angels that even though they sinned they could not die. Rather, he created them with a conditional immortality, "that if they discharged the obligations of obedience, an angelic immortality and a blessed eternity might ensue, without intervention of death; but if they disobeyed, death should be visited on them with just sentence."[12] Hence, when Adam in his sin forsook God, his falling away from God was the first death of the soul. Adam's fate was visited on his descendants, however, with the further condition that "those men who have been embraced by God's grace, and are become the fellow-citizens of the holy angels . . . shall never more either sin or die."[13]

In this manner, St. Augustine separated the affairs of Rome and Christianity and transformed the decay evident in the secular world of the time into a significant confirmation of the faith. Simultaneously, he held out the promise of that faith to everyone in reaction against the decay of the civic society of the time. Above all, within the framework of this philosophy of history St. Augustine integrated a major part of the thought and experience of his time; indeed, his philosophy of history was so skillfully adapted to the needs of his period that it dominated Western Christian thought for nearly a thousand years.

Wherever a pre-scientific society arose which permitted the appearance of secular intellectuals, such as the philosophers of the Greek city-states, it was these secular intellectuals who attempted to account for the society. The degree to which the concept of society may be cast into rational, unified form by pre-scientific secular intellectuals is revealed in Plato's *Republic*.

The inquiry opens with a systematic examination of the problem of justice, broadening gradually into a general examination of society.

A State . . . arises, as I conceive, out of the needs of mankind; no one is self-sufficing, but all of us have many wants. Can any other origin of a State be imagined?

There can be no other.

Then, as we have many wants, and many persons are needed to supply them . . . the body of inhabitants is termed a State.[14]

In its most primitive form, Plato argues, the state will consist at least of a variety of artisans and husbandmen producing the material necessities of life.

Let us consider, first of all, what will be their way of life, now . . . will they not produce corn, and wine, and clothes and shoes, and build houses for themselves? . . . And they will take care that their families do not exceed their means; having an eye to poverty and war.[15]

However, Plato urges that many persons will not be satisfied with the simpler way of life, but will want luxuries of many kinds.

Now will the city have to fill and well with a multitude of callings which are not required by any natural want; such as the whole tribe of hunters and actors; another will be the votaries of music—poets and their attendant train of rhapsodists, players, dancers, contractors.[16]

The country which was large enough to supply a small original population becomes too small. The state seeks to enlarge itself by engaging in war. The soldier appears. And with the increased complication of social structure more talent and training are required of the guardians.

The higher the duties of the guardian . . . the more time, and skill, and art, and application will be needed by him. . . . And the selection will be no easy matter.[17]

Under such conditions, guardians must unite the opposite qualities of gentleness and spirit.

From this base Plato systematically developed his personal utopian view of society. Education should be divided into gymnastics and music, for body and soul respectively. A careful censorship should be maintained over poets and writers of fiction (Homer and Hesiod, for example, would be banned from Plato's utopia because of their bad effect on the youth). Different schemes of education should be developed for ordinary citizens, for warriors, and for guardians. Social myths of the intrinsic differences between these social strata should be perpetuated. A condition of property and sexual communism should be created, though selective breeding by some device should be practiced.

The best of either sex should be united with the best as often, and the inferior with the inferior, as seldom as possible; and that they should rear the offspring of the one sort of union, but not of the other, if the flock is to be maintained. . . .
We shall have to invent some ingenious kind of lots [which grant access to sexual privileges] which the less worthy may draw on each occasion of our bringing them together, and then they will accurse their own ill luck and not the rulers.
And I think that our braver and better youth, besides their other honours and rewards, might have greater facilities of intercourse with women given them; their bravery will be a reason, and such fathers ought to have as many sons as possible.[18]

It is a misrepresentation of the social thought of pre-scientific societies to think of it, as is often done, as ineffective or inaccurate.

The large part of it is indeed accurate and effective, though often limited to the particular society. However, this is only part of the story. The myths and aphorisms of a Winnebago medicine man, the theoretical arguments of a St. Augustine, and the philosophy of a Plato were intended not only to explain their respective social orders but also to defend particular social arrangements within them. The Winnebago medicine man upheld the traditional order; St. Augustine was a spokesman for rising Christendom; Plato was a spokesman for aristocratic strata which had been displaced by the rise of radical democracy in Athens. Thus, their formulations had a propagandistic intent which has no place in a rigidly constructed scientific theory of society.

Even though the rise of a scientific theory of society carried with it the obligation to eliminate ideological objectives, early sociological formulations were drenched with ideological motives of their own. In the opinion of some scholars, this is still true.

> I . . . wish to stress the idea that although sociology has many potential uses and has been enlisted in support of various political faiths, it is by the nature of its key concepts and approaches intrinsically oriented toward the group rather than the individual, toward the herd rather than the lone stray. In connection with this emphasis, sociology stresses the notions of order, of collectivity, of social organization, irrespective of political labels such as "Left" or "Right." Thus sociology has an anti-liberal twist, and may even be considered as a critique of the traditional liberal ideal of individualism.[19]

It may be going rather too far to discern in mere employment of such concepts as "order," "collectivity," and "social organization" an "anti-liberal twist." If it were true, sociology would have a built-in ideological bias removing it as far from science as the mythology of the Winnebago Indian medicine man, the theology of St. Augustine, or the philosophy of Plato.

Although it is possible that some contemporary sociologists maintain a position as unpurified of ideological elements as the social lore of the Winnebago Indian medicine man, the primary objective of scientific sociology is to eliminate all forms of value bias from its formulations and to subject its hypotheses to rigorous scientific tests. One of the primary ways by which sociology distinguishes itself from pre-scientific explanations of society is its self-imposed task of purging non-scientific elements from its formulations. So far as the discipline of a scientific sociology succeeds, however, it may develop difficulties quite different from those of pre-scientific forms of social thought.

In the effort to subject their formulations to empirical test, scientists seek as much as possible to break them down into units verifiable under laboratory conditions. The difficulty that emerges is not the presence of bias in its concepts and findings.

Even to-day the sciences continue to achieve the most extraordinary results. The exact sciences, the natural sciences, have entered upon a phase of stimulating and rapid advance in respect of their fundamental notions and their empirical results. . . . In the mental and moral sciences, a vision that keeps close to the facts has become microscopically keen. There has come into being an unprecedented abundance of documents and monuments.[20]

The difficulty that may arise for the scientific approach to society lies not in its inexactness but in its loss of a total perspective of the whole as it becomes focused on particulars.

Owing to the vastness of the acquisitions of science and to the refinement and multiplication of its methods, there has been a steady increase in the preliminary knowledge demanded of those who belong to each successive generation, before they become able to collaborate in scientific work.[21]

A situation may arise in which even at the level of its detailed researches the loss of general perspective eliminates the lines between the significant and the insignificant.

Not science *per se*, but man in the realm of science, is in a crucial position. . . . There has arisen a sort of scientific plebeianism. People who wish to plume themselves as investigators draw empty analogies; they record any sort of data, make enumerations, pen descriptions, and tell us they are contributing to empirical science.[22]

There results such an endless multiplication of tiny research perspectives that even in a single science a decreasing number of persons have perspective on the whole.

C. Wright Mills was in part reacting to this problem when he turned his vigorous rhetoric against the tradition he described as "abstracted empiricism" in contemporary sociology. Contemporary sociology, he believed, tends to retreat either into ambiguously formulated concepts or into equally barren methodological preoccupations. Each is remote from social reality: "the methodological inhibition stands parallel to the fetishism of the concept."[23] This tends to "confuse whatever is to be studied with the set of methods suggested for its study."[24] For much of the resultant findings, "the thinness of the result is matched only by the elaboration of the methods and the care employed."[25]

Those in the grip of the methodological inhibition often refuse to say anything about modern society unless it has been through the fine little mill of The Statistical Ritual.[26]

There is little doubt that Mills' indictment against much of the industrious "busy-work" of contemporary sociology was well taken. Jaspers would have it that this is one inevitable product of specialization. However, Mills was not making a case for a scientific sociology. Quite the contrary, he felt that a scientific sociology was not possible. "Early social theorists tried to formulate invariant laws of society. . . . There is, I believe, no 'law' stated by any social scientist that is transhistorical, that must not be understood as having to do with the specific structure of some period. Other 'laws' turns out to be empty abstractions or quite confused tautologies."[27] It is evident that the consequences of specialization led Mills to reject the very possibility of social science itself.

In one respect the rise of a scientific analysis of society was inevitable. It was preceded by the rise of science to the dominant position in the intellectual life of Western man, and the dominant intellectuals of every age have taken up the explanation of their societies. In the nineteenth century the scientists had their chance. However, the scientific analysis of society faces a dilemma peculiar to it. So far as it maintains itself on a strictly positivistic level, it tends to reduce its problems to forms susceptible to rigorous quantitative and even laboratory manipulation. When this happens, Jaspers' criticism and, in part, that of C. Wright Mills are quite appropriate. The individual social scientist has a built-in mechanism which tends to make him lose perspective of the whole of his society. The loss of a sense of place for one's specialty within the whole has serious results, for it may lead to the failure to discriminate the trivial from the significant. The comprehension of one's society may be lost in a flood of irrelevant or semi-relevant detail—all carefully coded, tabulated, and presented in neat statistical tables. *The ironic end result is that there are many (of course not all) scientific students of contemporary society whose comprehension of our society is less realistic than that of Winnebago society by one of its medicine men.*

The highly critical reaction of some students to this tendency of the social sciences to become mired in irrelevant particulars is understandable if not completely excusable. It leads them (as it did Bramson and C. Wright Mills) to the view that whenever social science turns attention to the larger picture, it inevitably becomes ideological. From here, it is only a step to sociology becoming ethics or politics.

Social scientists' awareness of this dilemma—trapped between a detailed exactness and triviality on the one hand and a sweeping but non-scientific attempt at significant evaluations of the social order as a whole on the other—has led many to seek the salvation of sociology in "theories of the middle range." Merton, for example:

> The early history of sociology—as represented, for example, in the specula-tions of a Comte or a Spencer, a Hobhouse or a Ratzenhofer—is far from cumulative. . . . They typically laid out . . . alternative and competing conceptions rather than consolidated . . . accumulative product. . . . They were grand achievements for their day, but that day is not ours. . . . Throughout I attempt to focus attention on what might be called *theories of the middle range:* theories intermediate to the minor working hypotheses evolved in abundance during the day-to-day routines of research, and the all-inclusive speculations comprising a master conceptual scheme from which it is hoped to derive a very large number of empirically observed uni-formities of social behavior.[28]

Though this sounds like a most attractive compromise formula, it rests on an inexactly delineated configuration. The alternative which faces the theoretically inclined social scientist is not (despite Mills) simply the choice between grand, but empty, concepts and trivial factual studies. Moreover, Merton's formulations seem to imply that if a theory is general, it is necessarily empty. Other things being equal, the more comprehensive a theory, the better. Only when the detailed research is guided by more comprehensive, *genuinely empirical* hy-potheses can one hope to avoid social-science busy-work.

The real difficulty of sociology has arisen from the fact that many of the conceptualizations of more comprehensive social processes have been, in fact, ideologies rather than scientific hypotheses. The difficulty with grand theory was not generality but *value bias.* The answer to the false alternatives of large-scale ideologies *versus* grass roots fact-finding is not some sort of middle-range formula which is half of each, but the development of the highest powered empirical theories (most general and abstract) of which the science is capable. This is the theoretical task of a scientific discipline, whether it be in social or in physical science. The objections to the theories of Talcott Parsons, for example, either because they represent a "fetishism of the Concept" or because they are large-scale rather than middle-range, have no particular value. Parsons' theories are objectionable scientifically only if they are non-empirical or if they have less explanatory power than various alternatives to them. The more general a theory is, the more facts it should be able to explain.

THE TYPES OF SOCIOLOGICAL THEORY

The tendency for much of the enterprise performed in the name of Sociology to be pressed either toward ideological formulas for ethical and political strategies or toward blind empiricism, has resulted in a myth widespread among contemporary sociologists that sociology has been directionless and nonaccumulative. Unfortunately this myth has been repeated by a person of no less stature than Merton. In the same context as his previous citation, he states:

> We sociologists of to-day may only be intellectual pigmies but, unlike the overly-modest Newton, we are not pigmies standing on the shoulders of giants. The accumulative tradition is still so slight that the shoulders of the giants of sociological science do not provide a very solid base on which to stand. Whitehead's apothegm, affixed to the masthead of this introduction, is therefore all the more binding on sociology than on those physical sciences which have a larger measure of selectively accumulative advance: "a science which hesitates to forget its founders is lost."[29]

This myth appeases the conscience of all those who find it inconvenient to acquaint themselves with the richly varied, accumulated work which has marked the hundred years or so of sociology's existence. These traditions, which have been traced in some detail elsewhere,[30] present a different picture—one of continual and irreversible accumulation. Moreover, thanks in considerable measure to the foresight and initiative of The Free Press, a remarkable number of the classical works in sociology are currently in print and actively in use for both teaching and research purposes. This suggests a quite different conclusion than that early sociological work lacks significance for present-day sociology.

At least five major types of general sociological theory have been developed during the history of sociology. Contrary to the myth, accumulativeness may be seen not only within each type, but in sociology as a whole. Each of the five basic schools of thought arose in the first place partially because of ideological influences from the surrounding world. However, they were not abandoned for this reason, but because sociological theories developed from any one of them did not seem to account adequately for important features of social life. To understand the various schools of sociological theory simply as mutually exclusive alternatives is a distortion. To a considerable degree they supplemented one another in the exploration of various dimensions of social life. Furthermore, there has been no major school of sociological theory which has not permanently contributed to the growth of the field as a whole. Successively new areas have been added to the study of sociology.

A sociological theory consists of a set of systematic arguments intended to explain social life. When these are analyzed, some propositions will be found to be more basic than others. Those propositions which are not themselves further analyzable, but which form the foundation for other statements derived from them are the underlying assumptions (*basic hypotheses*) of the theory. Various generalizations about the nature, forms, and changes in items of social life which are logically deducible from the basic hypotheses are the *derived hypotheses* of the theory.

The first school of sociological theory to arise was powerfully shaped by ideological influences radiating from the surrounding social world in which the early sociologists operated. By the seventeenth and eighteenth centuries, the scientific approach had become established as Western man's characteristic method. Toward the end of the eighteenth century a powerful set of economic and political changes ushered in the modern world: the industrial revolution, the system of *laissez-faire* capitalism, and the modern democratic state.

It was inevitable under these circumstances that intelligent men in the nineteenth century should press science to the task not only of explaining the social changes which had taken place, but also of consolidating the world which had been established by the economic and political revolutions of the previous century. Appeals to the emerging scientific modes of thought for social purposes had already occasionally been made in the previous centuries. However, these appeals had been in the interests of bringing about social change, not in consolidating a social system brought into being by social revolution. This linkage of science and social reform continued in the nineteenth century with the rise of scientific socialism. Sociology, however, arose for the opposite reasons, in part as *a scientific answer to socialism.*

The two fundamental assumptions made by the founders of sociology (Comte in France, Spencer in England, and to a lesser extent, Ward in America) were (1) that social phenomena are as natural as any other and susceptible to the application of the positivistic methods of science, and (2) that social life consists of a unified system of inter-human activity which is like an organism in the integration of its sub-units into a working whole. In terms of these two fundamental assumptions, the first school of sociological theory can best be described as Positivistic Organicism.

The assumptions were neatly adapted to the ideological atmosphere within which the new science was born. In the first place, positivism took science out of the hands of the scientific socialists and put it at the disposal of the conservatives for whom the early sociologists spoke. In the second place, the concept of society as a great organic structure was brilliantly adapted to an anti-reformist social orientation. This has always been true of the organic analogy. It was employed by the ancient philosophical idealists (like Plato) with conservative import. Finally, by simple extension these two assumptions permitted the early sociologists to budget the problem of change into their scheme. Societies, like organisms, grow old and die. The nineteenth-century biological theorists had begun to study the way in which entire biological species evolve. A progress-evolution theory extended by analogy to society neatly transformed the concept of change from a revolutionary program to a conservative principle. Past injustices were the price of past progress; present injustices will naturally be overcome in the course of time, but meanwhile, they are inevitable. The first school of sociology, Positivistic Organicism, established the areas of social structure and social change, which were often described in the early period as social statics and social dynamics.

Ideological motives may play a role in the establishment of a scientific point of view, but they cannot sustain it permanently. The naturalistic and organic integrations of societies are hypotheses capable of being examined empirically and, on the basis of evidence, accepted or rejected. The application of scientific standards to various deductions from the theories of Positivistic Organicism constituted an important component in the rise of the second major school of sociological theory, Conflict Theory.

Like Positivistic Organicism, Conflict Theory assumed that social events were natural and subject to the positive procedures of science; in fact, it intensified the positivism of early sociology. However, all the postulates of harmony which flowed from the organismic theory of sociology left many early sociologists dissatisfied. As they saw it, one cannot relegate war, revolution, and other forms of conflict to past stages of social development; they are still with us. In fact there are few social situations which when examined carefully do not reveal quite a different mien from that suggested by the Positivistic Organicists: not a condition of harmony but a tense inter-penetration of opposed interests. There is, they felt, something wrong with the organismic theory of society, for it leads to an unrealistic view of the social process. Realism suggests that we conceive its most fundamental condition as one of conflict.

The realism of the Conflict Theorists is manifest in their closeness to the positions of people attempting to influence the actual course of events: the Marxian Socialists and the Social Darwinists. The Marxian socialists, who were spokesmen for the working classes of nineteenth-century society, not only conceived of conflict as lying at the core of life, but were certain that it had the special form of class struggles.

The history of all hitherto existing society is the history of class struggles.

Freeman and slave, patrician and plebian, lord and serf, guild-master and journeyman, in a word; oppressor and oppressed, stood in constant opposition to one another, carried on an uninterrupted, now hidden, now open fight, a fight that each time ended either in a revolutionary reconstitution of society at large, or in the common ruin of the contending classes.

The modern bourgeois society that has sprouted from the ruins of feudal society has not done away with class antagonisms. It has established new classes, new conditions of oppression, new forms of struggle in place of the old ones.

Our epoch, the epoch of the bourgeoisie, possesses, however, this distinctive feature: it has simplified the class antagonisms. Society as a whole is more and more splitting up into two great hostile camps, into two great classes directly facing each other: Bourgeoisie and Proletariat.[31]

In contrast to the socialists' theory of social conflict, some conservative groups used Social Darwinism to justify economic and political advantages which had often been acquired by force.

Darwinism was used to buttress the conservative outlook in two ways. The most popular catchwords of Darwinism, "struggle for existence" and "survival of the fittest," when applied to the life of man in society, suggested that nature would provide that the best competitors in a competitive situation would win, and that this process would lead to continuing improvement.[32]

In America, Social Darwinism became, for the time, a semi-official philosophy for right wing groups. In Hofstadter's terms:

> In the American political tradition the side of the "right"—that is, the side devoted to property and less given to popular enthusiasms and the democratic professions—has been throughout the greater part of our history identified with men who, while political conservatives, were in economic and social terms headlong innovators and daring promoters. From Alexander Hamilton through Nicholas Biddle to Carnegie, Rockefeller, Morgan, and their fellow tycoons, the men who held aristocratic or even plutocratic views in matters political were also men who took the lead in introducing new economic forms, new types of organization, new techniques.[33]

Because of its fitness to their needs, such groups in American society found vindication in Social Darwinism.

> American society saw its own image in the tooth-and-claw version of natural selection, and . . . its dominant groups were therefore able to dramatize this vision of competition as a thing good in itself. Ruthless business rivalry and unprincipled politics seemed to be justified by the survival philosophy.[34]

The main stream of sociological Conflict Theory flowed outside the more extreme political formulations and justification of either the Left or the Right. Moreover, it brought into the forefront of sociological thought whole blocks of historical materials which the postulates of harmony had led their predecessors to ignore. New attention was given to writers of antiquity such as Thucydides and Polybius. Among the Renaissance writers Machiavelli was revaluated. The great conflict theorist from the Arabic Middle Ages, Ibn Khaldun, was appreciated for the first time in the West; and among more recent Western thinkers, Hobbes received new attention.

The new apportionment of interests on the subject matter of sociology laid the foundation for the isolation of special areas of study. Their attention to the problems of force, conflict, and political struggle led the Conflict Theorists to establish political sociology. They even made a beginning in the study of a sociology of war and a sociology of law. Their attention to the conflicts of interests between social strata led to the isolation of social stratification as a special area of study.

Though sociology was enriched by the addition of new specialties and made more realistic, the appearance of Conflict Theory did not bring the development of sociological theory to an end. While Conflict

Theory solved some problems, it created others. First, it multiplied the number of alternative interpretations of social events without supplying adequate criteria for deciding among them. Second, the very act of making sociology more realistic—in shifting the process of conflict into the spotlight—it intensified the problem of freeing sociology from ideological commitments. Individual conflict theorists tended to be drawn to the support of either Marxist or Social Darwinistic politics, and away from the purely scientific task of the objective explanation of society. Although a core of able conflict theorists, such as Bagehot in England, Gumplowicz and Ratzenhofer in Austria, and Albion Small and George B. Vold in the United States, managed to keep Conflict Theory on an objective plane, the numbers of persons lost to the conflict ideologies of Marxism and Social Darwinism reduced the size and influence of the school. Meanwhile, a new set of influences was beginning to affect the discipline.

Positivistic Organicism and Conflict Theory, the two oldest schools of sociological theory, had in considerable measure been established by thinkers outside and independent of the colleges and universities of Europe and America. This circumstance of their origin encouraged a kind of freedom and universality of scope. Their exponents drew materials and points of view from any of a variety of sources—from philosophy, from history, from literature, from law.

It was a foregone conclusion that whenever sociology became an academic discipline much of the freedom and scope of an extra-university development in Western thought would have to be abandoned. For sociology to make its way without excessive conflict in the universities as one special study among others would require a narrower and more specialized definition of its field. This occurred between 1890 and 1920, when sociology first became established as a special discipline in some of the universities and colleges of Europe and America. Two new schools of sociological theory took shape during the course of this change of status: Sociological Formalism and Social Behaviorism.

The rise of Sociological Formalism was a product in sociology of the neo-Kantianism of the closing decade of the nineteenth century and the opening decade of the twentieth. The general reasons for the "return to Kant" at this time were bound up with the unparalleled extension of the scientific point of view in the nineteenth century. Whenever the scientific analysis is rigorously carried out, it brings about an extensive liquidation of traditional ideas and institutions. A century of such great application of science was also, inevitably, a century of great destruction of traditional values and faiths. However, when ethical, mythical, and religious forms which normally give meaning to life are destroyed by the extension of the scientific point of view, science often does not leave anything in their place[35] capable of substituting for the lost values.

The return to Kant in the late nineteenth century at a time when traditional religious and ethical contexts were being destroyed by the extension of the scientific point of view is understandable in terms of the historical background of Kantianism. The trend toward the separation of science, ethics, and religion into distinct compartments was no new phenomenon in the West. It had occurred in the eighteenth century in the separation between the rationalistic traditions of Descartes, Spinoza, and Leibnitz from the empirical traditions of Locke, Berkeley, and Hume. Cracks and strains were developing in the belief of Western men in the rationality of man and nature. They were being forced to choose between saving science and abandoning religion or *vice versa*. Coming at the end of this trend, Kant had made a major attempt to link these traditions once more and to fuse science, religion, and ethics into a single rational whole.[36] The nineteenth century opened with the Kantian synthesis of Western intellectual traditions. Hence, when the extension of science to many fields in the nineteenth century tended to set science, religion, and ethics into conflict once again, some thinkers had recourse to a neo-Kantian reaction. Kantianism in the eighteenth century and neo-Kantianism in the nineteenth belong among the attempts by Western intellectuals to eat their cake and have it too.

At this same period the movement of sociology into the universities was occurring with the demand that the field be precisely defined in a manner which would give it standing alongside other university disciplines. It was reasonable that the possibilities of neo-Kantianism should be explored for this purpose as well as for cementing the cracks that were developing between the humanistic and scientific aspects of sociology.

Since Kant had employed a distinction between the form and content of events in his attempt to solve his problems, it seemed reasonable to employ a similar device in sociology. Kant provided sociology with a special and limited location in its new academic setting. And his belief that the formal aspects of events are directly given to the mind without requiring elaborate investigation suggested a major departure from the positivism of the first two schools of sociological theory in the study of social forms.

Sociological Formalism assumed that (1) the peculiar essence of social life as studied by sociologists was not total societies or processes of conflict, but social forms abstracted from the content of social events, and (2) such forms require a method of analysis peculiar to them. The methodological problems of the Formalists led them to phenomenology and a form of controlled introspection as the proper procedure for discovering inter-subjective forms. The new emphasis of the Formalists led them to add new and special areas to sociology. The Formalists played a major role in establishing the theory of social relations as a branch of the discipline. They developed the details of the sociology of law, as a particularly important branch of the study of social forms, considerably beyond the Conflict Theorists. They also assigned greater significance to the sociology of law than did their predecessors. And they formally opened up the sociology of knowledge (the general analysis of cultural and knowledge forms of all types).

At the same time that Sociological Formalism was taking shape, alternative ways of adapting sociology to its new role as a university discipline were being explored in the various branches of Social Behaviorism. Pluralistic Behaviorism took shape in France under the influence of Gabriel Tarde and Gustav Le Bon; it migrated to America, where it was promoted by E. A. Ross and Franklyn Giddings. Social Action theory was developed in Germany by Max Weber, and in the United States by Thorstein Veblen and John R. Commons. Symbolic Interactionism, though not known as yet by that name, was being developed in the United States by William James, George Herbert Mead, Charles Cooley, and W. I. Thomas.

Like the Formalists, the Social Behaviorists were disinclined to take large-scale formations of social life such as total societies or the social process as units of study. However, they also objected to a separation of form and content as a foundation for a special science of sociology. In the end, they believed, social life always consists in specific acts occurring between specific people. They believed that in taking a total society or the social process as the unit of sociological analyses, the actual dynamics of social life tend to be lost sight of, for any one of these phenomena is in fact a highly complex series of smaller events.

Moreover, the Social Behaviorists were convinced that a genuine science of sociology required more than lip service to the possibility of applying the methods of the physical sciences to social phenomena.

Social phenomena are just as natural as any others, but they are a special class of events requiring the adaptation of the methods of science to their particular properties. Various branches of Social Behaviorism took the lead in the establishment of many of the methods with which contemporary sociology is identified. The Pluralistic Behaviorists promoted the development of Social Statistics; the Symbolic Interactionists developed the use of case and life histories; the Social Action theorists attempted to make comparative study more precise by means of ideal types.

As in the case of other theories, the special emphases of Social Behaviorism encouraged the development of new areas of sociology. The isolation of inter-human acts as the core materials of the science brought the individual actor into prominence. The Social Behaviorists were directly responsible for establishing such areas of sociology as collective behavior, the social psychology of personality, and social control. They also brought about major changes in many other areas of sociology including social structure, political sociology, the sociology of economic institutions, the sociology of religion, social stratification, and the sociology of law.

The last school of sociological theory, Functionalism, began to take on distinct form during World War II. Its founders (particularly Talcott Parsons and Robert K. Merton) looked particularly to the anthropologists, Radcliffe-Brown and Malinowski, for inspiration, though they also admitted influence from Émile Durkheim and Vilfredo Pareto among the sociologists. While this was occurring, Kurt Lewin was leading his followers from the field of Gestalt psychology toward sociology. Eventually, these two functionalistic movements, which may be called respectively Macrofunctionalism and Microfunctionalism, proved to have close affinities with each other, for they applied the same basic assumptions—the first on a large scale, the second on a small scale.

Although the acknowledged origins of contemporary Functionalistic Theory are among some selected anthropologists, sociologists, and in Gestalt psychology, the Functionalist analyses of social life were made from the standpoint of *social systems* conceived as organismic entities in a manner closely paralleling that of the Positivistic Organicists. The two most fundamental assumptions made about social systems were (1) the causal priority of the whole, and (2) the functional interdependence of parts within the social whole. To this revived organicism, which is not *in principle* different from that of the Positivistic Organicists, the Functionalists once more conjoined a purified positivism. The Microfunctionalists, particularly, carried out a vigorous program of laboratory experiments on small groups conceived as organismic entities.

The chief difference between Sociological Functionalism and Positivistic Organicism lies in the Functionalists elimination from consideration of the historical contexts, within which the Positivistic Organicists studied society. Furthermore, concomitant with this shift of attention away from historical contexts, the Functionalists sought to give their concept of social systems more universal formulation. The Functionalists have had the advantage of the considerable developments of methodology since the early days of sociology. Their methods, particularly those of the experiment-minded section of the school, have been quite sophisticated.

The areas of strength of modern Functionalism include social structure (social systems) and small groups. They have also done much to establish medical sociology as an area, and have played an important role in the re-structuring of the sociology of economic institutions into industrial sociology, which centers on the study of the primary group in industrial contexts.

The following table summarizes the basic assumptions and areas of interest of the main schools of sociological theory.

Contrary to the frequently expressed opinion that sociology has not been cumulative,[37] it requires only an examination of the courses offered by the major sociology departments to discover that as the various schools of sociological theory have added areas of interest and study, the range and richness of the field has been continually increased. It is quite possible that there are some sociology departments in which each of the areas outlined in the table above is represented by at least one course. As one area after another has been added to the growing body of material studied by the science, the task of developing an integrated explanation for the whole has become greater and more difficult. Before a new theory can claim generality, it must prove its capacity to account for the growing body of established facts.

THE PLACE OF
SOCIAL BEHAVIORISM

Both Formalism and Social Behaviorism have had the same kind of appeal in sociology that atomism had in physics or the cell theory

The Major Sociological Theories: Assumptions and Areas of Strength

Type of Theory	Assumptions	Areas Created by the School or Strengthened by it
Positivistic Organicism	1. Positivism 2. Total societies are basic unit of analysis 3. Societies are organismic unities	1. Social structure 2. Social change
Conflict Theory	1. Positivism 2. Social process as a basic unit of analysis 3. Conflict as the primary process	1. Political sociology 2. Sociology of war 3. Sociology of law 4. Social stratification
Formal Sociology	1. Anti-positivism 2. Basic units of analysis are social forms 3. Forms may be abstracted from content	1. Social relations 2. Strengthened the sociology of law 3. Sociology of knowledge
Social Behaviorism	1. Modified positivism 2. Basic units of analysis are meaningful inter-human acts 3. Large complexes of action, like groups and societies, should not be reified	1. Collective behavior 2. Social psychology of personality 3. Social control 4. Sociology of economic institutions 5. Sociology of religious institutions 6. Strengthened political sociology 7. Strengthened social stratification theory 8. Strengthened the sociology of law
Sociological Functionalism	1. Purified positivism 2. Social systems conceived as basic units of analysis 3. Social systems conceived as organismic unities	1. Revived study of social structure (social systems) 2. Study of group dynamics 3. Turned sociology of Economic institutions into industrial sociology

in biology. They offered some type of basic unit of analysis. This did not mean that any given meaningful social form or inter-human act was incapable of further analysis, but it did mean that such further analysis no longer dealt with social life but with sub-social phenomena. On the other hand, the analysis of social life as inter-human acts, which have varying meanings for their participants or forms, potentially could offer special insight into organized complexes, communities, or cultures (such as groups of such units).

However, while both Formalism and Social Behaviorism offered a basic unit into which social life could be analyzed and still remain social, the separation of form and content, at least in the manner of the early students, proved to be indefensible. Moreover, Formalism contained anti-empirical tendencies which alienated it from naturalistically inclined students, on the one hand, and sent the school on an internal evolution from neo-Kantianism to phenomenology on the other.[38] In the long run Social Behaviorism has so far proved to be the more rewarding alternative.

In contrast to all the other schools of sociological theory, Social Behaviorism brought the individual into sociological perspective. Positivistic Organicism's emphasis on total societies, Conflict Theory's emphasis on processes of group conflict, and Functionalism's emphasis on social systems, tended to shift the individual into the background. By contrast, Social Behaviorism's emphasis on unit acts as the ultimate social reality served as a continual reminder of the presence of individuals. When one is speaking of total societies and social systems or complex conflict processes such as warfare, it is almost automatic to assume that no single individual can make much difference. However, when one is talking about single acts, it seems equally self-evident that the properties of the individual may make *all* the difference. The alternative approaches to social life carried a tendency to play down individuality in all its forms in the one instance, to play it up in the other.

The most basic problem that has to be faced by any theory which aspires to generality is to explain those areas of behavior which it did not establish as well as or better than the school which established it. Thus, Positivistic Organicism and Functionalism can present themselves as general sociological theories only if they can explain the materials of the Conflict Theorists, of the Formalists, and of the Social Behaviorists. How difficult this is can be illustrated by Sherman Krupp's analysis of possible limitations of Functionalistic theory in the analysis of economic and other organizations.

A "harmony of interest" theme figures prominently in the heritage of modern organization theory. An element of harmony is injected into the analysis of organizations by preoccupation with the "functional" ordering of relationships. The functionalist approach characteristically assumes the unity or purpose of the whole and views the parts as they contribute to this unity. Like arms, or legs, or the brain, the parts work in harmony to serve or fulfill the good of the whole. But such an interpretation of parts and wholes is not the only one possible. Parts may be only loosely structured within a whole, or, more crucially, they may determine the nature of the whole rather than *vice versa*. The danger of the functionalist approach is that it may conceal harmony-laden teleologies. Thus, an interpretation of the business firm through the language of "group co-operation" may be analogous to a description of a jungle using a theory of the farm.[39]

If a theory subject to the serious limitations that Krupp finds in Functionalism is to retain its claim to scientific acceptability, it must either be modified or abandoned.

The fundamental task facing Social Behaviorism is to move out in its analysis from the field of collective behavior and the social psychology of the individual and other areas, where it has proved its efficiency, to the sociology of groups and institutions, the sociology of community, and the sociology of culture (including such branches of this discipline as the sociology of law, the sociology of art, and the sociology of knowledge). Powerful beginnings along such lines were being made by Max Weber at the time of his death. Many of Weber's followers and representatives of other sub-branches of Social Behaviorism have continued research in the fields of large-scale organization, community formation, and cultural change. However, Social Behavioristic theory has not been brought together in as systematically integrated logical form as has been achieved by some of its great rivals.

PART TWO

THEORETICAL
and METHODOLOGICAL
PERSPECTIVES

The two essays in the present section are devoted to phenomena which have been slighted in contemporary sociological theory: the relation that has in fact existed between a given set of theoretical orientations and methodological procedures, and the major shifts of orientation which sometimes occur in the theoretical perspectives of the outstanding figures of a discipline.

From time to time various sociological theorists have announced their intention to bring their theoretical reflections and empirical methodologies into working relationship. This was proposed by, among others, Auguste Comte, Herbert Spencer, Gabriel Tarde, Emile Durkheim, Franklyn Giddings, and Max Weber. One of the outstanding theorists recently to propose doing so is Robert K. Merton. He has had, he says in a work containing his major theoretical studies to date, two major concerns.

These are, first, the concern with the interplay of social theory and social research, and second, the concern with progressively codifying both substantive theory and the procedures of sociological analysis, most particularly of qualitative analysis.[1]

In his own particular theory, Functionalism, Merton states the relation between theory and method to be as follows:

Like all interpretative schemes, functional analysis depends upon a triple alliance between theory, method, and data. Of these three allies, method is by all odds the weakest.

Although methods can be profitably examined without reference to theory or substantive data—methodology or the logic of procedure has precisely that as its assignment—empirically oriented disciplines are more fully served by inquiry into procedures if this takes due account of their theoretic problems and substantive findings. For the use of "method" involves not only logic but, unfortunately perhaps for those who must struggle with the difficulties of research, also the theoretical problems of aligning data with the requirements of theory.[2]

It is quite startling to hear that its method is the weakest part of Functionalism. However, somewhat later Merton indicates that method is also one of the most "creative" parts of Functionalism. With what he views as considerable daring, Merton assigns creative functions to research.

With a few conspicuous exceptions, recent sociological discussions have assigned but one major function to empirical research: the testing or verification of hypotheses. . . . It is my central thesis that empirical research goes far beyond the passive role of verifying and testing theory: it does more than confirm or refute hypotheses. Research plays an active role: it performs at least four major functions which help shape the development of theory. It *initiates*, it *re-formulates*, it *deflects*, and it *clarifies* theory.[3]

While there is nothing wrong, in principle, with Merton's formulations, it is surely curious that although the intention is announced on page 3 of *Social Theory and Social Structure* that theory and research are about to be consolidated, one hundred pages later on (page 103) glad tidings of great joy are still about to be forthcoming for theory from research. This suggests the elaborate pantomimic gestures of ancient ceremonial priests preparatory to entering the sacrificial chamber.

Moreover, the very language has a legalistic character, not altogether consistent with rigorous scientific requirements. In the beginning it is proposed to *consolidate* theory and research ("the consolidation of theory and research and the codification of theory and method are the two concerns threaded through the chapters of this book").[4] This sounds like a business merger. It also suggests that Merton believes that theory and research are not now *consolidated*.

The language also has a political character when Merton speaks of Functional analysis as depending on "a triple alliance between theory, method, and data." The sociologist seems to have suddenly acquired the role of a statesman faced with the difficult task of bringing about elaborate coalitions of antagonistic forces.

One ought not be surprised, then, when this phase of Merton's discussion terminates on the same note.

It may be inferred that some invidious distinction has been drawn at the expense of theory and the theorist. That has not been my intention. I have suggested only that an explicitly formulated theory does not invariably precede empirical inquiry, that as a matter of plain fact the theorist is not inevitably the lamp lighting the way to new observations. The sequence is often reversed. Nor is it enough to say that research and theory must be married if sociology is to bear legitimate fruit. They must not only exchange solemn vows—they must know how to carry on from there.[5]

If "research and theory must be married if sociology is to bear legitimate fruit," one is tempted to inquire as to the sexual standing of the partners. Does theory father a finding, or give birth to an idea?

The ceremonial tone of Merton's remarks is related to his treatment of theory and research as independent activities. Theorizing is not an activity which can be separated from carrying out research, for it is never anything other than the conceptual phases of a research activity. Merton's elaborate statesman-like negotiation to bring theory and research together is somewhat in the nature of the search for a formula to mix the yolk and white of a scrambled egg. One is tempted to paraphrase Kant: empirical research undirected by theory is blind; theory unsupported by findings is empty.

That method and theory are merely two divisions of the research process has never been in doubt since the days of Comte. Their fitness to each other in any particular case, however, is a matter of special interest. Comte, for example, clearly perceived that if the unit of social analysis was the total society conceived as an organic unity, laboratory methods of scientific investigation were inappropriate to its study. As Comte saw the matter, laboratory procedure involved the introduction of artificial changes in an experimental case in order to determine the precise relation between one variable and another. Further, if the unit of study was the total society, such experimental manipulations brought about changes in social reality itself. Experimentation, thus, increased the irrationality of the object of study. The proper method of study of total society was by a comparison of the different historical stages of society with one another. To establish the correctness or incorrectness of Comte's particular formulations is less important than to recognize his clear perception that the theoretical definition of his subject matter from the onset rendered some methodological procedures relevant, others irrelevant.

In various ways both Toennies and Durkheim perceived that their sociological theories (which, like Comte's, rested on the conceptions of total societies as organic wholes) committed them to the employment of comparative methods with historical and ethnographic materials. On the other hand, when Gabriel Tarde reduced social reality to individual acts which either represented inventions or the imitations of inventions, it seemed natural to him to reduce the methods of sociology to two fundamental types which he described as archeology and statistics.

If archaeology is the collection and classification of similar products where the highest possible degree of similarity is the most important thing, Statistics is an enumeration of acts which are as much alike as possible. Here the art is in the choice of units; the more alike and equal they are, the better they are. What is the subject of Statistics unless . . . it is inventions and the *imitative editions* of inventions?

Statistics . . . follows a much more natural course than archaeology and, although it supplies the same kind of information, it is much more accurate. Its method is preeminently the sociological method, and it is only because we cannot apply it to extinct societies that we substitute the method of archaeology.[6]

And when some of Max Weber's theoretical formulations led him to make use of the comparative study of historical materials as an appropriate method, he elaborated the ideal type as a concept by which comparisons could be made with greater precision than is possible without careful attention to the terms of the comparison.

The following essay, on "Sociological Theory and the Ideal Type," consists of a detailed examination of some of the ways in which some theoretical formulations lead naturally to the employment of special kinds of methodological procedures. Similar types of inquiry are possible into the affinities of other types of theoretical formulations and the methods appropriate to them.

The second essay in the present section on "Talcott Parsons' Metamorphosis from Social Behaviorism to Macrofunctionalism" poses another kind of problem which, unfortunately, has all too rarely been explored by students of sociology: the basic shift in the suppositions of a creative sociological mind in the course of its explorations.

The fact that a thinker may change his mind in a fundamental manner in the course of his career has long been accepted in philosophy. It causes no dismay to students of contemporary philosophy, for example, that in a discussion of Bertrand Russell, it is necessary to specify the particular phase of his career under review. Nor is the fact that so distinguished a thinker may have changed his mind in a fairly radical manner taken as detracting from Russell's stature as one of the eminent men of our time.

By contrast to the freedom with which changes in the thought of eminent men are accepted in philosophy, literature, and the arts, the surprising position is held in sociology that it somehow detracts from the importance of a man if his career is discovered to display the phenomena of natural living growth. So, for example, radical opposition has been expressed directly against the essay on "Talcott Parsons' Metamorphosis from Social Behaviorism to Macrofunctionalism." Professor Loomis argues:

This chapter is an attempt to analyze Parsons' conceptualization of the social system. . . . Such an analysis, however, must be preceded by an overall view of Parsons' work which, taken *in toto* through more than two decades, is marked by a high degree of integration and inviolate unity. Nonetheless, its subtleties, complexities, and refinements, its frequent preoccupation with the border lines which sociology shares with other disciplines—such as psychology, economics, political science, and anthropology—and the continuously developmental stages of his works variously representing different levels of analyses have led to the charge (unfounded in the view of the present authors) that his theory is discontinuous and even contradictory through time. The essential unity and remarkable consistency of his conceptualized social system, although amenable to analysis by the PAS Model, cannot be communicated adequately without an attempt at a panoramic view of the whole together with a statement of his general theory.[7]

This is explicitly footnoted to the essay on Parsons.[8]

When such a sharp difference of opinion appears—as between the Loomis account and the essay printed in the following section—it behooves the reader to read Parsons and draw his own conclusions. However, it may be noted that further analyses along lines similar to that of the essay are to be found in *The Nature and Types of Sociological Theory*[9] and in the volume *The Social Theories of Talcott Parsons* edited by Max Black.[10]

A discipline that must find in its outstanding figures only "a high degree of integration and inviolate unity," and which can not tolerate in them the changes of strategy, the setbacks, and the exciting discoveries which characterize living growth, is applying to these figures attitudes appropriate, perhaps, to the heads of religious sects, but certainly not appropriate to the leading figures of a scientific discipline. It is in the nature of a truly creative mind to explode the formulas of its early training and find its way to new ones.

Though a few beginnings have been made with the examination of some major theoretical shifts in the careers of some outstanding sociological theorists—such as the shift of E. A. Ross from a branch of Social Behaviorism to Formalism,[11] of Znaniecki across two branches of Social Behaviorism to Functionalism,[12] of Merton from Social Behaviorism to Functionalism[13]—the study of the dynamic growth of ideas in the minds of major sociological thinkers has rarely been carried out. This is all the more unfortunate since the problems buried in a theory are often cast into dramatic relief by the changes in tactics of leading thinkers.

2

SOCIOLOGICAL THEORY
AND THE
IDEAL TYPE

THE DEGREE OF AMBIGUITY SUR-rounding the concept of "ideal types" in sociology may be seen by the fact that while some students have found them to be rather inadequate theories others have found them to be inadequate models of a mathematical type. Disregarding the common estimate of inadequacy, there is no consensus between these two positions as to whether ideal types are theories of methodological devices, for very different criteria are relevant to each case. Understandably, in interest of clarity, some students have been inclined to reject ideal types altogether, for even the most zealous exponent of their use seems to find it necessary to apologize for them. On the other hand, the most ardent critics of ideal types usually feel forced to admit, lamely, that they do have a place after all. Taken together all the diverse characterizations lend the problem of the ideal type in sociology the properties of a major mystery story. In reconstructing the scene of the crime, it is useful to go back to the state of sociology at the time the conscious formulation of ideal type occurred. We thus can attempt to uncover the motives and conditions that called it forth.

The present discussion will trace in rough outline the career of the ideal type in sociology, in order to clarify some of the problems posed by it and to locate some of the interpretations given to the ideal type. Particular attention will be devoted to Max Weber's concept of the ideal type, since the great bulk of modern discussion stems from it. Some of the contemporary revisions of Weber's type concepts and various substitutes and alternatives for the ideal types will be briefly sketched. Finally, a few of the more important criticisms of the ideal type will be examined.

In what follows I assume that a scientific theory is a logically interrelated body of empirical laws. Is the ideal type a theory? In the most recently published statement on the ideal type that I have been able to find (June, 1957), this is maintained. It is said that the ideal type "has the character of a *theoretical model*. As such, the type functions as an *explanatory schema* and as an implicit theory. The drawing out of this theory results in the explicit statement of hypotheses about the type."[1]

I assume that if anything has the character of a theory, if it functions as a theory functions, if it can be drawn out as a theory can be drawn out to produce hypotheses, then it is a theory. I do not, however, believe that ideal types are theories, for they are not logically interrelated bodies of empirical laws. McKinney is not alone in conceiving ideal types as theories; Watkins, Talcott Parsons, and others also have done so. Hempel accepted their conclusions but decided that as theories ideal types are scientifically unacceptable. On the other hand, in not treating ideal types as theories, I find myself in agreement with Max Weber, Robert MacIver, Robert Merton, and many others. All this is treated later.

Scientific method consists in the systematic procedures that institute an empirical proof. A hypothesis deduced from one's theory is tested and either confirmed, disconfirmed, or left in doubt. There are three general kinds of such systematic procedure for instituting a proof: experimental method, statistical method, and comparative method. The "logic of method" is the same in all cases. These subdistinctions arise in terms of the degree of precision of the theory and the amount and kind of control possible over the data to which a theory is addressed. In experimental method, procedure consists in instituting a controlled situation, the conduct of observation under controlled conditions, and the confirmation or disconfirmation of hypotheses in terms of the occurrence or nonoccurrence of predicted results. Statistical method deals with data arising from a repetitive operation (as, for example, from experiments, assembly lines, or recurrent natural facts such as births and deaths). Hypotheses are instituted with regard to quantitative data on the basis of mathematical models. The application of relevant statistical tests serves to confirm or disconfirm hypotheses. The oldest procedure of science is comparison. Comparison is an act intended to establish an item of empirical knowledge about which one is uncertain. Some idea guides the comparisons, and there is some theory, however crude, in the background.

The fundamental position taken in the present essay is that ideal types are neither experiments, mathematical models, nor theories but *devices intended to institute comparisons as precise as the stage of one's theory and the precision of his instruments will allow.* Just as one's theory determines the kind of situations set up in experimental procedure, or the kind of mathematical models selected in statistical procedure, so it determines the kind of ideal types developed in comparative procedure. Comparative procedure occurs most frequently in new sciences and on the frontiers of old sciences. Very often the success of comparative procedure leads to an increased precision of theory and method, gradually providing the basis for statistical and experimental procedures. If ideal types often give the impression of being provisional and jerry-built, it must be remembered that without the pioneers, civilization would not come to the wilderness. The evolution of the ideal type in sociology was determined by the attempts to transform comparative method into a more precise procedure. The place occupied by ideal types (and various alternatives for them) in current sociology is a testimony to the amount of sociological method still remaining on a comparative level.

TYPE CONSTRUCTION OF
EARLY SOCIOLOGISTS

Sociology arose in the nineteenth century with the attempt to combine an organismic concept of society with a positivism of procedure. Its basic theory was evolutionary; its materials were historical; its method was comparative.

Sociology was invented by thinkers with very special inclinations and talents: men with imagination, varied interests, wide information, and conservative temperaments. Comte, for example, was haunted all his life by the terror of disorder. He dreamed of a castelike society that would bring conflict to an end, and he even proposed a special technique of "mental hygiene" to secure individual peace of mind. Herbert Spencer was proud of the England of his day and suspicious of all elements in his society that tended to bring about change. As for Comte and Spencer, the source of social disorder was differently conceived, but the conservative temperament of each was all too clear. Each in his way carved out spheres from the old intellectual disciplines which they appropriated for sociology—a defensive image, in each case, against the forces of disorder.

Under the circumstances in which the nineteenth century sociological synthesis occurred, it is not difficult to see why the new field depended on a comparative method. The idea that society was an organism discouraged the use of experimental methods by the new science. Society was conceived as a vague superbiological organism often (as with Comte) thought to be coextensive with humanity itself. Comte largely rejected the notion of sociological experiments. Consistently with his theory, he argued that to change anything meant to change everything in the social organism. But it is impossible to observe everything. Thus, sociological experiments are almost out of the question. Spencer, who conceived all artificial interference with society as a change for the worse, was even opposed to sociological experiments on ethical grounds. The theories of the early sociologists, thus, ruled out experiment as an important sociological method. They could hardly turn to statistical method, since it had not been devised.

Their theories and their reliance on historical materials reduced method to a comparison of cases. Society was conceived as an organism that had evolved, developed, or progressed. The task of the new science was to trace this evolution, development, or progress. The facts that one studied were initially and primarily historical.

But if the first source materials studied by sociology were historical, new materials were soon added by ethnographic reports on non-Western peoples. The early reports were quite unscientific. However, they aroused immediate and great curiosity because of contrasts they presented to social phenomena familiar to the European. As early as Comte, the possibility was seen of systematically utilizing such data for sociological purposes. However, Comte steadfastly maintained that the materials for sociology were primarily historical.

To indicate the order of importance of the forms of society which are to be studied by the Comparative Method, I begin with the chief method, which consists in a comparison of the different coexisting states of human society on the various parts of the earth's surface. . . . By this method, the different states of evolution may be observed at once. . . . But we must beware of the scientific dangers of ending the process of comparison by this method. . . . It can give us no idea of the order of succession. . . . The historical comparison of the consecutive states of humanity is not only the chief scientific device of the new political philosophy. Its rational development constitutes the substratum of the science, in whatever is essential to it.[2]

If the method of the new science was comparative, the fundamental methodological questions that would sooner or later have to be faced had to do with the employment of this method in a manner which would give standard verifiable results. What was the unit of comparison? How was it to be set up? How could one be sure that different thinkers were comparing the same things? What are the criteria of a scientifically adequate comparison?

Early sociologists and ethnographers proceeded in blithe disregard of most of these questions. With rather smug ethnocentrism, the unilinear evolutionists assumed that their own societies and social circles (Victorian England, the Society of the Eastern Seaboard of the United States, The Society of Paris)[3] represented the pinnacle toward which world evolution was progressing. The latest ethnographic reports usually supplied the notion of what society had been in ancient times (the society of the Australian Bushman was a favorite). One then arbitrarily assumed that society had moved through successive stages from primitive beginnings to a high state of civilization occupied by the student. Such stages were often arrived at arbitrarily on the basis of quite extraneous considerations. Ethnographic and historical evidence was strung together like beads on a tenuous string of theory. When the thin thread of theory snapped, there was hardly anything to hold the miscellaneous "facts" together.

The collapse of the early theoretical formulations of positivistic organicism had a number of major and minor consequences familiar to all students of recent social thought: (1) The concept of "progress" and most forms of the concept of "social evolution" were abandoned by most social theorists. (2) Sociology broke most of its ties with anthropology. To many thinkers, the association seemed meaningless with the abandonment of the search for social origins and stages of precivilizational social change. (3) Sociology became apologetic of its dependence on history, showing increasing embarrassment in the use of historical data. (4) The comparative method was brought under critical review, and substitutes for it were sought. (5) Sociologists became increasingly sensitive about using large-scale concepts such as "culture," "civilization," and "society." The idea that these were superorganisms was dropped by almost everybody. The idea that "society" is the basic unit of sociological analysis was generally abandoned.

The naive and heedless enthusiasm of the early social scientists in constructing their pictures of social origins and development and the shocking way in which their creations were tumbled into ruins can easily obscure the nature of their conceptual activity. However, their problem, their data, and their method inevitably launched them upon programs of conscious and unconscious type construction. They assumed that mankind had undergone a regular and ordered development. Their problem was to discover what this was and what sequence of changes characterized it. Their data was ethnographic and historical; their method was "comparative." Specifically, they sought to establish the existence of certain types of society, types of social structure (particularly institutions) of smaller scope than society, and types of development or change. The names of many of the early social scientists are closely associated with the types they invented or used: Comte visualized society as developing through three basic types, Theological, Metaphysical, and Positivistic, which followed each other in sequence; Henry Sumner Maine traced social development from a patriarchal type of ancient society resting on social relations of status to modern types of political society resting on a contractual relation of the individual to the social whole; J. M. Bachofen thought one could discover an early universal prehistorical type of matriarchal family and society precedent to modern states and types; Herbert Spencer thought that one could trace social development from an ancient militaristic-theological type of society to modern peaceable and industrial types; Tönnies traced the general development of civilization from *Gemeinschaft* kinship, and neighborliness) to *Gesellschaft* (societies resting on psychological relations determined by political administration and the trading of the market place); Durkheim traced social change from a type of society resting on mechanical solidarity to a type of society resting on organic solidarity (ties of interdependence due to social division of labor rather than similarity due to friendship, neighborliness, or what not).

It is evident, thus, that a large part of the intellectual effort of early social scientists went into the setting up of types of society, institution, and civilization sequence. Although much of this type construction was methodologically unconscious (that is, not an aspect of deliberate procedure), it was not completely random and accidental. Comte thought his broad types of humanity were composed of more specific subtypes. Maine was of the opinion that although Ancient society resting on Status was a widely distributed social type found from India to Ancient Rome, its details varied from place to place. Maine and Bachofen both utilized legal materials in the conduct of their analyses and employed the principle of survivals to explain otherwise anomalous legal residues. Both Spencer and Durkheim were of the opinion that, in fact, societies existed in many forms more complex than their respective theological-militaristic, industrial peaceable, and mechanical and organic types. This automatically turned their types into generalized descriptions. Durkheim explicitly argued that comparison of societies only made sense when societies of the same type or at the same stage of development were compared. He had also advanced the idea that the type of legal relation found in a given society could be utilized as an index of its solidarity, distinguishing the problem of indices from causes. Tönnies recognized his societal types to be conceptual abstractions and simplifications. In all such respects, the type construction of the early sociologists was more intellectually responsible than may appear on the surface. Their ideal types were recognized to be conceptualizations rather than realities. Some of the problems of concept formation were seen.

TYPE CONSTRUCTION UNDER THE INFLUENCE OF THE NEO-KANTIAN AND NEO-HEGELIAN MOVEMENTS IN MODERN SOCIAL SCIENCE

The theoretical crisis in which early sociology found itself with the collapse of organismic positivism precipitated a heightened interest in the problems of methodology and theory construction. A not illogical form of the reaction to the crisis of the social sciences was the rejection of the positivism of early sociology. The "reasonableness" of this reaction was evident in the attempt by its agents to clarify the "organismic" elements of early sociology in terms of idealistic philosophy and the retention, in fact the strengthening, of the ties between sociology and history which had supplied the new field with its data. The rejection of positivism called into question the relation between the natural and social sciences. The neo-Hegelian movement, however, instead of trying to re-unite the natural and social sciences sought to sharpen the differences between them. This in turn led to the question of the capacity of the social sciences to establish general knowledge. Hence, there evolved the sequence of discussions between the neo-Hegelians and neo-Kantians.

This is not the place to review all the details of the transition from positivistic organicism to neo-Hegelianism and from there to neo-Kantianism. Some aspects of the thought of Dilthey and Rickert may serve to illustrate the manner in which the concept of "ideal types" was pressed into the service of the new points of view and given special interpretations.

Wilhelm Dilthey[4]

To Dilthey (1833–1911) the mind is teleological, pursuing its purposes and realizing its ends by the manipulation of the objects of the world. Man is the ultimate unit of social life and the social sciences which study man have quite a different relation to this unit than the natural sciences to their final units. In contrast to natural science, which arrives at its ultimate units by a process of analytical abstraction, Dilthey believed that the mind of man is given as an immediate reality. The conditions and states of society are understood directly from the inside.

The lines between social and natural science were sharply drawn. Natural-science knowledge is external and analytical; social-sciences knowledge is internal and synthetic. The basis for understanding the social world is found only in one's own experience. Only through "re-living" the experiences of the persons about us can we understand them. The devices and products of understanding fall into a number of groups: (1) Concepts and judgments, for example, have properties independent of the context in which they occur. Distinguishable from these are (2) behaviors flowing from and revealing the purposes that activate them. Finally, (3) there are expressions, written expressions, for example, or creative works which reveal to the understanding the totality of life. We know the physical world; we understand the social world.

Understanding consists in the selection of the significant. Meaningful types are the basic instruments of understanding. They may be types of society, social structure, institution or of some subinstitutional element such as law or art, even types of personality. Meaningfulness or significance depends on the relation of the individual to the *milieu* in which everything is in living relationship to the ego. An occurrence is significant to the extent to which it reveals the nature of life. Significance is immanent to life—it is a category of life—it is an ultimate fact beyond which reason cannot extend. The type is the significantly representative form relating the greatest number of possible facts to the whole.

So far as the social scientist or cultural historian is concerned with the establishment of actual facts, his procedure corresponds to that of the natural scientist. This, however, for Dilthey, is only the beginning of his true task of establishing the conditions and circumstances for understanding. The social scientist's task is accomplished only when he "re-lives" the experience of which the "facts" were conditions and external content, penetrating thereby its significance.

At this point, one touches the fundamental idealism of Dilthey's argument. One understands anything including the past only by penetrating its inner relation to the "I" of the present. Difference may be perceived only in terms of and against a background of similarity. The substratum of understanding in the social sciences is provided by the unity of human nature beyond time and place. The final court of appeal in determining human meaning is the ideal human type. Understanding of society and history is an endless process leading to ever new discoveries of the variety of the human spirit on even higher levels of experience: in every person, every community, every system of culture, in the spiritual whole of history.

Dilthey's solution of the problems of social science took the form of an identification of the social sciences and history. The social sciences and history together were placed in contrast to the physical sciences; each had a peculiar object of investigation, the psychical and physical respectively. The method of the two types of disciplines was also different, for the social sciences and history were thought to have immediate and direct contact with their objects while the objects of natural science could only be arrived at by external analysis. The break with positivism is evident. Natural science is a science of externals. Dilthey has nothing but pity for the social scientist who would imitate it.

Dilthey's solution to the problem of the social sciences was in one respect empirically motivated. The early materials for social science had, to considerable degree, been supplied by historical research. In identifying the social sciences and history, Dilthey was preserving at the time the sources of social-science data. However, with its implied devaluation of natural scientific knowledge and its separation of the various forms of knowledge into distinct kinds (rather than treating items of empirical knowledge as different only in degree) Dilthey could be expected to encounter opposition.

Heinrich Rickert[5]

The rationalistic tradition in Western thought takes the empirical world to be a unit, and scientific knowledge to be empirical conceptualization at its best. The neo-Kantianism of Rickert (1863–1936) illustrates both the opposition to Dilthey and the attempt to find an alternative solution to the problems of the social sciences.

As a Kantian, Rickert held that all empirical-scientific knowledge is based on experience. It is incorrect to set up a distinction in kind between knowledge of the psychical and knowledge of the physical, the one known directly, the other indirectly. Empirical knowledge regardless of its contents is knowledge of what is given in experience,[6] whether of physical events or mental events. One may know one's own self empirically only in so far as it is given in one's experience. Psychology is a natural science and psychological events are explained in terms of general laws of psychological phenomena established by the same manner as physical events—the same kind of methods as natural science.[7] The difference between psychology and the natural sciences is only a matter of the degree of exactness and precision of its concepts.

Dilthey combined history and social science. He sharpened the distinction between natural and social science, and rested the distinction ultimately on a difference in knowledge, direct and external. Empirical knowledge for Rickert was all of a piece; items of it differ only in degree. Although the natural and social sciences were in Rickert's perspective combined as a single kind of enterprise, both were sharpened in their distinctness from history.

For Rickert, both science and history are empirical disciplines. However, science is treated as one kind of explanation of experience; history as quite another. Science works with abstract concepts and attempts to explain the general or recurrent; history operates with individual concepts and attempts to explain the unique. The ultimate generalizing concepts of science represent objects in simplest form possible; the individualizing concepts of history represent a potentially heterogeneous array of significant elements.[8] History and nature represent two kinds of interest in empirical reality, two kinds of abstraction from it. As intellectual disciplines, both history and science utilize general concepts, but they are concepts of a different kind.

History and science, thus, represent two contrasting analyses of nature. The most general concepts of natural science, for Rickert, concern objects in the simplest possible form, while the most general concepts of history represent nature in complex integrated structure.

Hence in the materials of history the concepts of science have passed beyond their utility. The problem remains to determine the nature of historical individuality. Though the causal laws of natural science do not apply to historical individuals, this is not because they are uncaused. The peculiarity of historical materials lies in the individual uniqueness of the historical complex. Historical individuals receive this irreplaceable uniqueness from their relation to some value. The change or destruction of the value destroys the historical individual itself. The task of the historian consists in determining the value which constitutes the historical individual. This is not the same as evaluating historical individuals—passing moral censure or distributing praise and blame. Rather, the historian's purpose is to locate the historical individual in a more comprehensive whole.[9] In determining historical change, for example, the task of the historian lies precisely in isolating the significantly new, the teleological element which informs the totality of the development. Rickert rejected the concept of evolution, so central to the crisis of the social sciences, precisely because he felt that it tended to eclipse all historical stages but the last, shifting attention away from the estimate of each element or stage of historical development by referring it to a general value.

It may be seen that those aspects of social science activity accounted for by Dilthey as determinations of typicality and "meaningfulness" were accounted for by Rickert as characterizations of individual uniqueness in respect to a general value. Dilthey tends to assimilate social science and history to each other, separating them from natural science. Rickert fused the sciences into a single conceptual unit and excluded history from the circle.

In the course of the discussions of Dilthey and Rickert and their colleagues, the concept of "ideal types" tended to acquire connotations which in some quarters are still retained: devices for determining individual historical significance or "meaningfulness" as a part of a procedure of reliving, introspection, or *verstehen*.

CONTEMPORARY FORMULATIONS
OF THE IDEAL TYPE
DERIVING FROM MAX WEBER

Among contemporary sociological theorists there is by no means equal receptivity to the use of ideal types. However, the thinkers who have made basic use of the concept of "social action" for the analysis of social life have been not only most sympathetic to the use of ideal types but have consciously attempted to improve them. Social action, of course, is only one concept of contemporary sociology. The study of social action is concerned with but one area of sociology. Neither the concept nor the area is the exclusive property of any single sociologist or group of sociologists. Some of the sociologists utilizing the concept of social action as a basic one have been described by Sorokin as forming a school of sociology he calls "sociologistic"; some others using the concept have recently designated themselves as "functionalists." Ideal types are not the exclusive property of any single school of sociological theory. It was more the properties of the area covered by social action than a special theory that led to use of ideal types in connection therewith. These contemporary formulations go back primarily to Max Weber, who more than any other sociologist approached sociology by way of the concept of "social action."

Weber's discussion was cast in terms of the formulations by Dilthey as well as those of members of the neo-Kantian Marburg philosophers such as Windelband and historians such as Eduard Meyer. Weber not only attempted to avoid the semi-mystical conception of types as natural forms but reduced some of the presumed abstract theories of his day to mere ideal types. In Weber's opinion, for example, classical economic theory actually provided an illustration of the kind of "synthetic constructs" that have been conceived as "ideas of historical phenomena."[10] Classical economic theory presented not an abstract theory but an idealized picture of events in the commodity market under conditions of exchange operating in terms of free competition and rigorously rational conduct. Relations and events of historical life were selected and formed into an internally consistent system. Classical economics presented an idealization of certain elements of historical reality. Its "theory" was actually a utopia-like construct.

Weber went to some lengths to distinguish the ideal type in his sense from other notions with which it could presumably be confused. He urged that it was not an hypothesis, though it could be useful in formulating hypotheses. It is not a description of reality, though it aims, in part, at permitting unambiguous descriptions. The ideal type is not to be confused with ethical imperatives. "The idea of an ethical imperative, of a 'model' of what 'ought' to exist is to be carefully distinguished from the analytical construct, which is 'ideal' in the strictly logical sense of the term."[11] Ideal types are not stereotypes, averages, or abstract concepts. "An ideal type is formed by the one-sided *accentuation* of one or more points of view and by the synthesis of a great many diffuse, discrete, more or less present and occasionally absent concrete individual phenomena, which are arranged according to those one-sidedly emphasized viewpoints into a unified *analytical* construct. In its concepted purity, this mental construct cannot be found anywhere in reality."[12]

In the contexts in which Max Weber's fullest formal discussions of the ideal type are found, the problems of the neo-Kantian seem to have been uppermost in his mind. He urged that the basic purposes of the type is "to analyze historically unique configurations or their individual components in terms of genetic concepts."[13] Weber illustrates this with the concepts of the "church" and "sect." If we are interested in some historical phenomena such as Christianity in the Middle Ages, Weber urges, we must be prepared to admit that there exists in fact an infinitely varied mass of details with most varied forms and nuances of clarity and meaning. Study proceeds, Weber maintains, by asking what are the "Christian" elements of the Middle Ages. A combination of articles of faith, norms, church law, custom, maxims of conduct are fused into an "idea." The ideal types of the *sect* and *church* represent two idealized types of arrangement of the critical elements of religious institutions which may assist the student in the analysis of Christianity in the Middle Ages. Weber insists all expositions of the "essence of Christianity" are ideal types of only relative and problematic validity. Such presentations, however, are of basic value for research and systematic exposition. "They are used as conceptual instruments for *comparison* with and the *measurement* of reality. They are indispensable for this purpose."[14]

The argument is interesting for its similarities and contrasts to the conceptualization of Rickert. The type is offered as a device for the study of nature as history; it is, in this respect, like Rickert's historical individual. However, it is not conceived as resting on a general value on the basis of which all sub-elements derive "significance." A further illustration from Weber's argument brings the contrast even more clearly into focus. The ideal type, Weber says, is composed of both generic and ideal typically constructed elements.[15] The concept of "exchange," for instance, is a simple class concept. However, when this concept is related to that of "marginal utility" and the idea of "economic exchange" is offered, one has left the field of pure class concepts for the type in which typical conditions of exchange are assumed. Generic concepts merely summarize common features of empirical phenomena, but the ideal type is designed to aid the analysis of actual situations.[16] The critical element of the type is not—as for Rickert—a general value.

When Weber saw the main function of the ideal type in the analysis of historical materials and circumstances, he again was apparently following the neo-Kantians. However, there is no evidence that he accepted the dichotomization of history and science which would transform these two disciplines into opposites, each finding its boundaries in the other. Rather, with the neo-Hegelians, Weber seems to have felt that ideal type constructions represented the procedure by which historical materials were utilized by the social sciences. At the same time, in contrast to neo-Hegelians like Dilthey, Weber does not seem to have been willing to distinguish *in kind* between the knowledge of the social sciences and that of the natural sciences. In this last respect, Weber represents the partial return to the positivistic tradition of the founders of sociology. In sum: for Weber, ideal types were procedures by which historical materials were made useful for the general purposes of science. As applied to historical materials, he characterized ideal types as devices for description, as implements for comparison and measurement, and, under special circumstances, as procedures for instituting and testing hypotheses. The component elements of the type and the criteria for constructing them are particularly important. For Weber has also argued that the ideal type is not a description, not a general concept, not a law, not a moral or ethical judgment.

As noted, for Weber the ideal type contains both conceptual and observational materials, both being required for the type. Such conceptual and observational materials are not put together arbitrarily. The relationships expressed in a type are such as "our imagination accepts as plausibly motivated and hence as 'objectively possible' and which appear as *adequate* from the nomological standpoint."[17] Objective possibility and adequate causation are the criteria for forming conceptual and observational materials into a type.

The ideal type is a conceptual tool. Items and relations actually found in historical and social life supply the materials. These are selected, fused, simplified into the ideal type on the basis of some idea of the student as to the nature of social reality. Weber's discussion of the criteria for this selection and formation of elements into the type is not as unambiguously clear as it might be. It is unfortunate that the fullest statement of it occurs in the course of his critique of Eduard Meyer's historical methodology rather than in connection with his positive statements about ideal types. However, *objective possibility* seems to refer to the logical status of the items organized by the type.

In forming an ideal type, the student has in some sense extended his conceptions beyond the social reality presented to him. He has abstracted, sharpened, and extended relations actually perceived. Objective possibility as a guiding criterion of such conceptualization requires that the conceptual form so produced represents an empirically possible state of affairs. The ideal type is an imagined world. The criterion of objective possibility applied to this imagined world requires that it be an empirically possible world in the sense that it should not contradict any of the known laws of nature. An empirically possible world is *ipso facto* a logically possible world (the converse is not true). The terminology may be strange but the same could be said of every hypothesis of science. If it were not possible to test materially false hypotheses, science could not exist. The hypothesis is a conceptual formulation that guides investigation. No one knows for sure whether it is "true" until it has been tested. If one did, it would not be necessary to test it. However, to be capable of test at all it must express a material possibility. Similarly, the application of the criterion of objective possibility to ideal-type construction attempts to draw the line between science and metaphysics.

The second criterion for the selection of elements for the ideal type is that they be such as "appear adequate from the nomological standpoint." That is, the items should be "adequate" in terms of the causal laws of science. The special problems faced by the historian in making his estimates of events to include in his narrative is involved in this second criterion of the ideal type and its components. The historian often deals with complex situations resulting from the conjoint operation of a number of factors. The question is quite legitimate as to the extent to which some total given effect rests upon any one. "What is meant . . . if correctly formulated logically, is simply that we can observe causal 'factors' and can conceptually isolate them, and that expected rules must be *thought* of as standing in a relation of *adequacy* to those facts, while relatively few combinations are *conceivable* of those conceptually isolated 'factors' with other causal 'factors' from which another result could be 'expected' in accordance with *general empirical rules*."[18] Despite ambiguities, this seems to mean the historian, for his purposes, makes estimates of the combined factors that contribute to major events of interest. The laws of the science as established at the moment are the basis for his assignment of significance to some factors rather than others. If, on the other hand, historical materials are to be utilized for the purposes of science, the problem becomes a bit more complex. The causal laws of the science are employed to establish the significance of special items. Once established, these in turn may eventually help to reconstruct the laws of science.

The problems formulated by Weber in the concept of "adequate causation" have been taken up by Ernest Nagel. Ideally, Nagel maintains, explanation in history and science ascertain the necessary and sufficient conditions for the occurrence of a phenomenon. In fact, historical and scientific practice rarely achieves the ideal with any fullness. Historians particularly are often so removed from the full circumstances of an event that they can cite only the main, principal, or primary causal factors. Nagel rejects the notion that the "weighing" of causal factors in terms of their degree of importance is arbitrary and meaningless. He isolates a series of cases where such estimates are valuable:[19] (1) Two factors may be necessary for the occurrence of a third but not equally so; (2) Two factors may be necessary for a third, but a change in magnitude of one may have very different results from changes in the magnitude of another. (For example, industrial production may vary both with the supply of coal and the labor force but a given percentage change in the labor force may be far more significant.) (3) A variety of factors may be causally significant to event, but some may act as catalysts on others. (4) The frequency of total events may vary with items that do not exclusively determine them. In a whole series of such ways, it is Nagel's opinion, estimates of causal adequacy form a legitimate aspect of scientific and historical explanation.

In outlining the primary interpretation of the ideal type by Max Weber, a whole series of suggestions and interpretations distributed throughout his work must be ignored, however regretfully. The contexts containing Weber's fullest discussions were dominated by the neo-Kantian distinction between science and history. Some elements of the Kantian dichotomization seem to have brushed off onto Weber. The various passages in which such implications appear, as well as others which apparently suggest that the ideal type has relevance only for historical purposes, must, for want of space, be by-passed here. Such passages can be matched by others on the other side. At times, when social science interests were uppermost, Weber speaks of the appearance of types in almost pure form. For example, in his *Religionsoziologie* (Vol. I, pp. 436 ff., published in the *Archiv* 1915) in his discussion of various motives for religious rejection of the world, a series of types was outlined. Of them, Weber states, "The theoretically constructed types of conflicting 'life orders' are . . . intended to show that at certain points such and such internal conflicts are possible and 'adequate.' . . . They can appear . . . in reality and in historically important ways, and they have. Such constructs make it possible to determine the typological loss of a historical phenomena." Here the context suggests that types are used not for historical ends but that historical materials are to be used for scientific purposes.

There are other problems in Weber's account touching the problem of "adequacy." If one central and unambiguous meaning of adequacy is causal adequacy—that is, in accord with causal laws—there are other discussions of "adequate at the level of meaning." This, at times, in some passages, seems to refer to adequacy of an explanation in terms of ordinary common sense notions which may or may not be adequate in terms of the requirements of science. At times, however, a meaningfully adequate explanation is contrasted to a causally adequate one, in a way suggesting Dilthey's distinction.

However, the investigation of these and certain other passages to discern whether they are true or only apparent contradictions is of only incidental interest. More important is the status of the type in its most sound interpretation.

CURRENT USES
OF THE IDEAL TYPE
AND PARALLEL
CONCEPTUAL FORMATIONS

Despite the many possible ambiguities of Weber's account, the sober and intellectually responsible character of his formulation of the ideal type is evident. He pointed out the fact that one did not eliminate ideal types from science by ignoring them—one merely withheld them from critical analysis. His own treatment was marked by the attempt to extract what he felt were the sound points from early positivism, neo-Hegelianism, and neo-Kantianism. Types were used not to separate history from science but to mediate the use of historical materials for scientific purposes. Moreover, over-ambitious theoretical pretensions in social science and premature claims at having achieved abstract scientific formulations were denied, and their formidable structures revealed to be ideal types. Whatever the limitations, this bears the clear marks of intellectual honesty, and it is not surprising that many current sociologists whose point of approach to their problems is somewhat similar to Weber's have been inclined to employ their revised versions of the ideal type or obvious conceptual substitutes for it. A brief review of a few of these revisions of and substitutes for ideal types may illustrate the current state of thinking.

R. M. MacIver's Imaginative Reconstruction

The basic task of sociology, like all science, MacIver maintains, is to establish the existence of causal relations. These are to be established within the limits and on a "causal level" peculiar to the particular science. The basic procedure is to identify a situation in which the phenomenon occurs as against a comparable one where it does not, then to analyze out the cause. This is not always easy and may proceed by way of successive investigations with an ever more refined isolation of causes. A science performs its task most effectively where experimental control of the relevant situation is possible. In social science, where it is not, we often have to rest content with unrefined estimates of causes. Special interest attaches to procedure in social science precisely because we are so often unable to experiment.

The social scientist tries to follow a procedure very similar to the experiment setting up situation C and C_1, in one of which the particular cause (x) is present, in the other not. In the case of the social sciences, one of our situations C_1 is an *imaginative reconstruction*.

The very samples used by MacIver were drawn from those employed by Max Weber, Eduard Meyer, and others of the time when the problems of the ideal type were first discussed. "Where we cannot experiment we still follow the same process of analysis, but now one of our situations, C and C_1, usually remains hypothetical, a mental construct. We ask: what *would* have happened if the Persians had won the battle of Marathon? The alternative situation is not presented, cannot be reproduced in the world of reality. In the great majority of investigations into social causation, we must use what evidence we can muster, with whatever skill or comprehension we possess, to construct imaginatively an alternative situation that is never objectively given."[20]

Without the slightest ambiguity, MacIver's *imaginative reconstruction* may be treated as identical with the process of setting up ideal types.

Talcott Parsons' Use of Pattern Variables and the Production of Imaginary Societies

Parsons is certainly one of the most careful students of Max Weber among American sociologists. Parsons has been quite critical of Weber's use of the ideal type. As he saw it, for Weber, "The ideal type . . . is not merely an abstraction, but a peculiar kind of abstraction. It states the case where a normative or ideal . . . is perfectly complied with."[21] Moreover, Parsons maintains "ideal types call attention to extreme or polar" situations. The only system in which they fit is a limiting type of a kind "least likely to be found in reality even in at all close approximations," and this, according to Parsons, tends to shift attention away from the concept of a system as a balance of forces in equilibrium. "It leads to a kind of 'type atomism.' "[22] Parsons interprets Weber's ideal types in a manner that would bring them close to the formulations of Dilthey, a fact of which he seems heartily to approve. He does not, however, have much sympathy with Weber's use of types in a manner which would minimize the claims of abstract theory. Generally, Parsons' sympathies are more for than against Weber. At the same time, in view of his objections, one could expect Parsons to try to improve on the type as a conceptual tool.

Parsons seems to have found in the concept of "pattern variables" the device for securing the generalized abstract theory he felt Weber's ideal types could not obtain. A pattern variable is not a variable; it is, presumably, the schematization of directions or dimensions of some possible variation. In *The Social System,* for example, he attempted to establish "the pattern alternatives of value orientation as definitions of relation role expectation patterns."[23] If one may be permitted to translate this, Parsons is raising the question as to the ways in which the relations between two or more persons may be arranged or limited. For example, any person in a social relation, Parsons assumes, gets all he can out of it. In Parsons' inimitable language, "In motivational terms it may be presumed that the 'ultimate' interest of any actor is in the optimization of gratification."[24] However, it is also clear that in any social relation one person cannot get everything. There is a "polarity of affectivity-neutrality . . . in direct orientations to the social objects with whom an actor interacts in a role, and in its relevance to the structure of the expectations of his action in that role."[25] Again to translate: any relation between two or more persons may be limited in terms of the interest or lack of interest of the parties involved.

Without tracing through all the steps of the argument, Parsons argues that any social relation is describable in terms of five pairs of pattern variables of role definition:

I. The Gratification-Discipline Dilemma
   Affectivity *vs.* Affective Neutrality
II. The Private *vs.* Collective Interest Dilemma
   Self-orientation *vs.* Collectivity Orientation
III. The Choice between Types of Value-Orientation Standard
   Universalism *vs.* Particularism
IV. The Choice between "Modalities" of the Social Object
   Achievement *vs.* Ascription
V. The Definition of Scope of Interest in the Object
   Specificity *vs.* Diffuseness

To translate again: in any relation between two or more persons, one or other of the parties may be (1) interested or relatively disinterested, (2) selfish or unselfish, (3) interested in some immediate end or in a category of ends defined by a principle. The other party to the social act may be valued because of (4) what he can do (achievement—for example, because he is a great football player) or what he is (ascription—for example, because he comes from one of the "best" families in the town). Finally, (5) he may be interested in the other person in a social relationship for a very specific reason (a carnival barker wants nothing more from the sucker but his money) or in a general way (as when a young man loves everything about the girl). Parsons maintains that "If the derivation of these five alternative pairs from possibilities of the combination of the basic components of the action system has been correct, if they are . . . on the same level of generality and are exhaustive of the relevant possibilities . . . they may be held to constitute a system. Then, on the relevant level, which, as we shall see, is the *only one* which needs to be considered, their permutations and combinations should yield a system of types of possible role-expectation pattern, on the relational level, namely, defining the pattern of orientation to the actors in the whole relationship. This system will consist of thirty-two types."[26]

Parsons does not seem to have received all the credit he deserves for his handling of the ideal type. He seems to have done for the type what Henry Ford did for the automobile when he took it out of the bicycle shops and put it on the assembly line of the modern factory. Parsons, similarly, seems to have indicated the way to mass produce ideal types on an assembly-line basis, for he appears to have invented no less than a machine for their production. In this case, a set of five dichotomous action alternatives are set up. These are cross-tabulated. Certain permutations and combinations are counted. By the simple turn of the crank, thirty-two types of social systems are turned out.

Lest it be thought for one moment that Parsons has in any way escaped the problem so often raised as to the relation between the idealization involved in the type and the empirical reality, his comments on his application of the thirty-two types of possible social systems may be considered. When we examine actual social life, he states, "we do not find that empirically observable structures cover anything like the whole range of theoretically possible variability, that is, according to purely logical permutations and combinations of structural components."[27] The discovery that actual social systems are not as rich as the imagined ones is said to "serve a two-fold purpose for the sociologist." It not only permits him to short-cut investigation "of the whole range of structural possibilities and concentrate on a fraction of them" but "it can serve as a highly important lead into the formulation, and hence testing, of fundamental dynamic generalizations, of laws of social process, since the explanation of why the logically possible range of variability is empirically restricted can only be found in terms of them."[28]

There is a curious turn to these arguments. Apparently Parsons' assembly-line production of ideal types is so effective that, like the recent secretaries of agriculture, he is embarrassed by his surplus. The two main functions of actually looking at the facts are stated to be (1) to permit one to ignore some of the types and (2) to develop laws to explain why all the types cannot be found in fact. It is quite in accord with this surrealist atmosphere that Parsons permits himself to be startled by the fact that kinship has so much prominence in social structure,[29] which, he states, one would never expect from the thirty-two types. In explaining this surprise, Parsons is led to assign importance to all sorts of factors not even mentioned in his set of pattern variables such as the dependency of the human infant, the importance of sex to people, and the significance of child care, breast feeding, and the disabilities of women during pregnancy.

Howard P. Becker's Constructed Types

Although somewhat more explicit than Parsons, who employed the older terminology, Howard P. Becker has also been interested in the use of the type only after it has been purified.

The first innovation suggested to Becker is the renaming of "ideal" types as "constructed" types. This was in the interest of obtaining a vocabulary free from negative connotations of the term "ideal." Secondly, Becker suggests a breakdown of types into dated and localized, thought to be important for the historian, and undated and non-localized, being especially useful to sociologists.[30] Thirdly, Becker suggests a procedure for the setting up and use of types not quite paralleled in Weber's discussion.

If a sociologist is interested in some such phenomenon as revolution, Becker suggests, he must recognize the fact that no one revolution is ever quite duplicated by another. Hence, he proposes that the student examine as many revolutions as he conveniently can. On the basis of these, one may set up a series of types: revolutionary personality, processes, structures. This is after the student has formed a "highly provisional hypothesis" with the aim of developing a "constructed type" which can be employed as a tool. In social science "experimentation must be mental or selectively comparative. The process begins with a vaguely defined problem, the framing of a hypothesis, selective observation . . . with reference to it, and eventual construction of a type, or a battery of them. . . ."[31]

This is all quite different from Weber, who had assigned ideal types to a much more provisional stage of theory construction and empirical investigation. Constructed types in Becker's formulation appear as the end products or goals of research rather than as early and tentative formulations. Similarly, Becker suggests that constructed types either are hypotheses or together with an hypothesis they acquire direct predictive power. "The constructed type, in conjunction with an appropriate hypothesis . . . may have predictive power. . . . We can only say . . . that if and when these typical factors are given in this typical relation, these will probably be the typical consequences." This is somewhat qualified, however, for "All the constructive typologist ever says is that 'if and when' certain factors, which have been isolated as significant, recur in configurations which can be regarded as identical for the purpose in hand, then this in turn will probably occur."[32]

Weber, of course, had insisted that his types were not hypotheses or made up of hypotheses. The moment one treats them as such, rather novel consequences occur. The ideal type is never found in reality, being ideal precisely in the sense that it is an abstraction, accentuation, and extension of relations found in social life. If one takes the position that "if and when the factors" idealized in the type are found, certain other presumably idealized consequences follow, the result seems rare indeed. It would appear that the sociologist wishes to play "What's My Line?" with nature. He imagines a nonexistent state of affairs and defies nature to reproduce it.[33] This sounds like a social scientist who knows his own mind and is inclined to accept no nonsense, least of all from nature.

Merton's Paradigms

Still another device employed under similar circumstances and in much the same manner as the ideal type is Robert Merton's paradigm. Merton's brilliant study of the rise of the scientific attitude in seventeenth century England, using Weber's typology of the inner-worldly asceticism and Protestant rationality, reveals Merton's familiarity with and skill in employing ideal-type procedures. In view of this, his use of the term "paradigm" rather than "ideal type" seems to represent an unwillingness to quibble over minor issues and to find a neutral terminology. In any case, he has not only urged the utility of paradigms which he finds to have great propaedeutic value but has employed them as a device to interpret material felt essential for functional analysis, as a device for analyzing deviant social behavior, as an implement for isolating the problems in the sociology of knowledge, and as devices for investigating problems of intermarriage, social structure, and discrimination.

Precisely what Merton understands by the paradigm is not stated. Traditionally, of course, in grammatical analysis a paradigm was a set of forms containing some particular language element. The term also has been used to refer to a display in fixed order, to a pattern or to an example. The last of these seem closest to Merton's intention, for among the functions explicitly assigned to paradigms are the following: (1) bring into the open assumptions, concepts, and propositions used in sociological analysis; (2) isolate the skeleton of fact, inference, and theoretic conclusion; (3) provide an economical arrangement of concepts and their interrelations for description, having a notational function; (4) require that each new concept be logically derivable from previous terms of the paradigm or explicitly incorporated in it; (5) promote cumulative theoretic interpretation; (6) suggest systematic cross-tabulation of basic concepts; (7) assist codification of methods of qualitative analysis in a manner approximating the rigor of quantitative analysis.[34]

In terms of the various meanings of paradigm, pattern or model seems most nearly to approximate Merton's intention. However, there are various references to "formal" paradigms, "analytic" paradigms, "theoretic" paradigms, and "plain" paradigms. Whether all these have all the functions of paradigms is not noted. The various statements and examples leave much undetermined. Some statements suggest that the paradigm is merely an outline of the basic ideas of some particular study. At the other extreme, some statements suggest that the paradigm is a system of theory in which every concept is logically derivable, the paradigm being in fact a completed system of theory reduced to its most economical axiomatic structure, a calculus of concepts. Between these extremes, there are other statements suggesting that the paradigm is no more ambitious than a device for instituting systematic description.

Merton's paradigm for functional analysis, for example, seems to represent little more than a provisional outline of items that it is advisable for the functional sociologist to study. These are even phrased in the form of a mnemonic set of questions to ask oneself:

1. To what items are functions computed?
2. What situations can be adequately analyzed on the basis of observed motivations?
3. What are the sources of function and disfunction?
4. What is assumed to be functional?
5. How is the intervening variable to be validly established as a functional requirement in a situation where one can not experiment?
6. By what mechanisms are functions fulfilled?
7. How can we most accurately determine functional alternative?
8. How does a structural contact limit functional variation?
9. How is one to account for structural strains in the social system?
10. To what degree is functional analysis limited by the difficulty of locating adequate samples of social systems?[35]

This particular paradigm, which was described as a provisional codified guide for adequate and fruitful functional analysis, was said to lead directly to the postulates and assumptions underlying functional analysis. It was also stated to sensitize the sociologist to the scientific implications and ideological aspects of functional analysis. The paradigm consists of a list of items felt to be crucial and a set of questions to be asked at an early stage of study. The paradigm, in this case, is certainly not a systematic description or an axiomatic theory.

A much more interesting paradigm is present in Merton's essay on social structure and anomie. The provocative general proposition is advanced that social structures themselves may exert a pressure on individuals to engage in nonconformist or conformist conduct.[36] Developing the idea, Merton isolates two elements of social structure felt to be important for conformist and nonconformist behavior. Every social structure holds out to its members goals defined as legitimate; at the same time it regulates and defines the means and modes of reaching these goals. Merton urges that in a society where there is a very strong emphasis on the goals (success) without a corresponding emphasis on the means of achieving institutionally prescribed conduct, the latter can shift into the background. In this case, the society itself contains the pressures that lead to the breaking of its own norms. This, he maintains, is actually the case of American culture which "enjoins the acceptance of three cultural axioms; first, all should strive for the same lofty goals; . . . second, present seeming failure is but a way station to ultimate success; and third, genuine failure consists only in the lessening or withdrawing of ambition."[37] On the basis of this, Merton outlines a typology of individual adaptation. It may be noted that both presumed empirical laws and a set of specific historical conditions are present in the paradigm.

A Typology of Modes of Individual Adaptation[38]

Modes of Adaptation	Culture Goals	Institutionalized Means
I. Conformity	+	+
II. Innovation	+	−
III. Ritualism	−	+
IV. Retreatism	−	−
V. Rebellion	±	±

One may accept the cultural goals and the institutional means (conform), accept the goals but not the means (innovate), reject the goals but accept the means (be a ritualist), passively reject both goals and means (retreat), or rebel actively toward both goals and means.

In this second paradigm, Merton has all the elements and has conformed to the requirements of the ideal type as set down by Weber. A set of concepts was used to extrapolate from some relations found in actual social life. He analytically simplified and drew out the implications of certain selected tendencies. As far as our knowledge goes, three of his types—conformist, innovator, ritualist—are objectively possible. Undoubtedly, examples of a dyed-in-the-wool, simon-pure conformist or retreatist in everything could not be easily found—a fact in no way lessening the analytical clarification of possible combinations of social relations.

I am not familiar, from Merton's work, with any cases of paradigms which would fulfill the requirements of a closed system of concepts formed into an axiomatic theory. In view of this, it may be assumed that Merton's paradigms are, perhaps intentionally, a more loose version of what Weber intended by the ideal type.

John McKinney's Constructed Types

John McKinney's statement may be taken to illustrate the fact that ideal types have not gone out of fashion even with the youngest writers and thinkers at present. McKinney primarily follows Howard P. Becker's conceptualization, but his formulations have a strongly individualized property. It is argued that all concepts are constructs and creative "due to their abstract genesis." Since this is the case, it is urged "that the way is often to move one step further and create the constructed type." Such constructed types are characterized as being "a little more out of touch with perceptual reality than other constructs are." Moreover, a constructed type is said to be "a devised system of characteristics (criteria, traits, elements, attributes, aspects, etc.) not experienced directly in this form." The constructed type is said to be used for "comparison and measurement of empirical approximations" during which employment it reveals "nothing but deviations from the construct." This, it seems, is highly desirable, serving the purpose of "quantification in terms of the degree of deviation."[39]

Exactly why McKinney wants a quantitatively precise measure of the degree of deviation of types from reality is not clear to me. The point, however, seems to be important, for McKinney develops it further in a recent major volume on sociological theory. "Although examination of empirical cases never reveals anything more than 'approximations' or 'deviations' from the constructed type, it is essential that the type be formulated on the basis of empirical evidence. . . . Obviously, any variation or deviation must be a variation or deviation *from something*. To identify that something is necessarily to determine uniformity represented by the type."[40] Since the "uniformity represented by the type" is an imagined one, the intriguing suggestion of quantifying degree of fictitiousness remains.

THE CRITIQUE OF
THE IDEAL TYPE

It is evident that sociologists have been constructing ideal types consciously and unconsciously since the origins of the science. They have invented types of society, social change, family, religion, economy, politics, state, social movements, revolution, personality—the list is as extensive and varied as sociology itself. It is important to keep this in mind if one is to avoid some kinds of pitfalls. Schumpeter, for example, makes what he conceives to be a crushing criticism of Weber's use of types. "Some economists, among whom it must suffice to mention Max Weber, have felt the need of explaining the rise of capitalism by means of a special theory. But the problem such theories have been framed to solve is wholly imaginary and owes its existence to the habit of painting unrealistic pictures of a purely feudal and a purely capitalistic society, which then raises the question what it was that turned the tradition-bound individual of one into the alert profit-hunter of the other."[41] Schumpeter then proceeded to advance a scheme of ideal-typical forms of capitalism: early capitalism; mercantilist capitalism; intact capitalism; modern capitalism. If, under any circumstances, ideal types are going to be developed, scientifically responsible behavior would seem better served by recognizing this fact and bringing them under critical control. To withdraw such activities from scientific review reserves these areas for irrational activity. Moreover, the criticism of the ideal type on the grounds that it is unrealistic—that is, ideal— is the least rewarding form of criticism directed at the type.

The chief criticism of the ideal types in the earliest and most unreflective stage is that they were too vague to give consistent results. Some contributed to the development of sociology by making observation, description, or conceptualization a bit more precise than it had been previously. Some served their purpose and disappeared as they should have. Later developments in sociology provided the best criticism of early forms of ideal-typical procedure. They were ambiguous, inconsistent, and untrustworthy. From this standpoint, the assemblage and sharpening of the theoretical and methodological problems bound up with the type which occurred with neo-Hegelianism and neo-Kantianism represented a distinct advance.

The formulations of Dilthey, which would turn ideal types into configurations of "meaningfulness" guiding emphatic reliving of cultural and historical experience, and those of Rickert, which would make of them devices for assigning significance to aspects of historical individuals by referring these to some general value—such formulations have lost their interest for modern students. Even the most tender minded of contemporary students is inclined to see science as all of one piece. The insights produced by intuition, empathy, or some method of *verstehen* are to the modern student mere untested hypotheses. The funeral oration of the *verstehen* point of view was gracefully and ceremoniously performed by Abel in his *Operation Called Verstehen*[42] with his review of the claims of empathy to methodological standing and his disposal of it as an exercise in imagination that may, at times, be of secondary use in the sober tasks of proof. The positive values of the neo-Hegelian and neo-Kantian studies of the ideal type were: (1) pulling the various aspects of the problem of the ideal type together into one context; (2) focusing attention on the importance of social-psychological materials for sociology, paving the way for the appearance of a vigorous subdivision of sociology; (3) bridging the gap that was tending to grow up between history and social science, thus maintaining a relation that would permit social-science findings to bear on historical materials and historical data to become grist for the sociological mills. However, for the modern student the interpretation of ideal types as "meaningful *Gestalts*" is unacceptable. Whenever ideal types are given a significance similar to that assigned by Dilthey or Rickert, the modern student reacts in alarm.

An interesting type of criticism of the ideal type, at least of Weber's, has been advanced by Talcott Parsons. It will be recalled that Parsons interpreted the ideal type in a manner strongly suggesting the Dilthey-Rickert discussions, as a special kind of abstraction, one stating the case "where a normative or ideal pattern is perfectly compiled with." Weber, of course, had observed that there may be ideal types of brothels as well as ideal types of religions. However, this was not the grounds on which Parsons was critical of Weber's use of the ideal type.

Parsons urges that ideal types tend to concentrate on extreme or polar situations, tending thus to shift analysis away from the social system as a balance of forces in equilibrium. The ideal type is stated to be of utility only in analyzing a "limiting type" of system. Furthermore, Parsons argues, ideal types tend to lead to a "type atomism." The use of ideal types forms an obstacle to the formation of abstract theory. "Ideal type theory is . . . perhaps the most difficult level on which to develop a coherent generalized system. The concepts can readily be formulated *ad hoc* for innumerable purposes and can have a limited usefulness. . . . This, however, does not suffice for a generalized system. For this purpose, they must be arranged and classified in a definite order of relationship. Only then will they have highly generalized significance on either a theoretical or empirical level."[43]

The criticism that the ideal type concentrates only on polar or extreme situations and hence is adequate only for the analysis of a "limiting type" of system seems to entail a confusion between the analytical sharpening of relations in the type with extreme social situations. W. I. Thomas and F. Znaniecki, for example, in *The Polish Peasant* advanced a series of types to express the adaptation of the individual to changing social organization. They distinguished between the Bohemian, the Philistine, and the Creative Man. The Bohemian had so weakly internalized the social norms that he tended to overrespond to every social situation—to bend and twist, as it were, with every wind. The Philistine had taken over the conventional pattern in a narrow inflexible manner. The Creative Man had achieved a progressive, flexible, and responsive relation to his social order. These were types—analytical simplifications—of adjustment possibilities. However, far from permitting the analysis only of extreme or polar types of individual adjustment to social organization and change they proved to be an elastic system of possibilities ranging from individual disorganization to mastery of one's life situation.

On the other hand Parsons' criticisms that Weber's ideal types tend to result in a kind of type "atomism" standing in the way of the development of abstract theory seems to be well taken. To be sure, this criticism holds only for those instances in which ideal types are mistaken for abstract theory. When theory is taken to be a logically interrelated body of empirical laws, types cannot be theories. Weber, unfortunately, did not formulate his conception of social-science theory, but he did object to the notion that ideal types are theories. In fact, Weber believed that many social scientists had raised premature claims of having achieved abstract general theory. Classical economic theory provided Weber with an example of a presumed abstract theory which, he maintained, was merely an ideal type. Parsons and Weber were actually in agreement, but the criticism applies to anyone who does mistake ideal types for theory. When classical economics confused an ideal type for an abstract general theory, it was started on a course toward a metaphysics of ideal forms. Being strongly nominalistic and rather positivistic in inclination, Weber was decidedly suspicious of a kind of generalization he thought tended to become metaphysical. Weber's concept of ideal types, in part, represented the claims of empiricism against hasty over-generalization.

Of particular interest in connection with Parsons' criticism of Weber's ideal types is the criticism advanced by J. W. N. Watkins.[44] Watkins claims to find two kinds of ideal types in Weber's work which he calls "holistic" and "individualistic." Ideal types are constructed, on the one hand, by abstracting and expanding the outstanding features of a historical situation. These are organized into a coherent picture emphasizing traits of a situation as a whole. They are "holistic." On the other hand, some ideal types are constructed in a way similar to the modes in deductive economics, by formalizing the results of close analysis of some significant details of economic or social life considered in isolation. Such "individualistic" ideal types are constructed by inspecting the situations of actual individuals and abstracting such things as schemes of personal preference, kinds of knowledge of the situation or types of relation between individuals. The ideality of the type lies in simplifying the initial situation and expressing in abstract and formal ways the properties of the selected elements.

Watkins' criticism is simple and unambiguous and directed exclusively toward what he calls "holistic" ideal types. He argues that such holistic types involve one in the assumption that we somehow apprehend the over-all characteristics of social situations before learning about the parts.

On the contrary, Watkins argues, general knowledge of a social situation is always derivative. The basic principle of "methodological individualism" is that social processes and events should be explained in terms of the principles governing the behavior of individuals and descriptions of their situations. The methodological "principle of holism" would deduce behavior of individuals from microscopic laws which are *sui generis*, applying to the system as a whole. The fundamental reasons, according to Watson, for accepting the principle of "methodological individualism" are:

1. While physical things can exist unperceived, social things (laws, princes, prime ministers, ration books) are created by personal attitudes. If social objects are formed by individual attitudes, explanation of them must be individualistic.
2. The social scientist has no direct access to the structure and behavior of a system of interacting individuals, though he can arrive at reliable opinions about the dispositions and situations of individuals. Thus abstract social structures are best understood from more empirical beliefs about individuals.[45]

Watkins, of course, is not objecting to the use of ideal types as a conceptual procedure but to the use of ideal types in the service of a certain kind of sociological theory. Modern sociological functionalism appears to be precisely the kind of social theory that Watkins most opposes.

Talcott Parsons as one of the modern functionalists was impatient of Weber's actual typologies for precisely the opposite reason:

In formulating his classification of the four types of action, Weber neglected to develop the analysis of the structure of the total social system which is a logically necessary prerequisite of such a classification.[46]

By and large, Weber's work gives far more comfort to Watkins than to Parsons, for he had strong nominalistic reactions against prevalent forms of social realism. The extent to which Weber is both a comfort and source of despair to Watkins and Parsons transcends the problems of the ideal type.

A somewhat different type of criticism of ideal types has been advanced by Hempel,[47] not, in this case, confined to Weber alone. Hempel's criticism has been methodological, and it advanced from the standpoint of the methodological practice of the natural science.

The most general criticism Hempel has of typological concepts in the social sciences is that they tend to use the concepts and principles of classical logic, a logic of properties of classes. As a result, Hempel believes, they are incapable of adequately dealing with relations and quantitative concepts.

Hempel distinguished a variety of types: classificatory types, extreme types, and models. He urges that classificatory types tend always in time to be supplanted by precise formulations in statistical terms. To function legitimately, extreme types which are not class concepts must set up criteria for comparisons of more or less. They are destined to disappear as soon as operational criteria are found for proper judgment of "more or less" in a continuum. A scale of temperatures eventually replaces judgments of hot and cold, for example. It follows, Hempel maintains, that classificatory and extreme types are displaced as soon as statistical studies and operations are refined. They belong to the early stages of the growth of a scientific discipline. This brings us to models which are the basis for Hempel's discussion of Weber's types.

Hempel found in Weber's ideal types a good deal that was methodologically sound. For example, Weber saw ideal types as devices for the grasp of causal relations and meaning in concrete social and historical phenomena. The principles expressing connections were seen by Weber as "general empirical rules." Meanings discovered by emphatic understanding were admitted by Weber to be neither universally applicable nor always dependable. Weber conceived of the imaginary experiment as a dangerous and an uncertain procedure to be used only with caution in the absence of adequate experimental and observational data. Weber's discussion showed that he was aware of the close connection between contrary-to-fact conditionals and general laws. For Weber, the ideal type was an explanatory scheme embodying a set of "general empirical rules" which prompted conceptual grasp of concrete social and historical phenomena. By and large, Hempel found this to be a sophisticated and responsible set of ideas. He admits that imaginary experiments are also found in natural science where they may be intuitive or theoretical. Hempel's objection to Weber is due to his apparent reduction of the explanatory principles of sociology to meaningful rules of intelligible behavior and the reliance on imaginary experiments of an intuitive character.

Hempel is much more critical of Becker's reformulation of the type than he seems to have been of the statements by Weber. He noted that Becker argued that types function as hypotheses in the form of "if P . . . then Q" where P is the type evoked and Q is some more or less complex characteristic. However, in the nature of type construction, the consequence seldom, if ever, follows empirically, and the antecedent is then empirically false. From the occurrence Q, we can infer either that P was not realized or that the hypothesis "if P then Q" is false. Thus, when Becker has argued that all other factors being equal or irrelevant Q will be realized whenever P is realized, evidently no empirical evidence can ever refute the hypothesis, since unfavorable findings can always be attributed to a violation of the *ceteris paribus* clause. By contrast, in the formulation of a physical hypothesis, this clause is never used.

Hempel finds that in the physical sciences, too, there are ideal structures—ideal gases, perfectly electric bodies, and the like. Such concepts refer to extreme conditions which cannot be met in full. Their scientific value lies in the laws governing the behavior of ideal systems which are deductible from more comprehensive theoretical principles and confirmed by empirical evidence. Such types of models are of great value to physical science. On the other hand, perhaps the nearest approach to them is the kind of type concept found in analytical economics, such as the idea of a perfectly free competition, or of economically rational behavior. However, in contrast to the natural-science idealization, the principles are intuitive rather than theoretical idealization. The class of empirical evidence to which they refer is not always clearly specified. Only when operational meaning is attached to such theoretical parameters as "money," "profit," "utility," and the like, will the presuppositions of the theory acquire empirical meaning and become capable of test.

IDEAL TYPES AND
SOCIOLOGICAL THEORY

Hempel's treatment of the type is one of the most promising contributions of the recent discussions. Basically, he distinguishes three kinds of types: classificatory types, extreme or polar types, and the models of interpreted systems. The peculiar value of the classification is that it distinguishes between types on the basis of their methodological function, rather than in terms of some extraneous consideration such as whether they are going to be used by historians or by sociologists. There is little doubt that among the many concept formations described as types these subdistinctions apply.

Hempel separated the problems represented by classificatory and extreme types from models. Classificatory types, which it should be noted are not ideal types, are dismissed rather cavalierly as representing an old fashioned logic of properties and attributes not well adapted to study quantities and relations. Hempel's judgments are made from the standpoint of the natural sciences. The argument that classificatory types are destined to be replaced by formulations in statistical terms and that extreme or polar types are destined to disappear as soon as operational criteria are found for judgments of "more or less" in a continuum is indisputable. This, however, is no reason to scorn the significant (even if provisional) function of classificatory and extreme types in promoting description and establishing the limits of relations that may later be quantified. Precisely because the social sciences are in a less developed state than the physical sciences a larger burden of their elementary work is carried on by types. The moment adequate statistical conceptions are established and operational criteria for quantification are found, the types supplanted ought to be scrapped without further ado. One would hardly persist in distinguishing only hot and cold when a thermometer is available.

More important is Hempel's distinction between legitimate and illegitimate idealized models. Idealized models representing interpreted theories, such as are found in the physical sciences, were in Hempel's mind valuable applications of scientific theories. Ideal types were, he thought, illegitimate models, even though the principles expressing connections in ideal types for Weber were "general empirical tools." The idealizations expressed in the theoretical models of physical science were legitimate because they are deduced from general principles. By contrast, the principles of the ideal type were viewed as illegitimate, because they were intuitive rather than theoretical and often addressed to an only vaguely specified body of data. In any case, the model does not represent an axiomatic system explaining a body of tested empirical materials.

If the only types of legitimate models are those representing interpreted theoretical systems, one can only conclude that it will be long before the social sciences can achieve them. The long-range objective of presenting a theoretical system as a special case of a more comprehensive theory may be fine, but it will be a long time before sociology reaches this stage. Meanwhile, once again, invidious comparisons are introduced between sociology and the physical sciences. Wherever statistical and experimental methods have not been developed to a point adequate to its needs, sociology can only institute the most precise comparisons possible. This is precisely what ideal types were intended to do. In areas where quantification is incomplete and inadequate, mathematical models are, as yet, unavailable and where one, on the other hand, is not able to experiment, there is no choice but to find bases on which one can compare cases. It goes without saying that if one's comparison is between some actual state of affairs and the type, about all that can be predicted is nonsense. Rather, one compares two or more actual sets of affairs. The function of ideal types is to isolate the factors on which the comparison becomes critical. The degree to which the relations involved in the type are intuitive seriously curtails the extent to which one can generalize on the basis of them. However, in the early stages of science, one accepts help from whatever quarter.

Obviously, if one is looking for a permanent fixture in the achievements of science, the ideal type—at least any given one—can only be a disappointment. Whenever the ideal type is compared to the model representing an interpreted theory, the ideal type comes off a poor second best. This is inevitable, for the two are not comparable. Ideal types are not interpreted theories; they are devices intended to institute precise comparisons. Unless one wishes to assume that ideal types are not methodological expedients but transempirical forms constituting a kind of heaven of Platonic ideals in which actual events participate, one must assume that any given ideal type is destined to be surpassed. It must also be assumed, however, that ideal types will continue to be employed as long as sociology or any science relies upon the comparative method.

3

TALCOTT PARSONS'
THEORETICAL METAMORPHOSIS
FROM SOCIAL
BEHAVIORISM TO
MACROFUNCTIONALISM

A SCIENTIFIC THEORY IS A SET OF logically related hypotheses which form an explanation of a body of events. The two blades of the shears by which the scientist cuts out the pattern of his theories are logical consistency (of ideas) and empirical adequacy (of the explanation). Theory construction, this pattern-making process, takes time, and though the shears are continuously at work the patterns emerge only very slowly. Often, nothing is more futile than the question which blade of the shears did the most work at any given stage, for both are necessary, and particularly important is the fact that they cut against one another.

The two major patterns of theory that have been formed in contemporary sociology are Social Behaviorism and Functionalism. Many significant issues of social theory are bound up with the contrast. Some of the most important contemporary sociological theorists have been in the process of making the transition from one type of theory to the other. Perhaps the chief contemporary sociological theorist to make this trip is Talcott Parsons, who thereby internalizes in his personal development one of the central dramas of contemporary sociology. Moreover, as a charismatic leader of considerable influence, Parsons has trained students at different stages of his development who frequently talk past one another without apparent comprehension.

THE FUNCTIONALISTIC ARGUMENT
IN CONTEMPORARY SOCIOLOGY

Sociological Functionalism rests on the assumption that socio-cultural life is fundamentally organized into organic-type systems. The two general premises of Functionalism in which this assumption is contained are that (1) the organic-type system is the primary fact in socio-cultural events, which can be analyzed only from the standpoint of the whole; (2) any item in the socio-cultural system is in functionally interdependent relations within the whole; it is in reciprocal determination with the whole.

Although for reasons known only to themselves the Sociological Functionalists choose to trace their origins primarily to such anthropologists as Benedict, Malinowski, and Radcliffe-Brown, the position has profound affinities with those of such founders of sociology as Comte, Spencer, and Ward. Functionalism has become prominent in its recent forms since World War II.

The major internal issues in functionalistic theory have revolved around the questions: Just what is and how large is the system from the standpoint of which socio-cultural life must be analyzed? What are the basic properties of whole-part relations with respect to conditionality, indispensability, centrality, etc.? In terms of their respective solutions to these questions, two branches of Sociological Functionalism have emerged. Microfunctionalism, which takes a relatively small-scale system to be basic, is represented in the ideas of such persons as Kurt Lewin, R. F. Bales, L. Festinger, and G. Homans. Macrofunctionalism, which takes a relatively large-scale system to be essential, is represented in the recent theories of Talcott Parsons and Robert Merton.

THE SOCIAL BEHAVIORISTIC
ARGUMENT IN
CONTEMPORARY SOCIOLOGY

In commenting on the ancestors of the contemporary Functionalists, Robert Park long ago borrowed concepts from the philosophic theory of universals to characterize the difference between the Functionalists and non-Functionalists of his time. He described the Functionalists as "realists" (by analogy from the realistic conception of universals), that is, persons who explain social events from the premise of the causal primacy of the whole over the part. Park described the non-Functionalists as "nominalists" (by analogy from the nominalistic conception of universals), that is, persons who explain social life from the standpoint of the causal primacy of some kind of unit taken to be fundamental.

A richly emotive language has been created in the course of the conflicts that have emerged when Functionalists and Social Behaviorists have clearly perceived their respective theoretical differences. The Functionalists see the Social Behaviorists as blind "atomists" or "elementarists" who cannot see the forest for the trees; the Social Behaviorists perceive the Functionalists as mystically inclined "wholists" or "integralists" who cannot see the trees for the forest. Indeed, the basic tenets of Social Behaviorism are the reverse of the tenets of the Functionalists: (1) the only things that really ever exist are social acts; (2) all social group structures and the like are merely "as if" realities, fictions or conveniences of speech but not new entities with causal powers of their own apart from the causal aspects of the individual acts that make them up.

Just as subschools of Sociological Functionalism appear in terms of what constitutes the basic system and how such systems operate, so, subschools of Social Behaviorism emerged in terms of differences of conception as to what the ultimate units of social life are and what kinds of laws hold between them.

Though there were developments pointing toward Social Behaviorism before that period, this kind of theory came into its own after World War I and maintained its dominance over American sociology until World War II. By the end of World War I, three distinct subschools of Social Behaviorism had appeared: (a) Pluralistic Behaviorism (represented in the present by W. F. Ogburn and F. Stuart Chapin); (b) Symbolic Interactionism (represented by G. H. Mead, Faris, Blummer, and many others); and (c) Social Action theory (represented by Max Weber and R. M. MacIver). All these subschools of Social Behaviorism take the ultimate social reality to be some kind of behavioral unit. They differ primarily in the way this unit is conceived as acts, attitudes, or as meaningful social action. They all agree that social structures are nothing more, at bottom, than products of these units.

Despite internal variations, the Functionalists generally tend to think that the Social Behaviorists missed the boat altogether and never touch the real causes of social events at all. The Social Behaviorists, by contrast, have generally been convinced that the Functionalists are guilty of reification, of making things out of fictions. Society is the real entity that brings about conditions in its parts for the Functionalists; society, to the Social Behaviorists, is merely a name for the strategy of individuals, for society *as such* does nothing.

The extent to which Talcott Parsons stands astride the main theoretical trends of his time is revealed by the fact that he has undergone the development from one position to the other and from the worm of Social Behaviorism has metamorphosed into the butterfly of Macrofunctionalism. One may assume that so fundamental a change must have been accompanied by considerable inner drama. Perhaps some day Parsons will explain his reasons for the shift. Meanwhile, one can only account for the dramatic sense of excitement that clings to some phases of his work as a by-product of the radical nature of the theoretical change they contain.

TALCOTT PARSONS: PHASE I

The Structure of Social Action,[1] Parsons' first major book, was a review of the theories of Alfred Marshall, Vilfredo Pareto, Émile Durkheim, and Max Weber. Of these theorists Pareto and Durkheim were proto-Functionalists, Marshall and Weber were Social Behaviorists.

Durkheim, for example, took the critical property of society to be its solidarity or nonsolidarity (*anomie*). He went so far as to attribute even such individual phenomena as suicide to the social state of *anomie*. As his Functionalism reached full development in *The Elementary Forms of the Religious Life,* society was even conceived as the source of the basic concepts of logic and science. "Society is not at all the illogical or a-logical incoherent and fantastic being which it has too often been considered. Quite on the contrary, the collective consciousness is the highest form of the psychic life, since it is the consciousness of the consciousnesses. Being placed outside of and above individual and logical contingencies, it sees things only in their permanent and essential aspects, which it crystallizes into communicable ideas."[2]

In contrast to such extreme Functionalism, Max Weber formulated an extreme form of Social Behaviorism. Socially the only thing that ever actually exists, for Weber, is meaningful social action. Even social relations are merely fictitious entities. A "social relationship . . . consists entirely and exclusively in the existence of a probability that there will be, in some meaningfully understandable sense, a course of social action." This also holds for all social structures. "A 'state,' for example, ceases to exist in a sociologically relevant sense whenever there is no longer a probability that certain kinds of meaningfully oriented social action will take place."[3]

In Parsons' study, which is not particularly famous for its lucidity, it has often been noted that the discussion of Weber is the most clear. From a review of four social scientists (Marshall, Pareto, Durkheim, and Weber) Parsons deduced that a generalized system of action contains four types of elements: (1) heredity and environment, which are ultimate conditions of action; (2) means and ends; (3) values; and (4) zeal or effort.[4] Parsons' conclusions are in all essentials identical with Weber's. These are: (1) The act is the smallest unit of sociological analysis; (2) actions appear in systems—hence, system is the second structural concept; (3) systems may produce emergent properties not completely analyzable into the individual acts; (4) systems of social actions may, for convenience, be treated as structures, aggregates of persons; however, (5) structures have only a fictitious reality; in principle every structure is analyzable into unit acts, though this is slow and inefficient.[5]

The conclusions in Parsons' *Structure of Social Action* are most noteworthy for their thoroughgoing nominalism. At this time Parsons was a Social Behaviorist of the Weber type. The ultimate and only true realities are meaningful social actions. All structures are merely shorthand devices of analytical utility. In principle all analyses performed by use of social structures could be made more precise by analysis into social actions. The only indication of a potential break from this nominalistic orientation is the suggestion that systems of social actions may have "emergent" properties not analyzable into unit acts.

TALCOTT PARSONS: PHASE II

In his outline of a structural-functional theory of social systems in 1945,[6] Talcott Parsons made a decided break with his earlier "nominalism," moving toward a more "realistic" theory of social structure.

In this formulation, social system is the object of analysis, and "actor-situation" (rather than social action) is conceived as the unit part. While actors are the units of the social systems, a social system has a structure, *i.e.*, a relatively stable system of units. The role is offered as the concept that links two systems: the actor and the social structure. From the standpoint of the actor, social structure organizes expectations and defines proper behavior. From the standpoint of structure, an institutionalization of roles is the mechanism for integrating many different individualities.

Institutions are said to be systems of patterned expectation which control human participation in society. They are related to the functional needs of actors and the requirements of the social system in terms of the principle of functional differentiation. A threefold scheme for analyzing them is presented by: situational institutions (organizations of roles around natural or biological facts, as in kinship institutions), instrumental institutions (for the attainment of various goals), and integrative institutions (relating individuals to one another, as in social stratification and authority).

The contrast between this and the earlier formulation by Parsons is quite clear. (1) The ultimate units into which social systems may be analyzed are not social acts but roles. (2) The order of causal priority has been reversed and institutions define and cause the lesser units rather than being determined by them. Talcott Parsons' theory has shown a strong displacement away from the Weber type of analysis and in the direction of a Durkheim type of analysis.

By this time Parsons was finding himself in quite conscious opposition to Weber. He found Weber "suspicious of too much emphasis upon a functional approach to social science." Parsons quite correctly observes of Weber: "To him, departure from the 'whole' smacked of a kind of mysticism by which it was possible to derive far-reaching conclusions without adequate empirical basis."[7] In this context, Parsons launches against Weber the characteristic functionalistic complaint against the Social Behaviorist. Weber's whole methodology, Parsons maintains, tends to degenerate into a "kind of 'type atomism.' "[8] Without the slightest ambiguity, Parsons makes it clear that in his opinion adequate analysis proceeds *from the whole, not from the part.*

Phase II of Parsons' development was brought to its most systematic form in his statement before the American Sociological Society.[9] Here he indicates that the basic task of systematic theory is to carry out structural-functional analysis from the standpoint of the functional prerequisites of the system: biological and psychological provision for the needs of members and the structural provision for social order. Institutionalization and differentiation are the fundamental social processes. Institutions are the critical facts of society. This is quite consciously identified with Durkheim's position.

I think this is what is left of Durkheim's emphasis on the study of society as a phenomenon *sui generis*. This point of view should not, however, be interpreted to mean that sociology should be confined to the formal classificatory treatment of the structure of institutions. I should prefer the formula that institutions are the focus of its interest.[10]

In Phase II of his development Parsons has become deeply critical of the theories of Max Weber and increasingly receptive to those of Durkheim. The task of sociology now is centered in the interrelation of institutions, the motivation of individuals to conform to them, and the forms of institutional change.

TALCOTT PARSONS: PHASE III

Whatever genie operates at the base of Parsons' originality was inclined to give him no rest. Once again a new decade brought into being a new theoretical formulation first embodied clearly in *The Social System*.[11] The ideas of the previous decade were brought into a new synthesis. The elements of action are broken down into ideas, feelings, and values. Status-role (a person's particular place in a system and what he does in it) is conceived as the unit of social analysis. Institutions are conceived to be role-complexes of integrative, regulative, and cultural types. So far all this sounds familiar.

However, in this new phase social systems conceived to be the basis for the integration of value patterns and need dispositions become the units of analysis. A society is a social system meeting all the essential long-time functional requirements of individuals.

When social systems, comprehensive enough to be entire societies, become the unit of analysis, some device must be found to draw distinctions between them. Such a device has been presented by many traditional sociologists, as for example, Henry Sumner Maine in his contrast between *Societies Based on Status* and *Societies Based on Contract*, Tönnies in his contrast between *Gemeinschaft* and *Gesellschaft*; and Durkheim in his *Society Based on Mechanical Solidarity* in contrast to *Society Based on Organic Solidarity*. In recent times parallels have been found in Robert Park's *Sacred and Secular Societies* and Robert Redfield's *Folk Society* and *Secular Society*. Such societies have been differentiated in terms of such factors as kinds of legal relations, kinds of social bond, nature of institutional dominance, and the kind of evaluation by individuals of each other.

Parsons' device for arriving at a technique for analyzing social systems was to give abstract formulation to the various items in terms of which social systems may be compared. Parsons calls his new dichotomous formulations "pattern variables of role definition." For example, the pattern variable (I) Gratification *vs.* Discipline Dilemma refers to the fact that in any social situation one may be permitted to get emotionally involved or may be required to remain neutral. The members of a family, for example, are emotionally involved in and responsive to the situations of other family members. They may weep for a lost daughter or kill the fatted calf at the return of a prodigal son. Their relation to one another is one of mutual emotional involvement and gratification. A doctor in a clinic, by contrast, is expected to keep his emotions removed from his work in a disciplined manner. He is expected to give the same impersonal, scientific treatment to all persons who come to the clinic regardless of other considerations. One may generalize this contrast which appears between the ordinary family and the ordinary clinic. Any social group may differ from any other in the degree to which it permits emotional gratification on the part of its members or requires emotional discipline. Entire societies may differ in the same manner. In Parsons' inimitable language, societies may be compared in terms of the pattern variable of gratification and discipline. They will be found to be affective (emotionally permissive) or affectively neutral.

The numbered items, or as Parsons calls them, pattern variables, are the basic components of social system according to Parsons. They were put in a table together with parallel ideas from Tönnies to reveal their origin. But Parsons did not stop here. He argues that their "permutations and combinations should yield a system of types of possible role-expectation pattern. . . . This system will consist of thirty-two types."[12]

The starting point for Parsons' theory in this third phase of development is the old dichotomous classification of societies by the founders of sociology. Parsons' pattern variables appear to be abstract, dichotomous formulations of the items of such societal types. By working out their permutations and combinations Parsons is provided with a scheme

Parsons' Social Systems and Tönnies' Societal Typology[a]

PATTERN VARIABLES (DICHOTOMOUS ROLE DEFINITIONS)		GEMEINSCHAFT		GESELLSCHAFT	
Parsons	Tönnies[b]	Parsons[c]	Tönnies	Parsons[d]	Tönnies
I. Gratifications = discipline dilemma	Emotional relation	Affectivity	Personalized (like husband and wife)	Affective neutrality	Impersonal (like buyer-seller or lawyer-client)
II. Private vs. collective interest dilemma	Relation of individual to whole	Collectivity orientation	Status (each for all)	Self-orientation	Contract (each man for himself)
III. Value orientation	Responsibility of individual to others	Particularism	To particular persons	Universalism	To others legally: professional responsibility
IV. Modalities of social object	Basis for evaluating others	Ascription	For what they are	Achievement	For what they do
V. Scope of interest in object	One's interest in others	Diffuseness	General	Specificity	Specific or segmental

[a] Tönnies and Parsons approached their respective problems from opposite directions. Tönnies developed a typology of communities which he analyzed into a number of items which differed dichotomously in his Gemeinschaft and Gesellschaft. Parsons started his analysis with a series of five dichotomously classified items which he believed to be universally present in human society. He then envisioned the possibility that communities (social systems) represented various permutations and combinations of his pattern variables.

[b] The items in terms of which Tönnies analyzes his communities may be taken as equivalent to Parsons' pattern variables.

[c] If one takes together one pole of Parsons' pattern variables it may be seen that they are coextensive with Tönnies' description of the Gemeinschaft.

[d] If one takes together the other pole of Parsons' pattern variables it may be seen that they are extensive with Tönnies' description of the Gesellschaft. (Editor's Notes.)

of thirty-two types of possible social systems. Whereas the older theories (Durkheim, Tönnies, Maine) had two types of societies at their disposal, Parsons has thirty-two.[13]

When one applies this scheme, interesting novelties of procedure and verification appear. One of the first discoveries made in analyzing actual social systems from the standpoint of the thirty-two theoretically possible ones is the comparative barrenness of actual social reality: "In certain crucial areas of social structure we do not find that empirically observable structures cover anything like the whole range of theoretically possible variability." One immediate value of discovering the barrenness of social life is that it justifies the sociologist in "short-cutting investigation of the whole range of structural possibilities and concentrating on only a fraction of them." Apparently one is not only justified in ignoring most of the theory, but one is spurred on to find laws as to why the theory doesn't work. For Parsons urges that the discovery of nature's barrenness can serve as a "highly important lead into formulation, and hence testing, of fundamental dynamic generalizations, of laws of social process, since the explanation of why the logically possible range of variability is empirically restricted can be found only in terms of such laws."[14] This is Macrofunctionalism with a vengeance.

SUMMARY

The changes which continue to be made since *The Social System* have so far only altered details. Parsons' theory has gone through three basic changes: from a strict form of Social Behaviorism in which the unit of analysis was the meaningful social act, to stage two in which the unit of analysis was the institution (quite consciously identified as closer to Durkheim's position) to stage three. By stage three the metamorphosis from Social Behaviorism to Macrofunctionalism was complete.

How far Parsons moved from his original position close to that of Max Weber is revealed in the way the two thinkers handled Tönnies' societal types. Weber was familiar with Tönnies' ideas and found considerable utility in them. However, with his strict nominalism he could not use the *Gemeinschaft* and *Gesellschaft* as entities which determined their component parts. Weber transformed them into processes *vergemeinschaften* and *vergesellschaften*: movements toward community in contrast to movements toward society.

Parsons, in extreme contrast to such de-reification, formulated the properties of the *Gemeinschaft* and *Gesellschaft* abstractly and projected a system of thirty-two possible social systems. It is quite possible that Parsons is right: Weber might well have viewed Parsons' procedure as "a kind of mysticism by which it was possible to derive far-reaching conclusions without adequate empirical basis." There is little doubt as to the contrast. Weber has the spirit of the bank examiner who determines precise cash reserves. Parsons has the spirit of the business promoter who forms metaphysical holding companies.

It is easy to understand in terms of the sharpness of the contrast between the three different phases of Parsons' development why he has left a train of at least three groups of followers, each loyal to him, but unable to understand each other. Moreover, in the course of this personal evolution Parsons sums up a good deal of the development of American sociology, which was dominated by the various branches of Social Behaviorism until World War II but has since found room for the development of Functionalism. Parsons was one of the agents in this change.

The full motives for the rise of Functionalism alongside Social Behaviorism are not altogether clear. It *is* clear that the various branches of Social Behaviorism raised methodological problems they did not completely solve. Pluralistic Behaviorism pinned its hopes on the development of statistical methods (which it did yeoman service in introducing) but these did not fulfill all the expectations originally imposed on them. Symbolic Interactionism pinned its early hopes on case methods. These, too, proved to be only partly adequate, leading to the demand to make symbolic interaction researchable. Finally, Social Action theory depended on ideal types to make comparative study precise. However, it failed to convince many. These facts alone would have been sufficient to encourage further theoretical explorations.

Another possible reason for the emergence of Functionalism is the ideological atmosphere of the war and postwar periods. Social Behaviorism in treating society as a strategy was quite in accord with strong liberal trends of the interwar period. Functionalism, which treats society as a causal entity, is much more adaptable to the conservative trends of the war and postwar periods.

However, the precise reasons for the shift to Functionalism had best be stated by the persons who made the shift, and this they have not clearly done as yet.

PART THREE

INSTITUTIONS

and COMMUNITIES

The two dominant social theories at the present time are Functionalism and Social Behaviorism. The areas of primary strength of these two theories are quite distinct: Functionalism is most effective when dealing with groups and societies, while Social Behaviorism is most effective when dealing with social actions and social persons. However, if they are to achieve full generality, it is necessary for Functionalism to develop a theory of social persons, and for Social Behaviorism to develop a theory of social structure.

As the Social Behavioristic theory of social structure has been developed, some sharp contrasts have become visible between it and the Functionalists' theory. Functionalism, like its prototype, Positivistic Organicism, has approached the problem of social structure in organismic terms. Having conceived of societies in organismic terms, the Positivistic Organicists consistently treated social sub-structures—institutions—as organs. Talcott Parsons has formulated the relation between more and less inclusive social systems (societies and groups) in parallel ways.

The procedure of this paper has been to . . . define an organization by locating it systematically in the structure of society. . . . It seemed appropriate to define an organization as a social system which is organized for the attainment of a particular type of goal: the attainment of that goal is at the same time the performance of a type of function on behalf of a more inclusive system, the society.
It proved possible to bring to bear a general classification of the functional imperatives of social systems and with this to identify the particular mechanisms necessary to bring about the attainment of the goal or the organization purpose. The classification used has proved its applicability both for the level of the total society and for that of the small group. The present application to an intermediate level further increases confidence in its generality.
The classification distinguishes four main categories: the value system which defines and legitimizes the goals . . . the adaptive mechanisms which concern mobilization of resources, the operative code concerned with the mechanisms of the direct process of goal implementation, and finally, the integrative mechanisms.[1]

Though this formulation is far more abstract than that of the Positivistic Organicists, the assumptions are similar. It is noteworthy that the three levels of social structure (group, organization, society) are asserted to be identical in structure. Moreover, the significance of a group or organization lies in its "type of function on behalf of a more inclusive system, the society."

Surely the Functionalists live in a neatly buttoned-down world if an organization is a "social system" which is lashed tightly into place by no less than four "functional imperatives" and fitted into the more inclusive social system, the society, for which they perform essential functions.

In sharp contrast to this, Social Behaviorism always analyzes social reality into inter-human acts. From this point of view, to speak of groups as "social systems" already implies a fixity (reification) which does not exist in fact. To the Social Behaviorist, a group or organization is only a more or less stabilized pattern of inter-human acts—it is a *strategy of collective behavior.*

The notion of "social system" carries with it the impression of great stability—particularly when that system is held down by functional imperatives. It is like treating the activity of hiking as having the same kind of reality as a tightly laced pair of hiking boots. The idea of "strategy," on the other hand, suggests a dynamic fluidity, a continuous readiness for change, which is always in fact typical of human behavior.

One of the functional imperatives imposed on social systems, according to Parsons, is the "value system which defines and legitimizes . . . goals." Values are important for the Social Behaviorist, too; however, they are conceived as entering the sphere of action, not as a set of requirements clamped down from the outside, but as the objectives of strategy. Thus, for the Social Behaviorist, values are not like cast-iron pipes through which social life flows, but are like the uses to which they may be put. A strategy may or may not achieve its objectives. When it does, the strategy tends to be confirmed in its success; when it does not achieve the values for which it is designed, a strategy may be modified by a radical change of tactics.

In contrast to the Functionalist who sees fixity and stability everywhere, the Social Behaviorist sees groups and organizations as only more or less stable strategies, and life itself is thought to present a panorama of endless compromise, adjustment, and change.

Not only does the Social Behaviorist's conception of society differ from that of the Functionalist with respect to his conception of group and organization, but in some other important ways as well. The Social Behaviorist understands society (or community) as a total or grand strategy of collective behavior by a plurality of people. He sees no reason why the relation between groups and organizations and society should always be in harmony. As a matter of fact, he assumes that between a society (or a community) and some of its groups some conflict is inevitable. A society can arise only by the modification of groups in order for them to fit into a larger working whole. To some degree, the efficiency of groups is impaired in the process. One sometimes is in the unenviable position of having to weaken some features of the family to increase the efficiency of some features of the economy, or *vice versa*. One of the eternally challenging features of communal life, to the Social Behaviorist, is the modification and conflict between various groups and institutions wherever they are formed into communities.

Moreover, the Social Behaviorist cannot accept the view either that institutions are like "organs" of the social body or that the various groups and organizations of a society are constructed on identical lines as the total society. Society is a grand strategy of social life. To assume that such a grand strategy is identical with the smaller strategies that may be embraced by it, is like assuming that the total pattern of a war is identical with that of a single campaign. The Social Behaviorist, in fact, assumes that society and groups are always to some extent in tension.

Though ten years' time separates the following essays (the study of the family was written in 1947, and the introduction to Max Weber's *The City* in 1957), both are concerned with a Social Behavioristic interpretation of institutions and communities. The essay on the family accepts the institution as a pattern of behavior (a social strategy), variously subject to modification in terms of its affinities with other strategies from the surrounding social world. The introduction to Weber's brilliant study of *The City* is primarily intended to clarify his Social Behavioristic suppositions and his treatment of the city as a community made possible by the modification of the institutions of pre-civic communities such as the family and the clan.

4

THE VARIETY

OF THE

HUMAN FAMILY

MAN AS ORGANISM IS FIRST AND LAST
a living thing. Man and the microbe that may bring his death are only
very distant relatives, but the same stuff of life is in both. With the
monkey in the zoo, the alley cat, the rat, the flea, the microbe, man
shares the distinguishing characteristics of all life: the capacity to take
nourishment, to grow, to adapt to the physical environment, to reproduce. Among his closer relatives in the animal world, man numbers
the gorilla, the chimpanzee, the old-world monkey. Even the fine
points of his genealogy have been traced with fair exactness.[1]

The human family is built about the very things man shares with
all life: food, growth (of the young), adaptation (of young and old),
reproduction. It was inevitable that when man came to probe into the
mystery of his lost origins he should search the biological world for
clues.

In tracing the evolution of his hand, his upright posture, the
arrangement of his shoulders, man has had a high degree of success.
Even the differences between the human races have been explained as
minor variations of a single animal species.[2] Can he do the same for
the family? To phrase the question differently: Is there a protohuman
family out of which the wide variety of contemporary forms have
arisen? If there is, many of the doors closed to the sociologist will open
as if by a master key.

THE SEARCH FOR THE
PROTOHUMAN FAMILY

The search for a protohuman family would seem, reasonably
enough, to begin with man's nearest relatives, But students have by no

means stopped here. In the call of a bird, the trill of a frog, the curious dance of a salamander, they have found "courtship" patterns. In the dam of a beaver, the burrow of a prairie dog, the nest of a bird, they have discovered "home building." In the protection of its cubs by a mother wolf, the hatching of the eggs and feeding of its young by a mother bird, they have discerned analogies to the education of human children. Some thinkers, in fact, carry the search for clues back to the "social" insects: the ants and the bees.

The search for a protohuman family is far more difficult, however, than the search for a protohuman animal form. The animal form, at least, is an immediately tangible thing of flesh and blood or, at the very least, of fossil remains. A family, by contrast, is the result of a series of actions between the persons composing the group. It is an organized action *pattern,* and such patterns are not turned up by the spade of the archaeologist.

For analytic purposes two major types[3] of behavior may be distinguished. Behavior is *instinctive*[4] when it is directed toward fixed goals, when these goals or objects are biologically determined, and when the behavior pattern is hereditarily transmissible. The migration of birds south in the fall of the year, the return of the spawning salmon to fresh-water streams, the spontaneous croak of a frog in the spring, are examples of instinctive behavior.

By contrast, behavior is *noninstinctive* when it is undefined as to goal, when it is conditioned, in whole or in part, by other than biological factors in its execution, and when it must be learned. Though only a small part of noninstinctive behavior is "conscious" or "rational," rational action is the most extreme antithesis of instinctive behavior. The man who goes on a vacation has little in common with the migrating bird or spawning salmon. He chooses among possible vacation spots; he calculates his resources; he adjusts his stay to his time and general interests; and at the last moment his wife may change her mind. Without a road map he might get hopelessly lost in a way the migrating bird or spawning salmon never could. Similarly, a family resting on an instinctual basis will be objectively fixed, biologically structured, and hereditary; a family resting on a noninstinctual basis will be variable in pattern and subject to a range of adjustment in which accident and learning play significant parts.

The search for clues to a protohuman family may now be phrased in more exact terms. It is a search for a central core of instinctive actions—for a rough series of generalized drives. Furthermore, total behavior patterns of man and animal must be compared. Isolated similarities may be quite misleading. The "promiscuity" of a wren, the "homosexuality" of a pair of male chimpanzees in the absence of females, may bear little resemblance to comparable practices among men. The assumption that they are "natural" because they are found both among animals and men may be irrelevant.

INSECT SOCIETIES

The societies of the so-called "social" insects show a marvelous internal division of labor. A beehive, for example, is organized about the activities of the queen bee. The drones, once they have served the purpose of supplying spermatozoa for the eggs, are useless and usually die off in winter when food is scanty. The multiple activities of the hive, the construction of the intricate "cells," gathering the honey, the secretion of wax, guarding the hive, even the feeding of a special food that turns larvae that would otherwise be sterile workers into queens—all these are done by the workers. The hive functions as a communally guarded storehouse, nursery, and honey factory.[5] This community, however, organized with a completeness that would arouse the envy of the most absolute dictator, is only in external form in any way comparable to human society. Human society, too, has a division of labor and an integration of many activities into a working whole, but there the similarity ends. Before it is even grown, the larva is determined to be a worker or a queen by its diet. The physical structure that leads to the construction of the hive does not have to be learned— it is transmitted by the germ plasm of the insect. Instinctive behavior *par excellence!*

BIRD FAMILIES

The activities of birds toward their young sometimes seem to display a rather amazing intelligence. The bush turkey of the Solomons, for example, lays its eggs in heaps of vegetable matter and sand. The heat from the rotting vegetation serves to incubate the eggs. The blunt end of the egg points upward; the feathers of the fledgling point backward;

and when the chick hatches, every move serves to force it up and out of its natural incubator.[6] The bush turkey appears to have solved the problem of hatching its eggs without undergoing the inconvenience of sitting on the nest. Again, the robin seems to display real skill with her sculptured nest; the oriole appears to be a first-rate weaver when she contrives her silken bag on a swaying bough. And the naïve hunter is amazed when he finds himself deceived by the pretended disability of a mother partridge as she lures him away from her young. All these things are so ingenious as to seem not only intelligent but also consciously planned.

These actions, however, are uninspired by awareness or conscious intention. While there is great variation between the various species of birds with respect to ways of mating, nest building, egg hatching, or feeding, the behavior of any one species is biologically fixed. The fledgling hatched in an incubator and reared under artificial conditions reproduces the exact details of the life of its forest parents. Skills do not need to be learned but emerge complete with maturation. Sexual receptivity is periodic, appearing as the result of seasonal changes in the physiological processes of the bird.[7] The sequence of activities that constitutes the family arises automatically without learning. A sparrow does not learn new techniques from the nest of a robin; a crow is never tempted to append its nest like the oriole to the swaying branch-tips of a tree.

In the bird there is far greater latitude for accident and variation than is found among the "social" insects. There is, too, a surplus of energy that is expressed in play. Still, the fundamental behavior pattern involved in the family activities of the bird is biologically fixed and hereditary. It is definitely of the instinctive type.

MAMMAL FAMILIES

In contrast to the birds, mammals show a tremendous increase in capacity for learning. Beyond instinctive ways of behavior new "learned" patterns, habits, appear. Yet little can be gained from the study of the dam of a beaver, the tunnel of a prairie dog, the den of a mountain lion or fox. Sexual activity is in most cases confined to a special season. The inception of physiological changes in the mammal serves as a trigger mechanism to set off a chain of responses in which each response is linked to the preceding one in an invariable sequence. The peculiar house, hutch, den, or shelter is biologically determined in the species.

Interesting differences marking them off from other forms are nevertheless displayed by mammals. The period of gestation becomes longer. The time required for maturation is greater. There are fewer young, and this permits more "individual" attention. The latitude for individual variation on inherited behavior almost imperceptibly widens. And finally, learning, in the form of individual adjustment, learned responses, habits, can be discovered.[8]

**PRIMATE FAMILIES
OTHER THAN HUMAN**

The chief characteristic of the primate order is its simplicity and "generalization," or lack of specialization (that is, the animal is not limited to one purpose, as may be seen by comparing the hand to a hoof, a paddle, a claw). Most of the order lives in trees, and the whole of the order has characteristics resulting from life in trees, including upright posture and the tendency toward a generalized hand with a refined development of the power of grasp. Generalization is apparent, too, in the fact that mating is not restricted to a limited period, but occurs in monthly cycles throughout the year.[9] Above all, the further one moves up the scale of primate complexity the larger the brain capacity.[10] Again, the period of complete dependency on the mother is increasingly lengthened. The lemur is completely dependent for a few days, the monkey for a matter of weeks, the ape from three to six months, man a year; maturity is attained by the lemur in a year, by the monkey in from two to three years, by an ape in eight to twelve years, and by man in from twelve to fourteen years.[11]

From the lack of specialization of the primate order consequences of great significance to family patterns follow. It becomes inaccurate to speak of a *sex instinct*. Sex urge or drive would be better, for sexual activity is possible almost continuously throughout the year. As might be expected, the primates display an amazing amount of general sexual play.[12]

Both the male and the female primate are always to some degree in a sexually excitable condition, and the stimuli that can release their sexual responses are enormously varied. Any member of the social group, old or young, will stimulate sexual responses in another. A monkey will, as Hamilton has shown, also attempt to use kittens, puppies, foxes, and even snakes as sexual objects.[13] Sexual interest, in fact, seems to be one of the major bases, if not the most important basis, of more or less permanent male-female relationship.[14] The long period of dependency serves to bind parents and young together for a longer period.

Even the briefest survey reveals the wide diversity of family organization among the primates. The howler monkey studied by Carpenter in Panama[15] lives in groups of from four to thirty animals, occupying jungle areas with which they are identified by a process of mutual avoidance. The adult males act as defenders and protectors of the group as a whole, sometimes intervening in quarrels between the young, leading the monkey band on their noisy treks through the jungle. Other than such rough dominance by males there is no distinct organization in the howler bands; there are no distinct families. Copulation with the females during receptive periods is continuous and indiscriminate; the howler is genuinely promiscuous.

Quite another picture is afforded by the baboon. In Zuckerman's study, it was observed that the dominant males tended to build up harems which they defended to the death. At times when the proportions of males to females were roughly equal and when the males were of equal strength, a situation approaching monogamy appeared. Ordinarily, however, the dominant males gathered about them as many females as they could effectively defend. Thus the total family group consisted of the male overlord, his females and their young, and one or more bachelors which attached themselves to the family group.[16] The bachelors, in spite of an air of superb indifference, seemed to join the groups out of general sexual interest and were not always disappointed.[17]

In his native habitat the baboon does not seem to be as territorially bound as the howler monkey. During the day the large bands split up into solitary individuals or family groups and forage in the fields and plantations: by night they assemble in bands to sleep on the cliffs.

The gibbon of Siam[18] is monogamous, displaying a different family pattern. Groups ranging from two to six live within and defend areas of the forest. Gestation takes about seven months, during which copulation continues uninterruptedly. Infancy is prolonged; the infant gibbon is seldom out of contact with its mother for the first six weeks. The adult male's role seems to be primarily protective, and he may even intervene in intergroup quarrels. The young gibbons, brother and sister, intermate; sometimes a young male may even replace the father as sexual partner of the mother.

In his African setting, the chimpanzee is gregarious and nomadic. Individuals are associated in groups of two to a score, in which there ordinarily appear an adult male, one or more adult females, and a varying number of individuals between infancy and adolescence.[19] Food and shelter are readily available and the groups rove about building individual nests each night and living off the fruits of the jungle. Both monogamous and polygynous families occur, with polygynous patterns appearing more frequently. The remoteness of the areas and the shyness of the creatures have prevented systematic observation of the relative permanence of such families. The family life of the gorilla is roughly equivalent to that of the chimpanzee.[20]

In summary, the primates other than man are confined to tropical areas where food is plentiful. They live on fruits, berries, grubs, and vegetable matter, evidently without using special food-gathering techniques. There is, furthermore, at present no way of judging whether the territorial bands or groups of apes are instinctive or habitual, though the presence of a "territorial" instinct in birds has been proved.[21] The closest approach to shelter or house building among the apes is the crude "nest" built by chimpanzees and gorillas.[22] Perhaps more significant is the fact that the crude sleeping platforms of the chimpanzee are built for a single night, fitting into no permanent house pattern; the young sometimes build them in play. There is a decided difference between the various apes in the amount of time spent in the trees. The gibbon spends a majority of its time in arboreal activities; the chimpanzee spends about half its time in the trees; the gorilla is at best a clumsy acrobat. The gorilla, however, can stand erect and walk bipedally far more easily than the chimpanzee or the orangutan.

Of more interest are the "psychic" characteristics of the apes. The chimpanzee shows a definite fondness for rhythmic body movements and sometimes performs crude dances. While the gorilla has not been observed to dance, rhythmic pounding and beating is common. All the apes are gregarious and more seem to prefer group life, although as an ape grows older he is frequently solitary. Yerkes quotes Kohler: "A chimpanzee kept in solitude is not a real chimpanzee at all."[23] Rudimentary leadership based on size and strength appears in all the apes. The group is usually dominated by a male. While gibbons are found normally in single families, groups of families are found among both chimpanzee and gorilla. Finally, there seems to be distinct temperamental differences among the apes. The gibbon appears shy, timid, gentle, good natured, easily stirred to emotional response, quick to express resentment or anger; the chimpanzee is active, excitable, impulsive, and buoyant, with intense emotional responses,—temper tantrums are not unusual; the gorilla appears calm, deliberate, reserved, seems to repress or inhibit emotional response, and is on the whole brooding and moody.[24]

Yerkes and Yerkes note[25] that the term "instinct" seldom occurs in the literature concerning the chimpanzee. It does, in fact, tend to vanish from the literature concerning all the primates other than that about man. In place of biologically inherited instincts the monkey, and, more particularly, the ape tend to inherit less specialized drives or tendencies. One result of this is the formation of varying sized groups, another the multiple forms of sexual play. Most marked of all is the amount of learning, sociability, and emotional response. Family types range from promiscuous to monogamous. There is, however, no indication that any one kind of primate "employs" more than one kind of family form except where celibacy is forced on "bachelor" baboons, or monogamy results from an under-supply of females, or physical dominance leads to varying degrees of subordination.

THE HUMAN FAMILY

The most general survey of the characteristics of the human family indicates how far it has departed from a set of instinctively fixed actions.

Man lives under every variety of climatic condition from tropic to desert and from desert to pole. He does not simply accept his environment, but has positive and even aggressive attitudes toward it. He molds it to suit his needs. His house may be built out of skins, snow, bark, wood, stone, grass, mud, steel, or glass. He secures his own food supply through cultivation. He utilizes an amazing array of implements and instruments. Man's social life, too, is amazingly complex— sexual, political, economic, and many other elements are compounded in ways that are rarely twice the same.

Table 1.
A Tabular Comparison of Biological Families

Family	Sexual Basis	Social Groupings*	Social Dominance	Economic Status†	Behavior Patterns‡
		COMPONENTS OF THE FAMILY			
Insects	None after fertilization has occurred	Beehive or ant hill	Ant warriors	Communal economy	Instinctive
Birds	Temporary mates during mating season	Nest	Pecking order	—	Instinctive
Mammals	Mating promiscuous during rutting period	Herds, Packs, and Pairs	Strongest mammal	—	Instinctive. Some learning manifest
Howler Monkey	Promiscuous	Unorganized bands	Dominant males	No communal solution	Largely instinctive
Baboon	Polygynous	Groups of families	Dominant males	No communal solution	Instinctive. Some learning
Gibbon	Monogamous	Single family group	Strongest ape, usually male	No communal solution	Instinctive. Some learning
Chimpanzee	Monogamous	Single family group	Strongest ape, usually male	No communal solution	Instinctive. Some learning
Gorilla	Monogamous	Single family group	Strongest ape, usually male	No communal solution	Instinctive. Some learning

* Nothing comparable to a consanguinal family is apparent.
† Except in the case of the insects, a few birds, and mammals, nothing approaching a pure communal solution to economic problems can be discerned.
‡ No definitive study of instinct has been made among apes. A certain amount of crude education is discernible.

If instinctive and noninstinctive patterns are thought of as polar types,[26] the families traced fall on a scale. While insect societies represent an extreme case of instinctive social grouping, the families of human beings represent an extreme case of noninstinctive social grouping. It is noteworthy that as the role of instinct behavior diminishes there is increased scope for generalized drives, needs, or tendencies which not only permit but require individual adaptation and the increased application of intelligence. For a fixed problem with a single unlearned solution, there appear general problems capable of many solutions.

The search for a biological prototype of the human family, for a core of purely instinctive molds of behavior, has failed. The explanation of the human family has to be found in the nature of noninstinctive behavior patterns.

THEORIES OF FAMILY ORIGINS

To say that the search for a protohuman family has hitherto failed does not mean that the human family had no "origins"; it had to begin some time, somehow. Moreover, it is clear that the human family took its various forms step by step with the emergence of noninstinctive behavior. This does not mean, of course, that the family is in any way "unnatural." Noninstinctive behavior is as "natural" as instinctive behavior.

Since it is so vital to an understanding of the family, noninstinctive behavior deserves closer analysis. It has been shown to be based on generalized drives. Furthermore, an area of indeterminateness surrounds the action. Within this indeterminate area a variety of equally effective adjustments is possible. The most crucial question that can be asked with reference to noninstinctive behavior is, "Why, when many actions were possible, did this particular one occur?"

In the ape it was noted that "instincts" had largely vanished and in place of these were general needs, which are satisfied in a rough hit-or-miss fashion. The nest of the chimpanzee is extremely crude by comparison with the beehive. But no infant bee ever demonstrates the virtuosity of a young chimpanzee who constructs a crude counterpart of the nest in play. The chimpanzee's nest affords significant insight into the nature of noninstinctive behavior. Without fixed instincts to predispose him to a single invariable chain of responses, his actions become not responses at all but solutions of problems. The limiting conditions of the action are found in the satisfaction of the need in terms of the plasticity of the environment. The plasticity of the environment, in turn, must be interpreted in terms of the intelligence of the animal. The general needs of the ape are easily satisfied in a propitious environment; hence his solutions are quite crude and do not indicate any *extended* intelligent application—but intelligent they are.

The essential characteristic of noninstinctive behavior is found in the limited amount of intelligence[27] involved in the given case. Types of noninstinctive behavior may be constructed in these terms for the purposes of analysis.

The rat in the maze tries every available possibility, repeating the same actions over and over many times and at last achieving success by accident. Through many trials the maze is at last "learned" and the rat runs it swiftly and unerringly. The pattern of behavior consists in *random effort, leading to unthinking habit.* If this is set up as the lower limit of noninstinctive behavior in terms of the amount of intelligence involved, the most complete antithesis is the reflective action of a man at those times when he conscientiously plans a course of behavior in terms of an anticipated result. Between these extreme types of noninstinctive actions (random effort leading to unthinking habit and conscious planning and experiment) a number of intermediate types can be distinguished.[28]

Human actions do not occur singly. They are grouped and patterned in various ways. For this reason institutions and even total societies have been analyzed in terms of the kinds of actions that go into their composition. A society or family in which *traditional* and *sanctioned* actions predominate may be called a *sacred* society or family; a society or family in which *rational* actions predominate may be called a *secular* society or family.[29]

When the American housewife goes to the market and buys at the store that sells the product most cheaply, and when, further, her purchase is made in terms of a carefully calculated family budget, she is behaving *rationally,* and her behavior is a part of a *secularized* pattern. When the Irish countryman goes to the village and trades only at the shop whose owner has married a kinsman, he is behaving *traditionally;* his action is a part of a *sacred* pattern.

It is instructive to note that the predominant drift in times covered by written history has been from *sacred* to increasingly *secularized* types of social adjustment. The family has been deeply affected by such transformations.[30]

These considerations as to the nature of noninstinctive behavior are of great importance to the problem posed in the first section of this study. When the search for a protohuman family has not gone back to the biological world for an instinctive model it has sought for a common *sacred* family pattern, assuming that from it contemporary family types may have arisen.

The only safe conclusion that can be drawn from older studies of the family is that as a form of noninstinctive behavior it was, from the beginning, capable of assuming varied patterns. We should, perhaps, not speak of the "origin" of the "human family" but of "origins" of "human families"—recognizing that from the beginning of his differentiation from other animals man was a peculiarly plastic and adaptable kind of ape. The first family patterns no doubt originated in random activity that became fixed in unthinking habits. When such unthinking habits are socially transmitted—forced on the young or "learned" by the young—the patterned actions are traditional.

In at least one respect man's development, in spite of minor setbacks, has been continuous. Though the downfall of great civilizations testifies to the loss of techniques and tools *en masse,* once men have discovered or invented new tools they have tended, by and large, to extend the use of them. Man's forebears left the jungle and slowly through invention populated the planet—finally even boxing up a tropic atmosphere inside a house of snow in the Arctic wastes.

When man learned to speak, his capacity for varied adaptation to his fellows and to his environment expanded so terrifically that he was forever to be set apart from other animal forms. The first human families could hardly have been based on anything other than unthinking habits socially transmitted. They were traditionalistic sacred types. Changes must have occurred as a result of discovery and invention—brief flashes of rational insight that extended one man's control over others or the control of the group as a whole over the environment. In part the development of man has been his continuous advance into an environment he has made (or partially made) himself.

NONLITERATE FAMILIES
(SACRED TYPES)

The old illustrative method, miscalled "comparative," was not so much method as license. It drew its pictures of the family in the way the Greeks depicted the centaur—adding the torso of a man to the body of a horse and turning him loose on the wings of a bird. Illustrative studies of the family sketched in this eclectic style have been almost wholly rejected.[31]

A study of older theories calls attention, however, to the purposes of the various actions that make up the family. The actions that occur between members of the family or between the family and the wider social group may be sexual, affiliational, economic, magico-religious, esthetic. Some or all of these types of actions may be present and vital to the continued existence of the given family.

One of the most glaring errors of the older theories was the failure to take account of the total effect of all these actions as they were interrelated in the special case. Ordinarily, the minimum-essential social actions that must be taken into account are the sexual, the internal affiliational (those relating the parents to each other and to the young), the external affiliational (those relating the family to the wider group), and the economic. Magico-religious and esthetic actions are at times important, but it is not always necessary to reckon with them.

It should be noted that, in characterizing actions as sexual, affiliational, or economic, the emphasis has shifted to the defined *needs* the actions fulfill or the *purposes* they serve rather than the degree to which they are affective, traditional, sanctioned, or expedient.

On the basis of the sex relationship families have been classed as follows: (1) *promiscuous,* when every female is available for sexual purposes to every male and *vice versa*; (2) *group marriage,* when two or more brothers (kin by blood or classification) marry two or more sisters; (3) *polygynous,* when one man has two or more wives; (4) *polyandrous,* when one wife has two or more husbands; and (5) *monogamous,* when one husband has one wife.

In terms of affiliational dominance of the parents over the young and one parent over the other, families have been classed as (1) *genocratic* or *gerontocratic,* when the old men of the group are collectively dominant over the females and the young; (2) *patriarchal,* when the eldest male is affiliationally dominant; (3) *matriarchal,* when affiliational dominance rests in the woman.

In terms of the affiliations within and between the family and other groups of society, families have been classed thus: (1) *conjugal,* the immediate linkages between husband, wife, and children; and (2) *consanguinal,* the family based on a more or less extended kinship system. The chief types of consanguinal family are: (a) the *clan,* or *matrilineal clan,* when relationship is traced through the mother; (b) the *gens* or *patrilineal clan,* when relationship is traced through the father; and (c) *mixed,* when kinship follows some other principle.[32]

In terms of its economic functions the conjugal or consanguinal family may be classed as (1) *autonomous,* when it constitutes a self-sufficient economic unit, or (2) *heteronomous,* when it constitutes a part of a larger economic pattern.[33]

Too much attention has been paid to the classification of families on the basis of isolated traits; too little has been paid to the evaluation of the families as wholes. The classification of families as *nonliterate* (when the people did not possess writing) and *literate* (when the art of writing existed), *sacred* (when the actions that composed them were primarily traditional and sanctioned) and *secular* (when the actions composing them were increasingly affective and expedient), was a major step in the new direction.[34] This approach looks beyond the individual traits to the total family.

As has been indicated, the drives that underlie human behavior do little more than indicate the general problem. They do not predispose man to the choice of one rather than another means for its solution. The solutions of recurrent needs, however, are not random but patterned—this time patterned by "habit." The longer the period of infancy and dependent youth the greater the opportunity for the young to learn the habits of the parents.

A society built of such unthinking habits and not subject to intrusive outside influence tends to demonstrate a high degree of internal solidarity and a strong resistance to change—though adaptation to an advantageous set of intrusive conditions may occur dramatically, as in the case of the Comanche, who changed from a peaceable plateau people into raiders in a relatively short time.[35]

Left to themselves *nonliterate* peoples (and their families) are essentially conservative—tending to grow into their traditions rather than out of them. Innovation, of course, occurs constantly, and the accumulation of small changes in traditional behavior patterns eventually transforms the society. For the people within the society, however, there is often no awareness at all of change.[36]

The examination of a few nonliterate societies may serve the purpose of illustrating some of the varieties of sacred families. Since they represent long-established patterns from which slow internal adjustment has tended to eliminate antithetical elements, they indicate some of the ways in which sexual, affiliational, economic, and religious actions may be continued in stable patterns.

The Ovimbundu Family

The Ovimbundu of Benguela, South Africa, live primarily by agriculture.[37] The social structure in the past centered in two systems: (1) the Ovimbundu (those who do not eat flesh), who were commoners; and (2) a nobility (royal households of Imbangala stock). The line between these strata has tended to be blurred by intermarriage. The contemporary Ovimbundu peoples are divided into tribes feudatory to larger ones. The office of king centralized religious, political, and civil judiciary functions. The basic social unit is the village (*imbo*) under a headman (*sekulu*) who is technically the patriarch of the village.

The Ovimbundu household consists of a man, his wives (the family is polygynous), and their children. The household (*ocikumbu*) consists of domestic animals and possessions, as well as persons. Each wife, with her own hut, granary, chickens, and fields, forms the core of an autonomous economic unit. The wives are ranked—the first having pre-eminence.

Nearly all villages belong to a single *epata* or extended family. The two main kinship groupings are the *oluse* (paternal line) and *oluina* (maternal line). The *oluse*, consisting of local residence units,[38] controls education of children, ownership and inheritance of land, village office, and village worship (including agricultural festivals). The *oluina* dominates negotiable property, family observances, and rituals for specialized economic goods.

The Family in Lesu

A considerably different integration of family into social structure is illustrated by the Melanesians of New Ireland. Relatively propitious land and sea conditions make the gaining of a modest livelihood fairly easy. Pigs, taro, yams, bananas, and pawpaw are staples supplemented by coconuts, betel nuts, sugar cane, dates, breadfruit, and sago.[39]

The village, the primary locality unit, divides into hamlets consisting of from two to eight households with communal cooking facilities and, in some instances, with a men's house and a cemetery. Socially the village is organized into moieties and clans. Lesu has two: the Telenga (fishhawk) and Kong kong (eagle). The clans are composed of extended maternal families. Residence is matrilocal.[40]

At marriage, which cuts the lines of moiety and clan, the maternal clan functions as a unit. The child is a member of the mother's clan, which regulates education and property inheritance. The preferred marriage for a man is with the daughter of his father's sister's daughter's daughter. As in most sacred societies, sexual organization is pervasive. Women may not enter the men's house or attend its feasts and dances. Brush-clearing is a male activity, planting and cultivating female; cooking is a female prerogative, fishing and pig-hunting are male.

Among the contrasts with the family of the Ovimbundu are the importance of a matriarchal and matrilocal principle, basic differences in the relative economic independence of the household, and a different distribution of educational responsibility. These contrasts are definite enough to make it very clear that sacred societies or their components, although similar in many important respects, are often dissimilar in others.

The Trobriand Family

The family of the Trobriand Islanders described by Malinowski[41] stands in marked contrast to those already sketched. The islanders live in villages under the jurisdiction of a chief of noble blood. There is a sharp division of labor: the men do the heavier work of planting yam tubers, mending fences, housebuilding, fighting; the women do the lighter tasks, household work, weaving.[42]

The consanguinal family is matrilineal. The conjugal family is of two types: that of the chief, polygynous; of the commoner, monogamous. In contrast to the Lesunese, however, the man does not live in the wife's house but the wife in the man's. The maximum effect of the matrilineal clan is therefore prevented by a patrilocal principle of residence.

Economically the consanguinal family is autonomous, the conjugal family is heteronomous, *i.e.,* the conjugal household receives its yearly supply of yams from the wife's clan. The chief receives no tribute from his villagers, but each year the clans of his many wives contribute a share of the yams to his household. The vast stores of yams thus built up are used by the chief to finance wars, ceremonies, and expeditions.

The society is remarkable for the exceptional sexual freedom it tolerates. Sexual experiments among very young children are not uncommon. At adolescence the sexes are segregated, and young men live in "bachelor" houses. By this time temporary sexual liaisons are formed and broken. Marriage usually follows more or less permanent premarital liaisons, the motives being quite definite. A man cannot achieve full status in the community until he is married. Furthermore, the support of the household comes from a yearly gift of yams of the girl's clan. The final control of the clan over a displeasing marriage consists in withholding the support of the household.

Children are welcome among the Trobriand Islanders, and the roles of maternal uncle and father are the reverse of our own. Child training is accomplished with a maximum of ease. The child steps, at last, of his own volition from the situation of premarital sexual license into a monogamous adult role within which he is expected to be "faithful."

Marriage depends only upon the consent of the wife's clan. Divorce is as simple; the wife simply packs her belongings and returns home. With his economic support lost, the husband usually tries by means of gifts to win her back.[43]

The casual, free-and-easy aura that surrounds sex in the Trobriand Islands contrasts with the restrained attitude of the Ovimbundu, who ignored it when possible, and the Lesunese, who were quite ambivalent about it. A significant difference, too, is found in the way matrilineal descent and patrilocal residence tend to counterbalance each other. Affiliational dominance in the society is patristic.

The Eskimo Family

The economics of the Eskimo are all-absorbing; he is eternally preoccupied with the problem of survival.[44] So completely has he solved the environmental problem as he defines it, however, that little trading is done with the outside. While retaining some sentiment for the local area where he was born,[45] he may migrate over very long distances. Travel, in fact, is almost second nature.[46]

There is no definite political structure among the Eskimos. A chieftain is usually appointed for a single hunt, but his authority returns to its original status once the hunt is over.[47] The family is small and simple; it constitutes a self-sufficient economic unit with a division of labor typical of a hunting family.

Both polyandry and polygyny occur among the Eskimos, though polygyny is more frequent. The family lives in a common snow house sleeping on blocks of ice covered with skins. While indoors, heated to a considerable degree of warmth by burning animal oil, the family is naked, for the clothes are removed on entrance.

The Eskimos are ordinarily exceptionally mild.[48] Revenge takes the form, normally, of a wrestling match or a songfest.[49] The general friendliness is nowhere more completely illustrated than in the treatment of strangers, for no Eskimo would allow an acceptable stranger to remain long in his house without lending him a wife.[50]

In contrast to the families outlined so far, that of the Eskimo is simple. It is not integrally linked with a large kinship system nor with a political structure. The family is an autonomous economic unit which may be polyandrous or polygynous; sexual hospitality is widely practiced.[51]

The Atimelang Family

Du Bois' study[52] of Atimelang in Alor in the Netherlands East Indies provides still another example of the sacred family. Affected by the Australian landmass, Alor has a monsoonal climate with a wet season from January to March. With the gradual cessation of the rains, the sequence of crops from corn to rice and beans, followed by sweet potatoes and finally cassava, gives order to socio-economic life. At the end of the period, the land is burnt over and communal hunts for wild pigs are undertaken.

The villages of these former head-hunters are built around dance places of patrilineal lineages (*hieta*). These are surrounded by graves of prominent dead. The lineage houses are expressions of patrilocal residence.[53]

The kinship system has three groupings. The first patrilineal lineage, consisting of descendants of the eldest brother, is called the Eldest

House. Descendants of other brothers form the Middle Ones and the Youngest House.[54]

A second kinship grouping is found in the Male Houses. These relationships are recognized as the grouping of the given person's mother's brother and male descendants (Male House I), the father's male house (Male House II), the mother's male house (Male House III)—there are six in all. The third grouping is the Female House, consisting of all bilaterally reckoned kin not included in the above. It is made up of persons from whom supplementary ceremonial and "financial" assistance may be expected.

Marriage may be monogamous or polygynous. Taking a second wife is conditional upon considerable "financial" success, and it is only the older men who manage it. Marriage to any known kin is considered improper. Since the kinship system is relatively simple, marriage possibilities are wide. Mother-son, father-daughter, brother-sister relations are tabooed as incestuous.

Two major economic patterns intertwine among the Atimelangers. Women are theoretically responsible for cultivation and own all vegetable food, regardless of how much land and work by males is involved.[55] They therefore have very real power. On the other hand, men control the active "financial" system, operating with pigs, gongs, and kettledrums.[56] Such "currency" is invested primarily in the purchase of wives, burial feasts, and the building of lineage houses. The "financial" transactions may be complex enough to drag over two generations.

Interrelations between Families Studied

These five nonliterate families may serve to illustrate the way sexual, affiliational, economic, and other actions are patterned in a given family type. They indicate, too, the danger of taking any one trait apart from its context in the family and in the culture. Monogamy was found among the Ovimbundu, Trobriand commoners, and Atimelangers. In each instance the family was economically dependent (heteronomous). Polygyny appeared among the Eskimo and Ovimbundu, and the nobles of the Trobriands. In the case of Eskimo and Ovimbundu, the conjugal family was economically independent (autonomous); among the Trobriand nobility, polygyny had an important status as well as economic value. Polyandry appeared as an occasional marriage type among the Eskimos. Affiliational dominance was variously located in the family, the kinship system, or the village. The nature of the affiliational dominance and its location had an important effect on the type of relation that existed between family members and family and society. Premarital chastity was in no two cases given the same evaluation. Perhaps more significant than anything else, the qualities of personality values in a given family were nowhere identical. The Trobriand Islander is genial, hard-working, convivial; the Eskimo, sturdy, self-reliant, and friendly; the Ovimbundu is extraverted, expansive, aggressive, balanced in judgment, and dignified; the Atimelanger is mistrustful and introverted, with low self-esteem.

While these five family types are too few to be made the basis of sweeping generalizations, they do indicate some of the factors that must be considered if one is to discuss the family with any precision.

The older theorists talked frequently of *promiscuity.* Yet no people studied thus far have been proved to be "promiscuous." Even the ideas of "group marriage" are subject to some doubt, for there is some disagreement as to whether or not "group marriage" is actually present in the Australian tribes to which it has been ascribed, and a clearcut case is hard to find. Again, the assertion has frequently been made that monogamy always is bound up with the institution of private property. In none of these families sketched here was this true. Most significant of all is the fact that in no case was the family without a definite form. Each has its own specific rules and conditions and its own definitions of crimes and punishments.

LITERATE FAMILIES: SECULAR TYPES

The terms "sacred" and "secular," "nonliterate" and "literate," have been used as though they were parallel. This is only roughly true. It is difficult, *but by no means impossible,* to find a nonliterate society that is fairly thoroughly secularized. Such in fact were the Comanche, who developed into a raiding group on the fringe of advancing white culture. Expedient calculations had almost replaced the traditional patterns of the plateau.[57] Similarly, it is possible for peoples to possess writing and still to represent pre-dominantly sacred-type societies. Such were India, China, and Europe in the early stages of our Western heritage. Writing, in fact, may be a conservative force—such was the function of all "sacred" texts. Consequently, it may be said that in many instances writing facilitates the growth of what have been called, at times, prescribed societies. Oral transmission of sacred prescriptions is often amazingly effective, but the written word is even more so. Granting that affective nonrationality always remains or emerges in some form, the final test of secularization is always the degree to which expediently rational calculation has replaced custom-bound and sanctioned behavior.

However, in the progressive "rationalization" of human society, a development that has by no means been linear but has been filled with discontinuities, writing has a peculiar significance. It is to a large degree a rational invention in itself. It holds the face of the present before the mirror of the past. Even when the text is "sacred" and "inviolable" it tends to grow, if by no other means but the addition of bitter commentaries on the lack of congruence of the times with the ways of the fathers. Moreover, secularizingly destructive controversies about the exact meaning of a given prescription are likelier to arise if the prescription has been set down in writing.

A written record of the accumulated wisdom of the ages is more trustworthy than the span of the old man's memory. The recording of statistics, property settlements, and tax assessments permits government on an unprecedented scale. The codification of rules of social conduct, the transmission of messages through other than an intermediary—all these things and many others are possible with writing. As a net result, the presence of writing tends, by and large, toward an increasing rationalization of human actions.

The significance of writing as a secularizing agency can be seen by examining the problem of taboo. It is quite unnecessary, in explaining "taboo," to assume the existence of sexual jealousy, substitute symbolism, ambivalence, and all the rest. Social actions originated in the establishment of unthinking habits. The social transmission of these habits occurs because the young find it convenient to conform and acquire them or the old find it convenient to impose them. The unthinking accumulation of traditional actions is quite automatic. Training consists in the acquisition by the young of the body of traditional actions of the society. It is precisely offense against these traditions that is "taboo." The theological and magical interpretations of both tradition and taboo given by the society are often quite incidental.

No public force has been set up to enforce the taboo. The breaking of it may occasion only horror, or it may be punished by a solemn decision of the elders. The punishment may in turn become traditionalized.

With the development of writing, violations of taboos may be redefined as crimes. Punishments may be set down in a criminal code. The action now is universalized, standardized, and calculable in a new sense. In fact, the criminal may even weigh the advantages of the offence against the probability of the punishment in terms of a conception of reasonable risks.[58]

Among the secularizing traits that writing makes possible are the development of larger economic units such as would not be possible without some means of accounting; the replacement of a system of mores by legal codes with a consequent standardization of punishments; the appearance of contractual relations based on written documents maximizing the calculation of specific social relationships. In addition, the development of a monetary medium of exchange, if it has not already developed, is hastened, and this monetary medium of exchange in turn permits the translation of a wide diversity of values into standards units of value—"everything has a price." But the list is almost endless, for ultimately hardly a single sphere of human activity will remain untouched.

The more secularized the society, the more difficult becomes the job of analyzing the family in terms of the sum of the influences that play upon and within it. The nonliterate family, ordinarily, is located in a small unified culture. The nonliterate rarely comes in contact with more than a few hundred people during his entire life, and the effective society within which he lives may be far smaller than this. The secularized family is quite another story. So complex are the influences that may play upon it that they are almost impossible to list. Its members may participate in different groups and share with these groups values violently clashing with those held by parents or siblings. In many other ways the secularized family may be pressed on every side by competing appeals and conflicting interpretations. Remote changes in the far parts of the world may influence its economic status. The persons linked within it may wonder, in fact, whether there is anything certain beyond "death and taxes."

In contrast to the survey of nonliterates, where something approximating a total estimate was possible, the best that can be hoped for in examining a few types of literate families outside the United States is to isolate a small number of the major influences that play upon them.

The Irish Countryman

The Irish countryman studied by Arensberg[59] comprises small farmers concentrated in the south and west of Ireland. The typical farm is from fifteen to thirty acres in size. Rye, oats, potatoes, and turnips are grown. Pasture is kept, and hay is provided for a few milk cows. Pigs and chickens round out the economy, which is largely self-sufficient. Only the sale of cows brings money income to the household.

The division of labor between the sexes centers in the house and "haggard" (the family yard). The wife does the housework, takes care of the yard, the chickens, the milking, the churning. The man does the heavier work: mending walls, repairing, field planting, cutting peats in the bog for winter fuel. The children are early apprentices to father and mother in the chores and work of the farm.

Two types of affiliational distinction run through the family of the countryman. By convention a woman cannot inherit the land, which must if possible be inherited by a son—preserving the land in the family name. Women are subordinate in the scheme, but are economically essential in the completion of the farm work, and affiliationally essential for the production of sons. The other affiliational division is that of old and young, between whom much reverence and mutual respect is shown.

Marriage is of central significance to the whole system. It is arranged through an intermediary. It sets in motion the most crucial transitions of the society. The "boy" becomes a man. The old folks move into the special "west" room—the most hallowed part of the house. The sibling family is dissolved at this time, for other daughters and sons emigrate from the home. The dowry serves to compensate father, sisters, and sons for their loss.

Before one of the boys is married and settled on the parental farm, the countryman tries to make provision for his other children. If possible, the boys are apprenticed to a tradesman in the town. The girls are married to prosperous farmers or to tradesmen in the village.

Provisions for his children makes heavy financial demands on the countryman. He tends to hold on to the farm long; hence "boys" continue to grow older, and fret at the reluctance of the father to step down. Marriage occurs late; the system enforces celibacy and virginity.

Folk traditions and beliefs about the "good people" (the fairies) are strong and persist in spite of the fact that the public schools and the Catholic church preach against the fairy cult. But the Irish country-man is in transition. Folk beliefs are steadily "picked to pieces" in the schools. If the surplus youth were not able to emigrate, they would tremendously depress the subsistence level. The picture is that of a peasant tending to become a farmer—a sacred family in the process of being secularized.

The Japanese Family

In his survey of the manner in which Japanese sociology flourished after the Meiji restoration in 1868, Becker notes that though Japan has a rich variety of family types Japanese scholars have largely ignored them.

The family furnishes important and interesting object matter for concrete study, but up-to-date economists like Shiro Kawata and moralists like Kimio Hayashi have almost monopolized the field. The only sociological treatments worth noting are Teizo Toda's *Studies of the Family* (1927) and *Family and Marriage* (1935). When we take account of the fact that the family is one of the most important, constant, and universal of groups, and that Japan offers a rich profusion of family types, this neglect seems hard to justify. Hence we must rely chiefly on studies by Westerners.[60]

During the feudal era, tea-drinking had gradually been reduced to a ceremony in which the tea-drinker and his guest sat crosslegged in a relatively bare room sipping tea that had been precisely prepared. Host and guest joined in the contemplation of an art object such as a paint-ing, a vase, a symbolic arrangement of flowers. After the Meiji, the government revived the Tea Ceremony and Flower Arrangement—making them symbols for the grandeur of Japan. The Japanese code of feudal ethics, *Bushido*,[61] "The War of the Warrior," was also cultivated afresh. The Samurai (feudal warriors of Japan) were erected into ideals of Japanese manhood. The ethic of loyalty to the feudal chief was translated into the ideal of loyalty to the emperor. The highest expression of the loyalty was *hara-kiri*, ceremonial disembowelment.

The partially Westernized Japanese consist of university teachers, government bureaucrats, members of the foreign legation, and people brought up under the tutelage of missionaries. Even in the case of university professors and civil servants, however, the influence of *shukan* (custom) is strong. The people are devoted to their native costume, and prefer to sit cross-legged and without shoes. Ceremonial gifts of symbolic jellybeans are exchanged on customary occasions. Gratitude to a host is expressed by a ceremonious quotation from a twelfth century writer. The Tea Ceremony is a daily festival.

In the home and in society the Japanese man is completely dominant. The wife cannot argue, discuss ideas, or talk seriously with her husband. The Japanese woman is not a hostess, and can accompany her husband only on those occasions strictly required by custom. Her duty is always to act in accordance with custom, functioning as a servant of husband and children. She is not allowed to associate with men before marriage. Marriage is accomplished by agreement between the men involved. A woman of dignified status cannot work or earn money. The only schools of higher education for women in Japan are run by missionaries. Though peasant girls are utilized in the cotton factories, their presence is not voluntary but by agreement with the parents. The girls are confined to dormitories, and all spare time is devoted to schooling them in tradition and the arts of homemaking. At the end of the period the girl is returned to her parents. This arrangement brings in a small income to the family and supplies cheap labor for the factory.

The Japanese male has far more latitude than the woman. He is master of the household, its representative in society. For him the universities are open. His standard sexual outlet is the geisha, who is trained in the arts of dancing, love-making, singing, and entertaining.

It is rather ironic that the system of state capitalism tends to destroy the autonomy of the family. Industry requires the aggregation of proletarian workers. Urban centers that result create markets for farm products and turn the peasants into farmers. Correlated with such economic specialization is a differentiation of governmental function, and modern bureaucratic government tends to transform the feudal functionary into a civil servant. All these factors have tended to secularize the life of the Japanese man and woman.[62]

The Hindu Family

While the Hindu family is undergoing a transmutation,[63] it is interesting to look at the family as it was in a system that is now slowly crumbling. The family was inseparably bound up with the affiliational order; that order, in turn, was inspired by Hindu religion.

Affiliationally, India was divided by a system of castes which consisted of occupationally closed, mutually exclusive, and endogamous strata to which general honorific qualities were attached. The castes of India (*jati*) were, in turn, organized into four larger "colors" (*varnas*).[64] One general theory advanced to explain the origin of this social structure is that the word *varna* originally denoted the distinction between the Aryan (who came as a white conqueror into ancient India) and non-Aryan (the dark substratum of the native population) and that later Brahmanic interpretation invented the *jati* system to distinguish the castes actually found in practice.[65] Whatever the origin, there were four *varnas*.

At the top of the social system were the *Brahmans,* and these constituted not only a *varna* but also a caste. Then came the *Kshatriyas.* These were not a definite united caste. The name *Kshatriya* was simply a collective one assumed by such castes and families as were then dominant. In like manner the *Vaishyas* were not a caste. The name was merely a collective one comprehending the landed classes, cattle-keeping tribes, and clans of men engaged in commerce. The name *Shudra* is applied, as a collective one also, to various castes engaged in commerce and skilled trades, unskilled labor and household service, and other occupations held to be low.[66]

The four hundred million Hindus in India are divided into more than three thousand castes, most of these in turn having subcastes. The Brahmans alone have over eight hundred.[67]

The patriarchal Hindu family, consisting of male descendants, was located within the endogamous caste and bound together in a belief in progressive transmigrations of the soul. The system was further enhanced by the fact that only the male son could perform those rituals necessary to the transmigrations of the soul. The significance of marriage lay in the fact that a son was essential to family continuity.[68] A girl, on the other hand, was an economic liability. She left the house at puberty under a system of child marriage; hence she was of little use at birth or later. Infanticide of females was common.[69]

The son was most carefully awaited and carefully attended, and greatest care was devoted to his education under a Brahmin teacher, a *guru.* The education of the woman, however, was slighted or omitted completely. She would be lost to the household anyway. The woman could attain salvation only through her husband, who was her god and teacher (*guru*) in all things.[70] So important was the need for a son that if the woman was barren, provision was made for polygyny. Finally, after the death of the husband the woman was expected to follow him to death on the funeral pyre or, failing that, to remain a widow for life.[71]

In its original form the genocratic patriarchal family constituted an integral economic unit; recently, however, the industrialization of the country has made inroads on its autonomy. The system of child marriage and female infanticide has been legislated out of existence. In most places, at present, the *nautch* girl and *devadasi* have been eliminated. The strong tendency completely to seclude the women (the *purdah*) has been weakened. In one form or other the Hindu family is becoming secularized.[72]

The Latin American Families

The Spaniards and Portuguese came to the New World as conquerors; the main outline of the Latin American scene is in no little measure due to this fact. Generally speaking, the agricultural land is carved into huge estates, *latifundios*. In 1910 seven thousand families in Mexico owned nearly all the good land; 7 per cent of the population of Chile controlled the tillable soil.[73] This in turn has led to the sharp distinction between the extremely rich and the extremely poor.[74] It is the foundation, too, of the official contempt for labor that characterized the *hidalgo*.[75] Business has been largely dominated by foreign concerns.

The Iberians carried with them over the ocean a dynamic scheme of antithetical ideas about marriage, family, and sexual love. Catholicism enjoined celibacy and virginity as the highest service to God. Marriage had to be sanctioned by the church; it was eternal and irretractable. Birth control or even the thought of birth limitation by any means was sinful. As a direct contrast to this scheme the ideal of romantic love had developed. "The Romance misses no opportunity of disparaging the social institution of marriage and of humiliating husbands."[76] While the church officially enjoined eternal fidelity, the ideal of romantic love centered on adultery.[77] While the priesthoods and nunneries were sworn to celibacy and religious chastity, the development of concubinage in the clergy was a favorite theme of Boccaccio and Rabelais.[78]

The Mohammedan conquest of Spain, with the resulting diffusion of the ideals of polygyny and the seclusion of women, furthered the isolation of the romantic pattern in its Christian context. The more remote the lady became, the more irresistibly attractive. The more virtuous she was, the more valuable as an erotic object. The refinement of a dual standard of morality: of chaste secluded virgins, or dashing polygynous gallants, took place in this context. The higher the barriers about sex the more intense the passion—such was the "paradox of the Western attitude."[79]

This complex of ideas was transferred to the New World, and while the missionaries taught the ideas of monogamy, celibacy, continence,[80] the upper-class Iberians developed a flourishing system of concubinage and polygyny. The operation of a dual standard was never more marked. Not until well in the twentieth century has the Latin American woman been enjoying anything remotely approaching genuine freedom.[81]

Not the least of the differences between North and South America is the manner in which the two continents were conquered. The northern continent was secured by a constant flow of immigration and internal growth that displaced the Indian populations; the southern continent was secured by the spread, over the surface of the Indian populations, of a ruling hierarchy. This has resulted in the pressure of partially Westernized native peoples on the social order of South America.

In this connection, the study by Robert Redfield[82] of the folk culture of Yucatan has great significance for students of Latin American family life.

Yucatan lies between the modernized area of the northwest and the city of Merida. It is a Hispano-Indian culture devoted to the cultivation of maize, and of henequen from which sisal fiber for bags is made.[83] The maize is grown for home consumption; the henequen is grown for export and ties the economy of Yucatan with that of the outside world.

The study compares the city (Merida), the town (Dzitas), the peasant village (Chan Kom), and the tribal village (Tusik) in terms of family and class, Spanish and Indian cultural elements, cultural organization, economic problems, social problems, and religion. Interesting differences appear between these communities.

In the city, Spanish descent carried positive prestige, Catholic elements were weakened, the culture was highly diversified, mobile, and modernized, money was a true medium of exchange, individual ownership of land was universal, marriage choices were spontaneous and based on the conception of romantic love, the church was an association competing with other organizations, and folk practices were commercialized.

At the other extreme, namely, the tribal village, Spanish descent had negative status, the practice of Catholic ritual was more pervasive (and more modified in the direction of folk custom) commercial dealings within the group were almost completely absent, marriage was arranged by the patrilineal consanguinal family, the symbols of the church were more venerated, religion was practiced as a communal affair, and folk custom was a genuine expression of the sociopsychic life of the tribe.

The town and urbanized villages showed gradations between these extremes.

The value of the study lies in the insight it affords into the dynamics of the secularization of Hispano-Indian societies and families. In the tribe the consanguinal family is strong and effective. Marriage occurs by arrangement; the interests of the solidarity of the consanguinal family are paramount; property is owned corporately; monetary exchange between tribal members is almost absent. The consanguinal family is economically self-sufficient. While premarital chastity is not insisted upon, the "arranged" marriages are stable and even adultery is not grounds for a break in the family group.

All these elements tend to change as the family is traced in progressively urbanized centers. In the city the consanguinal family vanishes; marriage is individualistic and based on romantic choice; property is owned individually; divorce is frequent. In short, at least some of the Hispano-Indian families are tending to follow the model sketched as characteristic of the ruling stratum.[84]

The Chinese Family

The China in which the old-style family flourished was based on an agricultural economy. In contrast to the society of India, it never had hard and fast divisions of class.[85] The affairs of the emperor were administered by a body of scholars, the *literati*, who were skilled in the arts of calligraphy and learned in the sacred texts. These officials were chosen on the basis of competitive examinations open to everyone. The bureaucratic structure that resulted prevented the growth of a fixed nobility.[86]

The occupations of China carried varying degrees of prestige. Scholarship was the most honorable of occupations, farming ranked next, followed by craftsmanship and commerce. Actors, prostitutes, eunuchs, and slaves were regarded as socially inferior.[87]

The religion of the ordinary person was eclectic and tolerant—it was an "ethical" religion rather than a "salvation" religion like Mohammedanism or Christianity.[88] Two doctrines of popular religion were of great importance to the family. It was believed that two principles operated in the universe, known as yin and yang. "The yin stands for earth, the moon, darkness, evil, and the female sex. On the yang side are heaven, the sun, light, fire, goodness, and the male sex."[89] The other doctrine was that of the "five loyalties," which formulated explicitly the modes of conduct proper between prince and minister, father and son, older brother and younger brother, husband and wife, and friend and friend.[90] All recognized patterns of social conduct have specific religious sanction. And since the duty of son to father extends beyond death, a man and his ancestors are joined in a common socio-religious order.

The Chinese family was the specific affiliational unit that embodied these socio-religious principles. The consanguinal family normally lived in a single household. It consisted of the grandparents, the sons, grandsons, and grandchildren. It was genocratic; decisions were made by the older males.[91] It was an economically autonomous unit, normally engaged in agriculture. Often the oldest male in one of the larger families was the sole authority in a small village. In all cases the union between family and local political authority was close.

The son was essential to the family. He represented its yang, its hope. The rituals essential to the cult of ancestor reverence had to be performed by the son. Woman, on the other hand, represented sin, darkness, and earthbound passion (yin). The first importance of a woman was the possibility of a son, and this was too important a problem to be left to chance by the consanguinal family—marriages were arranged by the parents, often when the children were quite young.

In addition to ordinary marriage there was a system of concubinage that was not contingent upon the barrenness of the bride. The concubines were two types; those acquired with legal formality, and those purchased—often prostitutes from a brothel. Again, the imperial harem duplicated on a larger scale the constellation of the family. In the imperial harem there were a number of classes of concubines: the consort, three concubines of the first rank, nine of the second rank, twenty-seven of the third rank, eighty-one of the fourth rank.[92]

The slaves in China, at the time, were largely composed of daughters sold by poor families to the rich (to be used as servants) or to the brothels. These girls were taught singing, dancing, and playing the guitar-like *p 'i-pa*. Many of them hoped eventually to buy their way out of the houses. Some were purchased by husbands who were not satisfied with the marriage-of-convenience arranged by the parents in their anxiety to secure an heir.[93]

The status of the woman in the Chinese family was decidedly inferior to that of the man. The five loyalties, the ancestor cult, the doctrines of *yin* and *yang*, all reiterated the importance of the male. Girls were a liability and were lost to the family at marriage. Furthermore, the girl was not given any sort of formal education while schools, often taught by mandarins who had not been fortunate enough to get places in the government, were established for the boys. The wife had no property of her own, and achieved definite status only at the birth of her son.[94]

This old Chinese family which, Latourette remarked, "performed the functions which in the modern Occident are associated with sickness and unemployment insurance, old-age pensions, and life insurance,"[95] is passing away. The reasons for this are multiple: modern couples are leaving the consanguinal household, concubinage and slavery are no longer legal, divorce has been made easy, education (in the form of the public school) has been opened to women as well as men, women have been granted suffrage. All of these changes were well under way before the rise of Communism; they have now speeded up slightly.[96]

DYNAMICS OF FAMILY CHANGE

In contrast to the families of nonliterate peoples, which could be outlined within small compass, it has been possible only to trace a few of the central features of the literate families. This in itself calls attention to one significant difference between literate and nonliterate families; namely, difference in the complexity of the elements that play upon the family structure.

While no complete treatment of the problem is possible here, some of the dynamic principles underlying the transformation of the family, from a sacred to a secular type can be noted. In all of the five literate family types traditional and sanctioned patterns were disintegrating; rational calculations, sometimes accompanied by outbursts of affective nonrationality, were taking their place. Reference to the summary chart, Table 2, may prove helpful.

Table 2.
A Tabular Comparison of Human Family Types

Locale of Family	Conjugal Family	Consanguinal Family "Oluse"	COMPONENTS OF THE FAMILY Affiliational Dominance	Economic Status	Education
Ovimbundu	Polygynous		Elders of Tribe	Autonomous	Elders
Lesu	Monogamous and Polygynous	Clan	Maternal Males	Autonomous	Parents and Clan Elders
Trobriand	Monogamous and Polygynous	Clan	Males of Clan	Heteronomous	Maternal uncle
Eskimo	Polyandrous and Polygynous	None	Patristic	Autonomous	Parents
Atimelang	Monogamous and Polygynous	Male House	Patristic	Heteronomous	Primarily Parents
Irish	Monogamous	None	Patristic	Autonomous	Public School
Japanese*	Monogamous	None	Patristic	Heteronomous	Public School
Hindu†	Monogamous and Polygynous	Gens	Elders	Autonomous	Brahman
Latin American	Monogamous, Unofficial Polygyny	None	Patristic	Heteronomous	Public School
Chinese†	Monogamy and Concubinage	Gens	Elders	Autonomous	Public School

* The Japanese family represented here is by no means characteristic of the whole of Japan. It represents rather its most "Westernized" type.
† In the case of both Hindu and Chinese families the explanation centered about the old-style family that is now rapidly disappearing.

The consanguinal family tended to be weakened or to vanish altogether. With its disappearance, marriage by arrangement disappeared —there was no longer a larger group vitally concerned in the conjugal grouping and securing its own group interest in its control of the marital arrangements. Related to the disappearance of marriage for convenience, individual choice by the mates began to play an increasing role in the marriage. Marriage, too, became contractual; divorce, more simple and frequent.

Economically, in the change from sacred to secular the family ceases to be autonomous. The members of the family are incorporated in an expanded economic order. Other economic changes are apparent in society at large; the disappearance of barter, the appearance of the market. The peasant becomes a farmer; the trader becomes a retail merchant; the artisan becomes a factory worker or a semi-skilled laborer. The land ceases to be corporately owned. Group property becomes private property or the property of a contractual corporation.

Affiliationally, in the change from sacred to secular striking differences appear. Ultimate political control ceases to be local. It tends to be appropriated by a special organization—the town, county, or state government. The sexes tend to achieve equality. Taboo is replaced by law; custom is replaced by formal regulation. Education ceases to be a family affair and becomes the business of a specially planned school. The differences between age groupings are narrowed. The groups of the community (social organizations) become purposeful associations.

In all these spheres the range of rational choice continually widens; sexual, affiliational, economic, religious, and esthetic actions are less traditionalistic and sanctioned, and more subject to rational examination and individual choice. At times these choices are swayed by affective nonrationality.

The variety of family forms found in both nonliterate and literate societies constitutes both a promise and a warning, for the evidence unmistakably proves that while there is no one solution to sexual, affiliational, economic, and religious problems, these solutions are never unpatterned. The family can be changed and the hope of improvement need never be abandoned—this is the promise.

Yet there is an implicit warning in this very variety of family forms. Each culture has achieved its own patterned solution—a solution that it guards most jealously. The amount of variation within a pattern is carefully delimited, and individual transgression of culturally defined limits may subject the individual to scorn and contempt, excommunication, imprisonment, exile, or death. The community strikes back at the deviate.

The dream that unfettered freedom, sexual, economic, and social, is the solution to all human problems, the dream that man was born free and society has enchained him, the dream that human nature is "good" and institutions have corrupted it, are dangerous fantasies. Logically these notions are akin to the argument that since the earth resists the feet, walking would be perfect if there were no earth at all. But the earth and the friction of the ground to the foot are *necessary conditions* of walking; and existing social patterns are *necessary conditions* of social life.

The patterned solutions of family problems characteristic of any given culture constitute its conventional modes of behavior. These conventions are not only supported by specific punishments (spearing, drowning, imprisonment, exile, etc.) but by the structure of personality. Even if the delinquent offender is not discovered he is often stricken with guilt-feelings leading to cynicism, bitterness, disgust, progressive degeneration, and suicide. The internally secure and balanced individual is normally the one who achieves his individuality and freedom through the behavior patterns of his culture.

Thus, while the study of family varieties holds out the promise of change for betterment, *it carries the warning that ill-considered change may have far-reaching destructive effects on individuals and society.*

NEW DIRECTIONS

The literature on the family is vast; it has been possible only to sample it here. Yet in tracing families from biological to literate a number of general characteristics are evident.

The family is a behavior pattern which must be analyzed in terms of the characteristics of behavior. In the analysis of insect and animal families a distinction was drawn between instinctive and noninstinctive types of behavior. When the biological family was evaluated in these terms, it held little promise for the discovery of a protohuman family.

A review of nonliterate and literate family types reveals that no two families are quite the same. This lends support to the suggestion that there were probably many family types from the very beginning of man's history. Furthermore, these earlier families could hardly have been anything other than sacred types based primarily on traditional actions.

It seems clear that families have changed from the beginning. In times of written history this change has been, with many notable setbacks, a change from sacred-type families resting on tradition and sanction to secular-type families within which a high degree of rational calculation is possible. Sexual affiliational, economic, religious, and esthetic actions have all been increasingly rationalized.

In spite of the voluminous literature on families of the world, however, much of it, for lack of a trustworthy scientific method, is useless; it is only recently that the study of the family has come into its own.

One approach to analysis of the family that seems to hold genuine promise is that of Howard Becker and Robert Redfield, who have approached the problem comparatively on the basis of the type-constructs sacred and secular and folk and urban.[97] Such types necessitate (a) the refined study of individual family traits, while (b) they permit an evaluation of the specific family as a whole, and (c) they lead to scientific evaluations of the dynamics of family change. The superiority of this approach to the older anthropological and sociological approaches is twofold: (1) it avoids the meaningless classification of family traits; and (2) it permits prediction, and perhaps control, of family trends.

The same problem is approached in another fashion by Kardiner and his associates.[98] Their method consists in the acceptance of the uniqueness of the particular culture and applying to it of a revised version of psycho-analysis. The primary object of analysis, in terms of this method, is the individual family member. The child is particularly important, for the nature of the culture, in the final analysis, rests upon the traditions the child assimilates. His personality embodies many of the features that typify the culture.

The child is analyzed in terms of three behavior categories: *key integrational systems*, *projective systems*, and *reality systems*.

Key integrational systems consist of those phases of the child's training crucial to his development, viz., maternal care, nursing, sphincter control, emotional response, sibling attitudes, marriage, etc. The *projective systems* of the culture consist of "ultimate rationalizations," such as religion, magic, folklore, etc. The *reality systems* are those specific bodies of knowledge, those skills and techniques that give the people mastery over their material and social environments, such as boat building, wood carving, weaving, pottery making, scientific knowledge, and the like.

In surveying family types it has been stated that different families produce special personalities. Various writers have asserted that the Eskimo is self-reliant and good humored; the Kwakiutl of Vancouver Island is ambitious and competitive; the Trobriand Islander is generous and sexually easy-going; the Dobuan is suspicious and devious. The method of study proposed by Kardiner and his associates may permit a more exact analysis of the manner in which these personality types are developed. The family is the first school of personality. It is often the context within which personality assumes its characteristic shape, and sometimes the context within which personality achieves its most complete realization.

The analytical method of Kardiner, consisting of an analysis of individual adjustment, ideology, and scientific knowledge, of training, ideas, and activities promises more than the old illustrative method which isolated single traits from their specific contexts in family and community and "compared" these; it was incapable of explaining either the diversity of the traits or the significance of the special case.

These two developments in the field of genuinely comparative study—the *type analysis method* of Becker and Redfield and the *social-psychological method* of Kardiner and his associates—are complementary. The one aims at precise scientific knowledge of the basic patterns of family structure and change; the other aims ultimately at a more complete understanding of personality. New vistas may be opened by these new directions that the study of the family has assumed.

5

THE THEORY

OF THE CITY

> The closest approximations to a systematic theory of urbanism that we have are to be found in a penetrating essay, "Die Stadt," by Max Weber, and a memorable paper by Robert E. Park, on "The City: Suggestions for the Investigation of Human Behavior in the Urban Environment."
>
> Louis Wirth (A.J.S., Vol. XLIV, July, 1938, No. 1, p. 8)

NO SUBTLETY OF PERCEPTION IS required to determine that the contemporary American theory of the city is in crisis. Each season brings forth a new crop of books on the city. They are mere produce, not much as food for thought—dull fare as any teacher will testify when his students turn up for examinations with his city-texts unread. The student finds himself trapped behind a boredom so great that he would sooner face the prospect of failing the course. To change the imagery, too often in the presence of the materials of the ordinary city book one feels as if he is in the necropolis, the city of the dead from which all life has vanished. And the writers of the books seem to feel it, too, for as if in the belated effort to breathe life into their materials they argue that in response to the environment of the city the urbanite develops a "segmental" culture and "schizoid" mentality. There seems to be no stopping point in the interpretation of the city between visualizing it as a task exceeding the facilities of the department of sanitation or an insane asylum. Surely in this valley of dry bones one may ask with Ezekiel, "Can these bones live?"

The theory of the city somehow cannot account for what every journalist, poet, and novelist knows—the city is a living thing. As a system of life, the city penetrates the structure of biological evolution itself, creating new urban-insect and urban-animal forms. There are urban-insects like the silver fish, carpet beetle, bedbug, and the cockroach—as special to the city as the proletariat, as urban as the bureaucrat. The rat and the alley cat are animal denizens of the city with an outlook as urban as detachment and sophisticated cynicism. The city has its representatives from the feathered world in the sparrow, the starling, and the pigeon—dodging traffic with the same *sang froid* as the rest of the urbanites, disputing in the squares and holding council in the eaves—winning a livelihood from the by-products of commerce. There are moments in every city dawn when the circles, rectangles, polygons, and triangles—the geometry of the city—seem to float in the mist, like the essence of the human spirit emancipated from the earth. There are times, on starlit nights, when its towers and spires ram upward as if to tear the darkness loose from its riveting stars and the city seems to be a strident assertion of mankind against time itself.

When one examines the urban books it is not immediately apparent where they are deficient. It is certainly not in their statistical tables—since every city is a somewhat untidy statement in applied mathematics. It is an argument in millions of kilowatt hours, millions of short tons of coal, iron, steel, concrete, and brick. It is a metric assertion in linear miles of steel rails. It is a rebuttal in cubic feet of air space. It is a human petition in rates of infant mortality, and tuberculosis. It is a protest expressed in percentages of criminality, juvenile delinquency, prostitution, recidivism, mental illness, and senility. It is a suave assurance pronounced in volumes of transactions, in gross sales, in amounts of credit, in retail and wholesale values, in the size of payrolls, in cash reserves and balances.

Nor can one say the urban books are deficient in the kind of items they include. What is a city without political parties, bosses, machines, chambers of commerce, credit associations, labor unions, factories, newspapers, churches, schools, welfare agencies, philanthropic societies, humane societies, museums, art galleries, lodges, zoos, auditoriums, parks, playgrounds, slums, red-light districts, riversides or park avenues, main streets, jungles, sanitation plants and taxi-cab companies?

One may find anything or everything in the city texts except the informing principle that creates the city itself. One is reminded of Pirandello's piece, *Six Characters in Search of an Author*. Everything is present except the one precise essential that gives life to the whole. When all is said and done the question remains, What is the city?

The persistence in American sociology after all this time of the question can only be explained in terms of the peculiar developmental conditions of American sociological theory. Only recently has the question itself emerged in full clarity. This lends especial interest to the beginnings of a theory of the city in Europe among which the study by Max Weber stands out as of unusual importance. Weber's relevance to the question may be ascertained by way of a review of the stages of theoretical development of the concept of the city in America.

THE FIRST FORM OF AMERICAN CITY THEORY

The modern European city is centuries old; comparatively few American cities extend back of the nineteenth century. The American cities are cut off from the peculiarities of long-standing local traditions in a way that was true in Europe only in the newly-founded cities of the Germanic East. A newly-founded city possesses a relatively simplified structure as against its parent model, for its starting point is inevitably a simplified version of the terminal stage of a developed city. American cities were such simplified versions of civic forms current in England at the time of their founding. And while in Europe, generally, national power partly grew coextensively with the evolution of the city, in America the establishment of national power preceded the formation of most of our cities. The few cities incorporated before the American Revolution were chartered on the English pattern with limited powers granted to them by colonial legislatures. These powers were lodged in a council elected by limited suffrage. At the beginning of the nineteenth century only 4 per cent of the population lived in cities of more than 8,000 population. As cities began to appear in the nineteenth century they were largely modeled on an imitation of the state governments with a council of two chambers, one of which was elected by the city wards. The political activity promoted by this system was enormous for it facilitated avoidance of clear-cut responsibility. In the 1880's James Bryce insisted that city government in the United States represented the most conspicuous of all its political failures.[1] The events leading to this judgment were important for America's first urban theory.

As the effects of the industrial revolution were felt, the growth in size of the cities of the western world was enormous. In the 1880's, for example, Prussia's cities grew by two million; those in France by a million; the cities of England and Wales increased by three quarters of a million, and by 1890 London and Paris had more than doubled their populations as of the mid-century while the population of Berlin had increased fourfold.[2] In America the same phenomenon was apparent. By 1890 one third of the American population lived in towns of four thousand or more inhabitants.[3] Between 1880 and 1890 the number of cities with from 12 to 29 thousand population had increased from 76 to 107; cities of from 20 to 40 thousand population had increased in number from 45 to 91; cities of from 45 to 75 thousand population had increased from 23 to 39. In this decade Chicago increased from one half million to over a million. The Twin Cities had trebled in size. Detroit, Milwaukee, Columbus, and Cleveland had increased by 80 per cent. By 1890 there were already states and even whole sections where more than half of the entire population lived in cities of over four thousand inhabitants. (For example, more than three fifths of the people of the North Atlantic section filled this category.)

In the cities of both America and Europe the tremendous increase of population was correlated with a comparative decline of rural populations. In America the cities grew in considerable measure also by an increase in foreign-born populations. One fifth of all the denizens of American cities in 1890 were foreign born. There were as many foreign born persons in the cities as the entire population of the city in 1880. In 1890 there were only two German cities (Berlin and Hamburg) with greater German populations than Chicago; only Stockholm and Göteborg had more Swedes; only Christiania and Bergen had more Norwegians. One fourth of the Philadelphians and one third of the Bostonians were of alien birth. New York-Brooklyn was the greatest center of immigrants in the world: with half as many Italians as Naples, as many Germans as Hamburg; twice as many Irish as Dublin; one half as many Jews as Warsaw.[4]

The crowding of people into small space bears with it a tremendous increase in specialized demands. People need streets, public water supplies, public sewage systems, garbage disposal, police protection, fire protection, parks, playgrounds, civic centers, schools, libraries, transportation systems. A more complicated system of administration is necessary to handle the complex problems of engineering, law, finance, and social welfare. The unprecedented speed of civic growth accompanying the industrial revolutions carried unprecedented problems in all these respects. A few familiar illustrations from a much told story may suffice for us here.

In the 1890's in America not a single one of the major municipalities had adequate traffic facilities. The majority of streets were ill paved, turning into seas of mud during rains, or paved with cobble-stones or granite blocks. In the 1870's Washington laid more than four hundred thousand yards of asphalt. Buffalo and Philadelphia followed. During the same period Charleston, West Virginia, and Bloomington, Illinois, started paving with bricks which soon became popular, Des Moines, Columbus, and Cleveland leading the civic trend.[5] By 1900 Washington and Buffalo were the best paved cities in the world. Boston and the Borough of Manhattan followed, and Chicago was only beginning.[6] Meanwhile, since most cities were built on water-ways, bridge building was becoming a problem. The Brooklyn Bridge, completed in 1883 by the Roeblings, ushered in an era in the building of super-bridges. Before it was completed the New York traffic problem had become worse than it was at the time construction was started. Other cities were going through the same experience. Pittsburgh built the Seventh Street Suspension Bridge over the Allegheny; Philadelphia completed a cantilever bridge over the Schuylkill; Richmond built a suspension bridge.[7] Simultaneously the old horse cars, omnibuses and cabs from stage coach days were proving to be inadequate to move the urban masses. In 1879 New York completed an overhead railway which scattered oil and hot ashes on the unwary. It was so successful that a wing was quickly added. Other elevateds quickly followed in Kansas City, Chicago, and Boston.[8] In 1901 Boston had begun to burrow underground ushering in an epoch of city tunnel building that still continues. Cable cars were introduced in San Francisco in 1873 and followed in Chicago, Philadelphia, and New York and from there to other cities. A practical dynamo was finally achieved in the 1870's with the possibility of producing adequate supplies of cheap electric current. By the 1880's trial electric trolley lines were tried in Boston and Denver and after the success in Richmond, Virginia, they spread almost universally until 51 cities had established trolley systems by 1890.[9] The tension on communications was no less and by 1878 the telephone had already ceased to be a toy. And once the legal battles between Western Union Telegraph and the Bell Company had been solved, the full effects of Francis Blake's carbon transmitter, J. J. Carty's metallic circuit system, and Charles E. Scribner's switchboard could be felt. By 1880 eighty-five towns already had telephone exchanges with fifty thousand subscribers and thirty-five thousand miles of wire.[10] Meanwhile, the telegraph, at first slowly, continued to expand. Tre-mendous urban pressures led to the eventual consolidation, speeding up, and streamlining of the postal system. The sale of postage stamps increased from around seven hundred million to over two billion during the 1880's. The same period saw the tremendous pressure for efficient methods of lighting with the change from kerosene lamps to open-flame gas jets, to electric lighting made possible by the dynamo and Edison's invention of the electric light.[11] In the course of the competition of these utilities the process of making water gas was perfected. Moreover, the same time period saw the construction of vaults and cesspools, to accommodate the waste of the city with the development of drainage systems that poured sewage into nearby bodies of water and poisoned the water supply. Systems of disposing of garbage developed from dumping into the oceans by barge in the coastal cities to the feeding of garbage to swine in inland cities. The poisoning of the water supplies became acute with epidemics of disease and initiated civic improvements in water systems and a beginning of more sanitary disposal of sewage and garbage. After a dramatic series of fires (the estimated total fire losses in 1878 were over sixty-four million, by 1882 they passed one hundred million dollars, by 1890 over one hundred fifty million),[12] more efficient fire fighting systems, the introduction of new fire fighting devices and equipment, the increased use of fire resistant materials for construction, and initiation of fire protection ordinances and inspections got under way. The problem of housing mass populations was met by a building of shanties, rooming houses, hotels of many kinds, and inventions such as the tenement house which rapidly formed the slum sections of the cities.

Such details are not intended to be complete but illustrative of the opportunities and problems of the urban environment. The growing masses of consumers placed new values on standardizations and mass production. For if one only made a penny an item profit but captured the urban millions, he became a millionaire. Meanwhile the masses of aliens came in response to the need of great quantities of cheap labor. As the results of handicraft vanished from the product, skill disappeared from the producer. It was as if the new urban environment had to tear down before it could build up; it had to simplify before it could complicate on a new principle. And the city itself was emerging as a most desirable consumer. Instrumented by the credit arrangements of modern industry, it was possible for one generation to build what later generations paid for, the city was a monster with an endless appetite for anything that fertile imaginations could dream of supplying: brick, asphalt, concrete, steel, glass in endless arrangements and compounds. The city was also an economically important agent in other senses and able to grant monopolies in the form of franchises to an amazing series of "utilities" affecting access to and use of earth, water, and sky.

The first reactions to and interpretation of these phenomena hardly add up to a genuine theory of the city. They fall into two general categories: attempts to account for its location and its moral consequences.

Charles H. Cooley[13] tried to account for the location of cities. While in the past cities were located by proximity to a religious establishment or fort and while some cities have at all times been located by political considerations, the primary reasons for location of cities are found in transportation. A break in transportation, even if it involves no more than a transfer of goods from one carrier to another, involves much equipment and many facilities. Thus, it is at the mouths or key points of rivers, meeting points on hills and plains, and other such areas that city formations appear. When there is also a change of ownership with the possibility of temporary storage the center grows by leaps and bounds with stevedores, warehousemen, importers, exporters, merchants, money changers, accountants, secondary service personnel, and many other forms and types. The great majority of the larger cities of the United States are located on navigable rivers. The lake ports are among the American cities experiencing most rapid growth: Chicago, Buffalo, Cleveland, Detroit, and Milwaukee. New York depends for its importance on its location at the juncture of both land and water terminals.

Cooley's theory of transportation is evidence of the awakening theoretical concern with the city and the attempt, at very least to explain why cities locate where they do. A more general study of the same type is represented by Adna Weber's *Growth of Cities in the Nineteenth Century*.[14] This much quoted work performed a brilliant service in assembling a statistical picture of the recent quantitative growth of the city in the western world. Beyond this Adna Weber inquired into the causes of the concentration of people into cities concluding that this was primarily a product of economic forces and that those in turn were of the kind becoming significant with the industrial revolution: steam and machinery, trade and commerce, the solution of modern transportation problems, the industrialization and increased productivity of agriculture, the growth of commercial centers, transportation (with Cooley), industrialization and the factory systems. In addition to such primary economic causes of city growth, Adna Weber thought there were a series of secondary causes of an economic, political, and social type. In a secondary economic sense the city grows not only because of the revolution in transportation, finance, production, and commerce but also because of the lure of high wages and the inducements of more varied opportunities. Among the political causes of city growth Adna Weber listed the influence of: (1) legislation promoting freedom of trade; (2) legislation promoting freedom of migration; (3) centralized administration with its location of persons in civic centers; and (4) free forms of land tenure politically defended in the city. Social causes of city growth were found in the advantages the city offered for (1) education, (2) amusements, (3) a higher standard of living, (4) the attractiveness of intellectual associations, (5) habituation to an urban environment, and (6) a diffusion of knowledge of the values of city life.

Adna Weber was not at all convinced that the city spelled the moral ruin of mankind and he devoted a chapter to the *Physical and Moral Condition* of the cities in which he reviewed one of the most systematic indictments of city life in favor of the country.[15] The basic arguments of this treatise made by many other thinkers in other forms were that (1) the city-born reside in the poorest quarters of the city, (2) the city-born predominate in the lowest occupations of the lowest social classes, (3) the city-born contribute an unduly large proportion of degenerates, criminals, lunatics, and suicides, (4) the cities have a low rate of natural increase or even deficient births, (5) the city population consists of as many country-born as city-born, and (6) the typical city-class is incapable of self-perpetuation.[16] Adna Weber treated these propositions not simply as "moral" arguments but as testable hypotheses. After a review of the urban statistics he concluded that they are either mistaken or only partly justified. For example, Adna Weber denies that there is a distinction in America between rural and urban legitimacy rates. Moreover, in Europe while infanticide is more prevalent in the country, abortion is less prevalent there. Prostitution is profuse in the city, to be sure, but it is supplied in considerable measure by recruitment from corrupted country homes. Meanwhile "the amount of viciousness and criminality in cities is probably exaggerated in popular estimation" because of the facilities of the city press.[17] And against all these things, Adna Weber urges, one must not forget the many-sided advantages of the city.

While an awakening theoretical consciousness is evident in the work of Cooley and Adna Weber, at least with respect to the growth, size, and location of cities, another kind of theoretical interest is shown in Josiah Strong's concept of the moral effects of the city.[18] Strong thought that modern civilization shows a one-sided development of material in contrast to moral and spiritual properties. This material growth is manifest in the development of the "materialistic" city whose phenomenal growth was attributed to a redistribution of population because of the development of scientific agriculture, the substitution of mechanical for hand power, and the development of transportation. Society was seen as undergoing transformation from the farm to the city in an irreversible process. "We must face the inevitable. The new civilization is certain to be urban, and the problem of the twentieth century will be the city."[19]

A city, according to Strong, is materialistic when its intellectual and moral development are not commensurate with its physical growth. To illustrate: as a result of improper sanitation Strong believed there were at least 150,000 unnecessary deaths in the city in 1890. Among the basic problems the industrial revolution posed for the city was the adjustment of an aristocratic system of industry to a democratic system of government.[20] As civilization grows more complex the individual becomes segmental and dependent and performance failures on the part of the individual become more socially disastrous. As the city grows more prosperous and rich the administration of its interests affords increased opportunities for corruption. "If we have not sufficient moral sense or common sense to prevent saloon-keepers, thieves, gamblers, jail-birds, and prize fighters from dominating our municipal politics, we have as good officials as we deserve."[21] Homes are disappearing in the city at both social extremes. Among the rich, hotel and club life is being substituted for home life. At the other extreme appear homeless masses living in the lodging house, tenement houses, and a migrant idle class. The church grows weaker in proportion to the size of the city. "Ignorance, vice, and wretchedness, combined, constitute social dynamite, of which the city slum is a magazine."[22] In Strong's opinion these evidences of civic moral decline were correlated with and further exaggerated by the increase in numbers of foreign born and Catholics.[23]

Between the extremes of an attempt to account for the growth and location of the city and concern for a presumed "moral decline" occurring in the city lay the vast area of interest in and concern with politico-economic corruption which elicited reactions of an outraged citizenry. This was documented by the muckrakers, as illustrated by Lincoln Steffens in *The Shame of Our Cities*, and the organization of municipal reform movements.

These various developments cast up fragments of explanations, and materials for a theory of the city but hardly a theory. Cooley and Adna Weber, for example, do not offer theoretical explanations of the city. They assume its existence, only trying to account for its size, growth, and location. Their "theories" account only for the physical and external aspects of the city. On the other hand the moral reaction to the "materialism" of the city also constitutes only the most fragmentary of explanations of urban phenomena, quite apart from its domination of moral considerations. The city itself is treated as the "cause" of moral decline or—in Strong—at least, the foreign born populations, the Catholics, and the slum area. Precisely those individuals and groups most victimized by the processes of the city are blamed for their fates. This, again, is hardly an explanation of the city. Finally the muckrakers and their outraged publics, alarmed at civic corruption, locate the problem in government and their solutions in civic reform. But here, too, only fragments of civic phenomena were being conceptualized.

THE RISE
OF THE ECOLOGICAL THEORY
OF THE CITY

At the time that increased attention was being paid by American thinkers to the nature and problems of their cities, sociology itself was assuming more definite shape. By 1900 the first academic departments of sociology were being established. The new field had as yet to found its first professional society and its first professional journal. The movement from a pre-professional to a professional stage was accomplished in the first decade of the twentieth century. The first graduate school departments were set up. Moreover, if one were to find a point at which an autonomous science has appeared—not a mere area of special interest—it would be hard to find a more appropriate one than that time when assemblage by the discipline of its materials for study first hand occurs. Thereafter, the discipline does not rest on a mere re-hash of data gathered by some other discipline. Under the guidance of the brilliant staff assembled by Albion Small at the University of Chicago, many of these steps toward the professionalization of sociology and the establishment of it as an autonomous science were taken.

As a natural object of study for the new science of sociology, the city was subject to three kinds of requirements: (1) the search for a point of view permitting the approach to both aspects of urban phenomena, (a) the objective aspects of location, size, and growth (Charles Cooley, Adna Weber), and (b) the social aspects (noted by moral critics, Strong; reformers, Jane Addams; and muckrakers, Steffens); (2) an "objective" point of view—that is a point of view permitting simple understanding without *a priori* value commitments either to defend or to destroy; and (3) a point of view providing for the first hand study of the "facts" of the urban environment. All of these objectives were present in a series of papers, theses, and special research projects that were being promoted at the University of Chicago between 1915 and 1925. Eventually they were collected in the very appealing little volume, *The City*,[24] by Robert E. Park, Ernest W. Burgess, and Roderick D. McKenzie, which marks the beginning of a systematic theory of the city by sociologists in the United States.

Park provided the general framework for the ecological theory of the city, as this approach came to be known.[25] He took the position that the city is a "natural habitat of civilized man" in the sense that it represents a "cultural area" with peculiar cultural types. As a natural structure Park suggested that the city obeyed laws of its own and there "is a limit to the arbitrary modifications which it is possible to make: (1) in its physical structure and (2) in its moral order."[26] What holds for the entire city applies also to its sub-sections and every neighborhood takes on properties of the qualities of its inhabitants showing a historical continuity of its own. This, however, should not obscure the fact that the neighborhood tends to lose much of the significance it had in a tribal condition of mankind. Nevertheless, in the city, through isolation, the immigrant and racial colonies, or so-called ghettos, and areas of population segregation tend to maintain themselves.

Every device in the city facilitating trade and industry prepares the way for further division of labor and further specialization of tasks. As a result there is a continuous breakdown of older traditional, social and economic structures based on family ties, local associations, culture, caste, and status with the substitution of an order resting on occupation and vocational interests. Among other things, this means that the growth of the city is accomplished by a substitution of indirect "secondary" relations for direct, face-to-face "primary" relations. The church, school, and family are modified. The school takes over some of the functions of the family. The church loses influence, being displaced by the printed page. This may have the effect of separating the vocational classes so completely that they live in an isolation almost as complete as a remote rural community.

The selection of city officials by popular vote becomes impracticable under these conditions. To meet the emergency of the election crisis created by city life, two types of organizations appear for controlling the vote: the political boss and machine, and the good-government organizations (independent voters' leagues, tax-payers' associations, and bureaus of municipal research). The political machine is based on local, personal, and "primary" relations; good-government organizations rest on secondary relationships, depending upon organizing public opinion.

The great cities not only create vocational but temperamental types as well. Experience is of an increasingly fortuitous and casual character, excluding the more intimate and permanent associations of the smaller community. The individual's status is determined by conventional signs such as fashion and "front" and "the art of life is largely reduced to skating on thin surfaces and the scrupulous study of style and manners."[27] This is correlated with a segregation of moral environments, a multiplication of competing *milieus.*

One may sum up Park's conception of the city in a sentence: the city represents an externally organized unit in space produced by laws of its own. The precise statement of this external organization of the city in space—the badge by which the ecological theory is most quickly identified—was made by Ernest W. Burgess. The systematic statement of its inner "laws" was the work of Roderick MacKenzie.

The growth of the city was treated by Burgess in terms of its physical expansion and differentiation in space.[28] The expansion of the city, he thought, tends to take the form of the development of a series of concentric rings representing successive zones of urban extension. If nothing else interferes a town or city expands radially from its central business district like the Chicago "Loop." (1) This is the first area. Encircling the downtown area there is normally an area in transition, which is being invaded by business and light manufacture; (2) where property is being held for business use and while housing is poor, rent is low; (3) a third area is inhabited by the workers in industries who have escaped from the area of deterioration but who desire to live within easy access to their work. This area threatens to become the next slum. Beyond this zone is the "residential area," (4) of high-class apartment buildings or of exclusive "restricted" districts of single family dwellings. Still farther out, beyond the city limits, is the commuter's zone—suburban areas or satellite cities—within a thirty- to sixty-minute ride of the central business district.[29]

In the argument supporting this physical description, Burgess suggests that the phenomena of urban growth were a result of organization and disorganization in a kind of anabolic-katabolic process. Disorganization is preliminary to reorganization of attitudes and conduct and the newcomer of the city while discarding habitual points of view and traditional morality experiences mental conflict and personal loss. In the expansion of the city a process occurs which sifts and sorts and relocates individuals and groups by residence and occupation. Thus, within the "main stem" appears the "hobohemia" of homeless migratory men. In the zone of deterioration encircling the central business sections are always found the "slums"—submerged regions of degradation, disease, and the underworlds of crime and vice. And progressively as one moves outward the segregation and assemblage of other social adjustments are to be found.

The extent to which Park and Burgess had created an atmosphere actively promoting first-hand research into various aspects of the city is illustrated by the number of projects under their guidance at the time this essay was published. Some studies destined to be classics of American sociology were being conducted. Nels Anderson, *The Slum: An Area of Deterioration in the Growth of the City*; Ernest R. Mowrer, *Family Disorganization in Chicago*; Walter C. Reckless, *The Natural History of Vice Areas in Chicago*; E. H. Shideler, *The Retail Business Organization as an Index of Business Organization*; F. M. Thrasher, *One Thousand Boys' Gangs in Chicago*; H. W. Zorbaugh, *The Lower North Side: A Study in Community Organization*.[30]

Park and Burgess had assumed that the city presented a physical portrait characterized by typical areas and zones. They made numerous references to the laws which established them. The fullest statement of these so-called "laws" or "processes" was made by their colleague McKenzie.[31] Ecology was that phase of biology studying plant and animal forms as they exist in nature in relation to each other and to their environments. Human ecology was a parallel study of the spatial and temporal relations of humans as affected by the social environment. Society was thought to be made up of individuals territorially distributed by competition and selection. Human institutions are accommodated to spatial relations. As these spatial relations change social relations are altered, producing social and political problems.

The first use made of social ecology was to classify communities into four types: (1) Primary service communities are represented by agricultural towns, fishing, mining, or lumbering communities serving as a first step in the distributing process. (2) The second type fulfills a distributive function collecting basic materials from the surrounding area and distributing them in the markets of the world. These are commercial communities. (3) The third type of community is in the industrial town. (4) The fourth type lacks a specific economic base exemplified by recreational resorts, political or educational centers, communities of defense, penal or charitable colonies.

Communities are organized for defense and for mutual economic advantage. When a community reaches a point of culmination—the limits of the economic advantage that occasioned the population aggregation—it must either stabilize, re-cycle, or disintegrate. "A community which has reached a point of culmination and which has experienced no form of release is likely to settle into a condition of stagnation."[32] When it starts to decline, disorganization and social unrest follow. Competition becomes keener, the weaker elements are forced lower in the community or even forced to withdraw. Thus, beyond a point the economic competition that organizes a city, becomes keen and acts as a depressing element in it. At this time innovating elements tend to be introduced into the adjustment of the community, forming the first stage of an invasion that may lead to a complete change in the structure and organization of the community. As a community increases in size it becomes better able to accommodate itself to invasions and sudden changes in the number of inhabitants.

In the course of this process there is a development from simple to complex, from general to specialized. Increased centralization is followed by decentralization. The axial or skeletal structure is determined by the routes of traffic and travel. As the community grows there is a multiplication of houses and roads and a process of differentiation and segregation. As competition for advantageous sites becomes keener with the growth of population, economically weaker types of utilities are forced to lower-priced, less accessible areas. Residential sections also segregate into types depending on economic and racial composition of the population. Some specialized utilities do not appear until a certain point of development is reached "just as the beach or pine forest is preceded by successful dominance of other plant species. And just as in plant communities successions are the products of invasion, so also in the human community the formations, segregations, and associations that appear constitute the outcome of a series of invasions."[33] The two main types of invasions are due to a changed use of land and a new type of occupants. Invasions are initiated by: (1) changes in transportation routes; (2) obsolescence and physical deterioration; (3) creation of structures, buildings, bridges; (4) introduction of new types of industries; (5) changes in the economic base for the redistribution of incomes, and (6) real estate promotions. Invasions lead to a regular process of events with a distinct, initial stage, secondary stage, and climax. The climactic stage is reached when the invasion forces establish a dominant type of ecological organization able to withstand intrusions from others. Once a dominant use becomes established within an area, competition becomes less ruthless among the associating units, rules of control emerge, and the invasion of a different use is for a time obstructed. There are established, thus, units of communal life that may be called natural areas.

Thus the major processes that form the city are in order of importance, competition, concentration, centralization, segregation, invasion, and succession. Their operation creates the "natural areas" that form the physical structure of the city.

When one reviews the literature on the city from the days of this interesting assemblage of essays to the 1950's, it is evident that the second quarter of the twentieth century in American sociology has been dominated by the ecological theory of the city. The primary architects of this theory were Park, Burgess, and McKenzie. As early as 1928 it was clear that the sociological study of the city was assuming a standard form based on these ideas. Nels Anderson and Eduard C. Lindeman brought out their *Urban Sociology* in 1928.[34] The first eighty-nine pages of their book are devoted to an extended ecological description of the city and its environs. Another division of the book is concerned with the so-called "functions" of the city. This includes such topics as the supplying of the city, its waste and sewerage, transportation, recreation, and the mechanization of the urban environments. Another section is devoted to urban personality and groups, and breaks down into a review of some of the psychological effects of the speeded-up, mechanized urban environment on personality and the formation of urban social types with some review of the effects of professionalization on individuals and groups. The study is concluded with a review of problems of an urban environment: poverty, mental health, old age, the disorganization of the home, political disorganization, and so forth.

There is little value here in reviewing all the studies of the city, but a volume or two chosen over time may illustrate the fundamental fact that if the city in America had changed as little as the interpretations of it, its problems could have been solved long ago. In 1932 two very responsible volumes appeared by Davie and Carpenter.[35] Davie's volume even shows a reluctance theoretically to exploit the Chicago concepts. The book opens with the proposition that the development of urbanism is just about the most important thing that has happened to society lately. However, it is concerned so little with the theory of urbanism that the question, "What is the city?" is disposed of by a quotation from Munroe,[36] and after a rather quick review of the growth of the city based upon the study of Adna Weber, Davie took a quick look at city planning and the traffic problem and, dispensing with further nonsense, launched into a discussion of city problems. He devoted 119 pages to housing, 182 pages to health, 170 pages to education, and 149 pages to recreation. What did Davie contribute to the theory of the city? Nothing.

Carpenter's study is somewhat more rich theoretically, chiefly because of its continuities with the Chicago tradition. The first 188 pages were primarily devoted to the geology and ecology of the city. This was followed by a chapter on city growth and planning. The composition of the urban population was reviewed and some attention devoted to the effects of the city on personality. Once again the work trails off into a long review of the problems of the city—its effects on marriage and the family, the home, religion, and finally vice, crime, immorality, mental deficiency, mental disease, and suicide.

In both of these books much larger quantities of research were made available. They are, in this sense, more complete and up to date. But Davie reduces this to a mere review of problems without a particular integrating theoretical framework. Carpenter's study takes the ecological theory as unquestioned and only amplifies it in rather minor ways by somewhat greater attention to institutions.

How remarkably little fundamental change there has been since then is shown by two volumes appearing in 1955.[37] In the study of Rose Hum Lee the old topic of the growth of cities is amplified a bit by materials from Western Europe, Asia, Africa, and the United States. But the fundamental explanatory framework is provided by a demographic and ecological picture. The tendency is manifest to pay more attention to institutions—in fact almost ninety pages are devoted to urban institutions, somewhat less than one fifth of the study. The discussion of urban ways of life, leisure, personality, problems, and city planning are traditional.

In Bergel's study the same traditional formula is largely preserved. How little concerned he is with the basic theoretical meaning of the city may be indicated by the cryptic definition with which he is satisfied. "We shall call a city any settlement where the majority of occupants are engaged in other than agricultural activities."[38] A military base would seem to constitute an almost perfect case. Rose Hum Lee's definition is as cursory. "Cities are basically population aggregates which are large, heterogeneous, and densely settled within a limited land area.[39] However, more important than the lack of interest in theoretic issues is the maintenance of the traditional composition. Roughly the first 168 pages of Bergel's study is devoted to physical and ecological descriptions of the city past and present. A long chapter is devoted to urban demography. The examination of urban institutions is reduced to about eighty pages—a smaller proportion than is found in Lee's study. Almost twice as much space is devoted to urban problems and planning.

In 1958 Louis Wirth's estimate of the state of city theory is almost as relevant as it was in 1938. Moreover, Wirth was a charter member of urbanism incorporated—the Chicago school of ecological theory. In his brilliant study of *The Ghetto* he had carried out one of the most able studies of urban sub-communities to be made. He had contributed the annotated index to the Park, Burgess, McKenzie volume on *The City*. He was familiar first hand with the great majority of studies carried out under Park's auspices. Yet, writing in 1938 he argues:

In the rich literature on the city we look in vain for a theory of urbanism presenting in a systematic fashion the available knowledge concerning the city as a social entity. We do indeed have excellent formulations of theories on such special problems as the growth of the city viewed as a historical trend and as a recurrent process, and we have a wealth of literature presenting insights of sociological relevance and empirical studies offering detailed information on a variety of particular aspects of urban life. But despite the multiplication of research and textbooks on the city, we do not as yet have a comprehensive body of compendent hypotheses which may be derived from a set of postulates implicitly contained in a sociological definition of the city, and from our general sociological knowledge which may be substantiated through empirical research.[40]

It goes without saying that minor modifications of the original proposals of Park, Burgess, and McKenzie are hardly the answer for an urban theory. The concentric zone theory has been toyed with and minor alternatives to it have been offered. And a "separate nucleus" theory and a "sector theory" have been proposed. But they imply acceptance of the original postulates. More up-to-date studies of tuberculosis, recidivism, juvenile delinquency, housing values, prostitution have been offered from time to time. New and more recent demographic descriptions of the population by area and zone have been carried out. None of these proposals and studies touch the basic structure of the original "theory" and one may retain Wirth's critique unmodified.

Basically there are three major theoretical difficulties with the ecological theory of the city. First it started analysis off on the wrong track by orienting it to the geo-physical aspects of the city rather than to its social life. Social life is a structure of interaction, not a structure of stone, steel, cement, asphalt, etc. It is, to be sure, not altogether inappropriate to suggest that one can understand much about the activities of a household by a careful analysis of what passes through its sewerage system and what ends up in the garbage can—but this is true only if these are taken as by-products of activity and as evidence on which to establish inferences. Too much of the ecological study of the city was devoted to the establishment of the properties of various zones —natural areas, habitats, and what not—too little attention was paid to the life that produced these properties. An extraordinarily patient study was made of the scene of the crime; the criminal was largely ignored. The ecological theory of the city was in part betrayed by the demand to make the science autonomous, independent, exact. Too many of the charts, maps, overlay maps, diagrams, and statistical rates and ratios were present for their own sake.

A second fundamental difficulty with the ecological theory of the city was the unnecessary "primitivism" of its crucial concepts. These were summarized most compactly by McKenzie as including competition, concentration, centralization, segregation, invasions, and succession. Civic social life can indeed be accounted for in such terms—that is not the issue. The difficulty was that it could not be sufficiently differentiated in those terms. They could account as easily for rural life as for city life. They could apply to social life in the past or the present. They could apply to non-human animal life as well as to man's life; or to plant life as well as to animal life. One does not account for monogamous marriage by the presence of a sex drive. Such a sex drive will as easily account for sex outside monogamous marriage. One may account for the fact that he eats because he is hungry; this will not account for the fact that on some particular occasions he eats canapes and drinks cocktails. The basic conceptualizations of the ecological theory were insufficiently precise to differentiate the theory of the city from any other branch of sociological theory. In fact they were not sufficient to distinguish sociological theory from political or economic theory or even to distinguish sociology from some branches of botanical theory.

Thirdly, and in part growing out of the first two difficulties, the ecological theory of the city omitted precisely those concepts most traditionally sociological—groups, institutions, social structure. Nels Anderson's and Lindesmith's study of the city had no need for institutions—they were mentioned only incidentally with reference to social problems. In Davie's study as well, no formal admission of institutions is to be found. And after thirty years of development of the ecological theory institutions managed to find a place in the city texts but they are found to occupy less than a fifth of the space.

Positively the ecological theory of the city represented important advances. It facilitated the examination both of the external physical and internal social aspects of urban phenomena. Even more importantly the ecological theory demanded first hand research and the construction of an autonomous science. Finally, its very primitivism was a kind of advantage—it was so completely uncommitted theoretically that almost any kind of study could occur in its name. It was a sort of injunction: Go ye forth and gather facts. This favored the accumulation of a wide variety of data. Of course, this was an advantage won only at a great price, for ever and again the study of the city reduces to a mechanical framework for inventory the social problems of an urban environment. The framework is so loose that normative judgments are able to obscure the requirements of empirical social theory.

NOTES ON A
SOCIAL-PSYCHOLOGICAL THEORY
OF THE CITY

The observation that man thinks, feels, responds differently in the city than outside it is as old as the city itself. There is no more idle error than the supposition that the men of some previous age were any more unperceptive and unintelligent than we. Traditional evidence testifies to the fact that ancient men perceived and valued the special properties of their cities. A familiar concern of fathers for their children in ancient Egypt was that they learn to write and take up the "white collar" tasks of scribes in the imperial bureaucracy rather than suffer the privations of humbler occupations. Pressure and social ascent by way of an urban occupation are ancient. In nearby Babylonia the high value placed on specifically urban types of socio-political opportunities is shown in the care with which the attempt was made to restrict access to such opportunities to privileged groups of citizens. When the Jews were carried off into Babylonian captivity, they were permitted much freedom but carefully excluded from access to the priestly schools and the political positions correlated therewith. In Ancient China the desirability of the urban roles is indicated by the devotion, patience, and hard work the individual was willing to devote in preparation for the civil service exams and the extent to which his family and clan might finance his activities in training for the mandarinate. In classical Greece, the citizen was proud of his membership in the city, and he took this quality as a distinguishing difference between himself and the barbarian. Similar attitudes and evidences of civic pride differentiated the denizen of Rome.

However, it is one thing to recognize the development of a peculiar urban outlook, related to urban occupations and the city environment— this is as old as the city itself—it is another thing to isolate this as the peculiar core of urban phenomena making all explanations from it. The conditions that could lead to this rather curious result were present in the sociology of Georg Simmel.

Sociology was organized in the nineteenth century by non-academic thinkers like August Comte in France, Herbert Spencer in England, and Lester Ward in the United States. The founders of the discipline were rather breezy, imaginative, and not a little imperialistic. They were empire builders establishing a new field out of territories carved from the older disciplines. They did their work very well—so well that sociology was in process of establishment as an academic discipline during the lifetime of some of the founders.

Simmel belonged to the second generation as an academic sociologist. He and his colleagues faced quite a different task from that of the founders—the need to define the field with precision and in limited terms, not in ways that brought it into conflict with every other field. Philosophically Simmel was a careful student of Immanuel Kant; sociologically he was a leader in the school often described as Neo-Kantianism. Ignoring the details, Neo-Kantian social science attempted to arrive at a precise and limited definition of the social sciences by analogy with a procedure in Kant's philosophy. This consisted in drawing a sharp distinction between the form and the content of experience, and finding everything of a general value for science in the study of forms.

The task of the social sciences, according to Simmel, is to study the whole range of man's interactive life. The special task of sociology is to study the forms of social interaction apart from their content. Simmel assumed that the same social forms could encompass quite different content and the same social content could be embodied in different forms. It should be noted, moreover, that interhuman behavior does not by any means reduce to physical action, but includes ideas, sentiments, and attitudes.

If one grants Simmel's approach to sociology and brings the city under analysis, nothing could be more idle than to occupy one's self with demographic details and spend endless hours examining the physical characteristics of zones, neighborhoods, environs, and all the rest. A sociological analysis of the city finds its proper field in the psychic forms of interhuman life in an urban environment. Precisely the mentality of the urbanite is its primary object. Sociologically, thus, for Simmel there is nothing whimsical, marginal, or incidental about a topic like "Metropolis and Mental Life"[41]—quite the contrary in it sociology finds its proper field.

Simmel agrees with many modern observers that the city is peculiarly central to the destiny of modern man. He argues that the deepest problems of modern life arise out of the attempt by the individual to preserve his autonomy and individuality in the face of the overwhelming social forces of a historical heritage, external culture and technique of life. To the sociologist who wishes to understand this problem, it is important to comprehend the psychological basis of the metropolitan forms of individuality. This is found by Simmel in the intensification of nervous stimulation resulting in the swift uninterrupted transition from outer to inner stimulation.

The metropolitan man is subject to an unusual volume of stimulation, and he develops a mentality protecting himself against elements in the external environment which would uproot him. This means that he must react with his head rather than his heart—to yield to deep emotional reactions is to be crushed. His environment intensifies his awareness, not his feeling, leading to a dominance of intelligence. Intellectuality, which extends in many directions with the specialization of the urban environment, is characteristic of the city.

The institutions of the city confirm its mentality, for money economy and dominance of the intellect are intrinsically connected. Both involve a matter-of-fact attitude in dealing with men and things. Money is concerned only with what is common to all items of which it asks only exchange value, reducing all quality and individuality to the question: How much? It is, moreover, the natural institution of the market so central to the metropolis. City production is for the market, for completely unknown consumers who will never enter the producer's actual field of vision. The modern mind becomes ever more calculating. This calculation and the exactness which the money economy brings about also corresponds to the ideal of natural science which would transform the world into an arithmetic problem and fit its parts into mathematical formulae.

In city social life, punctuality, calculability, and exactness are required by the very complexity of life, intimately connected with money economy and intellectualism. Simmel believed that this also explains why original natures like Ruskin and Nietzsche who found the value of life in unschematized existence not only hated the punctuality and exactness of the metropolis but extended the same hatred to the money economy and the intellectualism of modern existence and science.

The same factors which enhance exactness and minute precision and form them into a structure of highest impersonality tend also to promote a highly personal subjectivity. A *blasé* attitude develops in the city as a product of the rapidly changing context of contrasting experiences. Over-stimulation results in loss of the capacity to respond. The essence of the *blasé* attitude is found in a blunting of discrimination. And here, again, the role of the urban money economy is evident and appropriate to the urban attitude. It is colorless and indifferent as a common denominator of all value. It hollows out the core of things—their individuality, special value, or incomparability. The larger the city, the more central the role of seats of money exchange and the more completely the purchasability of things is brought to the fore. Meanwhile the self-preservation of personality is bought at the price of devaluing the world, and can in the end only lead to the devaluing of the self.

The attitude of the metropolitan toward others tends to be one of formality and reserve. Simmel believed that the inner aspect of this reserve is not only indifference but a slight aversion or at least mutual strangeness and repulsion. Reserve with this overtone of aversion secures to the individual a kind of personal freedom impossible under any other conditions. In this connection Simmel thought that the great creativity of ancient Athens was due to its retention of some of the aspects of a small town in combustible tension with the stimulating intellectuality of the metropolis. While the number of persons makes the metropolis the locale of freedom, at a certain point in the economic, personal, and intellectual relations of the citizenry cosmopolitanism appears as well—this is manifest in the predominance of the city over the hinterland in a way growing in geometrical progression with the size of the city. Within the city, meanwhile, life has been transformed from a struggle for a livelihood with nature into an interhuman struggle for gain. And life is increasingly composed of impersonal components that displace personal coloration leading the individual to summon the utmost in uniqueness and particularization to preserve the personal core of the self.

Simmel's essay, *Die Grossestädte und das Geistesleben*,[42] did not seem to have nearly as much direct influence upon the founders of the ecological theory of the city as the treatment of the city by Oswald Spengler—which from its very phrasing appears in large measure to have been drawn from Simmel. Park's famous essay opened with reference to Spengler, not Simmel. "The city . . . is something more than a congeries of individual men and of social conveniences—streets, buildings, electric lights, tramways, and telephones, etc.; something more than a mere constellation of institutions and administrative devices —courts, hospitals, schools, police, and civil functionaries of various sorts. The city is, rather, a state of mind, a body of customs and traditions, and of organized attitudes and sentiments. . . . The city has, as Oswald Spengler has recently pointed out, its own culture: 'What his house is to the peasant, the city is to civilized man. As the house has its household gods, so has the city its protecting deity, its local saint. The city also, like the peasant's hut, has its roots in the soil.' "[43] While the description of urban mentality by Spengler is essentially Simmel's— as evident already in the ideas and quotation drawn from Spengler by Park—the framework for the interpretation of urban mentality is different.

Spengler developed his interpretation of the city in the *Decline of the West*[44] which was written during World War I and published in July, 1918. It became so popular that 90,000 copies were printed. Translated, it became a best-seller in the English speaking world. It contained powerful ideological themes from Western development. It is interesting to locate Spengler's study in relation to the German city.

The career of the city in Germany has been checkered. The Romans had established a system of fortress cities in German lands along the natural transportation routes represented by the Rhine and Danube rivers. These vanished with the fall of Rome. With the revival of trade in the late Middle Ages these old Roman settlements revived, for they were astride the routes for inner-continental trade. Later civic development in German lands occurred with the formation of cities into protective leagues like the Hanse on the North Sea and the Baltic, and the league of southern cities. Moreover, the pioneering movement of Germans into the frontier lands to the East was accompanied by the founding of many cities. These thriving cities underwent rapid internal evolution and formed the social basis for impressive developments in art, science, and literature. The religious wars, however, resulted in unbelievable devastation and impoverishment of the cities throughout German lands—the Thirty Years War left some cities with only a quarter of their former personnel and precisely the most civic types liquidated. Meanwhile, the opening of the new hemisphere reoriented trade away from continental Europe, cutting the very economic base out from under such civic leagues as the Hanse. City life was annihilated. City life began to revive again in Germany in the eighteenth century, but at the same time it was rural Prussia of the German northeast which led the way in consolidating the German Empire. By and large Prussia's policies were determined by the attempt to keep the city and its typical strata under political control, while political dominance—in the state, the administration, and higher ranks of the Army—was in the hands of rural aristocrats (the Junkers). Thus while in other Western lands and the United States urban types had the major voice in the affairs of the nation, in Germany the city man was peculiarly deprived of political responsibility.

As a result of these events in German lands, the urbanite tended to display an unusually intense concentration on urban talents and skills correlated with antipathy to and ineptness in politics. The strata that ran the government were shrewd, able chess players in the game of power, while they were remarkably crude and uncultured. The urban strata were over-cultured and politically inept. This supplied the basis for the savage tides of agrarian mysticism and the passionate rejection of the city which the Nazis could exploit. Spengler took over Simmel's description of the city and reset it in a frame of agrarian mysticism. The vast popularity of Spengler's work in post-war Germany is accounted for in terms of the fitness of this combination of agrarian mysticism and rejection of the city to the bewildered disillusionment of a defeated nation. The popularity of Spengler's work in America is to be accounted for somewhat differently—it provided a systematic rationale for the outraged sentiments generated in contexts of urban corruption and focussed to a point by the Pre-World War I muckrakers but dramatized by the heightened patriotism of war and the post-war let down.

The fundamental contrast in the order of human life for Spengler[45] is found between country and city. The roots of human life are always in the soil. Only in civilization with its giant cities do we disengage ourselves from such roots. The civilized man is an intellectual nomad, quite homeless, a microcosm, as intellectually free as the hunter and herdsmen were sensually free. World history is the history of civic men. The soul of a town is a mass-soul of a fundamentally new kind. The city quickly reduces the countryside to something experienced only as "environs."

Human civilization is cyclical. Every springtime of culture sees the birth of a new city-man and type of civism. It involves the creation of a situation in which man becomes more languid, while sensation and reason become ever more powerful. Man becomes "intellect," "*Geist*," "*esprit*." In the specifically urban form of understanding, all religion and science becomes intellectualized and more alien to the land, incomprehensible to the peasant.

We cannot, Spengler continues, comprehend political and economic history unless we realize that the city with its gradual detachment from the land eventually bankrupts the country. World history is city history and every culture is oriented in the type of the capital city, In all countries in the periods of late culture, great parties, revolutions, Caesarisms, democracies, and parliaments appear as the form in which the capital tells the country what is expected of it and what to die for. The classical forum and the Western press are the intellectual instruments of the ruling city. Moreover, all style-history is played out in cities where the life experience of man speaks to the eye in the logic of visual form. Gothic art was a growth of the soil, but Renaissance style flourished only in the city. The village peasant remained Gothic; the Hellenic countryside preserved the geometrical style. The Epic belongs to *Platz* and *Burg;* the drama in which an awakened life tests itself is city poetry.

The city is intellect, the "megapolis" is free intellect. Intelligence originates in resistance to the feudal powers of blood and tradition against which the bourgeoisie as an intellectual class becomes conscious of its own existence. As it develops the urban intellect reforms the religion of the springtime and sets aside the old religion of noble and priest for the new religion of the *Tiers Etat,* liberal science. The city assumes control of the land, replacing the primitive values in land—which are everywhere inseparable from the life and thought of the rustic—with the absolute idea of money as distinct from goods. Thus, the city not only implies intellect but money. And like money itself, genuine "megalopolitans" are at home wherever their postulates are satisfied. Money not only serves for understanding economic intercourse but subjects the exchange of goods to its own evolution. As the city expands the money market itself emerges for money is power. Money becomes for man a form of activity of waking consciousness no longer having any roots in being. Civilization always represents an unconditional dictatorship of money.

Finally, the city itself, the stone colossus, the "Cosmopolis" stands at the end of the life course of every great culture. The mass of stone is the absolute city. The final city is pure intellect. Civilization is nothing but pure tension; and intelligence is the capacity for understanding at high tension. In every culture the intellectuals are the final types of men. When tension becomes intellectual no other form of recreation is open to it but that of the world city itself—*detene,* relaxation, distraction. Civilized man tends toward sterility with a metaphysical turn toward death. And the last man of the world city no longer wants to live—at least as a type. This is the conclusion of the city as it grows from the primitive barter center to the city of culture, in the course of its majestic evolution flowering as civilization and wilting in a final destruction.

Louis Wirth[46] was far too much an urban type himself to find any comfort in the anti-urbanism and agrarian mysticism of Spengler. At the same time he was too theoretically perceptive to be satisfied with the substitution of a shallow external formula for serious study. Moreover, he agreed that the distinctiveness of all that is specifically modern is tied in with the growth of the great cities in the Western world. In reaction to the ecological point of view, he urged that "as long as we identify urbanism with the physical entity of the city . . . we are not apt to arrive at an adequate concept of urbanism."[47] Rather a sociologically significant definition of the city seeks to select the elements which mark it as a distinctive mode of human group life.

It is noteworthy that Park's famous essay began with almost the same idea and nearly the same phrasing. However, Park had Spengler in mind; Wirth took the point of departure from Simmel.[48] Urbanization, he urged, refers to the cumulative accentuation of the mode of life typical of the city. This is not to be confused with industrialism or modern capitalism. The central problem of the sociologist of the city is to discover the forms of social action and organization that typically emerge in relatively permanent compact settlements of large numbers of heterogeneous individuals.

The multiplication of the number of persons in interaction, Wirth argues, makes full contact of personalities impossible. The result is a "schizoid" property of urban personality. Urbanites meet in highly segmental roles. Their relations are secondary rather than primary. Contacts are impersonal, superficial, transitory, and segmental, leading to reserve, indifference, a *blasé* outlook, and the immunization of one's self against the claims of others. The superficiality, anonymity, and transitory character of urban social relations makes intelligible the sophistication and rationality of city dwellers. Freedom from personal emotional control of intimate groups leaves them in a state of *anomie* (a kind of normlessness), as Durkheim put it. The segmental character and unitary criteria of interpersonal relations emphasized the need for professional codes and the operation of a pecuniary nexus. A premium is placed on utility and efficiency and leads automatically to the employment of corporative devices for the organization of enterprises.

The simultaneous interdependence and instability is increased by the tendency in the city for the individual to specialize in those functions from which he receives greatest advantage. This further separates individuals. It becomes necessary to communicate through indirect media, and individual interests are articulated through delegation. Density reenforces the effect of numbers further by diversifying men and their activities and increasing the complexity of social structure. Hence, a premium is placed in the urban world on visual recognition. We see the uniform as denoting the role of the functionary, and are oblivious to personal eccentricities hidden behind it.

Groups and interests separate out under such conditions. Density, land values, rentals, accessibility, healthfulness, prestige, aesthetic considerations, absence of nuisances, such as noise, smoke, and dirt, determine the desirability of various areas of the city as places of settlement for different segments of the population. Place and nature of work, income, racial and ethnic characteristics, social status, custom, habit, taste, preference and prejudice are among the significant factors in accord with which the urban population is selected and distributed into more or less distinct settlements.

Nervous tensions deriving from personal problems and accentuated by a rapid tempo of life and complicated technology are always at work. The urban *milieu* tends to break down the rigidity of class lines and to complicate class structure.

Urbanism as a way of life, Wirth believes, may be empirically approached from three interrelated perspectives: as a physical structure with a population base, technology and ecological order; as a system of social organization with a structure and series of institutions; as a set of attitudes, ideas and constellation of personalities. With respect to the first, urban population shows selection and differentiation on a number of factors. There are more persons in the prime of life, more foreign born males, more women, more Negroes; there are fewer births, a failure to reproduce, and a higher death rate. As a social order, urbanism is characterized by the substitution of secondary for primary contacts. Related to this is the weakening of kinship ties, the declining significance of neighborhood, the undermining of the traditional bases of social solidarity, the transfer of industrial, educational, and recreational activities to specialized institutions. Along with this, since the individual actor is ineffectual alone and efficiency is only achieved in groups, there is a multiplication of voluntary organizations. Finally, urban personality and collective behavior show all the properties noted above along with increased personal disorganization, mental breakdown, suicide, delinquency, crime, corruption, and disorder.

The property that holds the conceptions of urbanism by Simmel, Spengler, and Wirth together is the location of the focal point of study in the "urban mentality." It can hardly be said that all the theoretical problems this poses have been resolved. Spengler's treatment is at once more complete and most questionable. Spengler's theory represents a reification of collective psychology. It is one thing to think of people as possessing a point of view, or system of attitudes; it is quite another thing to conceive of a point of view as possessing people. Nor does Spengler merely rest content with this. He not only assumes that collective psychology reified and visualized as a mass-soul has an independent reality, but that it is an organic phenomenon with a birth, growth, or death—in his rural imagery, with a springtime, summer, fall, and winter. And all spiritual entities when they die, it seems, return their spiritual potential to the all encompassing world-spirituality or proto-spirituality of the soil and peasantry. This is not responsible theory formation but the pyramiding of figures of speech. Such, it seems, is the technique for setting up metaphysical holding companies.

Simmel's analysis is at least theoretically consistent with his definition of the task of sociology as the discovery of the contentless inter-psychic forms of interhuman life. Consistently Simmel set about to epitomize the urban mind. On this topic he wrote an intuitive essay of great imagination, delicacy, and charm. However, neither his conception of sociology nor his treatment of the city is wholly satisfactory to the overwhelming majority of sociologists. It may be seriously doubted—at least it has been doubted—that the study of contentless inter-psychic forms is the task of sociology. In practice, it may be noted, Simmel never adheres to his own rules, but is at his best in the incisive comparisons of wide varieties of evidence. Moreover, the suggestion that form and content are intrinsically separable—that they may even have different origins—tends also to point toward the reification of forms. There is almost a Platonic note in this concept of a world of blue prints looking for a draftsman. Simmel has by no means completely avoided the reification appearing in Spengler's work. Finally, while Simmel does not make the mistake of presenting urbanism in a framework of agrarian mysticism, he tends to define his materials in a way that places them outside empirical study.

When one takes into account the fact that Wirth was a relatively hardheaded urbanite, it can easily appear strange that he was attracted by either Spengler or Simmel. To be sure, that he passed over Spengler in silence is understandable—Wirth was under no delusions as to the intrinsic superior spirituality of the country over the city. At the same time, he was not inclined to trade the parlor game of spinning our imaginative insights for the scientific process. Wirth's judgments become fully understandable only in terms of his obvious attempt to correct the simple-minded physics of ecological theory. His judgments, thus, have the properties of a corrective overstatement. To be sure, the social-psychological theory of the city exists only as a program possibility, not as an accomplished fact, and one is in a position only to criticize tendencies with all the risks this involves. Nevertheless, it seems to point toward a simple-minded psychological approach just as ecology led to an over-simplification on a physical level. There is a strong tendency for the relevant world of action to be reduced to mere matters of increase, density, and heterogeneity of population which have psychological effects. All indications point to the possibility that institutions tend to receive as cursory and incidental a treatment as they did from ecology.

Perhaps it is of some significance that though Wirth's brilliant statement is some twenty years old, the reconstruction in urban theory it demanded has not been forthcoming.

EUROPEAN DEVELOPMENTS IN URBAN THEORY

In the last quarter of the nineteenth and the first two decades of the twentieth century, the theory of the city was undergoing a remarkable internal evolution. Some peculiarities of American urban theory account for the fact that American theorists to a remarkable degree have cut themselves off from their European beginnings—except in the case of two, as when Spengler's ideas, because of their sheer popularity, forced themselves on attention, and when because of their sheer "urbanity" Simmel's views are belatedly taken into account. It will be recalled, however, that in the early days of the twentieth century when sociology became an academic discipline with limited rather than unlimited claims, it rejected its founders and their distinguishing peculiarities—which, incidentally, included the use of historical writings for sociological evidence. Sociology, in general, and urban sociology in particular, were striving to become autonomous sciences—gathering their own evidence first hand by their own methods. Moreover, the popular attitude toward the city in America was marked by the serious concern with current problems of urban corruption and the disasters to various areas of social life possible in urban environments. While European students of the city were oriented toward historical materials, American students were oriented toward the present. While European students had materials available from cities that had been going concerns for a thousand years, American cities were often not more than a few decades old. When an American student did happen to dip into the work of a European theorist, he tended to react to it as mere "ancient history." Once in a great while he was even willing to admit that it was interesting. He rarely saw in it any relevance to his own problems except as a curious contrast. Under these circumstances American students of the city largely cut themselves adrift from the urban theory of Europe.

Among the consequences for American urban theorists of cutting themselves off from research into the historical past of the city was the toleration of a degree of naivete that had been banned from other areas of their science. Human social forms, once they have been stabilized, and their difficulties have been worked out sometimes amount to something like solutions of a maximum efficiency to a given set of social problems. People are remarkably unwilling or unable to give up successful solutions. When they came to the new hemisphere, for example, they neither lost their language nor invented a new one. Sociologists who would not make the mistake for a moment of assuming that each new family represents a new family institution seem to have assumed something of the sort with regard to their cities.

A single illustration may suffice to illustrate the value of historical knowledge in interpreting some of the happenings in American cities. The patterns of city government in European cities evolved gradually and only stabilized after some centuries of development. As this stabilization occurred, the administrative focus of city government came to center in the structure of the mayor and council. American cities were set up by people of European culture, but the large majority of cities established in the nineteenth century followed the pattern of government of the state rather than the more normal European civic form. Sociologists might well have taken this as a kind of unconscious "experiment" in city government in America. Approached in this way, the American experiment—heralded as a device of securing greater democracy in the city—made possible the influence of every interest in city affairs except the public interest. Bryce has been quoted by everyone on the state of American civic affairs in the 1880's. City government, he thought, was the most conspicuous political failure in America. Under these circumstances a series of events began to occur which should have excited every sociologist in America—*American cities began to set up traditional mayor and council types of government along the European plan.* The more limited administrative structure and more clear location of responsibility were critical to the adequate functioning of city government in the system of institutions of the city. A certain degree of "visibility" as to its operations was necessary for the control of power.

This was a tremendous concession to the fact that the cities in America were "new" only in a physical sense—not in a sociological sense. The city was a peculiar system of institutions that had gradually arrived at an economical functioning in time. Within limits it could not be varied arbitrarily without paying an exceptionally heavy price. The price paid in nineteenth century America for its "experience" was the tolerance of almost unbelievable quantities of graft. Not only did most sociologists completely miss this point, but when the return to the more traditional relations of mayor and council occurred in American cities, the implications of this fact were radically misinterpreted.

The struggle for liberty has been a struggle to wrest power from one, or the few, and to lodge it with the many; that is, to decentralize government. When popular government fails, society is saved from anarchy by the strong man; that is, power is again centralized. The movement, therefore, to centralize government by transferring power from the council to the mayor was a confession that popular government in our great cities had failed.[49]

Thus, instead of seeing this as the partial return to a more stable community form, it was interpreted by Strong as a failure of democracy itself. Strong completely overlooked the fact that sometimes the decentralization of government permits the centralization of graft.

There are other examples of theoretical naivete. What are sometimes viewed as rather uniquely American contributions to civilization are enactments of a traditional civic drama. In 1901 in Galveston, Texas, the city stricken by wind and flood set up a commission which worked so well in meeting the disaster that it was continued as the governing organ of the city. Its success was copied, and it worked very well in small cities and was present in 327 out of 2,033 small cities of 5,000 or less population in 1945. In larger cities the city manager plan represents the equivalent of commission government. A city manager is appointed by the city council, which retains full authority to enact ordinances, make plans, plan developments, and select and discharge the manager. The city charter usually directs that the choice of a manager be made independent of party. He usually has power to choose all his own assistants and technicians. The plan was instituted at Staunton, Virginia, in 1908, and became nationally important following adoption by Dayton, Ohio, after 1914. In 1945 it was in effect in 350 cities of the United States of more than 5,000 population; the largest was Cincinnati with a population of one-half a million. Under the city manager plan a body of professional city administrators has developed who are fairly free of political considerations.

In America under the old system of diffused civic authority, such complex structures of party patronage developed that even the return to the traditional form of city government with a council and mayor was often unsuccessful. Such powerful party machines had developed that they immediately distorted city government to their pattern and continued to operate with hardly a pause. Commission government and the city manager are the exact parallel of the *podesta* system of the Middle Ages, arising for similar reasons and having somewhat the same results. There, too, party conflicts had become so destructive to the general interests of the citizens that an uncommitted outsider was brought in for administrative purposes and was free to choose his own subordinates. There, too, the *podesta* system led to the development of a body of professionals trained in city administration. Such examples illustrate the value of acquaintance with European urban theory to which we now turn.

The ancients, as André Piganiol observed, generally had little understanding of the city. Plato and Aristotle held the middle classes—typical urban strata—in contempt and wished to subordinate them to warriors and philosophers. Private property (that is, urban alienable property) was suspect, and money was thought to be dangerous. The location of the city on the sea was thought to be a mistake. Their own choice for a city was Sparta, hardly a true city but a permanent open military camp.

As "the city" increasingly presented itself as a problem to modern social scientists, one characteristic explanation was that the origin of the modern urban community was a survival of Roman cities. While there is little doubt that a considerable number of medieval cities took form at the same location points as old Roman garrisons and trade centers—such as Cologne, Mayence, Strassbourg, Rheims, and Paris—becoming feudal garrisons and episcopal sees, later evolving into modern cities, this does not explain the city but thrusts the problem it presents back into history.

There are two general properties of the theories of the city emerging in the late nineteenth and early twentieth centuries in Europe despite many differences between them—they all assume that the characteristics of any unit of social life are determined by institutions. Secondly, they all generally assume that human society is an evolutionary or historical product, hence explanation of social events consists in a discovery of origins. Thus, in contrast both to the ecological theory of the city and the rather fragmentary social-psychological theory of the city, European urban theory at the turn of the century held an *institutional theory of the city*. The explanation of the city was found in the peculiar order and historical primacy of its institutions. The various special theories differed in terms of the particular institutions they took to be central or original.

Fustel de Coulanges, who pioneered city theory, took the critical institution of the city to be a religion. The original nucleus of pre-urban society was thought to be the family finding its point of integration in the hearth, its religious symbol, and worship of the father as its priest. The union of several families could establish the hearth of the phratry.

The tribe, like the family and the phratry, was established as an independent body, since it had a special worship from which the stranger was excluded. Once formed, no new family could be admitted to it. Just as several phratries were united in a tribe, several tribes might associate together, on condition that the religion of each should be respected. The day on which this alliance took place the city existed.[50]

The critical point in the founding of the city was religious synoecism and establishment of the hearth of the city. The city assumed the form of a new sanctuary for common worship. The ancient city was a religious community.

Glotz considerably advanced beyond Fustel de Coulanges in his conception of the range of possible city types in terms of different relations of family and city to each other. Like Coulanges, he treated the family as the core structure from which both state power and individualism could emerge. Thus three stages in Greek city life were assumed, each with its peculiar institutional order.

The Greek city, while retaining the institution of the family, grew at its expense. It was compelled to appeal to individual forces which the original group repressed. For a long time the city had to fight against the *genos* and each of its victories was gained by the suppression of some form of patriarchal servitude.

We shall not see two opposing forces—the family and the city—but three—the family, the city, and the individual each in its turn predominant. The history of Greek institutions thus falls into three periods: in the first, the city is composed of families which jealously guard their ancient right and subordinate all their members to the common good; in the second, the city subordinates the families to itself by calling to its aid emancipated individuals; in the third, individualism runs riot, destroys the city, and necessitates the formation of larger states.[51]

This represents genuine advance over Fustel de Coulanges in that it conceives of the possibility of a more complete inter-institutional development making the city possible and of more varied city types. The family-dominated or patrician city is clearly visualized.

A third institutional factor was brought into central focus as determinative for the rise of the city by the students of comparative jurisprudence. Henry Sumner Maine, for example, in one of the great pioneering works[52] of social science argued that comparative jurisprudence proves that the original condition of the human race was one of dominance by the patriarchal family. From England to India in ancient times, he believed, society was organized in patriarchal families under dominance of the eldest parent with dominion extending even to life and death over his children. Law was the parent's word. Guilt was a community affair for which the kin had joint responsibility. At this stage kinship was the only ground for political functions. For all more complex social forms, Maine felt that the critical problem lay in the substitution of a principle of territoriality for kinship and a transformation of the legal order isolating the individual from his status in the family, freeing him for the plastic entry into multiple "contractual" relations. One social role after the other was freed according to Maine. The son was delivered from the *Patria Potestas* first, probably because it had always been necessary for him to become a patriarchal househead himself. The status of the slave disappeared, being superseded by a contractual relation between servant and master. In time even women won contractual freedom. As Maine put it, "The movement of the progressive societies has hitherto been a movement from Status to Contract."[53] The city in Maine's analysis is a legal structure resting on contract and territory rather than kinship and family. The effect of his analysis was to bring the relations of kinship and territory into central focus institutionally, shifting the attention of urban theory to the evolution of the law. This was the starting point for rich additional developments and the consideration of the importance of a whole series of legal or semi-legal phenomena for the development of the city. These include such things as (1) the importance of charters for the possibility of the city and the basis of its law; (2) the role in the appearance of the city of the development of special civic courts and law; (3) the importance for the city of the (Roman) legal notion of a civic corporation with a legal personality of its own.

Maitland, who did brilliant work on the evolution of the city in England, partly agreed with Maine. At least he urges that "the borough community is corporate; the village community is not."[54] However, its existence as a legal entity and as a fictitious personality resting its identity on incorporation as the result of the grant of a royal charter is a later stage of city development. Its origins trace back to the castle or burg or borough and to a special burgess obligated for the upkeep of the fortress. "It seems to me possible that the great men of the shire were bound to keep house and retainers, burgmen, *burgenses*, knights in this stronghold and place of refuge."[55] Maitland himself designated this as the garrison theory. Closely parallel with Maitland's garrison theory was the "military" theory of the city advanced by Keutgen in Germany. Towns were regarded as strongholds for emergency purposes, where the inhabitants surrounding the place could retreat for protection. In times of peace the lords kept a skeleton staff of retainers on duty; these were the first civic personnel. Some towns like Chichester and Canterbury in England at the time of Doomesday had between 100 and 200 houses attached to 44 and 11 manors respectively.

The attempt to explain the city in terms of economic institutions was made by Marx and others and much more completely by Pirenne.[56] He maintained the two attributes necessary to constitute a city are a middle class population and a communal organization. From this standpoint the *town* or *gorod,* originally enclosures where people might seek refuge in time of danger, were not yet cities. People might resort to them on religious occasions so that they became the sites of temples as well as the seats of officials. However, although they grew in complexity, they were still not cities. Historically the municipal system of Rome was identified by its constitutional system. In time Roman municipal centers declined until in the eighth century they were in extensive decay. Meanwhile the Church based its diocesan boundaries on the boundaries of Roman cities. This, in turn, meant that the cities where the bishops resided fell under episcopal domination as Roman cities decayed. Areas that had been centers of municipal administration under Rome lost their civil functions. In the ninth century *"civitas"* had come to be synonymous wtih the bishopric and the so-called episcopal "city." The episcopal "city" for Pirenne is a city in name only. The influence of the bishops became unrivaled precisely because the last vestiges of civic life were being annihilated. These centers often had a weekly market, where peasants brought their produce. Sometimes there was an annual fair. The bishop enjoyed both religious and secular power over them, for he even had loosely-defined police powers under which he supervised the markets, regulated tolls, took care of bridges and ramparts. These towns were fortresses as well as episcopal establishments. However, for Pirenne they were not cities, though many cities took them as points for development. They played a role in the history of cities as "stepping stones." Round about their walls cities were to take shape after the "economic renaissance."[57] The cities took form as a by-product of the activities of merchant caravans which settled outside the walls and in crisis could use them for defence.

Under the influence of trade the old Roman cities took on new life and were repopulated, or mercantile groups formed round about the military burgs and established themselves along the sea coasts, on river banks, at confluences, at the junction points of the natural routes of communication. Each of them constituted a market which exercised an attraction proportionate to its importance, on the surrounding country or made itself felt afar.[58]

The critical point for Pirenne was the development of a new class of merchants who found themselves at odds with the countryside and its institutions. They fought for a new code of laws, a private jurisdiction, free property, and eventually distinct communal organization—for Pirenne the city is the community of the merchants.

MAX WEBER AND
EUROPEAN URBAN THEORY

The abbreviated review of the highlights of European urban theory illustrates the variety of points of view and the accumulating mass of historical research at special points and for particular areas. Thoughtful sociologists recognized the need for a more special or more comprehensive theory of urbanism. Simmel and Weber were responding to the same problem. Simmel sought to solve the problems of the city by way of a specialization in terms of neo-Kantian formalism. Weber was familiar with Simmel's formulations, and he opened his study with the observation that the city is often thought of as a densely settled area of crowded dwellings forming a colony so extensive that personal reciprocal acquaintance of the inhabitants is lacking. But while recognizing the importance of this, Weber immediately pointed out that this could not serve as more than a fragment in the full theory of the city, for not only would it restrict the concept of the city to densely settled areas of large size but it would even then be inconclusive for cultural factors play a role in the point where impersonality makes its appearance in human affairs. It would be difficult to touch its limitations more quickly. Besides, Weber's theoretical starting point was different and in principle he could not have found Simmel's concept of the city completely adequate.

Max Weber's theoretical point of view may best be described as a form of social behaviorism. He was unwilling, like Simmel, to confine sociological analysis to the delineation of inter-psychic forms. On the other hand, he was strongly nominalistic and suspicious of any sociological procedure that had to invent artificial entities such as "oversouls" like Spengler's reified social psychology. Finally, Weber thought that the task of sociology was to explain human conduct in its meaningful dimensions and not merely externally. One can determine a person's loss of weight objectively by weighing him repeatedly, but it makes a lot of difference if he is losing weight because he is dying of an illness or because he is engaging in ascetic practices in connection with his religion. The task of sociology is to explain inter-human actions in terms of the meanings they have to the parties involved as well as in terms of specific physical changes they entail.

The idea of "social relation" for Weber was a kind of conceptual shorthand by which one speaks of the maintenance of a pattern in inter-human actions. If, when two people interact, one gives orders and the other carries them out, one may speak of a relation of dominance-subordination between the two. Weber was suspicious of the German tendency toward reification, and he was careful to insist that a relation exists only so far as inter-human actions actually occur.

Granting this meaning of "social relations," it is possible to take an additional step and conceive of the possibility of a complex "system" of relations. An institution such as a state, a family, a religion, or a system of law is a "system of relations." It has no different status from that of a single isolated relation—it has no further reality. The institution actually exists only so far as people act in certain ways. Just as the concept of "social relation" is a useful economy for expressing the comparative identity in a number of specific social actions, so "institution" is an economy for speaking about the occurrence of complex sets of social interaction.

In Max Weber's terms, all forms of European urban theory reviewed above are "institutional" theories of the city. They are different from each other only with respect to the particular institution taken to be central or original to the city. Weber's own position was not advanced by way of a review and critique of current urban theories—but as an independent inquiry into the nature of the city. But he automatically took these theories into account.

One of the values of Weber's approach to the problems of the city from the standpoint of the sociology of social action may be seen by further comparisons with Simmel. For both men society eventually reduces to social interaction or meaningful inter-human behavior. Simmel, however, would analyze this into form and content and confine sociology to the study of form. This reduces the science to an inventory of inter-psychic forms and leaves aside large blocks of the materials generally included by sociology. Max Weber, by contrast, set aside the distinction between form and content conceiving the task of sociology to be causal interpretation of social action. One of the most immediate consequences of this was the fact that Weber's theory of the city could encompass Simmel's, while the reverse was not true. There was room in Weber's theory for attention to mentality in the city. He was able, also, to recognize and account for the appearance in the city of most varied social types. As he put it, "The city . . . has always contained elements from the most varied social situations. Office candidates qualified by examinations and mandarins rub shoulders with illiterates despised as rabble and practitioners of the (few) unclean occupations in East Asia. Many kinds of castes carry on their activities beside one another in India. Blood relatives organized in clans appear together with landless artisans in the Near East. In Antiquity free men, bondsmen, and slaves emerged alongside noble landlords, their court officials and servants. And in the early medieval city ministerial officials and mercenaries, priests and monks, encounter one another in the city." Weber thus had provided for the fact that in the city all sorts of people meet and mingle, often without understanding one another. Slums may be separated from fine residences by a few hundred yards, but while they are geographically close they may be miles apart in points of view. He recognized the absence of psychological homogeneity such that the intelligentsia, middle class, political reformers, stand-patters, and go-getters, in Monroe's phrases, all pull apart to such an extent that city dwellers can only think effectively in groups. Weber's point of view permitted him to move in either direction—toward the mentalities, conceptual traditions, and segmented *milieus* of the city or toward the stablized patterns persistent through time, the institutions of the city. In fact, his theory required that he consider both.

With Simmel, Weber was able to recognize that in the city every occupation—including mendicancy and prostitution—tends to become a profession. The city dweller's mind is crowded with impressions with little time for reflection, developing a craving for novelty, an impatience with repetition, a yearning for the bizarre. Simmel's theory of the city was reduced to a sub-part of his own. However, this does not indicate how he dealt with the many conflicting institutional theories of the city. His procedure is a model of sound theory construction. He successively reviewed one type of concept of the city after another—the economic, the relation of the city to agriculture, the political-administrative concept of the city, the fortress and garrison concepts of the city, the concept of the city as fusion of fortress and market, the social and status concept of the city (legal concept of the city), the city as a sworn confederacy, the city as a body of militarily competent citizens—he attempted thereby to isolate and retain whatever was correct in each special concept of the city.

This may suggest that Weber's procedure was eclectic. But theory construction is not a mere matter of carpentry—sawing out little bits of existing theories and gluing them into a new inlay work of one's own. Theory construction is neither carpentry nor the solving of jigsaw puzzles with pre-cut pieces. Weber's procedure was no mechanical assembling of theoretically unrelated fragments but one of testing the various concepts of the city against the evidence noting what they do explain and what they do not. For example, in reviewing the economic concept of the city, Weber isolated the distinguishing property of the city in the conduct of life on the basis of non-agricultural activities. In terms of the dominant economic features of their life, a typology of cities is possible and one may distinguish producers' cities from consumers' cities, commercial from industrial cities, main and satellite cities with many sub-types. However, when all is said and done the economy of a city is a necessary *but not sufficient* condition of the city. Similar judgments apply to other concepts of the city and the evidences upon which they rest.

The concept formation in terms of which Weber brought together and surpassed the various forms of the *institutional theory of the city* current in his day was in the *theory of the urban community.* The relation of the concept "community" to other of Weber's ideas may be seen easily if his key concepts are outlined in terms of their comparative abstractness and complexity.

1. *Social Actions.* The ultimate units of analysis for the sociologist. These are inter-human behaviors having a meaning to the parties involved.

2. *Social Relations.* One may use this term to speak of the stable arrangement of elements appearing in social action. They do not exist

outside social actions; they merely represent the abstractly conceived arrangements or patterns an action displays.

3. *Social Institutions.* A similar way to abstractly conceptualize the social relations in a whole network of social actions. Social institutions bear the same relation to patterns of action that social relations do to single actions. In practice social institutions are always manifest as more or less stable patterns of behaviors. However important institutions are, they are not, by themselves, sufficient to account for all of social life, for individuals live out their experience in more than single institutions. They act as members of families, agents of economic institutions, as citizens of states, etc. How an individual acts in accordance with one institutional pattern like the family is modified by how he acts in accord with others. The state condones special kinds of marriage arrangements, not others; economic success or failure modifies activity in family contexts. One is led, thus, step by step to the total systematic units of inter-human life of which the institutions are separate aspects.

4. *Community.* In the concept of the urban community as a total systematic unit of inter-human life distinguished not by a single institution but by an order of institutions, Weber found a theoretical formulation which was able to take account of the many partial concepts of the city current in his time. As he phrased the problem, neither the "city" in the economic sense nor the garrison of inhabitants accoutred with a special politico-administrative structure necessarily constitutes an urban community. "An urban 'community' in the full meaning of the word appears only in the Occident. Exceptions occasionally were to be found in the Near East (in Syria, Phoenicia, and Mesopotamia) but only occasionally and in rudiments. To constitute a full urban community the settlement had to represent a relative predominance of trade-commercial relations with the settlement as a whole displaying the following features: (1) a fortification, (2) a market, (3) a court of its own and at least partially autonomous law, (4) a related form of association, and (5) at least partial autonomy and autocephaly, thus, also, an administration by authorities in the election of whom the burghers participated."

Weber's general procedure was to review the concept of the city in terms of the evidence from world history. On this basis he established the concept of the urban community. Any community, including an urban community, is not an unstructured congeries of activities but a distinct and limited pattern of human life. It represents a total system of life forces brought into some kind of equilibrium. It is self-maintaining, restoring its order in the face of disturbances. One need only recall the illustrations given previously of the unexpected consequences in corruption emerging in American cities facilitated by their awkward political structures. As noted, American cities were forced back into an older, more tested form of political organization. The city, as a limited pattern, obeys its own laws.

As a peculiar system of forces the urban community could not have emerged everywhere. Weber argues rather convincingly that it did not. It did not appear in Asia and only fragmentarily in the Near East in part for the very reason that the city was a center of state administration. Weber's arguments on this point are also relevant to-day for some capital cities, such as Washington, London, and Paris, precisely because they are centers of national government, lack some of the political autonomy of the normal city. They are prevented from becoming full urban communities.

The city as a peculiar system of forces could appear only under special conditions and in time. A good part of Weber's study is devoted to the gradual emergence and structuring of the force-composition of the city in various areas under different conditions and its gradual stabilization into a distinct form. As the changing composition of forces is traced from the ancient kingships through the patrician city to the demos of the ancient world, from the episcopal structures and fortresses through the city of notables, to the guild dominated cities on the continent, from the boroughs with their assigned garrison personnel through a peculiar evolution due to ties with kinship in England, many penetrating observations are made. And ever and again the complex processes accompanying the emergence of the urban community are laid bare. It is not difficult to accept Wirth's proposition that Weber's study is one of the closest approximations to a systematic theory of urbanism we have.

MAX WEBER'S RELEVANCE
FOR AMERICAN URBAN THEORY

If one grants that the analysis of the city as a peculiar community formation with a special arrangement of institutions is sociologically legitimate, a rather novel fact emerges: this kind of urban theory has been more frequent among American political scientists than among sociologists. Though this may seem startling at first, it is not difficult to explain. By the very definition of his activity the political scientist has to approach his problems from the point of view of one institution, the state. When he deals with the city his point of departure is found in city government. The moment he generalizes his problems and follows out their implications, his study becomes a more or less systematic review of the forces and institutions of the civic community by way of their bearing upon government, the charter, city law, city courts, the political party, the boss, the pressure groups, the good-government league, etc.

Two illustrations may suffice to show this tendency of the discussion of the urban community by political scientists to assume a form approximating Weber's.

In 1904 Wilcox carried out a study of the American city.[59] In a series of felicitous phrases he formulated the problem of the American city in quite sociological terms. He observed that in the city the sheer volume of stimulation to which the individual was subject inevitably places some pressure on democracy. "In the cities the gossip of the world comes buzzing in our ears twice a day at least, and perhaps through a score of channels."[60] All the forces affecting life in ways unfavorable to democracy tend to concentrate in cities. "The city is, indeed, the visible symbol of the annihilation of distance and the multiplication of interests."[61] Here all institutions tend to undergo change. "The neighborhood, the natural primary unit of local organization is weakened, and in many cases nearly destroyed. Home life is little more than a name, whereas a hundred people, often of different nationalities, live in a single tenement house. . . . Among the business and professional classes, a man's most intimate associate may be scattered over the whole city, while he scarcely knows his next door neighbor's name . . . there is an . . . organization of industry on so large a scale that, in cities, only an insignificant proportion of the people work for themselves."[62] Nor does the problem stop here for "the city is the distributing center of intelligence as well as of goods."[63] It tends to become dominant in the same way as a great employer of labor who deals with his men individually. The city transforms men as if by magic, and newcomers are absorbed and changed into city men. "There is little difficulty making city men out of countrymen; it seems well-nigh impossible to reverse the process."[64] And for many reasons the city assumes national importance. "Democracy . . . has been badly damaged by its contact with city conditions. . . . Secondly, the city, as the center of civilization and the distributing center of the nation's intelligence, tends to impose its ethical and social ideals upon the whole people irrespective of residence. Thirdly, as the accumulation of enormous wealth in the hands of one man without a corresponding responsibility for its use with reference to the social welfare, it is a positive menace to the general well-being."[65] Thus in a striking sense the approach to the city by way of one of its institutions, and in terms of the bearing of various social processes upon it, leads toward the kind of theoretical formation one finds in Max Weber's study.

With an exciting and distinctly "sociological" imagination Wilcox goes on to present "the street" as the symbolic model of the problems of the city. The street represents first and last the greatest material problems of the city, for here by the cooperation of the whole community, a free way is provided, an "open road," a challenge for traffic and transportation for all alike. "The street is the symbol of the free city wherein all cooperate to secure opportunity for all."[66] Similarly, one may locate dangers to the city here. "It is no wonder that the curtailment of the people's rights in the street through the grant of special privileges to individuals and corporations is widely regarded as a menace to popular institutions and a step toward the overthrow of the principles of free government. The control of the streets means the control of the city."[67]

It is difficult to imagine a more appropriate symbol of the city as a community. Every community is an organization of individual and general interest. Institutions determine at what points the line is drawn between these explosive forces. One may use the "street" as a symbolic meeting ground for the conflicts of private and public interest and hence for all the problems of regulation and control, of government, as well as for the penetration of private interests, by way of franchises and other monopolies to advantageous position over public life. The value of the street as a symbol does not stop here, and one could as well use it as a point of departure to all urban life.

That Wilcox's strongly sociological tendencies were no accident, but the product of an analysis of the city when made by way of one of its institutions, can be illustrated by Munroe's study.[68] After summing up the major aspects of urban growth and considering its basic causes as lying in an improved productivity of agriculture, the development of modern industry and commerce, and after reviewing various typologies of the city (for example, the primary service city, industrialized city, industrial-commercial city, and metropolitan city), Munroe raised the question as to just what the city is. His discussion bears comparison with Weber's.

Off hand one might say that it is a large body of people living in a relatively small area. That, however, would be a very inadequate definition, for it would convey no intimation of the fact that the city has a peculiar legal status, a distinct governmental organization, a highly complicated economic structure, and a host of special problems which do not arise when an equal number of people live less compactly together. A comprehensive definition of the modern city must indicate that it is a legal, political, economic, and social unit all rolled into one.[69]

Munroe goes on to urge that the city is a corporation at law endowed with an artificial personality such that it may sue and be sued, hold property, make contracts, employ officials and agents, levy taxes, borrow money, exercise the right of eminent domain. It is a unit of government with a charter proving its warrant for existence granted by the state. It has a form of government, a mayor and council or elective commission, or council and city manager, all with complex powers and functions. Economically the city is an agency of economic enterprise and purveyor of water and often gas, electricity, and transportation; it is an employer of labor, a purchaser of supplies and materials, a seller of services. The city is also an agency for promotion of social welfare with officials providing free education, health protection, poor relief, public recreation, and social welfare activities of many kinds. It was Munroe's opinion that the many problems faced by the city could hardly, in good theory or conscience, be blamed on the newcomers or foreign born in the city. If they have a general cause, it is probably the clumsiness of much governmental machinery.

American municipal development was interpreted by Munroe against a background of social-historical conditions. At a time when most sociologists either missed the fact altogether or misinterpreted it, Munroe saw that the corruption of the American city was made possible in considerable measure by the overly clumsy governmental machinery of the early nineteenth century civic structure. He correctly interpreted the civic return to a more traditional structure not as a failure of city democracy but as a product of the normal operation of its laws.

Furthermore, the development of municipal government was seen against a background of the social structure of the city. Munroe observed that even as a body of population the city has a peculiar social structure. In the city there is a reversal of many of the ratios of the countryside with greater numbers of women, greater numbers of people in the middle age groups. The city has rural influence which in part drains off many of the most intelligent persons of the country. Foreign born persons collect in the city, where they are subject to special concentration and special political manipulations. In the city birth rates fall, marriage and death rates go up. While there is no evidence of a change in physical virility as between country and city, in the city there is relatively higher intellectual achievement. Moral standards may possibly go down in the city, and certainly many crimes are peculiarly associated with city life: forgery, perjury, embezzlement, business frauds, all are peculiarly urban crimes. And beyond these phenomena there are psychological differences which emerge in the city. Here again, analysis moves step by step through the charter, city law, city court, political party, etc.

It should not for a moment be supposed that political scientists like Wilcox and Munroe fully carry out a sociological analysis of the urban community with its peculiar institutional order. They were political scientists, and as such ninety per cent of their analyses remained concerned with government and its problems. For the reasons already noted, in the remaining ten per cent of their argument they sometimes expressed a clearer sense of the urban community than many of their sociological colleagues. The task of carrying out theory construction on a full scale and the kind of sociological analysis of the city suggested by Weber remains.

A final point should be noted concerning the possible application of Weber's theory of the city. Weber found that one essential component of the fully developed urban community was the presence of a city fortification and a city army. This is the one element completely absent for the modern city. When one considers the multiple evidences from the historic past of the city which Weber brought to bear upon this point, the disappearance of the city fortification and city army cannot be without importance. In the ancient world outside the West, the presence in the locale of military-political powers different from the local residents often prevented the full emergence of an urban community. In ancient India at the time of the appearance of the great heterodox religions, Buddhism and Jainism, a considerable development toward urbanism was present. However, the cities of India were pacifistic and the "city" religions were very much so; this had as one consequence that at any time they chose the Indian princes could crush the cities. They did so choose. On the other hand, in all areas of the world the presence of a fortress and a local militia were powerful factors in establishing a nucleus around which the city could appear. Again and again the city took shape around the castle. In Europe, in contrast to India, when crisis deepened the burghers manned the walls and fought to maintain the integrity of the city.

It is of decisive importance which units of social life are able to maintain themselves by armed force. In many parts of the pre-literate world the ultimate military unit was the tribe. Feudal systems of the human society were determined by the decisive military importance of castle-based aristocratic landlords. For a time, in the Ancient Near East, more completely in the Ancient Occident and in the Middle Ages, the ultimate military units were cities, maintaining themselves in the surrounding world by means of their fortifications, their armies, and their navies. The ultimate armed units of modern society are not tribes, or castle-dwelling nobles, nor cities, but states. The modern city is militarily negligible even as politically it has become a subordinate unit. With atomic weapons the city may have become the great death trap of modern man.

The modern city is no longer a community with a firm military shell. The individual is no longer required to take up arms and man its walls—and with this the city no longer figures in his hopes and dreams as a unit of survival, as a structure that must marshal his supreme loyalties, since it may ask his very life. The destruction of the city no longer represents the extinction of the institutions of social life. Modern government, business, and religion are more interlocal with every passing year. At any time they choose the decisively militarily competent social formations of the modern world, the national states, can crush the city. This is not merely a possibility. In Russia, cities are governed by a city soviet elected by the workers in various industries and other units of the system. The city soviet is large, often with as many as a thousand members. It elects on nomination of the Communist party a president and praesidium or executive committee of eleven to seventeen members. Democratic civic autonomy in the Soviet Union is, thus, approximately what it was in classical Greece at the time of Homer, where the public assembly represented the occasions on which the decisions of the king could be announced and the people were permitted to respond by acclamation. Modern dictators have not been interested in permitting the independent urban community, for they know practically, if not theoretically, that independent communities support the formation of independent thought. In Italy Mussolini replaced elected syndicos and councils of a French model by a *podesta* appointed by the government in whom all authority was vested. In Prussia prior to World War I the government of the cities rested on a three-class system of voting in which membership in the city council was secured to a limited group of taxpayers, one third representation going to the relatively small group paying most taxes; a third to a larger second group; a final third to the rest. This taxpayers' council chose an executive board or magistrate of salaried professional officers, chairman, or a Burgomaster. The Weimar Republic introduced universal suffrage in German cities, permitting them to become more free and democratic. But the Nazis changed all this. The city was coordinated into the party structure, and the mayoralty and other principal salaried offices were staffed by party officials.

Max Weber's theory of the city, thus, leads to a rather interesting conclusion. We can grant the phenomenal increase and aggregation of modern populations as a concomitant of the industrial revolution. We should not, however, confuse physical aggregation with the growth of the city in a sociological sense. The urban community has everywhere lost its military integrity—its right to defend itself by military means. In many areas of the world it has, temporarily at least, lost its very legal and political autonomy—the same fate is possible everywhere. Meanwhile, within the city itself greater masses of residents pursue interlocal interests—as representatives of the national government, as agents in business and industries of the national government, as agents in business and industries of national and international rather than of civic scope.

The modern city is losing its external and formal structure. Internally it is in a state of decay, while the new community represented by the nation everywhere grows at its expense. The age of the city seems to be at an end.

PART FOUR

STUDIES
in NATIONAL
CHARACTER
and SOCIAL
STRUCTURE

The world-wide depression of the 1930's, the world war of the 1940's, the cold war and shift of the frontiers of the world to outer space in the 1950's have jostled the peoples of the world into a new and more intense awareness of one another. Hard times force a people back upon themselves in an economic and psychological defensive reaction. In the 1930's the nations of the Western world withdrew from each other, each to protect his own with cries of "Buy American" or "Buy British" or *"Deutschland über alles."* England, France, Italy, and Germany retreated behind protective economic and political walls while simultaneously launching upon an ideological build-up of self-image. In America the ideological counterpart of such conservative withdrawal was revealed in the shift from the gay, cynical literature and criticism of the jazz age and lost generation—the mocking, slashing attack on Philistinism, Sinclair Lewis' novels and H. L. Mencken's impudent critical assaults—to the elegiac paeans of self-congratulation evident in the transformed mood of Van Wyck Brooks' earlier works to that of his *The Flowering of New England.*

When World War II came it was as if the nations of the world had withdrawn into themselves and concentrated mood and resource, the more savagely to hurl themselves at one another in an orgy of destruction. The war intensified and exceeded the limits of each nation and simultaneously imposed new requirements of mutual knowledge. It was no longer sufficient simply to congratulate one's self that one's nation was not like others. It became desperately necessary to find a basis for agreement among friendly nations; it became a matter of life and death to possess a realistic knowledge of the enemy. In America a kind of "Know your enemy" literature developed in response to the war situation. The intensified self-awareness and self-preoccupation of the 1930's gave way to the painful other-awareness of the 1940's.

The post-war period has added still other components to the national consciousness of the world. While the war left each nation of the world with a more painful sense of its identity, it also created the powerful suspicion that the nation would never again be the self-sufficient unit of communal action it had been in the past. Who can escape the conclusion: No major modern war will be fought by the immediate contestants alone. The units of power have become vast international power blocs. Furthermore, however vast her resources, no single nation is alone capable of carrying out reconstruction after a modern war. The development of atomic weapons, inter-continental ballistic missiles, and the satellite weapons that can be anticipated in the near future, places a vast new capacity for destruction in the hands of any warring power.

There are still other respects in which the post-war world has experienced a heightening of and change in the requirements of national consciousness. In the first place, when wars are fought by power blocs, victory or defeat does not simply restore the world to its pre-war situation; it transforms the very landscape of power itself. Prior to World Wars I and II, England was the key to the European community of nations while Germany was its foremost rival. Neither nation will ever again seriously compete as points of potential integration for the communities of the world. The new competing centers of dominance have shifted to the United States and the U.S.S.R. This casts a whole new series of national and international relations into an unexpected prominence.

Meanwhile, as new lines of communal opposition are being drawn, man has moved to the new frontier of outer space. The first tentative steps are being taken, and the time approaches when man will begin shooting himself and other forms of life off the earth perhaps never to return again. The realization grows that the planet is a kind of space island held together as a limited unit by conditions that, however different and indeed difficult, are more closely related to each other than any conditions known or anticipated in the realm of outer space.

But such a dream of a world community is utopian. Man's waking life is obsessed by the growth and changing composition of the power blocs. That process of growth and change presents a peculiar irony. The most powerful communities of modern men are nations. Yet ultimate point of gravity of modern destinies lies in the composition of power blocs in which the limits of the nation are surpassed.

Nationalism is modern man's peculiar form of parochialism: the anchorage point of all that is reactionary, local, particularistic, sectional. The communities which at various periods in human history have ultimately integrated and distributed human activity have differed. There was a time when the majority of mankind was organized into tribal communities. In some areas of the world and in various ways, the communities represented by the peasant village provided a more efficient model of communal life than that offered by the tribe. In a still more limited manner at a later time the city community began to present itself as the most efficient model of socio-cultural life. Perhaps the high point in the development of the city community, the time when it represented the ultimate model of efficient human communal life, was the sixteenth century. Since then, despite tremendous quantitative increase, particularly as a result of the industrial revolution, the city has been declining as an integral community. Every loss to the city has represented a gain by the nation, as the true ultimate community of modern man.

It appears to be our destiny, in turn, to live in the very sunset period of the national community. For every modern observer knows that the ultimate activities of war and peace are the work no longer of single nations but of the power blocs. The units of the power blocs, however, are nations and the modern world is experiencing a kind of national crystallization process. India distinguishes itself as an individual nation from Britain, and Pakistan sharpens its national individuality against India. The Arabic nations sharpen their national identities against each other as well as against England and France. Algeria sustains a nationalization movement against France. And even an essentially ethnic and religious minority like the Jews in considerable measure has transformed its problems into nationalistic form in the movement and success of Zionism. No day passes without further evidence of the continued growth of nationalism in South America, Central and North Africa, and in the hinterlands of Asia. Nationalism is entering the final period of its most rampant growth precisely at the time when the problems of human kind have transcended its confines.

COMMUNITY FORMS AND SOCIAL TYPES

As every social scientist of the present knows, a community is an integrated total system of social life comprehensive enough to include all the activities, from birth to death, of a normal lifetime. It comprises the social actions surrounding birth, education, child care, marriage, earning a living, politicking, ageing and care of the aged, organizing one's relation to God or the supernatural, and administering the problem of death. A family, a religion, a state or any other similar unit of specifically organized social and cultural activity is not a community but merely one of the groups or institutions that make up the community as the comprehensive organization of the total activity system.

The variety of human communities is made possible by the almost infinite plasticity of human behavior. The continuity of the life of man in society rests on the stability of socially learned procedures. Savagery is never farther away from human society than the next birth; the highest and most exquisitely balanced achievement of human cultivation is never more remote than the next successful product of a society's educational processes. The continuity of a human community, thus, does not rest on a hereditary germ plasm like the communities of insects, but upon the success of the educational process in transforming the individual into its image. Every human community transmits behavior characteristic of and peculiar to it; if it does not, it ceases to be a distinct community.

The major communities of the past have left a residue of recognizable social types. In the older literatures of the world, we may discern the social type of the tribesman from the tribal community. In modern times, he rose to prominence once again with the European colonization of the western hemisphere. The European feared him, for he did not understand the tribal complex of his loyalties. Frequent attempts were made to enslave, for example, the American Indian, but these almost always failed, for the imposition of a way of life upon him which he defined as feminine tended to break his spirit so completely that he simply died in captivity or was driven to suicidal opposition to his enslavers. And the European found it necessary to import more adaptable peasant types from Africa to find a slave material adequate to his plantations and *latafundias.*

The tribesman was a social type outside the historical range of European experience at the time of the colonization of the Americas; the peasant was a known social type. Much of Europe was still organized into villages. The villager with his strong sense of property, capacity for hard work, calculating sense of self interest, suspicion of the outsider, and inclination to maintain his problems at a limited level sufficient to his needs but not beyond his personal control was well known in his moods, abilities, and loyalties.

The European was also familiar—as various other people and times have been—with the communal type of the city, the urbanite. He was known to be more articulate, subtle, and flexible, than the peasant. If he was less tenacious and traditional, he was more adaptable and suave. And if the urbanite tended to treat the peasant as rather stupid, the peasant was inclined to react against what seemed like characterless cynicism of the urbanite. There was no question to the European that these were recognizably distinct types of man.

Thus each community has produced its characteristic types: the tribe produced the tribesman; the village the peasant; the city the cosmopolitan urbanite. This is not to say that every tribesman is like every other, but merely that among tribesmen there tends to be a number of roughly comparable traits. And even though a Neapolitan may emphasize his distinctness from a Florentine, a Parisian emphasize still more his distinctness from a Berliner or a Londoner, and a New Yorker emphasize his difference from a Chicagoan, there is a recognition of similarity between cosmopolites the world over.

In the modern world all such ancient types are secondary and only of historical significance. The distinctive communities of modern man are nations, which tend to dissolve or assimilate all other structures. Modern nations dissolve and absorb the tribes in Arabia and North Africa, the peasant villages in India and Burma and the cities everywhere. And as these previous communities created their distinctive social types, so the nation creates its national types.

ANTHROPOLOGISTS, PSYCHIATRISTS, AND NATIONAL CHARACTER

If it is true that nationalism is rapidly becoming the peculiar parochialism of modern man, the contemporary world owes a very special intellectual debt to the teams of anthropologists and psychiatrists that have made their appearance in recent times. It is greatly to their credit that, at a time when it appears crucial to national and international understanding, they have reopened the discussion of national character. It may be suspected that the popularity their analyses and theories have enjoyed is due not so much to some of their challenging assertions, such as that whole nations may be compulsively anal erotic, as to their reopening of an area important to the understanding of our times.

While the present study shares the modern debt of gratitude to the anthropologists and psychiatrists, once again, one of the study's most fundamental aims was to develop alternative theoretical explanations of the phenomenon of national character. Before sketching these alternatives, it is of interest to consider the reasons why it was the task of the special combination of anthropologist-psychiatrist to take up the job of interpreting national character.[1]

The anthropologist-psychiatrist was responding to a socially felt need established by the sequence of world-wide depression, world war, cold war. The general reasons for this were sketched above, but if it were necessary to supply any further proof, this would be remarkably easy, even permitting of statistical confirmation. Anyone who surveys the literature on national character quickly discovers a very prominent fact: such literature increases during and immediately after periods of warfare, and declines sharply in volume in times of peace. National self-other awareness very evidently becomes a conceptual problem at times when the nations themselves have become problems to each other. In the United States considerable literature on national character was produced during and immediately after World Wars I and II. In Europe the same pattern is evident, and the volume of literature on national character increases in wartime. Many of the observations on comparative national character made by Europeans referred to in later sections of this study were made during the World War I period. Concern with the national character of Russia and the United States is one of the current preoccupations of Europe.

It is peculiar to our *milieu* that the anthropologist-psychiatrists have taken the lead in interpreting national character. In the nineteenth and early twentieth centuries, the interpreter of national character was more apt to be the journalist and ex-diplomat, and, at times, the political refugee. Such persons had the experience required for such a comparative task; they possessed skill in self-expression, and finally, they often had immediate personal motives for such analysis. These persons are, indeed, active interpreters of national character also at the present time, but to their observations have been added the unique interpretations of the anthropologist-psychiatrist, which tend to give the special color to current literature.

The emergence of the anthropologist-psychiatrist as the interpreter of national character seems most easily accountable by the unique combination he represents and by the peculiar demand of our times for authoritative professionalism. The intellectual world of contemporary man has been increasingly organized into specialties. The professional and the expert have usurped the right once reserved to clerics, philosophers and men of letters to pass authoritative judgment upon one area of contemporary experience after another. Modern man lives in a world of doctors, lawyers, dentists, psychiatrists, psychologists, demographers, statisticians, efficiency experts, marriage counselors, social workers, and morticians. The non-professional interpreter of human affairs increasingly finds himself without an audience, for automatically modern man turns for guidance to the expert and the professional. He will now pay hard cash to a psychiatrist or marriage counselor for information or advice that a few generations ago would be given gratuitously by the elders of the family, the minister, or even the family doctor. Small wonder that in matters of his national and international life modern man seeks the authoritative voice, just as he turned to the Kinsey reports for a biologically authoritative interpretation of his sex life.

It was the peculiarity of the professions of anthropologist and psychiatrist that fitted them to become in combination the authoritative voice on national character. The anthropologist is professionally trained to carry out comparative social and cultural observation of people. He has been trained to view societies as entire units and to study and interpret their properties as wholes. His central core of skills centers in participant observation which he has amplified and extended by the use of comparative techniques of many sorts, ranging all the way from kinship terminologies to linguistics. The one thing tending to limit the anthropologist's qualification as the paramount interpreter of national character is his popular identification with the study of backward, isolated, and primitive cultures.

The psychiatrist and psychologist, on the other hand, are the unique modern experts in affairs of human emotion. The reclining figure on the couch, the semi-darkened room, the relaxed and dreamy atmosphere, the omniscient but silent figure sitting taking notes are the very symbols of modern man unburdening himself of cruel frustrations and distressing anxieties. The psychiatrist is the professional who in considerable measure has usurped the role of the spiritual adviser and soul-healer of previous less cynical and less sophisticated ages. But even though contemporary man turns to the psychiatrist as an expert in the emotions, the psychiatrist has no particular claim to access by technique, training, or experience to the comparative observation of society and culture.

It is not difficult, then, to see why the combined anthropologist-psychiatrist so immediately struck modern man as precisely the right combination for the interpretation of national character. For did not such people conjoin professional expertness in cross-cultural observation with expertness in affairs of the human heart? A new coterie of international experts was not slow to answer the call. Its audience has not been disappointed with the result.

ANTHROPOLOGICAL-PSYCHIATRIC INTERPRETATIONS OF NATIONAL CHARACTER[2]

There are good reasons for believing that however appealing the new international experts have been to the modern imagination as interpreters of national character, the very properties that made them attractive might impair the quality of their interpretations.

The anthropologist has primarily been trained for the study of those early forms of human community that have persisted into the present, the tribe and the peasant community. Strangely enough, the argument is at times advanced that precisely this training uniquely qualifies the anthropologist for the study of all other community forms. But this would assume that the urban and national communities are constructed in the same manner as the tribal and peasant communities, an assumption radically at variance with the facts.

The critical differences between tribal and peasant communities on the one hand and the urban and national communities on the other lie precisely in a reversal of the order of institutional dominance. Some form of the family in its conjugal or extended form lies at the very core of the tribal and peasant community. All other institutions are ordered with respect to it. The family carries out the education; it is often not only the primary economic consumption unit but the production unit as well; it determines all major features of social rank; it regulates the ceremonial life; its males are the fighting force of the group; its elders the political leaders and key religious authorities. By way of contrast, in the urban or national community, some form of economic or political institution plays the critical role. The modern state, for example, supervises and controls education, regulates the economy, transforms the structure of the social ranks, establishes or controls all major social ceremonies, assumes an ever-expanding range of new social services, and transforms almost every other institution to fit its needs.

His training in the requirements of the tribal and peasant community inclines the anthropologist, when he turns his analytical talents on the more complex community forms, to approach all other institutions from the standpoint of the family and other primary group forms.

While his peculiar training often sends the anthropologist straight to the family as basis for his study, the psychiatrist he meets is there for different reasons. The psychiatrist's entire task consists in attending to the individual psychological casualties of the social struggle. Regardless of their ultimate origin, the individual's problems explode in his personal life. Furthermore, it is a rare situation for the psychiatrist to be able to transform the non-individual aspects of the problems brought to him. He must adjust the individual rather than transform the situation.

The very nature of this orientation means the psychiatrist must have a theory of individual problems that does not force him to transform the society of which the individual is a part. Such a theory makes his function possible. His theories must interpret the individual in terms of the individual's own history. In part the psychiatrist's function is to supply the individual with a rationale of his experience, with a way of accounting for the tensions that his existence engenders, of orienting his energies constructively toward those factors in his social situation he is actually able to control.

Thus when the anthropologist and psychiatrist join forces and launch upon a program of interpreting international politics they find themselves meeting on the same point. The one brings to the partnership a talent for comparative observation particularly of the customs of the family, clan, and other primary social grouping. The other is fitted out, from his clinical practice, with prefabricated explanations of individual emotional disorders as generated by family experience and the events of individual personal spheres.

There is a certain amount of charm in the products of this happy fusion of talents. The results are beautifully calculated to satisfy the requirements of a sophisticated international gossip. Remarkably complex events are neatly deduced from the presumed manner in which a given nation trains its infants. The most remote behaviors are transformed into products of the nursery. Whatever else may have been the case, events that have seemed alien and difficult before are made to appear quite close and familiar. The world is made to seem less strange, less frightful, when it assumes the form of comparative babyhood.

The scientific standing of these therapeutic little fairy tales is quite another story.

ALTERNATIVES TO THE
ANTHROPOLOGICAL-PSYCHIATRIC
INTERPRETATION

The purpose of the following essays is to explore some of the alternatives to the anthropological-psychiatric interpretations of national character. Theoretical considerations made this necessary.

If one were to ask for the rationale of placing the problem of the family at the core of national character, it would seem to require the assumption that the family is of primary importance to the national community. While it is not argued explicitly, the assumption appears to be made that the only difference between a tribe or peasant village and a nation is one of complexity. But the central assumption of the present study reverses this: the city and the nation are assumed to be something other than tribes or peasant villages writ large. Beyond mere quantitative differences they are here assumed to be qualitatively distinct forms of community.

The basic assumption made here is that any given human community represents a complete distribution of the possibilities of human life, forming a whole way of life. If one may be permitted such anthropomorphic language, a community is no more able than an individual to eat its cake and have it too. Human potential expanded upon one way of life is simply not available to be spent at the same time on another.

In order for mankind to form genuinely new communities, some activities that had formerly occupied human effort had to be abandoned. The precondition of the rise of the city and the nation was the breaking of mankind out of the families and clans of the tribe and the peasant village. These institutions had to lose much of their dominance over man's life in both practical and ideological ways. The human energies released by this process were then available for organization in quite new ways.

If this is correct, it is a radical error to derive national character from family structure, toilet training, child care, etc. To be sure, there is good justification for deriving the social types of the tribe and the peasant village from family-centered activities. These are, in considerable measure, family-centered community forms. By contrast, from the standpoint of the theory presumed here, the first step toward the understanding of the social types of the city and the nation is the recognition that one is dealing with communities that are not family-centered. The institutions that have importance in the regulation of life are present only in rudiments in the tribe and peasant village.

The general thesis explored in the present study may be phrased as follows: the social types produced by the nation are a product not of the family or any other single institution but of the peculiar socio-cultural structure of the national community.

SPECIAL VALUES
OF THE STUDY OF GERMANY
AND THE UNITED STATES

From the middle of the eighteenth to the middle of the twentieth centuries the history of Germany dramatizes to an unusual degree the potential of the modern nation for good and ill. It would indeed take an unusually unfair critic to deny the fabulous creativity of nineteenth-century Germany. It is one of the fundamental premises of the present study that Germany is an unusually worthy object of study, because her cultural contribution to Western civilization has been so remarkable.

Germany's period of creativity corresponds in some measure to the period in which it was being shaped decisively into a nation. If nothing else, this fact opens the interesting question as to the social conditions of cultural creativity. One could, for example, speculate that inasmuch as each newly formed community of human kind arises out of the materials of older communities, in the community's period of organization there are, so to speak, quantities of uncommitted energy available for creativity in a manner not true later. Or, perhaps, at the time when the communal solutions of a new community are still to be developed, the unorganized state of the community itself invites experimentation in a manner that is not true of communities in an older stage. Creativity would, thus, be a potential of the "youth" of a community form. From this standpoint one could perhaps relate national formative periods and creative products of some of the major European nations somewhat as follows:

National Formative Period and Creative Product

Nation	Formative Period	Creative Product
Italy	15th and 16th centuries	Humanism
France	17th and 18th centuries	Rationalism
England	16th and 17th centuries	Empiricism
Germany	18th and 19th centuries	Romanticism

However, even if heightened levels of creativity are a potential of the youth of a nation, this in no way accounts for the peculiar direction that creativity assumes in a given case.

Germany supplies more than an example of unusual national creativity and just as it would take a grudging critic to deny this, it would presume an unusually chauvinistic apostle to deny that Germany has been the delinquent child among the European nations. An amazing amount of German talent was subordinated to the intensification of the demands of national sovereignty; the risks were assumed of plunging the nation and the Western world into war. This has considerable interest quite apart from any concern with distributing war guilt or any other such ideological activity serving to mobilize emotion rather than to promote understanding.

Sovereignty was the principle which legitimized the dominance of the new national community over its parts. It was generated out of the ideological need of the modern state to justify its usurpation of the powers possessed both by local groups and the medieval church. The transformation of power from the medieval to the modern system was no sudden achievement, but a slow emergence which the principle of sovereignty justified stage by stage. Because the new consolidation of power was achieved slowly, counterbalancing forces accompanied the rise of the nation-state. These counter-forces served to limit the aggregation of power at any given stage. Whenever the national consolidation of force proceeded too rapidly (as during the French Revolution), it could explode in a series of international wars and crystallize opposition to the state at an international level.

Here again Germany arrived at the full implications of nationalism late and with a rush and intensity that dramatically revealed to the modern world, often to its horror, just what nationalism could mean when it was carried to its logical conclusion as an exclusive principle of communal behavior. The entire significance of German experience is lost if it is assumed that the operation of sovereignty there is unique. Both the way the notion of national sovereignty justified the fusion of all groups within the nation into a coordinated whole and the manner in which it was transmitted into a principle of international hostility, were not peculiar to Germans alone; only the unrestrained intensity with which it was pursued was unique. German experience was clarifying a principle contained in every nation.

Thus, whether one looks at the kind of intellectual and cultural richness made possible by the modern national community or at the totalitarian forms its political structures may assume, Germany has been like a mirror held before the face of the modern world. Other nations are as adequate for the contemporary examination of the problem of national types, but none offers more dramatic materials for demonstrating the full significance of such a study.

The value of the United States for the study of national character lies in a different direction from that of Germany. Germany was born as a nation out of pre-national community forms and within a surrounding circle of neighboring nation-states. The United States was a nation-state from its birth. The United States did not have to struggle for a national identity against ancient pre-existing peasant villages, manorial communities, or cities. It developed its national forms under frontier conditions; it faced an unusual task in the need to absorb more massive immigrations from the outside than any other modern nation. It represents a nation-state evolved more exclusively out of middle-class strata than any other in the modern world. Moreover, its middle classes have been in a very different situation from those of Germany. In Germany the middle classes were politically deprived for long periods under circumstances that led to the substitution of intellectual and artistic aspirations for political goals; in the United States the middle classes held virtually uncontested political power from the beginning, but were inclined to be anti-intellectual and anti-artistic.

THE FUTURE
OF THE GERMAN NATION

There is still another special reason for opening the theory of national types with Germany. More than any other single nation in the modern world, it critically raises the question of the future of a nation after the loss of a major war. Two major bids for the dominance of European society were made by Germany in the twentieth century. It is hard to imagine that Germany will ever seriously be able to make another.

The terror which these menacing gestures have generated in other lands is well known, for they even led to the startlingly barbaric suggestion that after World War II Germany should be transformed permanently into a rural nation. To carry out any such proposal would require a ruthlessness matching that of the Nazis themselves. It suggests an unprecedented experiment on mankind: the reduction of a national community to the status of a peasant community, the reversal of the course of modern history. Fortunately, the entire proposal was rapidly abandoned, for there are sociological reasons for assuming that it is unattainable short of the extermination of an entire people.

Meanwhile, two wars have left Germany sufficiently changed so that it will never be quite the same again. How much vitality Germany retains is, in part, indicated by the fabulous recovery powers of the nation. Since Germany was not permitted to expend its substance on militarism, its recuperation has been remarkably rapid. This evidence of inner dynamism sounds like the old Germany, but many other things do not. The partition of Germany amputated the Eastern agricultural area from political and social influence on the nation. Furthermore, when the Russians get done with the Junker, he will never again play his old role in the nation.

Moreover, it is a strikingly significant fact that after the Second World War, only the religiously conservative but politically liberal Catholic German south was able to supply the integral leadership of the nation. In fact, it appeared for a time to have been the only German group with sufficient internal coherence for the task. It is an ironic fact that it required the successive loss of two major wars before the fusion of intellectuality, liberalism, and political responsibility was permitted to form into an integrated structure at the top of the German Community. If this combination can persist, it will signify a new and more responsible era in German politics than before.

There is, however, a dark possibility in the emergence of elements from the German south into positions of political authority. The Catholicism of the German south historically forced the area toward a politically liberal position despite the powerful social and religious conservatism of the area. It was possible, thus, for Hitler and various rightist groups to find support in the area under the Weimar Republic when they were politically at odds with the official government. Hence the north German combination of official political authoritarianism tended to be counterbalanced by traditions of social and religious liberalism. South German areas often reversed the formula with combinations of political liberalism and social and religious conservatism. The possibility, thus, is ever present when the political leadership of the nation is drawn from the south of a new alignment of internal forces which would seek to crush out the social and religious traditions of the north.

Moreover, the social group that unites a nation after defeat in war always runs grave risks, for once it has performed its reconstructive work, it is often swept aside in a wave of reaction and blame for the very problems it helped to solve. Meanwhile, there are many unknowns. No one is yet able to assess the cost of the loss of German intellectuals, scholars, artists, and scientists to other lands. It remains to be seen whether East Germany will ever be permitted to return, and, if and when it does, what will be the influence of its transformed structure. It is too soon to say more than that some of the component parts of German national character of the past will never be manifest again. Germany is at one of the turning points in the evolution of her national character.

6

COMPARATIVE EUROPEAN
NATIONAL CHARACTER
AND THE PLACE OF
GERMANY

THE LAND THAT COULD PRODUCE THE literature of Goethe and Thomas Mann, the philosophy of Kant and Hegel, the music of Beethoven and Bach, could also produce Hermann Göring, Josef Göbels, and Adolf Hitler. The land that could make proud contributions to art, literature, music, religion, and science was also able to carry militarism to fantastic heights and engineer two of the most savage wars in the history of mankind. The land that could appreciate the delicacy of Heine could also sustain the unspeakable horrors of Buchenwald and Dachau.

These properties, which at once attract and repel, invite simultaneous formulation. Germany evokes an ambivalence even in its devotees; never calm appreciation, but love or hate often by turns. One is, first of all, attracted to Germany by its imagination, its creativity. Under the influence of the German environment nearly every theme of modern civilization was simultaneously clarified and extended. The same thematic body of enlightened thought and ideals was present in Voltaire and Goethe. In Goethe they undergo a statement in depth that is typically "Germanic." The themes of eighteenth-century rational and empirical philosophy were familiar to all the major philosophers of England and France. It required a Kant to perceive the implications of the critical analysis of Hume and to undertake a new solution to the conflict of rationalism and empiricism, and to succeed so well as to make his formulations the last great synthesis of the rationalistic phase of Western philosophy and the starting point for all modern philosophy. The materials of modal and tonal music, the first subtly responsive to melodic requirements, the second offering magnificent possibilities for a new aesthetic adventure into the world of simultaneous sound, were diffused through England, France, and Italy. It required a Bach to make the decisive synthesis of contrapuntal music, an integration so significant that it formed the starting point for all musical developments in the West thereafter. The music of romanticism and of revolution found a surpassing synthesis in Beethoven's fire and ice, passion and intellectuality. Such are a few of the familiar illustrations of the element so fascinating in German society and culture, its sweeping inspired imagination.

But the story never ends at this point. Ever and again the German imagination is a runaway horse. This may be illustrated by the German contribution to modern music which many observers have felt is the most German (and most distinctly Western!) of the arts, or the art where the German spirit has been most fully realized.

Modern music developed out of modal music, a music primarily intended to realize aesthetic effects of melody (successive sound patterns) resting upon pre-modern types of musical scales (modes) between which there was no true transposition, since each scale had a unique structure of its own. Modern music inherited these scales but gradually transformed them, giving them a parallel structure, forming them into a system of scales, and opening up immense possibilities for simultaneous sound effects and modulation from one scale to others of the system and the transposition of musical formation from one scale to another. Tonality was harmonically expressed by a series of chords built on degrees of a certain scale. These were formed in terms of a model. The scale in which they were constructed was determined by the relation of the keynote (octave) to the dominant (fifth) and the sub-dominant (fourth). However, from the beginning the practical laws of musical composition rather than mathematical and physical considerations determined usage, thus minor and diminished chords (occupying four degrees of the scale, while the major chords occupy only three), were employed. At first the requirements of tonality were narrowly adhered to and only chord types built upon its own degrees were permitted. However, modulation could considerably enrich the possibilities, and incidentally, increase the musically available tension and finally enhance the triumph of the original tonality. The decisive step to chromatism on the basis of the major-minor tonal system was made in its strict form for the first time by Johann Sebastian Bach, and formulated theoretically by Rameau. The art of modulation was brought to full development by Bach when, by way of chord types, modulation was carried to keys ever farther from the fundamental. For example, modulation to the subdominant minor became frequent. At the same time, one chord met with on every degree, the diminished seventh, begins to threaten the principle of tonality itself, for it belongs to every major or minor key.

With the appearance and employment of such "roving" chords, new possibilities emerged and were seized upon imaginatively by Wagner, who conceived of the possibility of an "endless melody." Harmony became complicated as more thirds were added and chromatism began to destroy the system of thirds itself. If, as Wagner frequently does, one moves from one of these "roving" chords not to chords strictly reducible to thirds but to another vague chord and so on to another, the result is the realization of Wagner's dream of an "endless melody"; but musical development is at the threshold of the destruction of tonality itself.[1]

The development in German music from Bach to Wagner is almost a paradigm of German development: brilliant creativity and unrestrainable force. Runaway development rushing impetuously to its own doom, unrestrainable short of the destruction of its own creation. It may be suggested that this is merely a by-product of the inner logic of an aesthetic development and does not by any means merit elevation to the status of a general principle, and particularly, assignment to a particular national character. However, one cannot overlook the frequency with which *the nineteenth-century Germans were "called" to carry through the logic of events.*

This has led many critics of German art to see in it a fundamental formlessness. It is certainly true that Italian and French art frequently achieve a serene harmonious lucidity of secular sensuousness or logical perception respectively. Both qualities are nearly always absent from German painting. German aesthetic passion presses toward violent contrasts of unrestrained fantasy or brutal realism, a drive toward boundless subjective expression. No wonder characterizations of its artistic genius as Gothic or Romantic are so frequent.

Along similar lines, the "form-giving" principle repeatedly seems to come to German art from the outside and to endure for a time until elemental forces thrust up from beneath shatter it. In the thirteenth century German art turns toward "die Welt des schönen Scheins" under the influence of French individuality and aesthetic sensibility— but quickly transforms it! In the fourteenth century illuminated Minnesinger manuscripts (*Manesse Codex* of Heidelberg and Wolfram von Eschbach's *Parsival*), motifs based on observation of nature increase. This naturalism helps emancipate painting from its ties to monumental decoration. Other artistic conventions are severed. From the work of the artists to whom Philip the Bold entrusted the decoration of the Carthusian Monastery at Dijon (Herman de Coulogne and his school), a lyric and semi-mystical quality appears which fired the enthusiasm of the nineteenth-century romantics. In the works of Konrad von Soest (*Crucifixion* at Rieder-Wildungen, 1404), naturalism triumphs in the rendering of fashionable dress, while the spidery-limbed bodies create tapestry-like effects. Linear rhythms begin to predominate. Naturalism continued to grow, and in Swabia Lukas Moser's (*Tiefenbronner* Alter of 1431) portrait, several incidents appear in the form of a continuous narrative. A delight in descriptive detail and sense for atmosphere appears. In the early fifteenth century, for example, Konrad Witz of Basel (1390–1436), problems of plastic form increasingly dominate until a kind of culmination is reached in the work of Martin Schongrauer (1445–1491), where there is frequent abandonment to the decorative fancies of the late Gothic. In *Maria in Rosenhag* (1473, Colmar) the form sustains a fascination with detail and a spiritual depth, but a decadent effeminacy is present. This sequence in which German art receives a form-giving principle from the outside, and then pours into that form a vital content until it cracks at the seams is, in the minds of many students, a typical drama in German art from the late Middle Ages to the present.

Left to itself, German art seems always ready to break down into subjective emotionality. This may be seen, for example, in the contrast between Dürer and Grünewald. Albrecht Dürer recovered a new sense of form in his two journeys to Italy. In his regeneration of German art, Dürer utilized expressive form to render simple, intimate scenes with powerful intensity. But the passionate emotion held in control by Dürer already bursts into a flood of subjectivity in his contemporary Matthias Grünewald.[2] In German experience, imagination rushes as a force uncurbed to the point of dissolving the very forms that make it manifest.

This had led many sensitive thinkers, including Germans, to the conclusion that Germany is *without culture*. While maintaining that the Germans individually have made the largest contribution of any people to the civilization of the world, Oscar Schmitz argued that they are without a national culture to harmonize instinct and intellect in a manner which can secure the respect of other nations. The great proportion of German people are wrongly educated or over-educated; they are book worms or pedagogues. In his opinion, nature has closed rather than fertilized the German intellect.[3]

Nor is this an isolated opinion. Nietzsche, too, insisted that there is no German culture; there are only great solitary figures like Goethe who wear their private cultures like the mists of solitary mountain crags. Nietzsche described German nature as a soft, swampy, treacherous soil on which every footstep of the foreigner made an impression and created "forms." He added that the Germans have no culture, for they have, as yet, no character.

NATIONAL CHARACTER

There are ancient parallels to the modern concept of national character. The classical Greek and Roman perceived a difference between civilized men and barbarians. The ancient Chinese contrasted their cultivated compatriots to the vulgar man of the steppe. The perception of differences between the *we-group* and the *they-group* is the core of all ethnocentrism, which is an important component of national character. The Eskimo drew a distinction between people and those who are only somewhat similar to people. But all these parallels do not quite touch the modern concept of national character, which is only formulated when the nation as a special community has achieved sufficiently coherent integration to establish social types of its own.

The theoretical background for the idea of national character was provided by the enlightenment attempt to reconcile the assumption that the distinguishing property of man is his reason, with the evident differences between men from place to place. Human nature was taken to be the same the world over. However, in fact very real differences between whole groups of men are to be observed. Hence, it was argued that the play of local circumstance on human nature must lead to a secondary differentiation of peoples. Montesquieu expressed the idea unusually well. "Mankind are influenced by various causes; by the climate, by the religion, by the laws, by the maxims of government, by precedents, morals, and customs whence is formed a general spirit of nations. In proportion as, in every country, any one of these causes acts with more force, the others in the same degree are weakened. Nature and the climate rule almost alone over the savages; customs govern the Chinese; the laws tyrannize in Japan; morals had formerly all their influence in Sparta; maxims of government and the ancient simplicity of manners once prevailed at Rome."[4]

To Montesquieu national character is a product of local circumstances. He advanced the thesis that government is sound only when it rests upon the national character of a people and expresses the spirit of the nation, for "we do nothing so well as when we act with freedom and follow the bent of natural genius," and he spun out many interesting observations on the possible relations between the government of a people and its national character. He argued that the more communicative a people are, the more easily they change their habits, since this quality is correlated with a delight in change. He maintained that the society of the fair sex spoils manners and destroys taste, for it leads to ornamentation in dress, a desire to please others, and assigns importance to frivolous turns of mind. Nevertheless, he thought vanity was advantageous to a nation, for it promotes industry, the arts, fashions, politeness, and taste. Pride, which Montesquieu thought important to the Spanish national character, is a great national danger leading to laziness, poverty, and general neglect. While the laws are the institutions of the legislature, Montesquieu maintained, the mores and customs are the institutions of the nation. If national customs are to be changed, it cannot be by way of legislation, but only by the introduction of other manners and customs. The customs of an enslaved people are a part of its servitude and those of a free people are a part of their liberty. Montesquieu was convinced one could develop principles for the effective judgment of national character.

Montesquieu also made numerous comparative estimates of national character. He thought that the ancient Athenians were like the French, mingling gaiety with business to such an extent that a stroke of raillery was as agreeable in the senate as in the theater. By contrast the Spartans maintained a character of gravity, seriousness, severity, and silence. One of the effects of pride, Montesquieu thought, is laziness. All lazy nations are grave. While the pride of the Spaniard leads him to decline labor, the vanity of a Frenchman forces him to work harder than others. National traits may appear in varied combinations; pride conjoined with ambition and notions of grandeur produced characteristic effects among the Romans. The Spaniards, famous for their honesty and fidelity, will often suffer death rather than reveal a secret, conjoining this with indolence. The character of the Chinese is formed by an almost opposite mixture of the same traits important in the Spanish character. The precariousness of subsistence inspires the Chinese with prodigious activity and an excessive desire for gain. While one never has cause to regret trading with a Spaniard, Montesquieu maintained, ordinarily only a Japanese merchant dares to trade in China. The ideal of a free nation was provided for Montesquieu by England. There disputes are occasioned by a violation of fundamental laws, and should a foreign power appear, there would be a revolution that would alter neither the constitution nor the form of government.

A revolution does not, in Montesquieu's opinion, change national character, for promoted by liberty, it becames a confirmation of liberty. A free nation may have a deliverer, but an enslaved nation can only have another oppressor. The enjoyment of liberty and even its continuation consists in every man's being allowed to speak his thoughts. A citizen in such a state will be able to say and write whatever the laws do not expressly forbid. National character generally was thought to be a phenomenon of a more fundamental character than wars or revolutions.

Unsystematically, but with a rich sense of its possibilities, Montesquieu delineated the essentials of the concept of national character. The idea was in the air. It did not escape Montesquieu's colleagues in other countries, such as David Hume. Hume was at once both a more penetrating logician and a more systematic and precise empiricist than his great French colleague. Although he turned his attention only briefly and incidentally to the problem of national character, he conceived it in thoroughly empirical terms, treating it as a set of shared habits (customs). Hume observed that any trade or class situation involves a core of basic activities (occupationally determined or fixed by life conditions) which institute a central system of habits in the individuals who practice them and around which other activities are arranged, attitudes clustered, and perspectives fixed. Hume was transforming the eighteenth-century notion of national character into a behavioral concept.

The idea of national character fitted the historical trends in the eighteenth century, for nationalism was evolving into a dominant social force. The large states created by the absolute monarchs found it necessary to destroy the patterns of feudal allegiance which obstructed the new national powers. The secularization of life and education and development of vernacular languages of the earlier period had weakened parochialism and sectarianism, making way for a new kind of territorial unification and identity. The new forms of economy reinforced the economic independence of the larger territorial units. The new theories of sovereignty and the concept of the rights of man were transforming the state from the private property of the monarch into the fatherland or motherland of all its citizens.

Montesquieu's national spirit or national genius and Hume's national character were given new intensity in the work of Rousseau, who had begun to conceive of the nation as a kind of organic unity. Rousseau's new emphasis on popular sovereignty led him to project the idea of a national will which was somehow superior to and not simply a statistical formulation of the will of the majority. Rousseau had begun to reify the concept of national character in a manner repugnant to Montesquieu and Hume.

The tendency to hypostatize was also present in the idea of a *Volksgeist* by German writers, beginning with Johann Gottfried Herder. He and his followers sought clues to its identity in folklore, folk songs, and primitive and popular traditions which were conceived to be the truly vital creative forces of a nation.

Once national character was reified in the idea of a folk spirit and fitted to the needs of German political nationalism, it quickly led to a glorification of irrational and instinctive factors conceived as the true elements of creative national genius. The reification had some positive results, for it inspired new researches in folklore, language, and tradition. However, it was also transformed into a metaphysical dogma by Hegel, for whom history itself was conceived to be the dialectical development of national genius.

In reaction to the excesses of German metaphysics and romanticism, the idea of a national character has at times been rejected outright. However, the eighteenth-century conception of national character never completely disappeared, for students have wished to recognize common properties of national behavior without hypostatizing them into a new kind of entity. This led Taine to give prominence to the *milieu* as a socio-psychological environment tending to generate characteristic behavior. More recently the concept of a *climate of opinion* has been revived from seventeenth- and eighteenth-century thought by Alfred North Whitehead and Carl Becker.

According to Carl Becker, common thoughts and even similar words typify an epoch. Typical or key words in the thirteenth century are *God, sin, grace, salvation,* and *heaven.* In the nineteenth century, on the other hand, *matter, fact, matter of fact, evolution,* and *progress* come most readily to men's lips. In the twentieth century such terms as *relativity, process, adjustment, function,* and *complex* seem most natural for expression of matters vital to us. In the eighteenth century, by contrast, no educated person could reach a conclusion without the use of such words as *nature, natural law, first cause, reason, sentiment, humanity,* and *perfectibility.*[5]

While Whitehead and Carl Becker have tried to revive the non-reified "behavioral" concept of national character, the Germanic "reified" form has also been revived. The Germanic forms of the concept of national character have been popularized by some anthropologists, such as Ruth Benedict (*Patterns of Culture*) and Margaret Mead (*Sex and Temperament in Three Primitive Societies*). The typical configurations which Benedict thought were produced by culture were drawn from German writings. In the course of his examination of aesthetic experience Nietzsche had argued that two fundamentally different ways of achieving the ultimate objectives of life could be distinguished. Manifest in two kinds of temperament, the Appolonian masters life and achieves its values through serene withdrawal, contemplation, emotional control, poise, and philosophical analysis; the Dionysian, on the other hand, seizes life in passionate embrace, ecstatically seizing its very irrational densities. The two kinds of temperament in which these life conducts are embodied appear in the contrast of dreams and drunkenness. Nietzsche, however, contrary to the majority of his German contemporaries, did not reify these temperamental contrasts.

In her analysis of the Zuñi of the southwest of North America, the Dobuans of Polynesia, and the Kwakiutl of the northwest coast of North America, Benedict utilized Nietzsche's categories to visualize these cultures as points on a scale from an Appolonian to a Dionysian life-form. As an exceptionally ceremonious people, the Zuñi, for example, were theorized to be controlled, repressed, exhibiting all the forms and customs of life typical of the remote, serene, unemotional objectivity of the Appolonian life-form. At the other end of the scale the Kwakiutl (with their complex winter ceremonials, initiation rites and dramatic ceremonies, the extensive rank striving of competitive noble clan-heads, their potlatches so destructive of property, and paranoic forms of social competition) were treated as Dionysian. Nietzsche's behavioral contrasts were reified and conceptualized as cultural contrasts.

The old Germanic notion of national character also reappears in the work of the culture configurationists and some other branches of modern anthropology. Ralph Linton, Cora du Bois, and James West, in collaboration with Abram Kardiner (see, for example, *The Psycho-*

logical Frontiers of Society), have developed a new version of the concept of national character in the idea of a "basic personality type"—personality configurations shared by the bulk of a society's members as a result of common early experiences. Personality was assumed to arise in the course of early training, particularly within the structure of the family (the Oedipus relation). Three major sets of activities were conceived to play a formative role: the key integrative systems (basic early training), reality systems (ways of adjusting to nature and man), and projective systems (folklore, poetry, literature, the "dream life" of the society). The way these three systems of activities intermesh establishes the basic personality of a people. The basic personality of nearly an entire society may closely approximate one of the individual personality formations originally delineated in the Freudian system of psychology; it may be strongly compulsive; it may be narcissistic; it may be sadistic or masochistic; it may be inhibited or repressed.

Current use of Germanic forms of the concept of national character are by no means confined to anthropological studies of primitives. Particularly since the rise of Fascism and Nazism, analyses of the national character of major national groups have grown in popularity. The Freudian type of analysis has been employed with particular frequency. German national character, for example, has been analyzed during and since World War II as an authoritarian personality formation determined by a peculiar Oedipal relationship found in the German family.

The present study, however, has the closest affinity to the views of Hume, Taine, and Carl Becker. National character is taken to consist of a typical system of behaviors. One can accept Hume's skepticism concerning the existence of a universally similar rational human nature and at the same time agree with him that collective behavior in fact often displays stable sets of habits. One can also accept the romantic thesis that lifts the emotional, irrational, and accidental factors to importance in the emergence of cultural identities without taking the metaphysical leap to the *Volksgeist* or an independent entity. Unlike the concept of *people's genius* or *folk spirit* the concept of *milieu* or *climate of opinion* does not lend itself to reification. German romanticism and philosophical metaphysics assigned causal priority in historical development to the folk spirit. By contrast the concept of *milieu* or *climate of opinion* locates behavior within a context which represents a similarity of response by a plurality of people.

In the present context national character refers to a configuration of behaviors which may come to typify various sub-sections of mankind.

As a peculiarly modern complex of institutions and customs, sentiment and loyalties, it is a social and cultural counterpart of nationalism. National character is by no means identical with personality, an individual's unique personal system of behavior; though national character can be expected to bear upon the kind of personality formation occurring in a given nation-state.

A national character is defined by a frequency of trait occurrence and to a peculiarity of trait combination in the behavior of the plurality of a national group. In view of the enormous plasticity of human behavior and man's infinite ingenuity, such stabilities are only temporary. In this fluidity lies the risk of over-hasty judgments of national character and over-strict constructions of their meaning. If there is neither frequency of trait occurrence nor a peculiarity of trait combination which can be independently observed and checked, judgments of national character are without determinable meaning. Moreover, the mere presence of a state does not guarantee the emergence of a national character. However, national character inevitably appears with the nation.

The processes by which a set of behaviors may arise out of institutions and play back upon them, are complex. When the set of behaviors appropriate to a national system of institutions comes to typify a population, a national character has formed. This calls attention to another error—in the present view—of the basic personality theorists who attempt to deduce national character from the family life of a people. As the most universal of all institutions, the family is the least plausible basis for the emergence of national character.

NON-GERMANIC NATIONAL CHARACTER IN EUROPE

The concept of national character and the facts it is intended to explain require neither the supposition that human history consists in the successive revelations of an inner folk spirit nor the assumption that the art, religion, literature, and politics of a people are the reflection of the toilet training of its infants. It requires only the occurrence of distinctive configurations of traits and behaviors.

Anything can be characteristic only with respect to something which is non-characteristic. Judgments of national character which refer to characteristic behaviors take form at points where the behavior of national pluralities may be experienced in contrast to others. Hence, the discovery of national character is always in some sense secondary. It is often made either by an alien visitor or by a native who travels abroad. For so long as one carries on life in an old familiar way, one does not perceive it as peculiar or distinctive. It does not even seem familiar except from a different vantage point which permits the contemplation of the unfamiliar. What is part of oneself simply "is."

National character, thus, is usually discovered as a reflected image. One needs only to recall the role played by foreign studies such as Tocqueville's *Democracy in America* in the discovery of the peculiarities of America. To a significant degree the configuration of America has emerged from the perceptions of foreign observers including, such English interpreters as Trollope, Martineau, Dickens, Herbert Spencer, Bryce, Wells, Chesterton, Belloc, and others. Among French (over 1500 volumes by French commentators have appeared) observers as Crevecoeur, Chateaubriand, Considerant, Chevalier, Clemençeau, and Siegfried, America saw its familiar self largely through unfamiliar eyes.

Many of the more subtly penetrating perceptions of the properties of America were possible to temporary expatriates who, like Henry James, discovered America in Europe. In a similar manner no one was more able to sound the keynote to British national character than Joseph Conrad. And these are not isolated examples. It is almost a fundamental principle that the precondition for the discovery of a country is a perspective permitting its familiar behaviors to appear peculiar and distinctive. It is clear why the post-World War I generation of writers whom Gertrude Stein described as a "lost generation," which included such persons as F. Scott Fitzgerald and Ernest Hemingway, discovered the thematic properties of the Jazz Age from the streets and cafés of Paris. Though our primary concern is with German national character, it is useful to review the formations of national character in the areas around Germany, since they form the context against which German national character appears as a special configuration.

England

The peculiar genius of the British in the minds of many students lies in the Englishman's capacity for action. A special temperament is required for greatest efficiency in the moment of the act. At this moment the dominance of behavior either by thought or emotion may be quite disadvantageous. It is not the time to have one's vision impaired by exacting insistence upon clear definitions and logically deduced theories. Action unfettered by intellectual requirements is freed for maneuverability. Moreover, the moment of the act is no time to have "buck fever." Action must be simultaneously freed from intellectual domination and unobstructed by emotion to produce consistent results.

Siegfried[6] was much impressed by British action orientation which, he felt, contrasts so sharply with the French. The Frenchman, he observes, has a small-*rentier* psychology, which leads him always to insist upon having a solution to every problem. But the Englishman operates on the principle that nature never presents herself in neat packages. All human arrangements are but temporary provisions for the continuance of activity. To Siegfried's mind, the Englishman is the prototype of the mariner in days of old who set his sails and charted the positions and course of the ship according to the changing winds and tides. So in his social and political life does the Englishman maneuver as in an unstable environment. Instability is accepted without resentment as an inevitable property of events.

Parallel to the nonchalant acceptance of the requirements of action is the simple acceptance of nature which characterizes the attitude of the Englishman. Lines extend from this naturalism to the most creative aspects of English thought. While Americans try to speed up the natural process, and the French to rationalize it, the Englishman simply accepts and works within nature. This philosophy was Francis Bacon's basic principle, the mastery of nature by employment of her laws. This same principle lies at the core of the special English contribution to modern philosophy—empiricism.[7] Empiricism requires the Englishman to keep in constant touch with experience, accounting for the avoidance of all types of thought which involve a separation from things. At its best empiricism becomes the instantaneous fusion of thought and action. Philosophical empiricism reflects this, for it even countenanced the program of deriving thought itself from experience. John Locke, who vigorously promoted this philosophy, also typified the English temperament in another way. Locke always stopped analysis at a sensible point, with a fine sense of when he was treading on thin ice—when further theoretic reflection would only lead on to self-contradictions.

It is the Scot, Hume, not an Englishman, who carried the logic of British empiricism to devastating conclusions. The result was an inescapable skepticism. Rational thought was revealed to be different from the rest of experience, and hardly derivable from it. The logic of empiricism may thus be conceived as pressing toward the abandonment of thought. But the British were typically unwilling to abandon intelligence, for this, too, would impair action. When Hume brought the older forms of British empiricism to an impasse, the majority of English philosophers simply ignored the whole messy business, and utilitarianism quickly filled the vacuum in British thought. Utilitarianism, like empiricism, has an inner affinity with English psychology. When utilitarianism is confused with selfishness it is misinterpreted. Utilitarianism is quite compatible with disinterestedness. At bottom, as Madariaga has observed, utilitarianism is the requirement, that action be fruitful. There are two common sense principles buried in utilitarianism: the idea that action is not pathological, but is motivated by the desire for happiness; and the idea that action represents a net increase in happiness for someone, and hence for mankind collectively. Of course one acts for a reason. Why act if no one benefits? This is a primary component of British psychology.

His attitude toward action dominates the Englishman's employment of his leisure time. He must be doing something physically. Siegfried, for example, observed when he served as an interpreter with the British Army during World War I that while the French general occupied his leisure hours by reading philosophical and historical works, the British general occupied his with a detective story or with playing endlessly with his dog; that is, when he was not throwing, kicking, or knocking balls about with his subordinates. A passion for playing with balls seemed to Siegfried to be particularly British.

In contrast to many other lands, games and sports are pursued in England not only by the leisure class but the middle and lower classes as well. In fact, the very standards of effective action are derived from sports which are promoted as sources of self-control, self-reliance, courage, tenacity, and team spirit. The rules of cricket tell of the English love of compromise between a particular freedom and a general orderliness or legality. Law and order in society are conceptualized in terms of cricket. "If everything in this nation of ours were lost but cricket— her Constitution and the laws of England of Lord Halsbury—it would be possible to reconstruct from the theory and practice of cricket all the eternal Englishness which has gone to the establishment of that Constitution and the laws."[8]

While the very norms for correct social and political conduct are drawn from sports and expressed in the concepts of fair play and sportsmanship, the English are puritanically reluctant to devise rules of deportment from art. The cultivation of taste, in fact, is perceived as a distraction, as an impairment of action. The national neglect of good food and wine has been universally noted, and Shaw ironically observed that "an Englishman thinks that he is moral when he is only uncomfortable."[9] When the French cultivate eating as an art, this only makes them appear the more suspect to the English, who generally abhor dietary unconventionality.

Theoretical subtlety is usually perceived by the English as a snare; in fact, the anti-intellectualism of the English is famous. Siegfried observed that to the Englishman the intellectual is a sort of mental acrobat, fascinating to observe, perhaps, but something of a monstrosity. When Siegfried was invited to give a lecture at Eton and asked his hosts for advice, they told him "don't be brilliant."[10]

Demiashkevich has assembled many pleasant instances of British anti-intellectualism.[11] For example, several hundred years after the establishment of the University of Oxford, in a memorandum by Eyre Crowe, it was stated: "There is no person or body in Oxford competent to declare what the functions of the university are. Among individuals the conception thereof differs immensely. . . . Oxford has never felt the necessity of declaring its purpose, because it has always found that purpose in its own traditions, moulded slowly by the pressure of economic and social revolutions."[12] As a by-product of this anti-intellectualism, the English are reluctant to undertake long-range planning, but seem to prefer rather to muddle through every crisis. There is some justice in Bernard Shaw's observation in *Saint Joan:* "If we can only have a treaty, the English are sure to have the worst of it, because they are better at fighting than at thinking." The suspicion of intellectuality leads to the formation of cabinets out of undynamic and "safe" rather than out of brilliant men. It has repeatedly led to the toleration of errors of almost unbelievable stupidity.

Charmingly, Siegfried observes that in some respects the Englishman remains fifteen years old all his life. He is young, as are young animals. Even his love of animals is a kind of perpetual adolescence. He was astonished, he stated, during his stay in London to read in the column of *The Times* letters to the editor like the following:

Sir: I noted two butterflies in my garden yesterday. This is two weeks earlier than usual at this time of year.[13]

That a great newspaper of a world metropolis should find space for a report on butterflies is most certainly symptomatic of national preferences.

The emphasis is on the importance of action, which inevitably thrusts the actor into prominence. Social stability is sought by the Englishman in good character for which he finds no substitute. For the same reason he seeks to develop a knowledge of men as the irreplaceable basis for effective conduct. A critical study of the work of fiction writers in England shows them largely to be concerned with the study of man himself. The study of man also forms the typical English point of approach to ethical, political, or social problems. One of the most favored volumes for study[14] beside the *Encyclopaedia Britannica* is the *Dictionary of National Biography*. A study reported by the *Book Review Digest* for 1922–1932 shows that ninety-one biographies and autobiographies of statesmen and public figures for these years were made in England, while France contributed twenty-six, Germany sixteen, and Austria thirteen.

Many students have noted the fact that the history of England is remarkably free from bribery, treason, and personal profit at the expense of the nation. Even mild cases of the abuse of office are rare, and insistence on good character is systematically carried out in practice. The English public is a remarkably good and strict judge of character. As a result of this emphasis on good character, a public figure can rarely survive a scandal. On the other hand, since the Englishman admires character as the highest human value, he is particularly careful in matters relating to the personal reputations of public figures.

France

French national character presents a number of contrasts with the English.[15] Not the least of these may be seen in roles played in France by a small peasant-proprietor outlook on the one hand and a general rationalism on the other; both of which perspectives are absent in England. The properties which differentiate French national character are in tension: the one, Siegfried observes, would make common cause with Sancho Panza, the other with Don Quixote.

The strong practical turn to the French outlook is traceable to the traditional attitude of the peasant who remained important in France long after he vanished from England. At home and in his private activities the Frenchman displays good sense and moderation. Like the peasant everywhere from France to China, he insists upon visualizing his problems as a unit. As far as possible he transforms the world itself into a sphere under his personal control. The peasant knows that life outside his local sphere is hard. This adds an element of materialistic calculation to his activities and a peculiar kind of stubbornness and tenacity in holding on to what he has won by hard work.

Only a step away from this peasant-like component of the French character is the mentality of the artisan and craftsman—which is quite distinct from that of a laborer of mass industry. The French workman, Siegfried notes, likes to put his individual signature on what he has made. He has personal identification with his work, and with his signature would stamp something of his personality on the object. For the same reason the French workman can generate little enthusiasm for the high level of individual but impersonal efficiency consistently maintained in England. To the Frenchman, the Englishman is a slave to routine. To the Englishman, on the other hand, the Frenchman lacks team-spirit, taking interest only in the game in which he can star. In any case, the Frenchman usually devotes himself passionately to work whenever it is creative. Invention intrigues him. However, he loses interest in a task the moment it becomes routine. Other nations have often reaped where the French have sown. Such basic inventions originated in France as the motor car, the airplane, and the movie projector, all of which were far more fully exploited elsewhere.

The small *rentier* and artisan qualities of the Frenchman, Siegfried continues, make him rather stubbornly self-sufficient and opposed to authoritarianism. He is nonconformist at heart. Moreover, he tends to be self-limiting. Once his security is assured, he limits his ambitions, emancipating his spirit by disconnecting action and thought. The negative effects of this may be a mixture of noble aspirations and inept attempts to fulfill them, often so typical of French egoism. No one has summed up these aspects of French character more precisely than Paul Morand: "There is a striking resemblance between us and the Chinese: a passion for thrift, the knack of making things last and repairing them indefinitely, a genius for cooking, mistrust, traditional politeness, an inveterate hatred of foreigners, but passivity, conservatism, interrupted by social tempests, a lack of public spirit, a great vitality amongst old people who have passed the age of sickness."[16]

The other major aspect of the French character is its capacity for analysis and rationalism. In France even the man on the street has considerable capacity for generalization, for isolating the principle contained in an issue, and deducing its consequences. Flowing from this proclivity for analysis is the average Frenchman's unrealistic faith in ideas. He also tends to accept as self-evident the notion that people can be swayed by an idea. Alfred de Vigny's definition of God in *La Bouteille à la Mer* is characteristically French. "The True God, the Almighty God, is the God of Ideas." Even André Gide confessed that ideas interested him more than men; in fact, "more than anything. They live; they fight; they perish like men."[17] During World War I, J. A. Spender was amazed by the diffusion of rationalism in French society. No Englishman, he thought, could have visited the French front without being impressed by the lucidity and skill with which anyone in command of anything, from the most illustrious general to the sergeant in the trench, could expound his job or enlarge upon the strategic situations.[18]

The finest flowers of French philosophy grow out as naturally from this soil as English philosophy grows out of its action-orientation. Descartes elevated this French everyday love of analysis to the level of a philosophical principle, seeing the way to truth not in intuitive insights or prophetic vision, but in the orderly methodological, preferably mathematical reasoning. His method of doubt consisted in the shearing off as irrelevant that which cannot be rationally proved in order to arrive at the mathematical certainties assumed to lie at the foundations of experience. Voltaire demonstrated in the realm of social experience the incisiveness of criticism flowing from the use of these principles. Rationalism reached fullest expression in the philosophy of the Enlightenment.

At the same times, Madariaga has sensitively observed, French intellectuality is perhaps more of a hindrance than a help to action. The Frenchman is irritated by the loss of conceptual control of a subject, which is often inevitable with immersion in experience. The natural result of the irritation is procrastination, the postponement of action. For the Frenchman, life becomes general staff work and a series of maneuvers. The vocabulary of action for the Frenchman, as Madariaga so aptly states, is studded with war metaphors: *attaque brusque, mouvement tournant, surprise, guet-apens, stratagème*. The Frenchman finds it difficult to take action as it comes; he rushes to it with a *furia francesca*. The calm of the Englishman is the lucidity of a man in his natural element. The Frenchman is lucid before and after action, but is overwhelmed in the spontaneous movement of life.

Irrationality leads in action the Frenchman to impose the intellectual category of order. He seeks ever more refined categories of explanation in defensive foresight. When action is forethought, tomorrow is, so to speak, transformed into an abstract problem of the present. To this wish for order Siegfried attributes the great vogue enjoyed by Taylorism (a system of work speed-up) in France around 1900, for it manifests a Cartesian spirit of sorts. Parallel to this attempt to organize economic life rationally is the Frenchman's attempt to organize society itself in a similar manner.

The Frenchman visualizes his social order as if it were official and imposed from above. He intellectualizes it and subjects it to artificial regulation, anticipating action by a complicated system of written laws which intend to foresee all possible cases. Within the network of *le droit* is a finer network of *les règlements*. Bureaucracy is to the state what *les règlements* are to *le droit*—derivations from a common rational principle. The demand for an intellectually conceived order established by authority dominates all public spheres.

French rationality, thus, transposes the form of sociability. While the Englishman enjoys a form of action in his leisure time, be it only playing with balls, the Frenchman would sooner converse. As Taine put it, the Frenchman instinctively likes to be in company. He talks with ease and enjoys good talk. "His conception of a good time leads him to seek something fine, light, lively, incessantly renewed and varied . . . he finds only in social intercourse; therefore conversation is his favorite pastime."[19] English observers have come to the same conclusion. It was Mill's view that a Frenchman is happiest in the period after supper in the private society of well-educated and intelligent men. "They converse and think in unison about the most exalted subjects, skipping from one to another in short, pithy phrases, and their general ideas, briskly launched, flutter like a swarm of insects."[20]

Intellectual conversation achieved its most developed and subtle form in salon wit. The social graces originating in the salon were transplanted to French café society, which performed the same service for the less wealthy that the salon did for high society. Some of the Paris cafés became centers of literary, political, and philosophical movements. The Café Procope, for instance, numbered such persons as Descartes, Voltaire, and Crebillon among its habituées. Beaumarchais waited there for the verdict on the first performance of the *Marriage of Figaro*.[21]

Rationalism and individualism have also been taken as general clues to the Frenchman's style of life. In domestic animals he prefers the cat, described by Demiashkevich as the most luxurious, rationalistic, and least mystically inclined of the creatures. In nature the unforeseeable is not a source of awe, as in Germany, or to be expected, as in England, but an occasion for distrust. The countryside around Paris, in a manner pleasing to Siegfried, has been made over into geometrically arranged parks (Versailles, Vincennes, and St. Cloud). The whole countryside has been cultivated until it is like a garden. The Frenchman has no more inclination to seek oblivion in alcohol than in a mystical immersion in nature.

Similar themes—clarity, balance, orderliness—are important for styles of personal deportment. In the control of experience rationalism and good taste play companion roles. Demiashkevich finds it typically French that Charcot, the famous teacher of Freud, could appreciate the genius of Beethoven while he despised Wagner who seemed overemphatic and formless. French newspapers pride themselves on the correctness of their literary style. Even small sheets devote space to literary subjects and linguistic problems. Siegfried has observed that while the English letter to the editor may be filled with Biblical quotations or zoological observation, a French letter to the editor is more apt to raise questions of grammar. Finished style is required even of the scientific technician. Henri Bergson observed that above everything else the French value the qualities of clarity and composition. "With us, no scholar can boast that he has written books which no one save a dozen fellow-scholars can understand. We do not have a caste of the high priests of science. We believe that clarity is the mainstay of democracy."[22]

As in the case of every national character, problems typical of the French are traceable to the same source as its virtues. Excessive demands for intellectual clarity often lead to the definition of problems so sharply that far from facilitating solution the problems become explosive. The intellectual ordering of collective life often seems an inadequate substitute for practical control, resulting in moral indifference or political intolerance. The failure to establish a practical equilibrium between individual interests and social loyalties is seen by many of even her most friendly critics as a characteritstic French failing. Moreover, fidelity to absolute truth may foster a multiplicity of points of view, while simultaneously preventing the intellectual compromises between them. One is reminded, by contrast, of Walter Bagehot's amusing comment that British democracy rests solidly on the stupidity of the nation. For, he said, even in parliament if everyone thought originally about every act, there would be as many amendments as there are members, and no business would ever be transacted. This often happens in France. The Frenchman tends to be theoretical rather than practical in politics.[23] While striving to realize his concept of the perfect form of society, he is reluctant to give up any part of the ideal for the sake of attaining what is practicable. As a result, politics become doctrinaire, permitting unscrupulous individuals to exploit the nation's dependence upon rhetoric. The masses are swayed by the belief that intricate problems may be solved by a simple rational formula.

Just as the French drama under the influence of a love of rational proof at times threatens to become an oratorical tournament, so the government and administration of justice become stages for rhetoric, often serving no practical purpose. The French have, not altogether unjustly, gained the reputation of being the most ungovernable, revolutionary people of Europe. In addition to the Fronde (1648–1663) and the revolutionary period (1789–1799), there were numerous other revolutions such as the July Revolution (1830), the February Revolution (1848), the Revolution of September 4, 1870, and the Communist Regime of March to May (1871). French rhetoric, moreover, has given a more colorful advertising to such periods than has been true for equivalent phenomena elsewhere.

Finally, the French tend to display the weaknesses which Demiashkevich described as systems D and C. System D (derived from *débrouillard*) refers to the art of improvising individual solutions to problems of equipment and training; this was forced on French soldiers and subalterns in crises, by the failure of superior officers to anticipate or prepare. Anything that does not fit a national scheme tends to be neglected. Thus in a crisis for all the many things that are planned, much remains for improvisation. System C refers to theoretical Quixotism, the inclination exemplified when the French High Command determined strategy in terms of some theoretical possibility so difficult to approximate in fact as to virtually guarantee defeat. As a result of this trait, the French can often accomplish difficult things with ease, while they do things which should be simple only with extreme clumsiness.

Spain and Italy

In this study tracing some of the formations of national character in Europe appearing around and playing back upon the German, the space available for such comparative review is too limited to permit detailed examination of secondary formations. The problem of the formation of national character in the interstitial regions and countries —the Saar, the Rhineland, Switzerland, Austria, etc.—must be ignored as well as the examination of the formations of national character in various secondary countries: Belgium, Holland, Greece, Czechoslovakia, Hungary, Poland, Finland, Denmark, Norway, and Sweden. However, because of the very interesting contrasts between German and general European characters, a very brief review of national character in Spain is rewarding. Spanish character has been formulated with exceptional insight by Salvador de Madariaga in *The Genius of Spain.*

Madariaga believes that the key features of Spanish national character fall into perspective the instant that the Spaniard is treated as a man of passion. The Spaniard is presented as a type who thinks by contemplation, awaiting passively for the object to reveal itself, until chance, coincidence, or sudden secret sympathy illumines the object in some new way. Thought is intuitive rather than discursive, revealing itself in an instantaneous contact of the life of the object and subject.

Intuition involves the whole subject at once. The opinions of the Spaniard are, thus, no mere ideas he carries in his head, but convictions he breathes. Spanish thought never exists as an impersonal objective structure. It emanates in rays from the intuitions which conceive it. Moreover, the final character of Spanish thought involves an inseparability of body and spirit, a kind of material spirituality or spiritual materiality. The usual contrasts between the sacred and profane, thus, are inappropriate to Spanish thought. While the conscious workings of intellect are reversible, this intuitive thought is as irreversible as it is spontaneous; it is final, integral. It can be neither verified nor begun again. The Spaniard's thought does not "progress," for intuition does not yield to a pre-established method. When a Spaniard has methodological pretensions, they are usually counterfeit. His method, if one calls it that, consists in watching unfold the events that his imagination may fire or fuse. Since the sources of intuition flow from nature, the Spaniard prefers to get his ideas directly in the course of his own contemplation of nature rather than seek them from others.

Left to itself, Madariaga maintains, intuition would probably bring from the depths of the subconscious nothing but pearls of thought. However, the psychology of the man of passion inclines him to establish passion rather than knowledge as the final aim of life. Thus, thought is subordinated to passion, and arbitrariness is guaranteed. As a result, Spanish thought is as rich in intuitive elements as it is poor in intellectual elements. If one were to employ the distinctions between genius and talent introduced into modern aesthetics by Immanuel Kant—genius referring to native ability and talent to ability developed by training—one could say that Spanish civilization is rich in genius and poor in talent. Moreover, since the efficiency of a cultural development depends on the combination of genius and talent, Spanish life achieves its highest forms in those arts (such as literature and painting) in which genius is more important than talent; it is weak in disciplines where talent is most fundamental (such as architecture and music).

The behavioral consequences for the Spaniard of his unique combination of traits is a peculiar form of individualism. The Spaniard follows a solitary path. He is inclined passively to behold life with resigned inactivity. Intellectual work is frequently visualized as local, partial, precise, mean and small, compared to the synthetic spectacle of the world. The Spaniard instinctively feels self-assurance and self-confidence; this self-assurance is a component in his low regard for intellectual leaders.

The man of passion, according to Madariaga, is in his natural element in a state of passion. A high degree of consciousness does not typify Spanish personality. In his passions he is at once more individual and more universal than the man of action. He knows only what he has assimilated; the knowing subject and object known are fused. Love becomes the precondition of knowledge. The ego moves to the center of all conceptualization, for everything springs from the sense of life, supplying the serenity and spontaneity of the Spanish type.

The substance of Spanish wisdom lies in its sense of and total involvement in the oneness of the whole. Individualism, humanism, and amoralism are the manifestations of the Spaniard's psychology, containing the defensive impulse of the man of passion against all social and intellectual forces which hinder the spontaneity of feeling. Collective life, thus, is dominated by the individualistic psychology of the type. This is also the key to Spanish egotism. All passions acquire true value only when incarnated and personalized in the individual. The standard of worth by which other entities are evaluated is found in the self. The rhythm of life oscillates between the ego and the whole, egoism and integralism. Intermediate stations between these poles are unable to provide equilibrium. Experience transpires in a landscape with a universal background. The most integral of all passions is the sense of life itself, compared to which other passions are ephemeral and partial. When he is most egotistical, the Spaniard becomes most universal, for his egotism is life in full spontaneity.

The interest in de Madariaga's formulations lies in part in the clear sense they contain that in the Spanish character one has touched one of the limits beyond which one passes outside the range of typical European experience.

In the development of national character in Europe, Italy is of immeasurably greater importance than Spain, not intrinsically but in relation to non-Italian forms. Italy was the transmitting link from classical Greece and Rome to European civilization. The few observations assembled on Spanish national character were intended primarily to call attention to the fact that there is no single climatically-determined Mediterranean character. The emotional excesses possible to Spain's man of passion flow outside the compass of Italian national character, as appears in their differential response to the Inquisition. Olschki has called attention to the potential in the Spanish character for indulgence in the emotional atmosphere of mass executions during the Inquisition. The hedonistic character that these mass executions could assume was revealed in the orgies of murder attended by the sovereigns, the courts, the prelates and an ecstatic mass of *aficionados*. By contrast, the Italians shrank from such types of hedonistic brutality. The attempt to introduce the Inquisition into Italy led to revolts in Milan and Naples and even in Rome, where the prisons and Holy Office were attacked as a result.[24]

It will be recalled that one pole of French thought was located in the petty-*rentier* mentality of the small independent peasant: a stubborn and at times greedy sense of the importance of property won by hard work, together with a willingness to limit one's claims in the attempt to secure a sphere of life completely under individual control and the belief that all problems have a solution were the result. By way of contrast, country life and a peasant mentality never played a primary part in the socio-cultural life of Italy, particularly Northern Italy. In the *piazza* of small towns and cities, where the managers met to carry out their agricultural transactions, contact between town and country was always maintained from Roman days.

Roman civilization itself had been welded out of the diverse cultures of the northern Etruscans and southern Greeks. It arose as a syncretistic form which dissolved the Italic tribes into the Roman commonwealth. Ruralism, tribalism, and racialism were melted down in the process. And when the decline of Roman civilization left the Franks in control, they ruled as a Germanic power, unwilling to grant any concessions to the Latins. The Lombard and Frankish nobilities and some subservient native elements thrust the countryside toward ruralism but never developed the moral code of fealty and justice of French feudalism. Their presence only sharpened the division between town and country without bringing the city under rural influence. The rural Germanic population never felt comfortable in the city, and the upper classes in the cities remained distinct from the foreign-derived rural nobility.

In Italy a balance between town and country, landowners and peasants, emerged institutionalized in the system of sharecropping, *mezzadria,* in which produce and risks were equally divided between the two parties. The influence of the city in the system is indicated by the speed with which the Italian city-states abolished rural servitude, long leading Europe in this respect. To be sure, permanent effects were left by German feudalism on Italian history: the country was impoverished, a breed of fair-haired mongrels was left in the north, and a feudal sense of hierarchy was diffused into all sections of society. In fact, one of the first acts by members of the communes, when they succeeded to power, was to assign themselves noble ranks. Apart from this, no major effects on Italian national character were left by the Germanic domination.

Comparable to the role of the mentality of the peasant in France was that of the urbanite in Italy. From the time of Dante, Italy was presented a spectacle reminiscent of ancient Greece, an agitated metropolitanism. The city-state supplied the matrix for political and social organizations. Italy's distinctive literature is of urban origin. Civic ethnocentrism sparks the rivalry between Milan and Pavia, Crema and Creoma, and exaggerates the significance of local dialects. The Italians even visualize themselves as urbanites, as children of the marketplace.

The modern communes were of critical importance for Italian mentality. As Max Weber demonstrated, they did not begin as revolutionary movements aimed at introducing democratic liberties; this only occurred gradually in the second half of the thirteenth century when democratic institutions of the city evolved out of the institutions of the *popolo.* The communes formed initially as a voluntary association of the urban strata for the purpose of controlling their own political affairs and monopolizing urban economic opportunities. The revival of Roman law was the work of the notaries and university professors of the communes. A new architecture was created when the cathedrals were rebuilt to serve their function as religious assembly places for the towns' expanding populations. The cathedrals were erected in cities and financed from public funds collected from the urbanites. The loss of many republican privileges with the rise of civic tyrannies did not substantially alter these trends, though popular assemblies moved from the cathedral to the *piazza*.

Civism is critical for the peculiar form of Italian particularism. The Italian is proud not of the fact that he is an Italian but more specifically because he is, for example, a Venetian or a Lombard. Sforza observes that an Italian feels uncomfortable when he meets a fellow-countryman whose accent does not at once reveal his home province or city. Such a person is de-particularized like an actor or a radio voice. The Italian, Sforza observes, even prefers a Levantine accent which at least identifies the speaker as coming from Para, Galata, or Alexandria. Similarly, a book preserving its affinities with the author's native province has a better chance of success than one identifiable only as a nationalized Rome or Milan. Even so universal a thinker as Benedetto Croce, Sforza observes, bears a sub-imprint as a Neapolitan.

In response to the requirements of the nation, official literature tends to be lifted outside particularistic frameworks, but the language of song, love, and laughter bears the stamp of the province. Even the cosmopolitan Boccaccio was so loyal to his city that he could not bring a rogue or hypocrite on the scene as a Florentine. His rascals were Milanese or Neapolitans. Sentimental attachment of the average Italian to his native city, the lack of internal migration, and the sense of legality contributed, in Olschki's mind, to passive acceptance of a regime of political realism, a dualistic education of a Jesuitical type, and a concept of political absolutism as an instrument of divine providence, all of which are major themes of the Italian character.

The city, however, was more than the *locus* of Italian particularism; it was central to Italian universalism, cosmopolitanism, as well. Cosmopolitanism, involving a flexibility toward thought systems, was worked out uniquely in Italy. In the fourteenth century Italy, according to Olschki, Averroism, centered in Padua, had achieved importance comparable to positivism today or to Darwinism in the nineteenth century. It was flexibly adapted to cosmopolitanism by the tolerance it represented and reinforced. Averroism permitted the coexistence of philosophic and theological truth, without giving rise to insoluble conflicts between them. The conceptual freedom required by the cosmopolitan temper was confirmed by it.

Under the influence of Averroism, theological universalism could develop without becoming omnipotent. As Olschki observes, large numbers of Italian popes subscribed to the idea of the fusion of Christian brotherhood with a worldwide sacerdotal, juridical, and political organization. Thomas Aquinas gave intellectual substance to this conception, though scholasticism as a discipline for churchmen had limited influence on the laity. Dante, on the other hand, integrated the theological and lay worlds, transcending scholasticism in a poetic synthesis.

However, as in the case of other national characters, the Italian has points of weakness. Many sensitive interpreters of Italy have noted that something of a moral vacuum tends to appear between the sacred and profane spheres of culture. Humanism was the unified view of life which arose in the Italian Renaissance and proposed to integrate these spheres. Although Humanism is identified with Petrarch, it transcends any single person. It formulates an attitude that is at once personal and universal. Poetry becomes a stylized vehicle for the expression of human sentiment. The ultimate rationale of life was found in the aesthetic development of man's own ego. The world was transformed into a problem of taste leading to the establishment of the new manner of deportment in the schools and courts. The movement evolved the ideal of a universal civilization, helping to revive the Latin language. Proponents of the new style found personal models of deportment in the ancients (particularly in Cicero and Seneca). Petrarch, for example, was constantly at work perfecting his personality with more care than he devoted to his verses, discovering the Italian people as a special community only incidentally, as it were, to the aesthetic discovery of himself.

Humanism synthesized the mood of the time, and the humanistic style supplied the Italian courts with modes of deportment for diplomatic exchange. The sonorous diction of Petrarch was adopted as an official court language. Petrarch's followers were found among diplomats, counselors, and secretaries to the sovereigns. Large segments of the urban patriciate participated in the revival of classical taste and culture, though it is doubtful whether the brutality of actual political and social conduct declined.

Humanism, which began as a movement of an intellectual aristocracy, increasingly became national in scope. Some modification of manners was inevitable. It spread as a sort of secular religion in local groups founded by its apostles. Its moods penetrated and transformed customs, art, and poetry. The general practice grew of entrusting the education of young noblemen and the sons of patrician families to humanistic tutors. As Olschki has observed, the didactic tendencies of humanism appear in the manner in which medieval doctrinalism was revived with the attempt to establish standards for the perfect prince (Datina, Patrizi), the perfect citizen (Palmiere), the courtier (Castiglione), the husband (Barbaro), and the family (Alberti). Meanwhile the continuing search for an ethical code for everyday life led to development of Ficino's mystical vision of the universe. The ecstatic philosophy of love diffused through secular society, assuming the form of a kind of universal eroticism.

Parallel developments of the cosmopolitan mentality are presented by Boccaccio who by artistic means intensified the psychological rationality of the period. Some of the tales represented in the *Decameron* were of general, others of local, diffusion. Boccaccio transformed them into a mirror of universal human qualities: folly and wisdom; deceit and honesty; cowardice and bravery. Skepticism and frivolity which so long typified Italian aristocracy were converted into forms of cosmopolitan sophistication.

Florence in particular became a center of literary and artistic naturalism. The bankers and businessmen were induced through a competition for status to invest their surplus gains in the patronage of art. The dangers that threatened their lives sharpened the poignance of their passionate affirmation of life and their attempt to perpetuate themselves and their families through monuments and foundation. While ideological Humanism pursued significance in the Platonic theology in which God appears as a universal noumenon and the human soul as an emanation of the Supreme Being, artistic naturalism was finding significance in the equilibrium of dramatic tension and structural harmony and in the geometrical proportion of parts. The arts (sculptures, reliefs, frescos, and paintings) assume the proportions of a secular religiosity in the presentation of an ideal reality synthesizing the spiritual and mundane.

The artistic style parallels the Platonic cult of divine proportions in man and nature with its insistence on measure and evidence. Parallels, in fact, appear between Dante, Petrarch, and the Humanists. Some kind of universalism even appears in Italian science. Copernicus rejected the old cosmological system with a sophisticated distaste like that which turned the Humanists away from the amorphous, the inartistic, and the forms of abstract scholastic thought. Motives seeking to link truth, beauty, and perfection in the formal properties of style were at work.

It is of critical importance, Olschki maintains, for the development of Italian national character that the counterpart of Humanism in politics was achieved at a time when Italy was losing its political independence. Niccolo Machiavelli died the same year as the sack of Rome. Francesco Guiccardine died in 1540 after the final subjection to foreign rule. The state was transformed in thought and practice into a transcendent imperium removed from everyday reality. Moreover, Spanish absolutism, established through the Company of Jesus and the Roman Inquisition, gradually secured control over the life of the nation; it reoriented its cultural powers and brought the individual conscience under control. Moral and physical torture, denunciation, spying, and secret prosecution all reduced the alternatives of the individual to submission or exile.

With the development of political and theological absolutism, the spheres of culture were transformed. The last two areas in Italian life to yield to the process were science (which with Galileo's denunciation and Bruno's martyrdom was brought to a close in Italy) and music. The ethic of everyday life which Humanism represented declined. The universalistic forms of science, art, and music spread outside the land of their birth, creating new movements wherever they touched, even while being stamped out in the land of their birth. Of the Humanistic cultural revolution, only an empty shell of eloquence and rhetoric remained. Once drained of its spiritual content, Humanism may appear (as many observers have often complained) only as a kind of windy bombast. There remains, as a minor compensation, a peculiar kind of moral uncommittedness damned as amoralism or praised as a Latin realism. Meanwhile the contribution of the Italian Humanism to Western civilization has been of permanent importance.

Russia

When one shifts attention to the east of Germany, a formation of national character comes into view more different from any of those so far reviewed than any of them are to each other. When in the strange cyclonic storms that occasionally stir culture, there occurs a westward movement in the winds from the east, the European experiences Russia as an unusual compound of familiarity and strangeness. In part Russia presents a kind of primitivism. Siegfried charmingly recalls a railway trip in which a Russian family in the next compartment unrolled its equipment and in short order had a samovar bubbling and a hammock with the baby suspended from the ceiling. It was as if a tent had been put up. The Russians, he observed, seem able to camp out anywhere, in an anteroom, a railway station, or even a railway compartment. It is by such signs that one recognizes the approach to Asia. But this primitivism is hardly the entire story, for Russia also displays a taste for subtle discussion suggesting an over-development rather than primitivism.

The very moment the European feels that he touches the essence of Russia, it usually dances tantalizingly out of reach and in the decisive moment moves outside the range of his experience altogether. When the Russian came to the West he became aware of elements in himself which fell outside the compass of ordinary western experience. Three major types of explanations[25] have been advanced by the Russians themselves for the difference between Russia and the West. Russian character has been explained on the basis of the extremes of a continental climate; on the basis of the conflict of Asiatic and European cultural influences (an explanation accepted by Tolstoy), and on the basis of the peculiarities of the Russian family (by Dobrolyubov, Ostrosky, Herzen, and Propotkin among others). Recently Tomasic has attempted to combine the last two types of explanation. He has argued that the culture of Russia is derived from two quite different sources: from the customs of power-seeking, egotistic nomadic horsemen of the Eurasian steppes and from the customs of Slavonic peasant folk, politically organized into self-governing villages and communally oriented with few distinctions of rank and class. From the first source Tomasic sees the derivation of tense autocracy, personal dependency upon and subordination to a stern distant father leading to a psychology of extreme insecurity, social irresponsibility, greed, self-seeking, and brutality. From the second source he sees the derivation of indulgence, sentimentality, optimism, pantheism, animism, an identification with nature, and emotional dependency. The organization of Russian society, according to his theory, was carried out by nomadic federations following the same pattern as those originally established by the Scythians and Huns in the area between the Ural Mountains and the Carpathians. These predatory warriors practiced a sadistic cruelty on the Slavonic communities from which they stole or purchased women and where they established families characterized by cultural dualism and tense internal conflict.

Thus the two contrasting family types, the Turko-Mongol and the Old-Slavonic, were theorized to be joined in the Russian extended household family community (*bolshaya semya*) with the communal family under the family head (*bolshak*) in which property was held in common and administered by a council (*soviet*) of married male members. In this family, it is argued, all the tensions of the early system were continued. The father imposed his will on its members by physical beating with the horse whip and birch rod. At a community level the same tension was preserved by power-thirsty rulers who employed brute force against the peasants. The peasants were, in turn, at times driven to such extremes that they murdered their princes. Folk tales relate violence of princes so terrifying that the very earth shrank and shriveled. The same narratives relate to the murder of their closest kin by such princes. This was the ultimate consequence of the imposition of the rule of nomadic warriors over the cultivators of the soil and led to the successive disintegration of the old ways of life and morals. The old Slavonic goddess of love, Lada, was relegated into the background before Bacchanalian passion and Dionysian orgiastic Larilo.

Anxieties and fears combined with a strong demand for indulgence, hatred and sense of guilt are asserted to be generated by the Russian society which resulted. The Russian saints, as portrayed in the hagiographies, are symbolic projections of these emotions; they are visualized as constantly tempted and intimidated by great hordes of fearful demons. A gloomy and terrifying view of life and death and apocalyptic pictures of the end of the world are offered by the church leaders.

If one disregards the over-simplification of this formula for the Russian character, derived in part from psychoanalysis and in part from the ideology of the Slavophils, in which everything arbitrary, uncertain and cruel, is derived from the Turko-Mongol and everything gentle, kindly, and communal, is derived from the Slav, the point is still valid that the Russian represents in some measure the result of a fusion of originally diverse ethnic differences. Moreover, the movements out of tribalism occurred more recently in Russia than in any other European nation.

However, the religious elements which were originally contributed by the tribes were certainly added to, complemented, and modified by Christianization. When Christianity was accepted by the Grand Dukes of Kiev beginning in 988 by Vladimir "The Saint," it was under the influence of the Byzantine Greeks. For two centuries after its establishment (1037), the Russian Church was subject to the Constantinople patriarchate, and most of the "metropolitans" and "bishops" were Greek. The effect, if not the intent, of the introduction and sponsorship of the Byzantine church by the Grand Dukes was to establish psychological and ideological grounds for the political integration of Russian lands. In the system of military theocracy that emerged, the function of a "messianic" ideology was, in part, to liquidate the forms of tribal religiosity and to fuse loyalties into new patterns of dominance-submission, protection-dependency.

The church was subject to the absolute will of the emperor. Its religious philosophy corresponded to political practice. The emperor was elevated to the status of a sacred, omnipresent, all-powerful symbol. The Russian Orthodoxy that emerged was similar to Byzantine Orthodoxy in that it was based on monasticism. However, the monks of the Russian church were more sharply separated from secular affairs than the Greek, and they conducted lives of asceticism oriented toward the achievement of personal salvation. Native Russian, Byzantine, and Turko-Mongol institutions were fused into an amalgam under imperial control. (In fact, with respect to religious beliefs—contrary to Tomasic's view—the Mongol rulers were more tolerant than the Grand Dukes, for the shamans of Asiatic people were not organized into a priestly class and the Mongol emperors did not see in them either a threat or a means to imperial power.)

The special form of fusion of church and state in Russia colored all other socio-political phenomena. If the only ideology that is officially permitted is religious, all opposition is forced to take a religious form. Any nationalistic movement which sought to democratize the Russian state inevitably had to assume the demeanor of religious fanaticism. Expansion of the state and messianic world-redemption were ideologically linked. Social and political action assumed the form of compensatory or salvation devices. Feelings of humility, self-abasement and inferiority, which in other lands are confined to religion, typified every day experiences in Russia. Moreover, any protest against existing conditions inevitably assumed the form of religious heresy.

As one comes into modern times, the social ferment accompanying the rise of the modern national state in Russia is correlated with the appearance of all sorts of prophecies and apparitions. Saintly men and prophets, who were often mentally unbalanced, appeared in the streets openly to protest against the czar and his government. Such "idiots" were considered saintly both because of the daring of their behavior and the incredible hardships and cruelties they often endured. Very characteristic of the Russian people was the appearance of pseudo-czars among the masses and of prophets who were healers of body and spirit. Also typical of Russia was the practice of *yurodsty* ("being a fool for Christ's sake"), accepting, even insisting upon, the humiliation and mockery of the world. The manner in which protest against existing conditions always assumes religious form is further evident in the great number of Russian religious sects like the *Dukhobortsy* (spirit-wrestlers) and *Molokane* (milk drinkers). The resentment toward the authorities by such sect members was very strong, inclining them to receive every act of an official character with passive resistance. Among the Dukhobortsy even the authority of the family was resented, and the very names "father" and "mother" were replaced by the terms "old man" and "old woman." It is little wonder that so much of Russian thought should have a religious coloration and that as a newly constituted form of political power, Russian Communism should make one of its first acts (1917) the disestablishment of the Russian Orthodox Church, while at the same time assuming a form that observers almost universally describe as religious.

However, while some properties of Russian national character can be gauged only in terms of its form of Christianity, there are others which must be approached from the standpoint of czardom. The major objectives of the Muscovite rulers were the internal consolidation of the power of the czar and territorial expansion. Religion served both ends. Meanwhile the hereditary magnates, the local princes and *boyars,* were obstacles in their path. It was theorized that the best way to break the power of the landed aristocracy was by making it economically dependent on the czar through expropriation, resettlement, and imprisonment. During the process suspicion, mistrust, abusive domineering and insistence on blind subordination typified official policy.

Since the days of Czar Nicholas I, the secret political police (the Third Section), implementing the growth of central power, was placed above all ministers and directly subject to the czar. By the time of Ivan the Terrible, the power of the independent landed aristocracy had been suppressed and the aristocrats reduced to the status of service nobility, given lands on condition that they render service to the czar. The presence of an ever-watchful secret police generated enormous feelings of insecurity. Another aspect of the strengthening of central power appears with Peter the Great's attempt to Westernize Russia as "first carpenter of the Empire," after his trip abroad. The old system of administration based on the service nobility was now replaced by a system of salaried officials organized into a new military and administrative bureaucracy directly dependent on the czar. Moreover, Peter carried through a whole series of reforms while "paying off" the old nobility by making them hereditary owners of their estates. The great *dvorianstvo* thus obtained hereditary rights to their lands at the very time that their service to the state ended.

One can most easily approach the social movements beginning in eighteenth- and accelerated in nineteenth-century Russia from the standpoint of the newly formed landed gentry appearing during Peter the Great's reforms. It became a leisure class without power. It had nothing to do but occupy itself with improving its estates or following Peter's advice—traveling, visiting, and studying in Western lands. Its members went to schools of Western political movements and social ideologies. From its circles the first political opposition movements were recruited among whom were some interested in constitutional government.

The emergence of an independent intellectual life began in Russia with eighteenth-century Free Masonry. The first Masonic lodges arose in 1731–1732. Some of the "best" Russian people were Masons. It was Russia's first free, self-organized society. In the Freemason Novikov, it found an active figure of Russian enlightenment; he edited works of the western mystics, the Christian theosophists, and the fathers of the Church. Masonry provided a vehicle for the expression of some things hitherto missing from Russian life: the anticipation of aspirations; an element of cosmopolitanism; an emphasis on humanitarianism and Christian love; social justice; an interest in schools and charitable institutions. Its ideals penetrated the officers' corps and a number of military societies. The "Decembrists" who revolted (December, 1825) had been trained in Masonic lodges and were strongly tinged with religious mysticism. It is a significant comment on Russian society that it was the nobility that created the Decembrist movement; such is the possible consequence of creating a group with social and economic, but not political, power. Out of aristocratic ranks proceeded the first liberation movement in Russia, opening a revolutionary century. The Decembrists had passed through Masonic lodges; so, too, had a great number of the early Russian thinkers. Pestel and Turgenev, for example, were Masons.

By the beginning of the nineteenth century Russia had gone to school in Europe. Young Russian gentlemen had often studied in France. They could usually speak French, and were familiar with French literature. Moreover, the French Revolution had brought French royalist refugees to Russia in search of asylum. Currents of thought had begun to differentiate. Opposition to the czar took two forms: one was pro-Western, seeking development along humanistic, liberal, and juridical lines; the other was anti-Western, a reaction to Western rationalism, materialism, "heathenism," and cosmopolitanism. The Westerners accepted Peter's reforms and sought to continue them. The Slavophils believed that a special culture belonged to the spiritual soil of orthodoxy and that Peter's reforms were a betrayal of Russia. They found inspiration in Hegel and the German Romantics (rather than in Voltaire and the Encyclopedists), and found the ideal of Russia, its utopia, in Russia's historic past. According to Slavophil interpretation, the Old-Russian Slavic community was founded on the principles of obedience, responsibility, social justice, equality, Christian love, and humility. The *mir* represented the basic institution in which the organic totality of body and soul, faith and reason, man and society, were maintained.

The Slavophils placed great emphasis upon the importance of the family, an idea ridiculed by the Westerners. So, for instance, K. Leontyev denied any particular sense of family among the Russians. Berdyaev, a contemporary Westerner, maintained that most people of the West, particularly the French, have a far greater family sense than do the Russians. But the argument of the Slavophils was utopian rather than factual. They saw the commune as the foundation of Russia and the basic difference between Russia and the West. While seeking to restore the archaic group value of the Slav folk and the peasant commune, these revolutionaries exhibited the same messianic power-oriented drives as did the ruling classes of czardom.

The effects of the European revolutions of 1848 and the defeats of the Russian armies in the Crimean War (1854–1856) led a section of the intelligentsia to the belief that the czaristic system was not invulnerable. Plans for action were developed by the anarchists. With czaristic traditions of unconditional power in mind, they proposed the preemption of the right to cheat, steal, lie, destroy, and kill as a way of disposing of the ruling classes. By the second part of the nineteenth century the process of disintegration of the old order had gone far. Serfdom was abolished; many manorial estates were in ruins; the gentry was partly impoverished and pauperized. In the new society even the position of the clergy became precarious. Russian Orthodox seminaries became fertile grounds for the diffusion of revolutionary propaganda. From the divinity schools and priestly families came such nihilists as Chernyshevesky and Dobrolyubov, such terrorists as Nechaev, such Bolshevists as Stalin.

Berdyaev has observed that the intellectual left in this time began to assume the character of a monastic order with all of the phenomena of asceticism, capacity for sacrifice, endurance of suffering. It lived in acute conflict with the empire. Many students from impoverished states had to depend on public and private munificence to finish their studies. For meager incomes, some became police informers. The declassed nobility of priests' sons, former clerics, sons and daughters of government employees and unemployed professionals, became known as the *raznochintsy*. Its members led bohemian lives and engaged in literary activities and journalism.

From the *raznochintsy* intellectuals freed from fear and awe of God, czar, and father, and simultaneously politically frustrated, developed the ideologies of destruction. These ideologically aimed at the liquidation of all basic institutions and authorities of czardom: family, religion, property, power of the father, church, and the czar. The ideology of these nihilists of the sixties even attacked philosophy, since it might turn men aside from action.

The anarchists sought ways by which extreme hatred could be promoted. Stepniak insisted that the terrorist is twice noble and irresistibly fascinating, since he combines two sublimities in himself— that of martyr and hero. Bakunin conceived of a secret society which would organize a disciplined membership under rigidly centralized authority eventually resting in one man. It was urged that only a minority of professional conspirators dedicated to ruthless terror could accomplish social revolution. The secret revolutionary groups that were formed came to be known as the *podpolie* (underground).

In the seventies the development took a new turn. It was the time when the *Narodnichestvo* flourished and the intelligentsia went to the people to redeem its guilt and to repay its debt to them. The *narodnik* intellectuals mingled with the people, seeking to enlighten them and improve their economic position. This movement took on a revolutionary character only after the government began to persecute its adherents. At times the peasants themselves handed the *narodniki* over to the authorities.

Details could be added without end, but this is sufficient to provide a provisional framework for the isolation of Russian national character.

It has been observed that Russia is a prime example of a kind of value in backwardness: the possibility of choice is great. The one thing most completely absent—the very absence being characteristic of Russia in contrast to the West—is the lack of any influential bourgeois ideology. Thus neither the rationalism nor the romanticism of the West, both of which flourish among middle-class strata, find real reception in Russia. Russian romanticism is a product of frustration from which exalted emotionalism takes rise. The lack of a bourgeois ideology is tied in with the complete lack of a middle class in the Western European sense.

Many other characteristics of Russia are related to its lack of a middle class and of the values and virtues of town life so characteristic of the West. The discipline of the guilds and the habits of thrift are missing. So, too, is the absence in Russia of a veneration of culture. As Dostoyevsky put it, the Russians were all nihilists, and Berdyaev added, either apocalyptists or nihilists. In any case, skill, efficiency, success, and the virtues of integrity, industry, and thrift to which Western moralists ascribe the superiority of their civilizations are treated by the Russians as spurious.

Mr. Dillon, who was for long St. Petersburg correspondent to the *London Daily Telegraph,* even maintained that the Russians lack the reverence for the facts which lies at the root of the Anglo-Saxon character. He maintained that a Russian can no more bow to a fact, acknowledging it as final and decisive, than he can to a mere opinion. Along with this de-emphasis of facts is the tendency to raise intuitively discovered "truth" to the level of an unquestioned dogma. As Berdyaev (*Nouveau Moyen Age*) observed, the Russians are probably less honest than Western peoples, a fact bound up with their very virtues.

The virtues and vices of the Western European in his relations both to property and to problems of truth were in accord with his situation as a propertied man of the middle class. While the Western European treats property as sacred and is not prepared to be robbed without a bitter struggle, he has a materialistic ideology as well. A Russian, on the other hand, even when a slave to cupidity and avarice, has no ideological justification for private possession of property. The Russian, in short, does not have the middle-class individual's justification for or responsibility toward property.

The intellectuality of the Western European also shows the influences of the middle-class situation from which it is ultimately launched. There is a hesitancy toward the metaphysical elaboration of thought which loses touch with a factual base. Russian thought, by contrast, often manifests a preoccupation with theory and an acceptance of intuition as absolute to the exclusion of facts. Philosophical intolerance which cannot accept a factual basis of agreement and which rejects all compromise is an inevitable result.

Russia is dominated by an acute dualism. Inhumanity, cruelty, injustice of man were objectified in the Russian state, alienated from the people, and turned into an external power. This dualism emerged in Russian thought at every turn. The Slavophils developed it in the direction of religion and faith, the Westerner toward revolution and socialism. In both cases there was a striving toward integrality and a totalitarian view of the world that would fuse theory and practice.

The Marquis de Custine (*Lettres de Russie*) had phrased the same point. Physically Russia's climate and morally its government, he thought, tend to devour in the bud everything that is weak. It is a country of wild passions or weak characters, of revolt or automatons. There is no middle ground between tyrant and slave, saint and animal. And Berdyaev saw all Russian ideology, whether theocratic or socialistic, as totalitarian. The Russians are "maximalists" and precisely what looks like utopia in Russia is most realistic.

As a people, the Russians are polarized. They are a conglomeration of contradictions, tending to seek virtues in extremes. This can result in the use of violence and terror to settle disputes as in modern times. As Chaadaev had asked: so long as societies are in a state of uncertainty without convictions and rules even for everyday affairs, and so long as life is not regulated, what chance have the seeds of good to ripen? He went on to observe that foreigners who admire Russian audacity forget that the same characteristics which make them bold and reckless rob them of depth and tenacity, sensibility to good and evil, truth and falsehood, and an impulse toward progress. To all observers there is a lack of balance, a fusion of contradictory elements. In the same Russian one often simultaneously finds humility and pride, idealism and cynicism, virtue and vice; he may go from one extreme to the other with unusual ease. Even in recent times Soviet representatives at international affairs find it so easy to combine charm and brutality, amiability and rudeness, that one never knows which to expect. They are, as Siegfried put it, like Merovingians strayed into the twentieth century; or it is as if the Russian missed a stage in psychological development between the Middle Ages and modern society.

A considerable number of outstanding Russian intellectuals display in their personal lives what Western observers see as a lack of emotional balance. They often move from one ideological camp directly into that of their most bitter opponents. Dostoyevsky stated: "In all things I go to utmost extremes." Moreover, lack of moderation and emotional instability were a favorite nineteenth-century theme of Russian *belles-lettres*. Ideologies which seek universal salvation through identification with Christ (Slavophilism) have their counterpart in ideologies which demand universal destruction and identification with anti-Christ (nihilism, terrorism). This very fact gives to Russia an unusual vivacity, spontaneity, and fantasy. The heightened creative spirit was correlated with nineteenth-century Russian bohemianism.

Russian intellectuals in the nineteenth century moved freely outside the established contexts of Western European thought patterns with some of the freedom for recombining its themes which is sought by the bohemian artist or expatriate writer. Chaadaev, Hertzen, Khomyakov, Bakunin, Dostoyevsky, Tolstoy, Soloviev, Michailovsky, Leontyev not only developed highly personal orientations but also recombined the major themes of Western thought in novel ways. They presented political points of view ranging from monarchical absolutism to socialism, religious positions ranging from materialistic atheism to absolutistic Byzantinism, methodological orientations ranging from violently anti- to powerfully pro-science. Their "bohemian" freedom for a recombination of intellectual traditions was undoubtedly a component in the numerous Russian scientific developments of the time; for example, Lobachevsky's non-Euclidean geometry; Mendeleev's periodic table; Ilya Menchnikov's establishment of the role of phagocytosis in resistance to disease; Pavlov's physiological experiments and psychological theories; Zhukovsky's contributions to areodynamics; Fedorov's studies of crystallography; etc. And parallel to the freedom with which nineteenth-century Russian intellectuals moved outside the routine trends of thought was the Russian's lack of a sense of time. Even his meals, Siegfried notes, tended not to be taken on time.

The iron discipline of czardom clamped down on Russia, and the lack of any means by which participation in government was possible left all humaneness at the level of individual experience and gave every social or political movement a form simultaneously of protest and of religion. Almost always Russian thought in the nineteenth century was religious, ethical, and social in nature. Spengler had described Russia as an apocalyptic revolt against antiquity, the forms of which have no place in Western tradition. At the same time, the residual human being is paramount. Impersonal justice does not appear, for man himself is more important than any principle. Pity for the fallen and humiliated is typical. This combination appears repeatedly in outstanding figures. Tolstoy, for instance, felt himself in revolt against the state which he saw as organized violence, and found the simple laboring people the object of his love. The same phenomenon appears in the intensity of the community spirit upon which the Slavophils fastened.

A basic religiosity is thus never absent from nineteenth-century Russian thought. The social revolutionaries bore the stamp of asceticism. Tolstoy, Dostoyevsky, and Soloviev, however different from each other, are similar representatives of religious *narodnichestvo*. The need to struggle against social sin informs their activity. Tolstoy expressed a religiously based nihilism, a consciousness of guilt toward the people and repentance. In *The Cossacks,* in *War and Peace,* and in *Anna Karenina,* the truth of primitive life and falsity of civilization are affirmed. The truth of life is to be found near to nature in the profundity of birth and death. There is a religious density to Tolstoy's formulation as well as a sense of sin and guilt that are absent from Rousseau, who seems otherwise similar. Similarly, the anarchist theories expressed by Bakunin, Prince Kropotkin, and Tolstoy are directed toward authority and the state in a manner that gives them a religious cast. Bakunin's anarchism was an extreme form of human development: human animality, thought, and revolt—the last indicating that man is rising to a higher level. Bakunin's militant atheism has a religious intensity. The Russians are in a sense never sceptics but always dogmatists. Darwinism, which in the West had the form of a hypothesis, in Russia acquired a dogmatic character. Materialism itself immediately becomes a matter of religious faith. All things are assessed in terms of orthodoxy and heterodoxy.

Religious themes are everywhere common. Identification with suffering marks the work of Dostoyevsky. He even viewed his own sufferings as a blessing. Russia identified herself with the crucified Christ. In a similar manner, Russian juries and peasant courts were ever ready to acquit repentants. Further, Russian writing was preoccupied with social, political, religious, and psychological problems.

As Berdyaev observes, the burning of one's self alive as an exploit in religion is a Russian national phenomenon. From the theme of indigence and poverty that informs religious poetry to the emergence of mystical and prophetic sects with their thirst for the transfiguration of life, the religious theme of Russian national character is manifest.

GERMAN NATIONAL CHARACTER

When national character is defined, as it is here, as a set of behaviors and attitudes that tend to characterize the members of a national community, it requires no very extensive review of the facts to assure one's self that it is in fact a valid concept. Even this brief review—for comparative purposes—of the major countries around Germany brought into focus marked differences of behavior and attitude. Undoubtedly endless argument is possible about the details as well as the estimate of the relative importance of any given component of a particular national character. This is inevitable for any formation as loosely patterned as national character. The surprise is not that there is some difference of opinion, but rather, that there is so much agreement as to the genuinely essential components of a given national character, an agreement underlined by the very fact that national character almost more quickly than anything else tends to elicit patriotic and ethnocentric types of judgment prejudicial to cool scientific estimates. However, a given national character is only a relative stability developing gradually out of the history of local institutions and providing the social matrix for any new developments. One could expect German national character to be distinctive if only because its location was central to the system of national characters as diverse as those reviewed.

A number of social and historical influences and processes played a role in the formation of German national character.[26] The first structure of culture was supplied by the Teutonic tribes that appeared on the borders of Rome in the first century before the Christian era. Emil Ludwig has maintained that they are the basic source of many of the essentials of German national character. The Teutonic tribes had tents, wagons, and harnessed horses. They were weaponed with clubs, long swords, and tall shields, and they rushed into battle bound together with ropes. Dressed in animal pelts, living on oatmeal, skimmed milk, and beer, these intruders were lured on by the wealth of Mediterranean lands, and possibly pressed on by others from behind. The brutality, bravado, courage, and treachery reported of these tribal peoples have been conceived by Emil Ludwig, for example, as forming the most fundamental component of German national character. But there is no need to subscribe to a "racialism," as did Ludwig, simply because one deals with land so productive of racial ideologies.

Rome left an imprint on these Germanic peoples who were partly shaped through its typical institutions—family, property, government, treatment of the individual—which were applied to whoever lived under the *Pax Romana*. Permanent residues of Roman culture appear in the Rhine Valley, accounting for certain distinctive similarities, for example, between Württenberg and Baden, in contrast to the Prussian provinces to the east. It was in this area, too, that the French Revolution, much later, had its most determinable influence on Germany. In any case, it is often observed that a German from the south and particularly southwest often has much more in common with the French than with a Saxon or Prussian. It is here, too, that the sense of well being and joy in the home and primary group that the Germans describe as *Gemütlichkeit* is most typical. The Germanic tribes were partly formed into a homogeneous unit by Rome.

Another factor important as a formative influence is the extensive ethnic variation in Germany. The proportion of Slavs in the population is large, for between A.D. 400 and 700 the Slavs invaded Eastern Germany to the Elbe, and the whole population of Central and East Prussia, of Silesia and Saxony, are mixed with Borssians, Lecks, Wends and Serbians. Not until the Middle Ages was this area reconquered by the Germans under the organization of the Teutonic Knights, who established the Marches of the East. The mixture of races and ethnic groups not only indicates the actual early cultural voriety but also reveals the futility of all racial interpretations of Germany.

In addition to the influences rising from the long domination of the Holy Roman Empire on the one hand, and feudalism on the other, German history is marked by the belated persistence of the frontier. Historically, many areas of Germany were Christianized only quite late. Moreover, while the countryside of France has been transformed by the labors of man until it is like a garden, in Germany much of the aspect of raw nature remains. The history of Berlin, for example, Siegfried notes, is relatively short. To late development he attributed its aggressive modernity—like most American towns—as if stamped out whole in the middle of the wilderness and displaying all the earmarks of a recent movement of civilization.

The peculiarity of Germany in the nineteenth century was not so much to be found in the diversity of elements that went into its composition as in the unmodified persistence long after a time when somewhat similar factors had been integrated in one way or another in surrounding nations. Until the threshold of the nineteenth century, there was a persistence of medieval elements long in process of transformation in Italy, France, and England. The Holy Roman Empire, also a medieval institution, held on as well, preventing the formation of national power and the reintegration of social elements around the nation-state. However, the best of the Middle Ages, the cities, also persisted in vigorous form at a time when they were in process of being melted down as autonomous communities in France and England, and in contrast to Russia, where they had never reached very full development. Although Germany had a developed middle class similar to Italy, France, and England, and in contrast to Spain and Russia, and although these middle classes became the bearers of cultural nationalism against the reactionary Holy Roman emperors, when the nation-state came at last in Germany, its powers were consolidated in the hands of the Prussian landed aristocracy, the Junkers. The German middle classes were systematically excluded from power. Hence, when the German character began to jell, it was very uncertain; and those elements which could give it greater stability were sealed off from full influence on the whole.

A peculiar kind of uncertainty emerging from these influences had been observed by Nietzsche as a property of German national character. The Germans, he said, are "a people made up of the most extraordinary mixing and mingling of races, perhaps even with a predominance of the pre-Aryan elements, as the 'people in the center' in every sense of the term"; they are "more intangible, more ample, more contradictory, more unknown, more incalculable, more surprising, and even more terrifying than other people are to themselves." Nietzsche added: "It is characteristic of the Germans that the question, 'What is German?' never dies out among them."[27]

The property of a "people in the center," as Nietzsche put it, has struck many German observers. Karl Julius Weber, for example, had noted that whenever in his travels abroad he met a person too obliging to be a Frenchman, too ceremonious to be a Briton, too simple for an an Italian, too supple for a Spaniard, too lively for a Dutchman, too modest for a Russian, but at the same time one who obtrudes himself with sidelong bows and incredible deference to all whom he thinks are more distinguished than himself, he recognizes a compatriot. A search for a definition of oneself in external formulae is typically German and was already recognized by Kant, for whom France was a land of fashions, England of humors, Spain of ancestors, Italy of magnificence, and, in contrast to all these, Germany was a land of titles. In the popular story a number of individuals pass the time on a long train journey by defining themselves. The Englishman wrote "I am," the Frenchman "I love," the Russian "I sin," but the German asked to be excused so he could "think it over."

Even a brief comparison of national character in Germany with that of each of its major neighbors is revealing. Of all the European national communities, it is nearest to Russia, with which it shares many characteristics that each does not hold in common with other nations. The influence of the East penetrates to Germany; Europe primarily from Germany has extended influences to the Urals. Two properties frequently observed to be uniquely present only in Germany and Russia are a certain kind of externally imposed discipline or passive obedience and a proclivity to revolution. These, to be sure, are somewhat differently organized in both places: Russian obedience is somewhat more resigned and passive than German. The set faces and detached looks are encountered in Russia, but they have a kind of oriental contemplativeness lacking in Germany. Moreover, while the Germans idealize order and dominance, the Russians idealize community and brotherhood.

Germany and Russia both have inclinations toward mysticism. However, unlike the German mysticisms of race and blood, Russians incline to a mysticism of soil. Moreover, German discipline and passivity have the form of a kind of armor or, in the imagery of Siegfried, a kind of orthopedic corset to hold up too weak a spine. But when all is said and done, the German submission to all authentic manifestations of power reminds one of Russia; it is the form of the Russian *nichevo*, lasting only as long as opposed by a force greater than their own.

So, too, there is a similarity to the Russian in the other aspect of German experience, its revolutionary impetus. In the middle of the nineteenth century, Arnold Ruge had observed that German patriotism, like the national religiosity of the Russians, was always directed toward the future.

Corresponding to their similarities, Russia has always been able to receive more from Germany than from any other country of Europe. In contrast to the relative shallowness of the Westerners (deriving influence from Italy and France) is the relative profundity of the Slavophils (deriving influence from Hegel and German Romanticism). It is quite appropriate that Karl Marx should have his greatest influence, not on Europe and its proletariat with which the manifest content of the doctrine is concerned, but on Russia and the peasant-based movements that could respond to the Germanic elements of its latent content.

Of all the formations of European national character, the Italian seems to mix least easily with the German. Perhaps this is because the Italians have been so anciently cosmopolitan and the Germans so anciently rural. Even in north Italy, where Germanic domination long held sway, the Germanic country-dwellers never felt happy in the city, nor did the urbanite feel any affinities with the countryside. Compromise social mechanisms developed in time, permitting these two component elements of the society to remain quite separate. This contrasting role of urbanity in Italy and Germany was still observed in the late nineteenth century by Nietzsche. As he put it, a poor Venetian gondolier cuts a better figure than a Berlin *Geheimrat*, and is even a better man. Slyly Nietzsche urged, "ask any *woman* what she thinks." And while the German prides himself on the superiority of his morality to that of the Italian, he lacks the latter's cosmopolitan restraint. As Alfred von Tirpiz had observed, the corrupt German is infinitely worse than the corrupt Italian. Karl Weber has insisted that while the clue to the Italian's psychology is imagination, to the Frenchman's it is wit, to the Englishman's understanding, and to the German's it is remembrance. Certainly above all in the German and Italian arts the difference in Italian lightness, grace, and form is manifest in contrast to Germanic heaviness and "depth." This seems to have been uppermost in Friedrich Hebbel's mind when he urged his countrymen to be suspicious if any Italian should ever compliment a German on his artistic achievement. For, Hebbel maintained, even if the compliment is honestly intended, it is no more than an expression of amazement at finding that a bear can dance. It is never admiration of the dance itself.

Though culturally, politically, and militarily they are eternal competitors and professional enemies, the affinities of the French and German are somewhat greater than those between the German and the Italian though they are certainly less close than the ties between the German and the Russian. French "logicality" has often appealed to German imagination, while German romanticism has had some minor reception in France. French admiration for German scholarship has often been great, but beyond this, contrasts appear. The French feel an almost instinctive repugnance for anything immoderate or chaotic, and have little use for the favorite German adjective, "*Kolossal.*" While German thought feels most at ease in flux, in the abstract, resisting all that circumscribes or limits, the French cannot extract a sense of profundity from the obscure. The same contrast appears in a comparison of their attitudes toward nature. Germanic communion with the oversoul and the search for God through nature appear to the Frenchman as irrational preoccupations. While in French philosophy eclectic doctrines have been characteristic, in English philosophy dualistic and pluralistic forms have been most frequent. In contrast to both, German philosophy inclines toward monistic formulations. The fact of monism seems more important than any particular form, and the German often slips from a spiritualistic to a materialistic form of monism. The demand for wholeness also appears to be a basic motive for the development of *Gestalt* psychology.

As Germany during the eighteenth and nineteenth centuries became ever more fully self-conscious, her best thinkers repeatedly expressed admiration of French flexibility. Kant, for example, observed that while in the treatment of any subject the German commonly erects a ponderous system from which it is ever after difficult to move him, in France an idea—such as mesmerism—becomes a fashion for a time, but soon afterward completely disappears. The same observation was pleasingly formulated by Jean Paul (Fr. Richter) in the early days of the nineteenth century: When Mendelssohn defined pain as a break in continuity, Richter observed that this at least correctly identified the German's pain. For Germans seemed unwilling to move out of an old position. Richter opined that Germans probably even turned over in their beds less often than the French.

But it was French wit and social ease that most frequently captivated the German intellectual. Ludwig Börne had noted that the wit of the German is a sword with an edge but no point, while French wit is a rapier with point but no edge. Börne believed that in the long run the stabbing always conquers the hacking weapon. And Heinrich von Kleist argued that while at his best the German speaks with understanding, the Frenchman speaks with wit. The German wanders around the subject; the Frenchman catches the ray of light it casts and passes to another subject. The same idea was in Börne's mind when he asked who could take a German volume and guess its content or its purpose without its title page. The building materials of stone, marble, glass, and all the rest are present, but no completed structure.

Social and political contrasts lie at the basis of these differences, and while France revealed herself in her civilization, Germany has experienced a succession of saviors to a point where many observers tend to treat Germany as a land of becoming and of potential rather than realization. Heine observed that there has never been a German people in the same sense as there has been a French people. Nobles, middle class, and peasants are even more heterogeneous than they were in France before the Revolution.

The search for an extraneous source of stability so characteristic of Germany, as Saphir had observed, even affects the social intercourse in the two societies. While the Frenchman goes into society as a good companion, having left not only his hat and coat but his minister, banker, clerk, and deputy in the anteroom, the Germans rarely meet in society. When they do, everyone brings his office, his title, and hangs them like napkins before his mouth, lest anything merely human escape. At a personal level Heine found the French more reliable as acquaintances because they are less given to dreaming, and one is not so apt to meet a Frenchman some morning and be insulted because he dreamed that he was insulted or that his grandfather was kicked by yours.

While Germany's artists and philosophers have most often envied France, her politicians and statesmen have most often admired England. In Germany in modern times a whole series of major political figures from Bismarck to Hitler have expressed respect for England. Bismarck had likened Germany to a self-made man and England to an old aristocratic peer. It was the theoretically unobstructed capacity for action in England that Bismarck admired in contrast to the German tendency to develop enormously elaborate theories and yet to act quite inappropriately, if at all. Goethe had the same thing in mind when he observed that while Germans torment themselves with philosophical problems, the English develop great practical intelligence. They laugh at the Germans and conquer the world.

It is not, to be sure, true that the German does not respond to the facts. But he is apt to take a rather academic view of them. Prince von Bülow had noted that the theoretically-minded German often insisted on deriving his opinions from books or the depths of his ethical convictions, while the Englishman based his judgment on immediate observation. The approach to reality from the standpoint of a rather complex system of theoretical possibilities is typically German and very unlike the English. Georg Christoph Lichtenberg long ago observed that the German frequently spends his energy suppressing something which ought not to occur at all. There are occasions when a German does not laugh only because laughter would be inappropriate, while in the same situation it would not occur to an Englishman to laugh.

The English "genius" for action is related to a concern with character and a considerable capacity to make accurate judgments of character. The German, by contrast, is most apt to be deficient in his judgments of people. An English military man observed precisely that if one gives the German a human being to study, he will probably make a mess of it; but give him a thing to study, and he will do a better job than anyone else.

English efficiency in action was related both to a suppression of theory (negatively related to "bungling through") on the one hand and a tendency to play down the emotional elements of every situation on the other (British understatement). Germany is overdeveloped on both scores, excessively theoretical and emotional. At the same time, this very fact makes possible a much more vigorous and free atmosphere in England. Maximilian Harden during World War I was astonished by the contrast in freedom between Germany and England. He observed that at the very depth of the war, anyone in England was free, if he wished, to write his opinion that the German cause rested on a firmer basis of justice than England's. At the same time, Germany felt a compulsion, as it has in all times of solemn decision, to clamp down the lid on free expression, leaving only the alternatives of silence or of "bleating the tune struck up by the government." All men love liberty, but, as Heine observed, how differently: the Englishman loves liberty as his lawful wife; the Frenchman loves liberty as his chosen bride; the German loves liberty as he loves his old grandmother.

From this range of comparisons made by so many sensitive observers, it is clear that Germany developed a distinctive national character of its own, sharing something with each of the others, differing from all.

7

GERMAN

NATIONAL CHARACTER

AND

SOCIAL STRUCTURE

LIKE EVERY COMMUNITY THE NATION as a way of life is a combination of the forces composing human interactive behavior. Only as a system of forces could a nation display any continuities in time, for otherwise it would blow up, break down, or fall apart. Like all other communities, it is only relatively stable. Communities may be founded; they may develop, change, weaken, and be destroyed. The graveyard of history has many monuments to communities that flourished for a time.

A nation is neither a physical system (like an internal combustion engine) nor an organic system (like a living creature), but a social system, a way of life. No nation ever acts; only people act. The component parts of the nation, as of every community, are the various special modes of action. As a social system the nation represents the adaptation of one mode of action to another, forming the way of life.

It follows from these propositions that the set of behaviors which peculiarly identify the nation, its national character, always constitute a composition of forces. Forces that are partially opposed or antagonistic to one another have been brought into relation with each other, making the action in system cyclical or recurrent. The operation of any one force in part prepares the system for the next. One has not touched the essence of any particular national character until the antagonism of forces operating in the given case has been isolated. There is, thus, always a paradoxical property to every national character. National character represents, so to speak, a kind of controlled explosion. It is an assemblage of forces which, if not turned against one another, could potentially blow the system to bits.

The nature and form of these forces, and the formula that relates them, of course, may vary tremendously. The English national character was peculiar in that its point of integration was located in action. The force conflict in France was evident in the tensions arising out of the contrary pull of a peasant mentality on the one hand and rationalism on the other; the point of French integration is most frequently found in thought. The basic conflict in Spanish national character appears in the constant alternation between egoism or integralism. The conflict that Italian national character formulates has long been seen to lie in the tension between particularism and universalism; in Humanism Italy found an ideal synthesis. The violence of the tension of forces in Russia appears when at every point all things are calculated in terms of orthodoxy and heterodoxy. In every case one deals with a system of partially antagonistic forces.

In Germany the peculiar force composition of the national character takes the form of a rigid outer shell and an inner ferment, a surface calm and an inner insecurity. Love of discipline and need for order imposed from without is the converse of an anxiety over disorder within. Thus, behind its rigid outer surface, Germany is a country of indecision and perpetual change, a revolutionary country ready to accept any new saviour. As Siegfried penetratingly observes, the German spirit, so rich in possibilities, is always seeking a form in which to express itself. Goethe saw this characteristic of his countrymen, and maintained that Germany had two souls. Nietzsche observed that the Germans constantly alternate between surrender to foreign influences and a vengeful longing for originality. It has often been noted that the most productive of the Germans (like Mozart and the German historians) are mediators of the surrounding world, often fitting the forms of other cultures to a rich German content.

Noting this insecure search for form, Nietzsche commented that oftentimes the Germans do not experience the passions they seem to manifest. They are, he thought, afraid lest one should not credit them with passion and they make grimaces and commit excesses, not because they are moved by strong emotion, but in order to make one believe they are. This attempt to organize its inner life has been seen by many thinkers as taking two forms (recent students include Emil Ludwig and Demiashkevich)—the drive for a worldly wholeness (totalitarianism) on the one hand, and a mystic identification with the other-worldly (religious mysticism) on the other.

Between such extremes in its attempts to compose its inner life,

Germany has often been observed to manifest only the greatest insecurity. The bitter factionalism (*Parteisucht*) of the political parties of the Weimar Republic (1919–1933) was experienced by most people as unusually exhausting. Kayserling has argued that the Führer understood this peculiarity of the Germans, for if the German is offered the choice between going to heaven directly or hearing a lecture about it first, he will most certainly choose the lecture. The abhorrence of wit has been thought to spring from the same source, a solemn horror of disintegrating ideas. Goethe had captured this brilliantly in his observation that it is easy to be witty when one has respect for nothing. Nietzsche, as usual, attempted to force maximum realization upon his countrymen of this aspect of their behavior. "The German soul," he said, "has passages and galleries in it; there are caves, hiding places, and dungeons therein; its disorder has much of the charm of the mysterious; the German is well acquainted with the by-paths to chaos. And as everything loves its symbol, so the German loves the clouds and all that is obscure, evolving, crepuscular, damp, and shrouded: it seems to him that everything uncertain, undeveloped, self-displacing, and growing is 'deep.' The German himself does not *exist*; he is *becoming* and developing himself."[1]

When he renounces his claims on the world, the German has a tendency toward an extreme ecstatic piety freed from all connection with action or a quasi-mystical pantheism. When the German is oriented toward the world, the same tendencies tend to take the form Spengler described as an impetuous formlessness inclining toward caesarism in government. Nietzsche seems to have had the same thing in mind when he insisted that the Germans are a dangerous people "expert at inventing intoxicants." One can never be sure where a new manifestation of the same tendencies will appear. In a letter to his son, Field Marshal von der Glotz stated: "I thoroughly enjoy the wild poetry of war, and I have formed a perhaps un-Christian fondness for it, against which I cannot defend myself." Hitler understood this and correctly interpreted his compatriots in *Mein Kampf*: "The future of a movement is conditioned upon fanaticism, the intolerance with which its supporters present it as the only right one" (p. 485). Bismarck was disturbed by the same thing. The German, he thought, always has a tendency toward discontent. The people in other lands will work hard, secure a comfortable life, and, perhaps in their fiftieth year, begin to taper off and simply maintain their security. But the German who begins work by running errands for the office is unsatisfied until he owns the factory. Then for the first time his ambition is loosed and he is ready to purchase the city. Bismarck had observed that while this unlimited ambition has good aspects, it is very questionable from the standpoint of political contentment. Bismarck and Hitler had the German's peculiar ambition in mind, but Hitler was in process of fomenting a political movement, and Bismarck was trying to stabilize a regime in power. Such ambition is produced in part by contradictions that the German has not succeeded in reconciling, leading many observers to the view that the German is both sentimental and at the same time brutal and cruel with somewhat greater frequency than any other Europeans in the nations outside of Russia. He often appears to enjoy the very catastrophe he has caused. In the critical hour he tends to become destructive of resources, human life, and states, rushing always to the edge of the abyss.

Many observers within and outside Germany have called attention to a series of properties related to this German tendency to live in extremes and the inability to find a stopping place short of them. The lack of inner control in political life has been paralleled by a lack of tact in social life and of taste in art. In fact the lack of inner control is seen, at times, as Germany's greatest defect. The country's most efficient states and most powerful armies have led the country to ruin. The absence of a sense of moderation, the precondition of judgment, makes it particularly dangerous to unloose passion. Balance, common sense, even moral sense, are cast to the winds, and the German often slips with equal facility into the *Kolossal* or the petty. With an obsession for information, the German frequently obscures the significance of that information by an excessive concern for detail. With a praiseworthy passion for analysis, his conclusions are often disconcerting. The lack of security, which Goethe believed characteristic of German art, he attributed to a lack of taste in turn resting on an absence of skill in the use of euphemisms. Schopenhauer observed that Germans have a tendency to search in the clouds for what lies at their feet. The lack of a capacity to embellish the everyday fact observed by Goethe is inevitably correlated with the need to search the remote for the romance one is incapable of finding near at hand. Friedrich Hebbel attributed Schiller's popularity to the German's fascination with haziness. In Hebbel's opinion Schiller never offers anything quite poetic, but panders to the German love of the hazy and indefinite.

In social intercourse the lack of moderation and measure is manifested by the absence of tact. Daisy, Princess of Pless, was struck by differences in discretion which she found very evident between English and German newspapers and complained about her people's lack of tact. A century earlier Joseph Görres maintained that the Germans had elevated uncouthness into an art and had developed boorishness into a system. In the early days of the Weimar Republic, Prince von Bülow repeatedly expressed surprise that so many educated Germans fail to understand the importance of good form in international intercourse. Germans abroad, he thought, too often gave offense by boorishness, arrogance, and boasting. The conceited "Herr Doktor" and "Herr Professor" and callous man of commerce were most at fault. It was as if the true German was embarrassed to be found uttering a conceit. In Germany, Goethe had suggested, one lies when one is polite.

This same combination of virtues and vices identifies much of German scholarship. The Germans, said Nietzsche, think they are profound when they feel heavy and melancholy. They take sweating as proof of "earnestness." But, he insisted, their souls are boorish and the spirit of beer is potent even in their ideas. The lack of taste and tact (and judgment in scholarship), Nietzsche thought, has often made German scholars prone to superstition and eager credulity—intellectual parallels to their vices of old—drink, a tendency to suicide (spiritual exhaustion), and the use of spiritual intoxicants such as music. As Julius Langoben noted, when the professor lectures or the scholar writes, be it out of conscientiousness or deficient self-restraint, the German is prone to overdo. Scholarship tends to become "official." Ludwig Börne maintained that the German scholar regards himself as a state functionary. His books are documents, his study is an office, his science is a mystery. He appears to have taken an oath to leave his understanding at home whenever he goes to his "office." Heinrich von Kleist wondered whether German scholars, for all their preliminary labors, ever attain their goal. They constantly whet swords they never use. So passionately do they learn that they often leave no time to accomplish the objectives that originally set them on their courses. With his treatises overflowing with notes and quotations, the German professor, in Goethe's view, is forever making side excursions. He suggests they are like dogs which tug at the leash to lift their legs against all sorts of questionable objects so that it takes all day to cover a few miles. William James, in his charming characterization of Wundt, touched many of the features of the typical German professor. "He isn't a genius, he is a professor—a being whose duty it is to know everything connected with his *Fach*. Wundt has the most prodigious faculty of appropriating and preserving knowledge, and as for opinions, he takes *au grand sérieux* his duties here. He says of each possible subject, "Here I must have an opinion. Let's see! What shall it be? How many possible opinions are there? three? four? Yes! just four! Shall I take one of these? It will seem more original to take a higher position, a sort of *Vermittelungansicht* between them all. That I will do, etc., etc." So he acquires a complete assortment of opinions of his own; and, as his memory is so good, he seldom forgets what they are. . . . Was there ever, since Christian Wolff's time, such a model of the German Professor?"[2] This conception of the professor's role has led German scholars to collect enormous masses of information, observation, and classification. Too often the result is a kind of compilation or thesaurus without form. To French observers like Siegfried, this relates the German to the barbaric son of Asia, and separates him from the spirit of classic Greece. The very style of writing in Germany seems to express a denial rather than an affirmation of form. Every German sentence, Bruno Frank maintained, is a sort of miniature Wagnerian music-drama. In the end one receives redemption, but only after a purgatory of heavy tedium and obscurity.

Few things in German aesthetic and artistic development sum up the properties of its national character better than its romanticism, which Demiashkevich believed is a Dionysian revolt against classicism. Romanticism was anti-rationalistic, locating the source of human value in sentiment and imagination rather than in reason and form. It sought revelation in the mystical. It led to explorations of the depths of individual and collective psychology. It attempted to penetrate the latter by the study of folklore. In literature the romantic mood was anticipated by the Storm and Stress movement (named after Klinger's drama, *Sturm und Drang*), a rebellion against the themes and forms of neo-classicism. German romanticism appears in the fact that all great plays and operas are tragedies. German poetry is most at home with the themes of world woe and death (*Weltschmerz, Todesgedanken*). Some critics have suggested that only a deficient sense of humor could sustain such romantic *Sehnsucht* and such rather surprising attitudes as the fear of a split personality that often characterizes not only German literature but German life.

Manifest as is the attitude toward nature in German literature and life, the romantic mood assimilated pre-modern animistic cultural forms to itself. Interest revived in the songs of the *Minnesinger*, in which various natural phenomena of forest and field mysteriously aid the hero in love and war. The Germans retained this ancient communion with nature in contrast to the French, who have assimilated an organized and cultivated countryside to society. The pantheistic devotion to the divine creative mother nature (of Johannes Scotus Erigena and Meister Eckhart) is a German rather than a French manifestation.

The German has an aversion to detached analysis. To engage in reasoning for its own sake always seems cynical. The average German pursues interests remote from the witty interchange of the salon. Hiking, camping, and travel are his preferred means of relaxation. In their military memoirs German high commanders attend more to the phenomena of nature than do the French. Siegfried has observed that there is no spectacle more typical than a German Sunday, whether under Weimar or the Nazis. Even American soldiers stationed in Germany, themselves from a culture of ardent picnic goers, are amazed. No one ever seems to seek an individual distraction, but people of all ages march and hike about the countryside as though, in Siegfried's imagery, to a conquest, tramping in line with flags flying. Perhaps as a consequence of his fraternization with nature, wherever he goes the German farmer easily transplants his skills and is acclimatized in a new country more rapidly than almost any other group.

A number of properties typify German national character: (1) extremism combined with stubbornness and inflexibility; (2) the expression of this extremism in monasticism or mystic religiosity; (3) a lack of inner control and moderation, expressed in such deficiencies as the lack of taste, tact, or form; (4) romantic sentimentality; (5) a revolutionary spontaneity that penetrates the shell of every form imposed on it and is manifested on the one hand as a chaotic formlessness or even as a negative, form-destroying force, yet on the other—in the very fact of pressing beyond limits—in a capacity for reopening every issue for new creative development; and (6) a drive toward discipline, externally secured, ranging from delight in work for its own sake in everyday life to the willing acceptance of caesarism and totalitarian-authoritarianism in government.

COUNTRY AND CITY[3]

When a nation arises as a new community, it necessarily modifies in a fundamental way the communities which preceded it. For a long time its chief competitors are the communities it supplants. The relative importance of and the relationship between rural and urban aspects of national social structure inevitably have basic influence on national character, for they represent not simply special institutions but relatively fully equipped sub-communities that are potentially competing total ways of life.

Moreover, rural and urban communities have quite different consequences. Rural life binds the individual close to nature, making him dependent on the incident of local terrain and accident of weather. The cycle of social life always shows some adjustment to the organic rhythm of growing things, to the cyclical growth of crops. The daily rhythms of animal care set limits upon the rest of activity. By contrast life in an urban environment is adjusted to an artificial or man-made environment. It is detached and remote from the more immediate determinations of organic growth, being bound more directly to the requirements of other people. Rural life fosters attitudes of self-reliance, traditionalism, passivity in the face of national disaster or fatalism, while urban life develops sophistication, fashionableness, the enjoyment of novelty, rationality, and experimentalism. The very terms "urbanity" and "cosmopolitan" recall the origins of a typical outlook or "mentality" in the urban environment. The historical fates of country and city in Germany have important bearing upon its national character.

Archaeological finds show that Germany passed through a number of agricultural stages. Stone age rock carvings show men plowing. The aboriginal Germans lived in lean-tos or roofed dugouts with their domestic animals. Cattle were kept for dairy purposes only; sheep were kept for wool. Chickens, geese, and ducks were raised. Horses were used for riding, carting, and for meat; domestic work was performed by women and slaves. Such was the general status of German agriculture in the time of Tacitus.

During the first Christian centuries two developments affecting agriculture in German lands were of importance. The Slavs moving from the east reached the Vistula and the Elbe, crossing lands formerly occupied by Germanic tribes. The agriculture of these Slavic peoples (including Wends, Poles, and Czechs) was more primitive than that of the Germans. Their fields were small, their way of life primarily pastoral. Meanwhile in the remaining area of German occupation the clearing of forests had begun, in part in response to attempts to set up younger sons of the family on lands of their own. Later clearing of the land was undertaken systematically by monastic orders and by the landlords with larger holdings who appropriated large tracts of the king's land. In the old German area of Carolingian times (bounded by the Rhine, Elbe, North Sea, and the Alps) there were numerous isolated farms and marsh villages established on the plains of the northwest by Low Saxon peasants. In Franconia, Thuringia, and Bavaria many nucleated villages appeared. On open plains and in the valleys of the Lower Rhine and Saxo-Thuringian regions, an ancient peasantry was settled.

In the Carolingian Era at the time the clearing of forest land began, a reorganization of rural society was taking place. Primitive tribal organization was being replaced by the feudal system. Tribal chiefs were subordinated to the counts of districts (*Gaugrafen*) and of the frontier districts (*Markgrafen*). The counts were bound to the emperor by oaths of fealty, and were kept under control by royal commissioners (*Sendgrafen*) sent out as inspectors from the royal court. Society was concentrated in rural villages, where the soil was held by freemen subject to military service, and worked by bondsmen and serfs. The holders of fiefs sought to make them hereditary. Meanwhile the increased use of horses and the cost of military equipment were transforming military service into an almost intolerably expensive burden for the ordinary free peasant. Peasants turned into serfs who in return for personal service at the manor had a small share of the agricultural produce for their own. Free land-owning individuals were pulled into the system by their military helplessness, turning their properties over to the lord or church (*commendation*) in return for military protection. As the feudal system grew, it pulled other social forms into its framework.

The feudal system and its extensive pacification of the social life, which restricted warfare to the landed aristocrats, freed the great mass of individuals from the hazards of war and accelerated the process of land clearing, which was increasingly organized by large landlords and monastic orders. A growth of population, reversing a trend of ancient Roman society, was made possible by such conversion of social life to peaceable pursuits. The old Germanic area of settlement thus rapidly became too small and the reconquest of old Germanic land to the east began. This was accomplished more by the plow than by the sword (though when necessary, force was unhesitatingly used). Much of the colonization was accomplished by contractors (*Locatores*) who procured settlers in return for a considerable portion of the settled land. Only in the beginning was it necessary for the German frontier districts (*Marken*) to be settled under special royal officials (*Markgrafen*) as a defense measure against the Slavs and invading Mongols. The *Markgrafen* of Eastmark on the Danube and Northmark on the Lower Elbe were pioneers, but later the monastic orders (particularly the Cistercians and Premonstratensians) increasingly undertook colonization. In fact, peaceable arrangements with Slavic princes were frequent. Whenever swampy soil or alluvial lands had to be reclaimed, special inducements were made to Flemings and Hollanders to secure them as colonists. By the end of the thirteenth century, settlement extended from the Vistula to the Scheldt in the north, from the Rhône to the Drave, and from the Danube and Alps to the North and Baltic Seas.

The clearing of forest, the formation of the feudal system, and the colonization of the east were simultaneously carried through, as revealed in the way the monasteries of the Middle Ages assumed a manorial form. In addition to its church, the monastery had living houses, farm buildings, wine cellars, presses, baking houses, shops for craftsmen (smiths, tanners, saddlers), and buildings for manufacturing glass. They often produced salt as a regular industry. The monks worked in mines and built bridges and aqueducts. They were architects and engineers as well as religious men. Field and pasture were united in the same farm.

As this system of cultivation was extended, the herdsman was declassed (*unehelich*). The great estates and monasteries, meanwhile, provided experimental laboratories for improvements in agriculture and cattle breeding. The shift from pastoralism is reflected in the fact that grain replaced meat and dairy products in importance in the economy.

The feudal system persisted in Germany longer than in other western European countries. At the beginning of the nineteenth century it was still a major force. Eighty per cent of the population was rural, and characteristic institutions of medieval economy such as serfdom were retained. The open field and three crop system prevailed. Because of his hereditary dependency, the serf lacked marital freedom, choice of occupation, and movement in the districts east of the Elbe on the landed estates under the Junkers.

Military events forced rulers to action after the overwhelming defeat of Jena (1806). The Prussian kings and their ministers saw the need to institute a series of reforms to modernize agriculture. The serfs were freed, but this was in the interests of the nobles. Very little land was given the common people, for only well-off workers who had previously held enough land to support a full plow team received the rights to the land they worked. The Junkers were interested in breaking the hereditary claims to land use which stood in the way of agricultural rationalization, and had no intention of standing idly by before the rise of the new class. Since the Junkers furnished the higher ranks of officers of the Prussian army, as members of its political ruling groups, they were in a position to exploit the political and economic developments in their own benefit. The new land laws and laws freeing the serfs became occasion to divest many of the former peasants of lands they had traditionally worked. Many peasants were reduced to the status of agricultural laborers. Thus while in west Germany the old feudal manorial economy (*Grundherrschaft*) was destroyed, in the east a new estates economy (*Gutsherrschaft*) took its place. Junker families maintained their position in the Germany army and increased their importance in the political structure. The Bismarck Constitution of the German Reich (1871) in effect made the Reich government the extended arm of Prussian government. The Junkers enjoyed political ascendancy within it.

The emancipation of the serfs set in motion activities to untangle the property right of the open field system. Even in the twentieth century five or six years of litigation were required to straighten out the property rights for a single village, because a holding that had been large enough to support a single large family could comprise up to three hundred separate strips. The enclosure movement set in motion by the land and enfranchisement laws cut costs of cultivation by one fourth, while increasing production by one third. Production was further increased in the second quarter of the nineteenth century through cultivation of potatoes, sugar beets, the use of legumes and green manure with red clover in place of fallow-land, nonsystematic crop rotation. Between 1800 and 1870 the yield of rye and barley was doubled. These improvements largely benefited the Junkers, who formed an Agrarian Party in order to promote legislation favorable to their interests.

The economic crisis of 1870 and the world economic crisis of 1873 shattered the price of agricultural products and increased farm indebtedness. The Junkers pressed for protective duties on food stuffs, primarily cereals, which were secured in 1879. The burden of food tax fell upon the industrial worker. The cycle between 1890 and 1913 was exaggerated by the increased use of fertilizers and employment of agricultural machinery, while legislation helped the Junkers fully to exploit their monopolistically closed home markets.

Distribution of Farm Ownership in Germany before World War I

Size of Farm (in Acres)	Approximate Number	Agricultural Area (in Per Cent)
Under 5	3 million	5
5 to 12½	1 million	10
12½ to 50	1 million	33
50 to 250	250 thousand	28
Over 250	25 thousand	22

During World War I German agriculture felt the strain placed upon it: farm prices were fixed, the government requisitioned horses for military service, cattle were killed because of the food shortage. The farm crisis continued in the post-war period. Though land reform was desperately needed, the post-war food crisis mitigated against immediate reform. The army was reduced to 100,000, but was left in the hands of the Junker aristocracy. Reactionary judges applied the laws of the Republic. Hence, by the time the agrarian crisis was over, the Junkers were again in strategic control of the rural economy, and were quite disinclined to yield power. Meanwhile the estates had become rallying places for the flotsam of war. Vigilante armies were organized on big estates, and in Pomerania a new Agrarian League was created. Inflation benefited the Junkers, for the export premium created by them guaranteed a monopoly of the home markets while permitting them to liquidate their debts at the expense of the nation.

The comparison of agriculture in Germany and France today is revealing. Both have a large class of peasants who cultivate their farms by their own labor. The typical peasant of France works on a smaller scale than the German, though in southwest Germany, where, on small holdings of five acres (grapes, fruit, tobacco, etc.), the individual cultivators are able to support their families, a close approximation of the French pattern is found. But in contrast to France, Germany had a far greater number of large estates; nothing in France corresponded to the German class of Junkers in the region east of the Elbe. The self-limiting mentality of the peasant that played so important a role in the French national character could not become a major component of German character. The declassed peasant and the Junker set the tone for German agriculture.

The story of German agriculture is thus based on the strength and persistence, of the feudal system, followed by its peculiar successor in the agriculture of the Junkers, who remained one of the most powerful components in the state. By contrast, the story of the German city is one of many fits and starts, of splendid development and of unexpected reverses.

In the eighth century, after four centuries of decline, an increasing demand for luxury goods lured growing numbers of traders and merchants into German lands. These traders gathered around the major castles for protection and began to collect permanent groups of customers. Old areas of Roman settlement revived (exemplified by Cologne, Regensburg, Mainz, Worms, Constance, Zürich, Trier, Augsburg, and Basel). Carolingian sites such as Magdeburg, Dortmund, Cambrai, Goslar, Wurtsburg, and Bamberg also began to expand. By the tenth and eleventh centuries around many such strongholds (*urbi*), a new settlement (*suburbium*) had formed. The strongholds sometimes represented a bishop's see, an imperial palace, or a center of feudal administration. With the revival of commerce, the sites along major rivers such as the Rhine and Danube developed with particular speed. Freemen appeared in the towns and organized into fraternities or guilds. These townsmen established regulatory activities and their commercial and craft populations introduced coinage and promoted urban rather than rural economic and political policies.[4]

By the twelfth century the market settlement had developed into a functional unit called a "forum"; its settlers were "mercatores." The ensuing civic communities began to seek rights from the rulers of strongholds. The first grants of communal rights in German lands are recorded at Cologne (1106) and soon after at Goslar. The city was a new community which had a seat of handicraft and trade and a walled fortress. It was a self-governing jurisdictional entity and had a new system of social classes. There were around two hundred cities in Germany by the year 1200. During the twelfth century new market settlements were founded by dynastic families who had begun to see their value as sources of profits. Freiburg and Lübeck are examples of cities so founded.

Also by the twelfth century the growth of imperial and free cities and leagues was well under way. The long struggles from the tenth to the twelfth century of the burghers to wrest political power from the dukes and bishops, ended in victory for the cities and the appearance of considerable power of self-government in them. Most cities were governed by a city council and other officials. They maintained public baths, streets, water supplies, and building inspection. They started postal systems and maintained educational activities. Groups of cities attempted to secure freedom from external threats by associating in leagues. In the north the Hanseatic League eventually embraced over ninety cities. The Swabian League formed in the southwest.

By 1400 Germany had over three thousand towns. Those (like Cologne, Mainz, Frankfurt, Ulm, and Augsburg) along the Rhine and Danube trade routes were among the most highly developed urban areas of medieval Europe. In the north the original Hanseatic towns of Hamburg, Bremen, and Lübeck were joined by many others in the north German plains for the exploitation of internal commerce as well as sea trade. By the end of the Middle Ages the population of the Holy Roman Empire was about twelve million. About 15 per cent was in the towns—a high percentage for the time. Twelve of the Reich's cities had a population of over ten thousand.

A number of factors brought about a reversal of urban development in Germany. The discovery of America reoriented European commercial life to the Atlantic and together with the rise of the Dutch cities led to a decline in the internal trade routes. Northern towns began to stagnate until, in 1630, the Hanseatic League dissolved. The collapse of the Italian and Levantine trade in the eastern Mediterranean with the emergence of Turkish power in the Balkans and the Near East led to an extensive decline of the cities of southern Germany. To these forces were added the disasters of the Reformation and the Thirty Years' War. Widespread destruction of cities occurred. The Peace of Westphalia left Germany divided into three hundred sovereign states with nearly fifteen hundred quasi-sovereign principalities and imperial cities. The merchant aristocracy was destroyed by the religious wars. Powerful urban leagues were abandoned. The urban middle class was largely liquidated. Moreover, after the Thirty Years' War, dominated by the Hohenzollern electors of Brandenburg under the Great Elector, Frederick William (1640–1688), the Empire had no intention of restoring civic autonomy. Cities which had formerly enjoyed independence under the rule of patrician merchants and the guilds were now brought to heel under state control. Their councils were subordinated to traveling tax commissioners. The administration of justice was centralized in the state, and the power of the state police was extended into urban areas.

In the early stages, city growth had supplied the princes of the states with sources of wealth quite beyond the potential of the feudal countryside. However, in the long run the growth of the states inevitably brought them into conflict with the cities. The leaders of the states had not the slightest intention, when they were not forced to do so, of permitting the cities to run themselves, determine their own taxes, and maintain their own military forces. This was the state of affairs when Napoleon abolished the Holy Roman Empire and demonstrated in the defeat of the Prussians the weakness of the political-military system. Hence, after the decline of Napoleonic power and the Russian disaster of 1812, Prussia took the lead in expelling the French in full realization of the need for reform. To restore the economic foundations of socio-political power, Freiherr von Stein and Prince Hardenberg initiated a series of local reforms including the elimination of serfdom, the granting of considerable self-government to the cities, the abolition of old restrictions on the guilds, and the granting of social and political rights to Jews. Urban life rapidly recovered its vitality, and was further stimulated in the middle of the nineteenth century by the Industrial Revolution. Coal mines were opened in the Saar and Ruhr. Old craft towns, Rhine-Ruhr, Rhine-Main, Saxo-Thuringian, and Silesian areas were rapidly industrialized. In the south, Stuttgart, Munich, and Nuremberg became manufacturing centers. Hamburg and Bremen developed new commercial importance in the northwest. Berlin became a major economic center in the east. The population of Germany increased from forty million in 1870 to sixty-four million in 1914, representing largely an increase of urban dwellers.

The rise of the large commercial and industrial city with a population greater than one hundred thousand is a phenomenan of modern Germany, a product of the Industrial Revolution. In seventy-five years the metropolitan areas (*Grossestädte*) in the Reich increased from eight to fifty-two. By 1933 one third of the German population was concentrated in such *Grossestädte*. An additional fifth of the population was located in five hundred cities with populations of from ten to one hundred thousand. By the time of the outbreak of World War II, only a third of the population was distributed in rural communities with populations less than two thousand.

Despite state supervision, the cities under the Empire enjoyed considerable autonomy. Under Weimar only limited changes of civic structure were made, the most basic being the introduction of universal suffrage and proportional representation in city elections. A great increase in partisan politics at the local level was one by-product. The Nazis once again reversed all this, eliminating local government, strengthening the central administration, and abolishing democratic and representative features of the old system. They strengthened the position of the chief mayor and introduced Nazi party controls at all levels of municipal government.

The towns and villages of Germany were composed of large families, relatively younger populations, and higher birth rates than were its cities. These differences tend to distinguish city and country everywhere. Country people present many traditional differences in dialect and religion. Urbanites show greater uniformities in life style and a weakening of religious convictions. But peculiar to Germany is the maintenance of the landed nobility's ancient relation to the peasantry and rural workers and its tendency to retain its strength. Also in Germany merchant and artisan groups of the small towns retain to an unusual extent their traditional form. In the cities, on the other hand, there has developed a small upper class of capitalists, a dwindling original middle class, and a proletariat with many complex variations in social stratification.

Only in terms of the continuities in German rural history and the discontinuities of German urban history can some of the features of its national character be clarified. The first period of the flowering of German cities saw also the flowering of its artistic and intellectual life. With the reversals of this early period of civic development, there was a break in its culture as well. Hence major scholars, artists, and scientists like Erasmus, Dürer, and Kepler of the first period had no immediate successors. There is some justice in Emil Ludwig's argument that everything constituting the glory of the German spirit has come from the German burghers. He maintained that while in other nations city-dweller, nobleman, and king are often at odds, in the great periods their cultures coincide. But in Germany, he urged, "whenever the Reich was strong and united, it starved in spirit; and whenever it was weak, the spirit thrived." Ludwig derived this paradox from national character rather than national character from it. He believed that the separation of force and culture was due to the uncultured disposition of the princes and nobles. Meanwhile, the citizenry, having been excluded from political leadership, pursued art and scholarship, as Ludwig put it, "after the fashion of women and old men left at home when their menfolk are out at war. This, in turn, forfeited them their political sense, their interest in government. Sensing the contempt of the domineering Junkers, the German burgher shunned responsibility. He threw himself into gainful work, and when he had amassed enough wealth, or when as a son or grandson he had means and leisure, he went in for science or the professions, while the artists rose directly from the ranks of the artisans. A desire for freedom hardly ever emerged."[5]

There is little doubt as to the accuracy of Ludwig's linkage of certain features of national character to the role of the relation of city and country, but it would seem more plausible to reverse the implications he draws from that linkage. One may add to Ludwig's observations those of Gershenkorn: "Agrarian mysticism with its 'praise of rural life,' its promise of the 'Kingdom of Blood and Soil,' its ideal of '*Bodenständigkeit*,' of autarchy as a preparation for war, [its] hatred of 'urban and nomadic Jews,' [its] weird nationalism with its Hottentot ethics, its political solipsism, and its sovereign contempt for international obligations—all these are familiar elements of the present system in Germany. They are also the salient attitudes and policies adopted and pursued by German agriculture ever since the critical period of the late seventies of the past century."[6]

In German national character, rationalism, urbanity, sophistication, cosmopolitanism—the typical attitude formations of the city—were under-represented or suppressed. Traditionalism, religiosity, and the peculiar parochialism natural to the country were over-represented. Moreover, the forces of the countryside were imposed upon city culture. Agrarian mysticism, excesses of romanticism, and anti-intellectualism seem to have been inevitable properties of German national character.

THE SOCIAL CLASSES[7]

The most powerful of all forces on national character are the sub-communities within a nation, for they represent points of alternate synthesis. Germany's urban and rural components locate the primary tension points important for its national characteristics. More detailed distinctions are possible the moment one cuts below this surface to the hierarchical ordering of people within a society. The structure of the social classes in a nation and, particularly, their relation to one another have an importance for its national character second only to her sub-communities.

There seems to be little doubt that if one were to eliminate all distinctions of social rank, the requirements of conjoint action would establish a new set almost immediately. In society men pursue a life in common. They formulate group decisions, take conjoint actions, produce and distribute various kinds of values. The very fact that people join in action entails a differential participation in activity with varied claims upon it fruits. At every hand hierarchical orderings of individuals arise in terms of decision-making (power), in terms of execution (work), and in terms of access to value (economic value and social status). Human hierarchies are complicated by the fact that they become habitual (traditional) in the given society, and individuals come to have quite different potential access to values by the fact of birth alone. Traditional organizations of access to social values are constantly being disrupted by discrepancies between tradition and ability. There are further disorganizations due to the appearance of new social forces which render old social forms obsolete.

If one's object is to study social stratification, there is great value in distinguishing between class, power position, and status. Class refers to a plurality of persons who share a common set of economic opportunities (capitalists, farmers, landlords, skilled laborers, shopkeepers, etc.); power position refers to one's opportunity to make binding decisions upon other persons of the society (the president of the state, a cabinet officer, a legislator, a bureaucrat, a judge, a policeman, the boss of a political party, etc.); status refers to one's comparative claims to social honor or prestige. When one is interested not in analyzing the sub-elements in social stratification but in locating the general properties of the society which emerge out of the conjoint operation of economic class, power position, and status, the concept "social class" may be useful when it is taken to refer to a stratum of individuals sharing the same hierarchical position in the society as a whole. Members of a given social class share a closely linked series of class situations, have access to a range of typical power positions, and claim special social honors.

The concept of social class is important for the understanding of national character. National character refers to a set of behaviors characteristic of the nation. These behaviors are never equally appropriate to all the social classes of the nation. Some social classes more than others determine, set the style for, and appear as representatives of the whole.

The Landed Nobility

The landed aristocracy enjoyed an unusual predominance. A number of sub-formations were found in it. The *Uradel* determined rank in traditional terms. It was possible for a prince such as Chlogwig Hohen-Lohe-Schillingfürst to scorn the eastern gentry. The Junkers, for their part, disdained the newly knighted who had won rank for service to the state or eminence in science, art, or business. Bismarck, who himself had started as a simple "von" (his mother had been a commoner, and his wife was excluded from élite noble functions) was made a count and a prince only at the time of his dismissal from office ("Herzog von Lauenburg"). The landed aristocracy as a whole derived its lauded position and its correlated powers from its feudal heritage. In the period immediately prior to the rise of Hitler, the estates of the aristocrats embraced over 20 per cent of the arable land of Germany. East of the Elbe such estates encompassed up to 40 per cent of the land. The stratum involved has been seen to be a historical development, from the feudal period opposed to the bourgeoisie, and in a position to use the state to dominate German society.

The events reviewed in the previous discussion of the changing ratio of city to country in Germany found their point of focus in these social strata. In the nineteenth century the transition to agrarian capitalism reinforced the strengthening of the nobility. The process had begun in the eighteenth century. When, as a war measure, Frederick the Great introduced the system of Landschaften, fusing estates of the nobility into credit cooperatives, the districts were pledged collectively for debts and military cooperation. The sale of any portion of such landed estates was prohibited by law. At the same time, acquisition of new land was made possible. A force had been created that could grow only in one direction. Estates were bequeathed in entail. These legal protections continued into the nineteenth century, helping to consolidate the estates while preventing the bourgeoisie's penetration of them by way of purchase.

To this accumulation of power, as already noted, was added the effects of the liberation of the peasants by the edicts of 1809 and 1811. The nobles were in a position to reduce the peasantry to a landless agricultural proletariat, releasing themselves from traditional obligations for their support. Over 2,500,000 acres of land were acquired by the aristocracy and added to estates converted to large-scale production with free labor. A kind of agrarian capitalism replaced feudalism.

The agricultural proletariat formed in response to agrarian capitalism did not exhaust the rural labor supply. Peasants near the large estates were drawn upon for part-time labor. The estate owners, moreover, employed their political power to control this labor. A law in 1854, for example, forbad workers from striking. During World War I repeated measures operated the same way. The Servants Ordinance (1910–1918) bound agricultural workers to the estates by yearly contract. In the middle of the nineteenth century, labor organizations were illegal in rural areas. Manorial local government (*Gutsbezirke*) gave the owners legal control over inhabitants of a district. The nobility thus had at its disposal a free laboring class without responsibility for its welfare. At the same time it retained semi-feudal control over its labor. It came very close to eating its cake and having it, too.

The growth of industry speeded migration of rural workers to the city. To compensate for the labor shortage that ensued, seasonal migration of workers from Poland was allowed. By 1845 the number had mounted to half a million a year. The growth of industry, however, also strengthened the *bourgeoisie,* which attacked the privileges of the aristocracy. The *bourgeoisie* had an interest in agricultural free trade, for high food costs caused discontent among the poorly paid workers. The fall of Bismarck and the rise of Caprivi marked the changing tide of conflict. The latter concluded various commercial treaties and tariffs (1892) at the expense of agriculture.

The angry agrarians thereupon formed the League of Agrarians (*Bund der Landwirte*) in 1893, by whose pressure after 1894 a series of chambers of agriculture were formed which agitated for favorable agrarian legislation. This resulted in a continuation of the agricultural policy begun in the crisis of the 1870's (a world economic crisis and the competition of Russian and American food stuffs). Economic protectionism thereafter remained basic to tariff policy. Modifying influences proceeded from the practice of the agrarians after 1870 of investing less in peasant lands and more in industry, commerce, and banking. Intermarriage began to occur between members of the *bourgeoisie* and members of large estates. The members of the *bourgeoisie* had their eyes on rural rank, and the Junkers had their eyes on *bourgeois* wealth.

In World War I the agrarians wanted to defeat Russia as an agricultural competitor and to annex parts of Poland and the Baltic estates for expansion of their holdings. This was a powerful factor in the war on two fronts. They had control of the army. Their economic position was good, for profits were increased through government measures, and agricultural labor was bound to the soil by war decrees. Moreover, prisoners of war were placed at their disposal. With the loss of the war and the outbreak of revolution, the aristocracy was temporarily overwhelmed by the formation of workers' and soldiers' councils and unable to control a portion of its own troops. But, the Social Democratic government left the old officers' corps in charge of the army, and the agrarians quickly formed volunteer corps which they placed at the disposal of the Social Democrats for suppression of radical elements. Despite the fact that the agrarians were having things their own way, the more aggressive officers and aristocrats refused to work with the parliamentary government. This aggression culminated in the Kapp Putsch of 1920.

The republican government protected private property, and inflation ended agrarian indebtednes as the aristocrats paid off their debts with worthless marks. When stabilization of the currency once more aggravated the rural economic crisis, the government rescued the agrarians with a series of agricultural credits. The agrarians cut production costs, rationalized production, and increased the use of machinery on their estates. They also fought to raise tariffs on agriculture. They formed a coalition with the German *Volkspartei* (the party of big business), and welcomed Fascist dictatorship.

To a considerable degree the style of deportment of a nation is established by its highest ranking class. The power of the Junkers in the German nation is clear. Even as late as 1918 the three-class system gave the landed aristocracy disproportionate representation in the Prussian Diet. Here they fought reform, maintained feudal codes of honor, and opposed parliamentarism. In all things they pursued policies of narrow self interest. Such behavior, Lowie notes, called forth Fontaine's *Irrungen, Wirrungen,* and Lili Braun's reminiscences. As late as 1910 the titled Prussian lieutenant, with full popular support, held industrialists and merchants in contempt. The hold over the army was extensive. The *élite* regiments in Prussia were monopolized by the aristocracy. Even sons of financial magnates were excluded from commissions in the cavalry. To consider Jews as candidates for officer's rank was out of the question.

As often noted, the typical Junker understood little other than farming and hunting. Though responsible for the state, he hesitated to manipulate it completely to his advantage. His ignorance and lack of cultivation were notorious. Baring-Gould has collected many instances of Junker boorishness. Gross errors in grammar were so common among Prussian generals as to be castigated by Baron von Stein. In *Münchhausen* Immerman observed that there were whole districts where noblemen found it contrary to their station to read a book. Their preoccupation with fox hunting, gambling, and church-going was viewed by

Fontaine as exhausting their contribution to German culture. While cultivated noblemen even east of the Elbe were known, as shown by the brilliant Humboldt brothers and the classical scholar von Wilamowitz-Moellendorf, they were exceptional. By and large only the older nobility, particularly that from the south and west, patronized the arts—as did Beethoven's patrons or those of Goethe, Friedrich Hebbel, and Franz Grillparzer. This has been illustrated by Ludwig I, who corresponded with Goethe and visited the poet in Weimar to congratulate him on his birthday, or even by Ludwig II, who patronized Wagner.

As the Junker rose to prominence in the German aristocracy, he tended to be characterized by an arrogant rank consciousness in contrast to the British rural aristocracy which fused with the urban patriciate. In England a model of gentlemanly deportment diffused through the middle classes. Alien to the British was the exaggerated retention of rank discriminations which existed even within the German nobility itself. While in England rank was inherited only by the eldest son, in Germany rank was retained by all the members of the family. The effect in England of the inheritance of rank and title only by the eldest son resulted in a wide distribution of family ties between the nobility and the rest of society. Thus, in England the nobility was not so remote, and its behavior was not so sharply differentiated from that of persons of lower rank. On the other hand, in Germany a consolidation of rank was an inevitable product of the inheritance of rank by all members of the family. This placed the relatively powerful social force of the family behind the strengthening of rank differentiations, just as in England the force of family ties served to mitigate the sharpness of rank distinctions between eldest and other sons. In one satirical formulation (Nestroy's *Freiheit in Krähwinkel*) the German aristocracy is represented as conceiving of humanity as limited only to persons of baronial rank. Lowie notes that intensified rank consciousness existed even among children. Helmut Gerlach (*Von rechts nach links*) could not organize a mock battle among the servants' children, for they fled in terror when he advanced, and Lili Braun reported in her memoirs (*Memoiren einer Sozialistin*) that in play children cringed before their genteel age mates. Such factors, to be sure, did not prevent impoverished Junkers from seeking the daughters of financiers and industrialists as brides.

Intensified rank consciousness, vulgarity, ignorance, and extreme and selfish provincialism, all were among the contributions made by the Junker to the national character. Germany in considerable measure thus presents a case of the precise reverse of the more usual status situation in which the *nouveau riche*, as for example in the Renaissance or in eighteenth-century France, would naturally express his competitive strivings in the struggle for self improvement in the arts and social graces. Considerable social crudeness characterized the highest ranking class, and, accordingly the *nouveau riche* sought to prove that they had made good by assuming an exaggerated boorishness.

The Upper Middle Classes

The middle classes include a number of sub-strata. In Goethe's time, for example, Frankfurters recognized six social grades: burgher-patricians, holders of university degrees, merchants, craftsmen (and shopkeepers, innkeepers, and brewers), peasants, and day laborers. At this time and place each grade was subject to sumptuary laws, and a master craftsman's wife could not wear furs or other finery appropriate to a merchant's lady. The highest ranks among the upper middle classes were occupied by the burgher patriciate. This development is true of such Swiss towns as Bern and Basel, which had a patriciate equivalent to that of the Cabots and Lodges. In Hanseatic cities (Hamburg, for example) the patriciate developed a formalized cultivation. Hamburg men still kiss ladies' hands.

The *bourgeoisie* is defined, in part, by its relation to private property as opposed to feudalized property or socialized proletarian property. The first section of the modern *bourgeoisie* emerged in the course of the expansion of craft production and marketing and the ensuing struggles for private property and the right of private accumulation of capital. The Industrial Revolution gave a new turn and a new intensity to the development. The German *bourgeoisie* was originally patronized by the absolutistic rulers who realized that commerce was a source of liquid wealth. Despite the great reverses earlier, by the end of the eighteenth century, the *bourgeoisie* had shown significant economic, political, and cultural growth. The obstacles it faced were many: the tax policies of the states, the monopoly rights of the medieval guilds, and the monopoly of land by the aristocracy.

When the French troops occupied Germany, they proved to be of unexpected help in breaking down these traditional obstacles and were often received by the *bourgeoisie* as friends and allies. Napoleon aided the *bourgeoisie* in many ways by the abolition of tariff frontiers, the transformation of the tax system, the abolition of exclusive landowning by the nobility, and the elimination of numerous craft and guild monoplies. But Napoleon had the instincts of an aristocrat, and the continuation of the Napoleonic blockade had negative effects on commerce. The continental blockade practically destroyed shipping. Taxes grew ever more oppressive; the French tariff wall was restrictive. *Bourgeois* groups thus helped overthrow Napoleon.

Bourgeois opposition to the Germany monarchy began to form in the nineteenth century, but the state guarded its political prerogatives jealously, making only a few economic concessions. Prussia abolished internal customs, reformed the revenue system, passed a uniform low tariff, and finally formed the *Zollverein,* which tended to become a *bourgeois* force. Economic legislation of 1867–1887 carried further that of the *Zollverein.* This promoted rapid accumulation of capital and especially favored economic concentration and centralization. The government itself was a member of the Rhenish-Westphalian Coast syndicate. Technical schools were established, scientific societies supported, and economic relations between government and business were promoted by the chambers of commerce.

Foreign policy also shows the influence of the upper middle class. After 1879 tariffs on industrial products monopolized local markets for German-made goods. Colonies were acquired for their raw materials and markets. German consulates often became institutes for market research. A strong merchant marine was built with government subsidies, and the navy protected German business abroad. After 1900 the anti-British foreign policy reflected the opposition of the German *bourgeoisie* to its chief competitor.

The outcome of World War I was of basic significance to the *bourgeoisie:* territories, raw materials, and capital investments were lost; patent rights were annulled; the merchant marine was destroyed. A socialistic working-class government appeared imminent. The *bourgeois* attempts toward political control of the republic were aided by conservative policies of the Social Democratic government, which obtained raw materials, opened markets, floated foreign loans, established industrial credits, subsidized a new merchant marine, repaid foreign business losses, aided concentration in industry, banking, and commerce, promoted industrial research, kept tariffs high, and even reduced the wages of labor.

Among the upper middle classes special interest attaches to the holders of university degrees who ranked somewhere above other sections of the middle class but below the patriciate. Especially interesting is the extensive rank-consciousness in this stratum. Since the educational institutions of a society are responsible for maintaining the normative order, one can expect an unusual sensitiveness to the principles on which the upper stratum of a society behaves. Educational practices tend to capture and intensify this. In England social strata with a level of education equivalent to that of the German Junker display a profound respect for the norms of sport, and judge social relations in terms of whether they are or are not "cricket." In the United States the equivalent strata operate on norms very similar to those of business. By contrast to both England and the United States, the outstanding trait in educated German circles was an exaggerated sense of rank differentiation. Elementary schools sharply distinguish between *Fachlehrer* (subject teacher) and *Oberlehrer* (principal). The elementary school hierarchy is in turn sharply distinguished from the secondary school hierarchy: The *Studienrat* (subject teacher), the *Studiendirektor* (principal), the *Oberstudiendirektor* (district supervisor) and his substitute, one rung below, the *Oberstudienrat*. At the university, rank consciousness caused the student to have cards printed *stud. med.* and *stud. phil.* Having passed his examinations and filed the required copies of his dissertation, the young scholar was permitted to have his cards printed with *Doktor designatus*. A full-fledged Ph.D. with permission to lecture is *Privatdozent* but without appointment is *Dr. phil. habil.* The doctorate has so much prestige (baffling outside the German cultural sphere) that medical degrees are sought without intention of practicing medicine simply for the prestige of the degree and the right to use the title. The same motivation appears in the agitation (since 1899) to secure doctorates for graduates of technical schools. A professor and holder of a doctorate in two fields may sign himself *Prof. Dr. Dr.* In addition to the academic ranks of *Privatdozent, Professor extraordinarius, Professor ordinarius,* is the head of a university titled *Magnificenz.* In a manner reminiscent of the American regular army, at faculty affairs, the wife of a *Professor extraordinarius* dares not contradict the wife of a *Professor ordinarius.*

In Hamburg, to be sure, only lawyers and physicians normally retain their titles outside academic circles, and a scholar is not automatically a privy councilor. But, as Lowie noted, this is exceptional, for even Goethe never overcame his awe of hereditary ranks. At public gatherings titled persons sat aloof from the common herd. At Göttingen University students sat on reserved benches. The only parallel in the United States is presented by the role of the sons of Boston patricians at Harvard. According to Cleveland Amory, by 1749 all students were ranked by the president according to social standing. This determined the order of chapel seating, marching in college processions, and precedence for class reciting and serving one's self at the table. The social distance from the Harvard freshman and the president was so great that it led the Harvard *Lampoon* to suggest that a place in Harvard Yard be commemorated by a monument to mark the spot where President Lowell once spoke to a freshman.[8]

The contrast with Germany appears in the fact that this class consciousness in academic life was but a marginal phenomena in the United States; in Germany it was typical. The same is true for the excessive formality which may be exemplified by the typical behavior of a Prussian state archivist such as Meinecke. Lowie reports that when in 1887 Meinecke began his career as Prussian state archivist, he had to hire a taxi and call on each of his senior colleagues in dress suit and white tie. Frock coat, buttoned kid gloves, and silk hat were mandatory on official visits, and on New Year's morning every archivist called in swallow-tail coat to pay his respects to the director.

The style of life of the upper middle class shows the powerful influence of the aristocracy. It appears in the need to maintain servants: a cook and maid and even a French governess. Lowie again assembled many illustrations. When he married (1895) Meinecke found that he needed an apartment with a minimum of five rooms, furnished with suitable furniture and in which he might entertain at least eighteen guests at a time. In the suburbs of Berlin Mommsen kept three maids. An amusing variation in the upper-middle-class style of life was provided in Munich academic society, where women spent their afternoons drinking coffee and knitting, while their husbands met their cronies at the tavern. Unexpected visitors at night gave their orders to the maid, who had them filled at a nearby restaurant, and was paid and tipped by the guest. At times, particularly in Heidelberg and Berlin, academic households assumed the properties of the salon.

In the upper middle classes cultivated men, poets, and artists formed many associations. The formation of voluntary associations is symptomatic of both the presence of strongly felt needs in the social groups concerned and the presence of unstructured areas of life not organized either by official institutions or by traditional practice. The closest parallel in the United States to this formation of clubs for literary and artistic self-improvement in German academic circles is the club formation of middle-class women. In his youth Fontaine belonged to four literary clubs. The Tunnel over the Spree, a Berlin Sunday Society, was founded in 1827 by the satirist, Saphir, and survived for half a century. Paul Heise belonged to the Tunnel, and when he moved to Munich in 1854, he formed the Crocodile. There were many such clubs.

Heavy drinking patterns had status value in these strata which, in emulation of the coarseness of the Junker, tended to rate abstinence as effeminacy. As often noted, even academic persons frequently cultivated alcoholism as an art. This obvious imitation of the boorishness of the Junker also extended to the preservation of dueling patterns. Not all students of fraternities or all fraternities were given to fencing, and the Catholic organizations rejected in it principle. However, the *Burschenschaften* fenced and maintained an intricate code for settling personal affronts. Under the Weimar Republic as late as 1923 the University of Innsbruch listed a number of *Schlagende Verbindug*. Scholars who accepted the practice included Max Weber (who as a young man had to win his dueling scar), Friedrich Naumann, and Wilamowitz-Möellendorff. It was as necessary for a young would-be aristocrat to win his dueling scar as, by comparison, for a young athlete in the United States to win his letter.

One major middle-class ideal was the harmonious development of individual potentialities; this ideal, however, was not the old humanistic one but an artistic superman ideal. To thousands of young Germans Goethe was the model of creative achievement, self-cultivation, and aversion to politics and social reform. This intensified neo-humanism led to idolatry of great men, with whom first-hand contact was sought. Like a most anxious *parvenu*, the neo-humanist attended concerts and art exhibits; he drew, painted, wrote poetry, and played a musical instrument in a veritable frenzy of self-cultivation. A successful businessman often took up painting, the piano, or the violin, testifying to a strong sense of cultural deficiency in the face of often great business success.

The German upper middle classes present the conflicting influence of contradictory behavior models: that of the gentle, cultivated, older traditional aristocracy of the south, and that of the boorish, rusticated, unintellectual Junker aristocracy of the north and east. The former offers an ideal of deportment more easily achievable in academic circles; but the latter is of more recent vintage and reflects more direct access to actual social and political power. In some careers, as for example that of Max Weber, the pull of both ideals may be seen. As a young man, he drew many of his ideals from the latter, but as time went on he showed increased responsiveness to the former ideal. The simultaneous function of both ideals often baffles the outside observer who cannot see how a German intellectual can simultaneously show deep and genuine learning coupled with a proclivity for browbeating his subordinates and employing a language against his opponents more appropriate in a fishwife.

The anxious pursuit of culture was often fused into a combination of snobbery, conservatism, political indifference, and intemperance. Schopenhauer thought the masses were stupid, a sentiment many times echoed by Nietzsche. Treitschke took for granted that only an élite minority could enjoy culture. Such persons as Max Weber, Rudolf Virchow, Theodore Mommsen, Ernest Mach, and Anton Menger were exceptions. The tendency of German scholars to behave in an abusive and self-aggrandising manner toward each other is well known. Bülow sounded the universal complaint against the lack of taste of German scholars. In its extreme form, no one can achieve recognition without denouncing someone else. Schopenhauer deliberately gave his lectures at the same time as Hegel. In Vienna students only clandestinely dared to listen to Freud lecture. In his "Considerations of an Unpolitical Man," written during World War I, Thomas Mann preaches self-development and regard for art as the most ethical forms of activity. He treats liberalism and democracy as shams, he repudiates utilitarianism, and he warns that if the conservative German spirit is democratized, it will perish. The deportment of the upper middle class could hardly be more neatly summarized.

As in the case of the landed aristocracy, the upper middle classes sound some of the major notes of German national character. Ever and again this separation of social precedence from political activity may be seen to have its effects. The antipathy of the upper middle classes to politics expresses their actual situation. The cult of one's self appears as a compensatory formation, but it does not assume the form of the cult of a responsible political self. The indifference to the lot of the masses which they distrust and the excessive concern for aesthetic affairs in contrast with an ineptness at and ignorance of public affairs, all express the various features of the actual social situation of the upper classes. All are central themes of German national character.

The Middle Classes

The middle classes include numerous strata ranging from the upper layers of the proletariat to the lower layers of the *bourgeoisie*. They have been undergoing change. The old middle classes, the product of the first developments of urbanism, include artisans, small craftsmen, shopkeepers, independent professionals, *rentiers,* and pensioned persons. The old middle classes were organized in the guilds which were built around the roles of master, journeyman, and apprentices with ceremonial promotions marking each stage. The guilds restricted competition, fixed prices, maintained quality, and developed qualifying examinations for subordinates. In time they often became restrictive of economic and social opportunities even to the point of utilizing guild promotion as a device to force the marriage of the master's daughters. Women, illegitimate children, slaves, and foreigners were not usually admitted to the guilds. At their best, the guilds standardized production, maintained standards, and eliminated unfair competition. Many guild customs were alive in nineteenth-century German society at a time when they had vanished from France and England.

With the change to urban society, new social types appeared: officials (policemen, firemen, postmen), new types of vendors, *rentiers,* superintendents of residences, and new types of service and bureaucratic personnel (civil service personnel and white collar employees). These social types grew up outside the old guild system. The new middle classes include non-independent professionals, national, state, and local officials, office and clerical workers, timekeepers, foremen, and managers. The new middle classes presuppose an economics of large-scale production and industrialization dependent on quantity rather than quality and handicraft production.

The life conditions of the new middle classes are determined by its lack of economic independence. The members are recruited primarily from families of the old and new middle classes. They are better educated than the workers. As white collar persons, they have the capacity to sustain a better level of life than most workers. They are motivated by the feeling that they have a better chance for social and material advancement than the workers.

The emergence of the new middle classes was a product of the same forces that created the *bourgeoisie.* The relation of the new to the old middle classes is somewhat like that of rural feudal strata to those of agrarian capitalism. The abolition of the guild restrictions on production during the Napoleonic era was a blow to the handicrafts. The embattled strata affected by these measures had a hand in the Revolution of 1848. A general Congress of Craftsmen (1848) meeting at Frankfurt am Main proposed heavy taxes on machinery, conceiving machinery as an agency of social destruction. However, the rise of large-scale production could not be stopped, and after 1871 the disintegration of the old middle classes was rapid. Through an ordinance of 1869 the government tried to aid the artisans through a partial restoration of the guild system. Reform measures (1881) transformed these guilds into corporations with juridical rights. New regulations of 1887 increased their power. But none of this could halt the tides of change.

After 1860 attempts to strengthen the economic position of artisans led to the formation of cooperatives for artisans under Schultze-Delitzsch. The General Federation of Cooperatives had 3,699 member cooperatives, with an individual membership of 1,200,000, a business capital of 650 million marks, and business transactions of 2 billion marks. In 1898 the government organized a central coperative bank to furnish them with cheap credit. Such measures slowed the disintegration of the old middle classes which were tending to disappear even though economic concentration in retail trade was much less than in industry.

The displacement of the old middle classes by the new is by no means confined to Germany, but represents a structural development in Western society. In America some of the changes in its composition have been documented by C. Wright Mills, one of the most able former students of Hans Gerth.[9] A brilliant analysis of the ethos of the new middle class in the United States is contained in William H. Whyte's *The Organization Man*.[10] These studies prove beyond any doubt the strong parallels in the mentality of the new middle class wherever it appears. In one sense the events in Germany differ only in the slowness with which the destruction of the old middle class and the creation of the new occurred.

After World War I the German government tried to gain the support of the middle classes, though it did not change their economic base. Though private property was guaranteed, the old middle class suffered most from inflation, which wiped out persons with small fixed incomes while rents were held controlled. *Rentiers* could not subsist on their income. Shopkeepers were unable to replenish their stock with dpreciated paper money. The old cooperatives were largely ineffective. The new middle class suffered far less than the old because its income rested on salaries which had a better chance of keeping pace with inflation. By 1924 the old middle classes found themselves with only 10 per cent of their pre-war capital. The new middle classes, dependent on large-scale capital, were affected by the same crises as the industrial worker. However, they had no unions at all or, at best, weaker unions to meet the threat. They, too, though to a lesser degree, faced proletarization.

The style of life of the middle classes was fixed by two major facts: its political importance as a voting block and as the core for a mass party was far greater than that of the *bourgeoisie;* however, it was trapped only a step above the proletariat. Its style of life was characterized by pathetic imitation of the *bourgeoisie.* In *Das Tägliche Brot* Clara Viebig expresses the shabby vestiges of a woman's claim for prestige: she has had an affair with a lodger who was a doctor, and never tires of insisting that she had almost been a *Frau Doktor.* This class frequently made fantastic sacrifices to finance a favored son toward a doctorate. Often with nothing to set itself off from the proletariat more than a thin veneer of culture, it is little wonder that when faced with complete disaster this class was ripe for Fascism.

The rank-consciousness of the higher classes found its counterpart in the middle classes. Salesgirls and bookkeepers of Berlin, for example, would not willingly associate with female factory workers. In Saxony, Lessing, a pastor's son, shocked his parents by hobnobbing with actors. If the *bourgeoisie* found its deportment modes in the aristocracy, the middle classes, old and new, took over striving toward higher culture from the upper middle classes.

The Industrial Proletariat

The industrial proletariat is a product of the same forces of modern society already sketched. At the base of the economy these forces created the propertyless worker, formally possessing full rights but in fact often in a situation where the exercise of his rights was impossible. Out of the propertyless strata of society the concept of socialized ownership took shape. The conditions of the early industrial worker in Germany were as bad as in other Western countries in the early days of industrial capitalism. Child labor was prevalent, twelve to fourteen hours of labor a day were frequent; and the wages of heads of families were so small that wives had to contribute to family support by taking jobs as laundry-women, sewers, knitters, and peddlers. The homes of workers were crowded, with children often sleeping in the same bed with lodgers of the opposite sex.

As in other lands, attempts were made to meet the problems of the worker by union organization. Ferdinand Lasalle (1825–1864) founded

the *Allgemeiner Deutscher Arbeitverein* which had a program for reform of national labor conditions. He petitioned Bismarck for universal
suffrage and the improvement of working conditions. Bismarck denied
the request and advanced labor legislation of his own intended to pull
the teeth of the socialist's program. Marx (1818–1883) and Friedrich
Engels (1820–1895), after repeated defeats in attempts at reform, repudiated dealings with those in power and advocated a program of
international revolution by the workers of the world. Bismarck, meanwhile, utilized two attempts against Emperor Wilhelm's life (by non-
socialists, incidentally) to introduce a bill outlawing the Social Democratic party, exiling the agitators, and suppressing anti-government
publications. Despite such official suppression, the strength of the Social
Democrats grew from 124,000 in 1871 to 3,000,000 by 1903 and 4,250,-
000 by 1923. It is never easy, Bismarck discovered, to legislate a social
force out of existence.

Bismarck's refusal to permit the German labor movement to operate
within the framework of existing political forms was a strong component in the formation of an international, revolutionary, and utopian
(rather than a revisionistic) socialism. At the same time Bismarck
slowed the pace of change. Only after the interactionalists and re-
visionist socialists united in 1875 did a unified Social Democratic party
make general headway. One of the prices paid by the laboring groups
for unity, however, was the internalization of the conflict between the
two wings. Meanwhile, Bismarck's provision of some social legislation,
while intended to disarm Social Democrats, showed that even without
a program there was value in the labor movement. The state also tried
to force arbitration conditions which were unpopular. A systematic
policy was pursued of supporting only those unions emphasizing national unity. However, all such policies fired the revolutionary concept
and the full development of trade unionism proper only became possible
with the repeal of the anti-socialist laws in 1890 which permitted the
branches of German labor to work together toward a common goal.

Another development of importance for German labor involved consumer cooperatives which had been initially formed in 1860 under
Huber, Pfeifer, and Schultze-Delitsch as middle class organizations.
In the 1880's consumers' cooperatives were formed among workers in
Saxony, initially affiliated with Schultze-Delitsch groups. When accused of socialism, however, they broke from the central organization
in 1902 and formed an independent organization, becoming closely
affiliated with the free trade unions. In 1912 they formed a unified

organization, and by the time of the outbreak of the war, they had close to one million members.

During the war, despite the propaganda of the internationalists, the trade unions remained loyal to the fatherland. There was, indeed, some dissatisfaction among the metal workers, and the small active Spartacus group retained a revolutionary ardor of the Marx-Engels type. Toward the close of the war, following repeated military reverses, a number of strikes broke out. With the fall of Germany in 1918, the radical movement spread in the ranks of German labor. With defeat came revolution. In every city, town, and hamlet, in the army, in the factories, workers' and soldiers' councils were formed and ready to take over the reins of government. The Spartacists hoped to set up a proletarian dictatorship. However, the new government moved with great timidity: it neither ousted the capitalists nor socialized key industries. The workers' and soldiers' councils were suppressed. Volunteer troops formed by the Junkers were used by the government to smash radical labor formations. The Social Democratic party was manipulated into doing the work of the industrialists and the landed aristocrats. In the period that followed, unemployment increased cyclically, reaching six million in 1932. It was a time of progressive loss for labor. The eight-hour day was abolished; unemployment insurance and government relief were reduced; the unions were weakened.

The difference between American and German labor at this time is significant and revealing. In the United States in the 1920's there were anarchist and "red" scares and a strong anti-trade-union movement. However, the prosperity of the United States in this period of industrial expansion had spread to all levels. The American worker simply was no radical. He found his identifications with rather than against the middle classes. In Germany the lines between worker and middle class became increasingly sharp.

The anti-religious tendencies of the German working class were intensified by the official use of religion as a weapon against labor. The strong shift in the trade union movement in the direction of utopianism and revolutionary socialism was a response to the powerful forces in German political life which blocked the trade union movement and thrust it outside the pale of existing society. Göhre reported his own religious animosity. Workers' letters (Adolf Levenstein, ed., *Aus der tiefe: Arbeiterbriefe*) repeatedly document the same thing. An iron worker is apologetic because his mother was pious; a collier calls religion the concubine of capitalism; still another becomes atheistic because of contradictions in the Bible. At the same time, the reactions of German labor to World War I demonstrated that it was neither unpatriotic nor unwilling to work within the order if given half a chance.

The tendency of each class to take its ideal deportment models from the class above it is evident in the strong manifestation of the German worker's cultural interest. Throughout German labor there was an extremely high appreciation of knowledge, an interest in abstract topics, and a fascination for the arts. Societies for adult education were promoted by labor organizations such as the Heidelberg *Arbeiterbildungsverein* over which Wilhelm Wundt presided. Distinguished scholars like Frederick Albert Lange and Rudolf Virchow often took part in such ventures. The implementation of these cultural interests made German labor one of the most cultivated in the world.

Agricultural Proletariat and Peasant

The formation of an agricultural proletariat, a stratum of non-propertied rural workers, is a nineteenth-century German phenomenon. Before this, rural dwellers were land owners or serfs or semi-peasant craftsmen. The *Bauernbefreiung* of the early nineteenth century actually freed the land from peasants who had cultivated it for centuries. It was a profitable arrangement, for the landlords were then able to hire only as much labor as they needed without assuming responsibility for the welfare of the workers at other times. On the other hand, in the south and west many landlords found it profitable to buy off the feudal obligations from emancipated peasants. The new free agricultural workers were paid in cash and produce or, in the case of seasonal workers, wages and board.

Seasonal workers were usually small peasants or village dwellers with one occupation in winter but dependent on their summer earnings. The Poles, a most important group of the seasonal workers, numbered about one hundred thousand a year. A number of economic types of agricultural workers appeared: those receiving cash and produce and a dwelling place on large estates and those leasing a barn, house, and land from the estate owner and working part-time on the estate. Peasants with small holdings were transitional between the landed and landless rural proletariat, furnishing part-time labor on estates or working as seasonal day laborers.

Wherever medium- to large-sized peasant holdings existed, a number of associated phenomena appeared. In the peasant household there were often persons other than family members, such as sons of neighboring peasants who were owners or prospective owners. All or part of the wage of such persons was in kind or room and board. Freedom of movement of members of this group was much restricted by their aims. Their wages lagged far behind the general wage. The agricultural proletariat in the nineteenth and twentieth centuries often lost energetic individuals through migration to the cities or to other lands. Between 1885 and 1905 it is estimated (Searing) that over one million migrated from East and West Prussia, Pomerania, Posen, and Silesia.

The substantial implications of property for social freedom were familiar to eighteenth-century rationalistic thinkers like John Locke. To speak of men as free without permitting them to acquire the property that would make them so was doubletalk. The freeing of the peasants which was, in large measure, a freeing them of their property was an act that left them exposed to rural society without anchorage to make their social claims felt. Because it had some political skill, conscious or unconscious, only part of the peasantry was reduced to the status of a proletariat. From the standpoint of official society, this created divisions in their ranks. The independent peasant-proprietor was not in the least inclined to join the landless proletariat, but inclined by the structure of his economic position to take the point of view of the Junker. Meanwhile the presence of an additional series of subdivisions between independent peasant proprietorship and full proletarization further subdivided these groups.

By and large, agricultural workers remained the least organized stratum of German society. At the same time the rural proletariat could only hope to improve his economic situation by organization. Before 1914 there were signs of ferment among agricultural workers and trade union organizers were making some headway. During the war, however, they were bound strictly by the government, and unrest declined since there was some general improvement in the rural conditions. In 1918, however, their lot grew worse, and they joined the socialists and Christian trade unions in some numbers. This radicalization of the countryside culminated in a series of strikes by agricultural workers in east Germany in 1923. These failed because of the antagonism of the government and trade union leaders. Thereafter membership in the rural unions declined. In 1924 the government introduced compulsory arbitration, and the landed aristocracy began to force still lower wages. The peasantry was now ripe for Fascism.

The modern free peasantry, an outgrowth of the rise of the

bourgeoisie and the breakdown of the feudal order, had as its primary ideal ownership of its own private property and production for profit. This group is also generally opposed to the development of agrarian capitalism. But there is no unity of outlook in the countryside. The property-owning peasantry was a bulwark for the *bourgeoisie* and landed aristocracy against socialism. Since the government defended private property, the peasantry was always on the side of the state. Many peasant attitudes were politically vague to begin with, and peasants with larger holdings carried on capitalistic activity of their own, developing interests similar to the aristocrats. Thus the rural strata divided into groups all in favor of private property, but some for and some against the aristocrats. Thirty per cent of the landlords cultivating about 47 per cent of the land fell into this group. On the other hand, the great majority of *Parzellenbauren* like the *Kleinbauer* had holdings too small for a livelihood, and were closest to the proletariat.

The grievances of the agricultural workers centered in long hours, poor pay, the existence of yearly contracts difficult to break, and laws prohibiting, under penalty of imprisonment, organization or striking. In many cases pay was so low that a worker was expected to bring his wife and children into the fields. Furthermore, he was not only expected to show extreme respect for the landlord, but was often physically beaten for his pains. His attitudes tended to be narrow. When he had half a chance, he was greedy for profits. He strongly rejected innovation and had a limited knowledge of the outside world toward which he felt no obligation.

The social psychology of the peasantry stands at opposite poles from that of the urbanite. He achieves his life goals not by working in some organization but by a self-sufficient independence on his holdings. His life is adjusted to an organic cycle of living growth and not to the mechanical structure of the machine. His attitudes are traditional. He is the natural soil of religious traditionalism, which was frequently scorned until the political powers perceived it as a buttress to their needs.

Summary

Various of the national characteristics of Germany emerge as the peculiar deportments of some given class and as a product of the relation between various social classes. (1) A large section of landed aristocrats show an inordinate rank consciousness conjoined to social bad taste and ignorance with some remnants of an older, more humanistic aristocratic outlook. (2) The *bourgeoisie* displays an inordinate development of interest in the arts, which appears in part as direct compensation for deprivation of the right to determine its political fate. Together with this are numerous imitations of the worst features of the deportment of Junker aristocracy (drunkenness, coarseness, bad taste). (3) The deprivation of the power of self-determination in the middle classes was nearly complete, a fact opening the possibilities of imitation only of the cultural interest of the *bourgeoisie,* strong rank-consciousness, and a pitiable terror of proletarization. (4) The proletariat had a strongly utopian mentality conjoined to an anti-religiosity produced by the socio-political weapons employed against it. It also displayed a strong, sometimes pathetic, craving for culture. (5) The agricultural proletariat together with various formations of the peasantry had a somewhat formless character due partly to being at the bottom of the heap. The peasantry are bearers of the most traditional of social and religious forms.

RELIGION

In German national social structure rural and urban components form semi-independent communities. The social classes represent categories of people which partly cut across the rural and urban community formations. In Germany the countryside provides the anchorage for the highest and lowest of class formations: upper nobility and Junkers at one extreme, and the peasants and agricultural laborers at the other. Intrusive between these class formations are strata domiciled in the city ranging from the urban patriciate to the industrial proletariat. The social classes constitute lines along which new community formations may arise in Germany. This is shown after the crisis of the 1870's by the increased intermarriage between the landed aristocrats and the daughters of financial magnates, bankers, and industrialists of the urban environment. Moreover, after 1900 it was among agricultural workers that the trade union movement native to the urban industrial proletariat began to make headway. It may be assumed that if such processes could operate uninterrupted over time, one single unified community would eventually replace the semi-independent communities represented by town and country.

But social structure may be sub-divided by other distinctions than urban and rural communities and social classes. It is also specialized in the organization of special sub-areas of inter-human behavior. A community is an entire way of life for a plurality of people. A social class is a category of persons occupying equivalently graded ranks within the community. An institution is an organized subactivity of the total community; such as are provided by the family, religion, the state. Inevitably some aspects of national character will be associated with the specific institutions as well. No institution is more important for national character than religion. One need only recall the importance of Protestantism for national character in England; Catholicism for national character in France, Spain, and Italy; Russian Orthodox Christianity for national character in Russia; Confucianism for China; Islam for the Arabic countries; Shintoism for Japan; and Hinduism for India.

The religious institutions of a community consist of the organized collective behaviors directed toward matters in the given community which fall outside the everyday routine—the accidental (sickness and health), and the ultimate (death and life)—and which they attempt to form into a meaningful unit. Christianity, which is of concern here, for example offers an explanation of the events lying beyond those making up everyday life and of the relation of everyday events to these events. Typical ideas and attitudes are represented in the notions of "God," "Heaven and Hell," "sin," "prayer," "conversion," "redemption," "salvation," etc.

What constitutes the unknown, mysterious, and inspiring varies with the nature of the community and the state of knowledge. The rain which the rural dweller may receive as a blessing from heaven may be viewed by the urban dwellers as merely a disagreeable addition to their day. The man armed with the knowledge of the modern scientific age is not inclined to view a bolt of lightning as the "fist of God."

The career of the city in Germany, as has been noted, has been unusually checkered and subject in the hours of its finest growth to unexpected reverses. The career of the country has been, up to World War II, subject to reinforcing continuities of development of such a kind that it was lifted into strategic position over the economically and culturally superior city in recent times. It may be expected, then, that many elements of German religiosity have been fixed more by a rural than by an urban outlook.

By and large rural populations tend to be both more conservative (resistant to innovations from the outside viewed, often correctly, as destructive to local values) and more religious. The rural linkage of traditionalism and religiosity is related to the omnipresence of birth and death, for the rural environment is one of living things. Moreover, the hazards of weather, insects, and animals are always present. Existence is close to nature and bound to the organic cycle. The bounty of a good harvest is its natural product, and this is often counterbalanced by the specter of natural disaster. In the northern climates all that is biologically potential is accented in the phenomena of generation concentrated in the spring of the year. Under such conditions a communion with nature or the profound sense that nature is personally alien are always possible. In classical Greece the staid, rational, tempered, and sophisticated Apollonian cult of Olympus was typical of the city, but the emotional, ecstatic, bacchanalian cult of Dionysius was typical of the countryside. Generation cults, fertility rituals, ecstatic rituals of death and rebirth are all phenomena of a rural religiosity.

The spread of Christianity over Europe was completed only in the Middle Ages. In the course of this diffusion, complex adjustments occurred with the beliefs of tribal and peasant populations and in many instances the superstitions of rural Christians were hardly distinct from tribal and original peasant beliefs.

When the cities began to develop in the late Middle Ages, they transformed the *milieu* to which Christianty had to respond. The need to adapt the church to changing social requirements is illustrated by the fact that from Pope Innocent II in 1215 to Leo X in 1512, no less than nine world councils were held with church reform as the primary item on the agenda. However, since it is infinitely easier for the political powers to carry on their business with the aid of religion, religious and political institutions tend to interweave. As a result, religious reform ceases to be a simple religious matter. The so-called "causes of the Reformation" actually refer to the multiple lines of tension emerging between the religious spirit and changing social circumstances. Practices that had long been usual in and outside of the church became objectionable. The church sold offices and justice. A section of the clergy lived in a state of concubinage. The wealth of the church was great, and tithes and taxes were collected. The clergy paid dues to the curia and recouped themselves by charging high fees for their ministrations. Simony, the sale of appointment to office and of justice, was widespread. Pardon for practically all crimes was obtainable for a price. Meanwhile a special source of ecclesiastical revenue had been found (during the Crusades) in the sale of indulgences, remissions from sins, and penances in this life instead of the pains of purgatory. The practice which arose as a means of assuring Heaven to warriors fighting the infidel was generalized into a money-making device. Moreover, some priests not only had concubines but kept taverns, gambling rooms, and brothels.

As the new religious spirit developed in the urban communities, it took the form of an objection to the sacramental theory of salvation. This was the idea that grace is imparted to the believer by means of the rites of baptism, confirmation, eucharist, penance, extreme unction, holy orders, and matrimony. Against this, the view took form that salvation was a product of personal belief and deportment. To the idea that ascetic other-worldliness—the monastic ideal—was the source of highest religious value, another was being opposed. The sweeping denunciation of these worldly pleasures and forms did not make sense in the thriving civic world. An idea more in accord with the times was that this worldly activity itself can be a means to salvation. To the view (popular in rural areas) that the worship of saints is a path to the holy was opposed the passionate emotional rejection of such practices as a hagiolatry approaching polytheism. Parallel to this was the rebellion against the traffic in relics, which at the time included a wide variety of spurious articles: wood presumed to come from the cross, shin bones of the ass on which Christ rode, whole bottles of the Virgin's milk. Finally, the new spirit took the form of an insistence on the separation of spiritual and temporal power, since their fusion was conceived to be responsible for corrupting the spirit.

The strong rural component in German religiosity appears in the mystics. Master Eckhart (1260–1327) preached that God is the only true Being, and that man is able to reach the absolute. Henry Suso (1300–1366), a student of Eckhart, expressed an ecstatic piety and advocated personal salvation through self-denial and good works. Tauler (1300–1361), a Dominican of Strassburg, placed great weight upon good works. All honest work is the service of God. Pure religion consisted in being intoxicated with God and "melted in the fire of His love." The mystics had powerful ties with the countryside, and the idea was always present that nature is good. There is a divinity in nature which is the handiwork of God. It is radiant with His glory.

Such was the ferment in Germany while it was still a great rural area to the north of Rome.[11]

At the same time, the social changes correlated with urbanization called for religious reform, and Germany experienced a vigorous development of cities. The religious ferment was evidenced not only by the German mystics but by the observations of Erasmus and the experience of the Hussites. When Martin Luther, an Augustinian Friar, university professor of Wittenberg, and also, significantly, the son of a peasant, expressed his indignation against current church practices by drafting the Ninety-five Theses on the indulgence system, he only sparked the demand for reform. The fuel was at hand for a general conflagration. In Luther's three treatises in 1520 a positive program for the establishment of a national church free from papal interference was projected. There is little doubt as to the popularity of Luther's program. Furthermore, the success of the movement he initiated was in part made possible by three-hundred-odd independent German states owing little more than nominal obedience to the emperor. Here was a program at once popular and an occasion for pursuing political independence from both the Emperor and the Pope. The revolution that had been set in motion could be utilized to advantage by the princes, but it also spread to all classes and resulted in the Peasant War. Though at first welcoming the peasant revolt, Luther eventually turned against it and sanctioned its bloody extermination. The first wave of the development was not brought to a close until the Peace of Augsburg in 1555. At this time, when Protestantism was near its height, possibly 70 per cent of the Germans (including the Austrians) were Protestant.

The Peace of Augsburg was only a truce. The period between it and the Thirty Years' War was used for the assemblage of forces for further struggle. In 1555 Pope Paul IV initiated Catholic reform. The Counter Reformation took the field against heresy implemented by the Society of Jesus and began by reforming the monastic orders. The Inquisition and the Index were freely employed. Meanwhile, the Anabaptists at Münster split off from the main body of the Protestant movement in one direction, while Calvinism spreading from Switzerland attracted many Lutherans. Lutheranism was ripe for counterattack. The Thirty Years' War was actually a series of four wars: the Bohemian and Palatinate War (1618–1623), the Lower Saxon and Danish War (1624–1629), the Swedish War (1630–1635), and the Franco-Swedish War (1635–1648). The series of struggles left the Empire weakened and the Emperor reduced to the mere shadow of power. Thereafter the Hohenzollerns, whose subjects were Protestant, ranked as the second most powerful force in the Empire. The Reformation left an intellectual ferment in its wake with an intensified interest in the founding of schools, a deepened interest in spiritual things, a widespread interest in the Bible and religious literature. Finally the war and its associated famine, disease, and emigration is estimated to have reduced the populations of the Empire from sixteen to six million. In Württemberg, only one sixth of the population remained; in the Lower Palatinate, only one tenth.

The Thirty Years' War was in large measure responsible for the destruction of the Empire. Though a rural area, Prussia emerged as the dominant political center. In Prussia the state church was Lutheran, and the king was head as *Summus Episcopus*. This left some problems, for the Hohenzollerns became Calvinists in 1613. The problem was eventually settled in 1817, when Frederick William II united the two churches into the Evangelical Church. Similar amalgamations occurred in Nassau in the same year, in the Palatinate in 1818, and in Baden in 1821. Under pressure of the Napoleonic conquests, confiscations of Catholic church lands occurred. After the defeat of Napoleon the church attempted to regain its power but met with serious opposition by the special states. For example, in Bavaria in 1818 an edict limited the rights of the Catholic church, and under Fredrick William III (1798–1840) Prussia asserted its sovereignty over both Catholic and Protestant churches. The Catholics sought emancipation of their activities from state control as well as freedom of instruction and the press. Their demands corresponded with the liberal demands of 1848. In 1850 Prussia permitted both churches some freedom.

After formation of the Empire, Bismarck undertook the destruction of the Catholic church. The Catholic Center party had come into existence in the 1860's, quickly becoming a state's rights party; its membership was recruited largely in the liberal Rhineland, Westphalia, and the south German states from elements antagonistic to domination by Prussia. Bismarck's bitter *Kulturkampf* closed with the repeal of most of the measures taken against the church except for compulsory civil marriage in Prussia and the prohibition of Jesuits. The latter measure was not repealed until 1918. The struggle crystallized the tensions, but once persecution ceased the Catholic Center party became a bulwark of the national state so far as the rights of the Catholic minority were not interfered with.

The Revolution of 1918 gave the Protestant churches some further freedom from state control, but it did not separate church and state. The state guaranteed many old privileges of the Catholic and Protestant churches. The government continued to consider everyone a member of a church unless he had formally resigned. Both churches had the right to levy taxes which took the form of a 10 to 15 per cent supplement to the income tax. In Prusssia the revolutionary government appointed three commissioners to head the church after the flight of William II left the Evangelical church without an official head. At this time the population of Germany was about one third Catholic and two thirds Protestant. Jews constituted less than one per cent of the population of the Reich. The relation between the Catholic church and the state governments was unchanged except for Bavaria, where a Concordat (1924) gave the church complete freedom to regulate its own affairs. However, there the state still collected taxes for the church and continued to pay an indemnity for property confiscated in the Napoleonic period.

Before the war religion was compulsory as a school subject. The revolution did not achieve the socialist goal of eliminating religious instruction from the schools. The state defended the belief and practice of the religious bodies, and Section 161 of the Penal Code punished blasphemy, public vilification of religious bodies or their beliefs and ceremonies with imprisonment for a period not to exceed three years. Numerous arrests and convictions of communist and socialist freethinkers were secured under this regulation. In general, the revolution led to an increase rather than a decrease of religious influence by the church. The weakening of central power which was Protestant and which had checked Catholic influence opened up the possibility of generally increased religious influence. This was in accord with the mood of the times, the fear of radicalization and the concept of the church as a bulwark against this.

In Prussia the backbone of the Evangelical Church was in the agricultural regions. The appointment of ministers was under government supervision. The Evangelical Church had stood for God, the Kaiser, and the Fatherland. It retained this form. Under the republic the Catholic Church in part came into its own. The Weimar Republic was formed with its support. The Center party was in a position to shift its political program to the left to satisfy the radical leanings among its followers. The Center party was thus a basic stabilizing force in the regime. It is not without significance that the last most tenacious resistance to the Nazis was anchored in Catholic groups, and only the

Catholic south had sufficient inner coherence to form the point of integration of the German nation after World War II.

Religion and the church supported the state. Thus, when in the nineteenth century German labor found itself outlawed by the state and by state-controlled religion, various forms of Freethinking arose. At an earlier period the *bourgeoisie* had been placed in an identical situation. In 1861 the German Freethinkers' Society was formed from left wing groups, from the liberal *bourgeoisie* and middle class elements. With the growth of Social Democracy an atheistic movement developed among the workers. However, even though many Social Democratic leaders were atheists, party officials refused to commit the party to an anti-religious program. The forces, however, remained and in the early days of the 1930's the Internationale Proletarischer Freidenker claimed a membership of five million. It conceived religion in Marxian terms to be the "opiate of the masses," and looked forward to the day when a communist society would be set up and the church would disappear.

Some of the bearing of religion on German national character is already partly clarified by the capsule review of Germany's religious history. Protestantism under Luther turned out to be an instrument for the political integration of non-imperial forces in German lands. The Thirty Years' War devastated the empire, destroyed her cities, and left a situation that Prussia as a Protestant nation would eventually be able to exploit. The Napoleonic invasion further weakened the Catholic forces of the South German states. As Prussia consolidated her forces in the nineteenth century, Protestantism was used as an instrument of social and political domination. The state secured almost complete control over the ministry, which in turn became spokesman for the most reactionary of political interests. This, together with the active attempts by Bismarck to smash the Catholics, gave Catholicism as an embattled minority a strong impetus in the direction of liberalism. The Catholic Center party thus became the spokesman for religious freedom and state's rights. Meanwhile, in the other direction the employment of official Protestantism as a weapon for the smashing of the trade union movement gave the more radical wing of the socialist and trade union movements a strong push in the direction of free thinking and atheism. The same forces earlier in the nineteenth century had created a movement toward free thinking among the *bourgeoisie* and middle classes. But while these are characteristically German phenomena, they do not exhaust the significance of its religion for national character.

Wherever Protestantism has appeared it has tended to give a

peculiar cast to experience. The sacramental theory of the church provides in the sacraments an automatic means to salvation. Moreover, since the sacraments can only be administered by the clergy, a strongly authoritarian element is added to the individual's moral and religious life. In the most decisive moral and emotional life-crises the individual has a system of institutional authorities to fall back upon. And, in ordinary conduct, so long as one has conformed to the religious pre-requisites, he can proceed about his affairs with the same uncommitted freedom as a child in its play pen, always aware of protective sides and of a responsible watchful eye.

The branches of Protestantism vary considerably in their manner of doing so, but all of them shift emphasis from the sacraments to the individual's relation to God as the ultimate religious fact and deter-minant of salvation. A personal equation is thus substituted for a set of institutional procedures. Religious significance then potentially attaches to every act, to every thought. The whole of life is transformed into a field for religious strategy.

In addition to establishing the religious significance of everyday conduct on a new, more intense level, Protestantism strongly modified the role of the clergy in religious life. At all of his moral and religious crises, the individual stands alone with his conscience and his God. In the end he and he alone must accept full moral responsibility for his acts.

No sensitive observer of German national character has failed to note the effects of the Protestant orientation. There is an omnipresent religious insecurity, a yearning for the infinite. There seems, at almost every point, to be either an inclination to neglect earthly comforts and pursue the kingdom of God or else to pursue everyday activities as a salvation device. There is a tendency toward melancholy, a kind of pessimism, and an inclination toward a dejection psychosis. The emergence of the typically German fear of split personality, something a Frenchman would consider incredibly strange, can be understood only in terms of this context. At the same time, the recovered religious significance of everyday activities provides an unusual intensity to work. Work has, as many observers repeatedly note, more than the significance of a boring necessity to the German. He often plunges into it as if into sin or as if to escape from guilt. Moreover, diffused throughout Germany is the idea that religion is absolutely essential for continued social and political life. When religion has, as in the case of the freethinkers, been turned into an obstacle in their way of political growth, atheism and freethinking generally acquire a religious intensity.

Again this touches upon a basic clue to German national character. In such an atmosphere all activities acquire a religious or quasi-religious form. Materialism and skepticism, for example, developing in the latter nineteenth and early twentieth century were pursued with religious intensity in politics, literature, the theater and press, culminating in orgies of neo-sophistic, hedonistic individualism. The neo-romantic revolt against materialism discernable in such phenomena as the *Jugendbewegung* (youth movement), with its variety of organizations like the *Wandervögel* (Migratory Birds), *Freideutsche Jugend* (Free German Youth), *Pfadfinder* (Pathfinders), etc., also generated a quasi-religious form in the cult of naturalism and communion with nature. Flowing from this same atmosphere, the power to hear voices remains a valuable asset in German socio-political life at a time when it is only indicative of insanity in other lands. Adolf Hitler, who had appropriately been called the German Joan of Arc, was quite ready to supply this need.

ECONOMIC INSTITUTIONS[12]

Economic institutions, the organized social behaviors associated with getting a living, also stand in close relation to some of the behaviors that compose national character. It has already been necessary to take the economic institutions into account in estimating the role of city and country and the social classes upon national character. Rural economic institutions have already been sketched in sufficient detail for present purposes. Some further insight is possible, however, into the implications of the industry and commerce of Germany for its national character.

In the Middle Ages industry was concentrated in the towns and controlled by the guilds. Every town had a variety of handicrafts. The large cities were the location of more specialized crafts. Foreshadowing an era of non-local industry, even at the time some industries were located outside the towns: iron and glass making, for example, which required the use of bulky materials such as ore and charcoal. Metal working, which followed the mining communities, also tended to develop outside the towns. As water power came into increased use, industries dependent on it for power took on a more permanent character. However, industry which underwent an early development in Germany suffered the same fate as urbanism. At the lowest point of its political integration, Germany was divided into more than three hundred fragments, a political situation highly unfavorable to the development of large-scale industry. Napoleon started the process of unification. After the victories culminating in Jena (1806), the country was re-formed into about forty states.

In 1806 there was still no Germany: no common currency, taxes, law, systems of roads (those of one state rarely coincided with those of another). Each state had its own customs, tariffs, and transit tolls. Prussia, the largest state, had over sixty tariff districts. At the beginning of the nineteenth century Germany was still in a medieval industrial state. About 80 per cent of the population of Prussia was rural. While a thousand places had town rights, only seventeen had a population of over ten thousand. In 1800 the average annual income of the Prussian subject, it has been estimated, was twenty dollars. Sombart believes that aside from the landed nobility there were not one thousand persons in Germany with incomes exceeding 2,500 dollars.

The most important single commercial change in the early days of the nineteenth century was the formation of a customs' union, the *Zollverein*, which wiped away many tariff frontiers and made possible the extension of trade. In 1834 it covered about two thirds of the area and population of Germany. Political support for industry also appeared after 1800, and gains were made in the manufacture of cotton and wool. Steam power grew in Prussian industry from 7,500 hours power in 1837 to over 600,000 in 1875. Iron production was increased from 26 tons per worker in 1860 to over 70 in 1870. The firm of Krupp early achieved leadership. The founder, Friedrich, died in 1826, leaving a son and four workmen. The business grew to 67 in 1835 (at the time of the introduction of the first steam engine). By 1873 it had grown to 1600, and Krupp steel was unexcelled for small arms and artillery. However, until 1850 German industry was still in an apprenticeship stage. In 1860 only 12 million tons of coal were produced, indicating the small progress in employment of steam power and large-scale production.

In 1879 the system of peasant master craftsmen, journeymen, and apprentices was still typical of German industry. However, after 1870 German industry assumed a rate of growth almost beyond belief. The phenomenal growth of industry and commerce beginning in the 1870's shows some aspects of the German national character at its best—just as in some aspects of its political development some properties of the national character appear at their worst. But it will be useful to review this development, before attempting an estimate of it.

In 1871 Prussia established a single German state, adding the provinces of Alsace and Lorraine, which were rich in agricultural and commercial resources. An indemnity of one thousand million dollars was extracted from France at the close of the Franco-Prussian War. Germany was still 60 per cent rural, but was not so for long. In 1840 there were only two cities with a population of over 100,000; by 1913 there were forty-eight. In the 1870's the very character of industry was transformed. The Thomas-Gilchrist process (1878) permitted use of the phosphoric ores of Lorraine for steel production. Other advances in iron and steel processes reduced the amount of coke required for fuel. The production of lignite was stepped up. Distillation of coal and lignite were correlated with profound advances in the chemical industries. In the 1880's electricity began to be produced in power plants. By 1890 vertical integration was already emerging in the heavy industries of the Ruhr. Coal production increased ten times from 1875 to 1913. Pig iron and steel production increased seven times; steel ingot and casting production increased 70 times. The production of industrial horsepower which was at 62,000 in Germany in 1855 exceeded 6 million in 1911. By 1914 cartels in heavy industries were developed under the leadership of Krupp, Thyssen, and Stinnes.

A number of major socio-political events played back on German industry from the time of the end of World War I to the rise of the Nazis. In 1918 the Armistice was signed, and the country was in revolution. In 1919 the Peace of Versailles was concluded. German currency was undergoing inflation. In 1923 the Ruhr was occupied and the currency was in collapse. In 1924 the Dawes Plan was put into effect with internal stabilization and an inflow of foreign funds. In 1929–1930 the Young Plan was devised with further influx of foreign funds. In 1931 a moratorium on war debts was declared, and credits were frozen.

During the republican period the cartelization begun in the Imperial era was advanced at full speed, for loss of plants in Lorraine encouraged syndication. The runaway inflation of 1920–1923, moreover, permitted large concerns to buy out small ones and amalgamate them into ever larger units. After 1924 under the Dawes Plan foreign funds were invested in German big business, still furthering the process. The peak of cartelization was reached in 1926. The United Steel Works comprised one half of the iron and steel production. Six concerns of the Ruhr accounted for 80 per cent of the crude steel and 35 per cent of the coal. Twenty concerns controlled 90 per cent of the coal output in the Ruhr in 1937. The Krupp concern, on the verge of bankruptcy in 1927, was rescued by credits from American and Dutch bankers. It became chief armaments maker for the Nazis. The chemical industry began with the first synthetic drug in 1888 and the opening of research laboratories at Elberfeld in 1896. The first syndicate (1905) expanded to become I. G. Farben in 1925 with headquarters in Frankfurt. The industrialists were also active in international cartels in coke, steel, nitrogen, and rayon. The first international cartel was formed in Brussels in 1926. The British Steel Federation became a member in 1935. American producers joined to form sub-cartels in 1938. This may typify the form of German industrial development.

A few indications of the tremendous substantive change in the twentieth century may be added. Coal production reached 150 million tons in 1928. It was at 190 million in 1943. Production of lignite (brown coal) was at 165 million tons in 1928; 253 million tons in 1943. Oil production was at 100,000 tons in 1929; it had reached 3,500,000 tons by 1941. Germany has the greatest electric potential of all the countries of Europe, with over 7,000 generating stations. Sixty per cent of the production was in public owned plants. In 1927 four fifths of production was from coal and lignite, one fifth from water power. Iron occurs in Germany in small quantities in scattered areas. Before 1918 Germany's iron supplies were mainly drawn from Lorraine (20 million annual tons, 70 per cent of the supply). In 1937 Germany imported 20 million tons, half of which came from Sweden and 15 per cent from Lorraine. Total production in 1950 was 11 million tons. In the pre-war period Germany was second only to the United States as a producer of iron and steel. Peak production was in 1939 with an output of 18 million tons of pig iron, 22 million tons of steel.

As the industrial era opened in the second quarter of the nineteenth century, the economic policy of the German statesmen, flowing from the political composition and traditions of the German principalities, was, and could only be, cameralistic. Modern technology and business thrives in an impersonal and cosmopolitan environment. It could only get under way in Germany with the removal of tariff frontiers and other obstacles to trade and communication. The furtherance of trade and industry by German statesmen was initially of a negative or, at best, permissive sort—the removal of restrictions previously enforced. It was a reluctant concession to necessity—a typical act of German "freedom." The imperial frontiers became a device for making the Empire into a self-sufficient entity to be employed in supplementing international politics.[13]

Industrial progress was regulated primarily by tariff regulations. Beyond this, economic activity of the statesmen was directed to building railroads (as a military strategy) and subsidizing ship building. Important effects flow from such political policy. As Veblen indicated, German mineral resources and coal resources were fair, but comparatively only second best. The soil in Germany varies, but over-all it is not very good. The one large asset of Germany was an industrious and intelligent population. Had a free trade policy been pursued, Germany would have painted quite a different portrait. The coal and iron would not have been so fully exploited. A far larger proportion of these materials would have been imported. German industry would have gone much farther in the production of export goods. There would also have been radical differences in agricultural activity, which would have quickly declined and lost its comparative importance. German national policy radically depressed the economy out of its "natural" course with the consequent emergence of distorted compensatory forms. Another incidental product of the political aim at self-sufficiency was the drive to the acquisition of colonies in hopes that the raw materials and markets would make the Empire independent of foreign nations. Thus the distortion due to German political policy, tending to shift economic relations radically from the course they would otherwise have followed, also altered its position in international economy and politics. Here German behavior rapidly assumed the form of intimidating threats and use of power politics. It is significant that when the average German emigrated, he wished to go anywhere except to the German colonies, where he would often have been under more ruthless repressive control than at home.

There were many obstacles to German industrialization: lack of capital and absence of the habit of investment in industrial enterprise. The habit of investment, however, quickly appeared with the need for it, as did the required banking institutions. It soon became apparent that the Germans had no serious aversion to making money. On the other hand, Germany was in a position to acquire the industrial knowledge of the modern world directly at high level without going through the tedious steps of trial and error. Machine technology is far easier to acquire than skill, for it operates on scientific principles with wide applications. The special training for service as operators of machines is far less exacting than the training demanded of individuals under a handicraft system. Moreover, it should not be forgotten that in moving directly from a medieval economy to nineteenth-century industrial economy without going through the transitional stages, Germany was in a position to take over only what was best. Moreover, it was not chained to a vast investment in an obsolete technological plant.

In composition and intelligence the German people were quite the equivalent of the British. The rate of introduction and expansion of industry rested only on the discretion of those groups in control of the political economy. Here again some advantages in the German community were apparent: the classes in a position to profit from the introduction of an industrial technology were used to a low rate of economic return; the natural resources to be used were lying idle and could be obtained cheaply; a supply of workmen was at hand and the break with earlier traditions in trade and industry was so complete that Germany was peculiarly unhampered by conventional restrictions. It was not necessary to break down one set of industrial skills and retrain for another.

There is an aspect of technological unemployment that can act as an obstacle to industrial advance. One might assume that it would be just as easy to retrain industrial personnel as to train the pre-industrial types Germany had to work with as it entered the merry-go-round of industrialization. However, this is to ignore the significance of human factors that accompany given levels of technological skill and their displacement. When a worker has over the years worked himself into possession of a special technical skill, it is a source of personal pride and crucial to the social standing he holds in his own social circles. He may be as personally proud of his own skills as the most thick-skulled archduke is of a new stud. When the worker finds himself technologically displaced, the whole foundation of his existence is dissolved. Usually he is simply untrainable for the jobs that have displaced his special skills; they are usually technically simpler and more lowly paid. He is frequently a psychological casualty of industrial advance. At the time of her industrialization, Germany had neither an obsolete industrial plant nor an investment in obsolete technological skills. While this is an advantage that could last for only a generation or two, it was important. The same phenomenon partly appears in the twentieth-century industrialization of Russia.

There were other special factors at work of a type to enlist Veblen's enthusiasm. German captains of industry did not come from a training school of retail business, real estate, or political jobbery. They were born under the competitive test of industrial competition itself. They had neither obsolete equipment nor outmoded trade relations to contend with. They were pure captains of industry rather than of finance or politics. As Veblen observed, they chose their associates purely for technical reasons rather than for their astuteness in financial politics. Moreover, there was a supply of educated men in the German community eager to find employment in some blameless occupation. Much of the responsible staff and corps of the industries came from the universities rather than from the country store or lawyer's office, and these men were capable of appreciating theoretical and technical industrial requirements. Furthermore, the labor force was not made up of a pauperized population of a congenitally ineffectual type such as were at times produced in English industrial towns by the early stages of capitalism.

German industry integrates the activities of a number of strata. The entrepreneurs who assumed the risks in Germany were in a peculiarly favored and yet disfavored position. Socially it was long disfavored and excluded from intermarriage with the landed aristocracy, intermarriage becoming more frequent only after 1870. It found itself prohibited from *élite* posts in the army and from most higher political positions. At the same time, in the interest of war potential and economic self-sufficiency, the Empire was forced to promote its economic claims. Business, moreover, was politically encouraged precisely in concentration and centralization of industrial potential.

These events bear comparison with developments in the United States in the same period. At a critical stage of its development, modern industrial technology required great consolidation moves that would crush the local formations and establish the huge industrial aggregates capable of exploiting the new mass markets they helped create. In the United States this consolidation was the work of the robber barons and industrial tycoons who operated in a ruthless manner on extra-legal and even completely illegal grounds. In the United States their rise was accompanied by the passionate agitation against the trusts, by the era of the muckrakers, and the repeated waves of outraged popular opinion expressed in explosions of civic reform. The rise of German industry shows almost the reverse of the American phenomena. Thus many of the economic aims of the *bourgeoisie* were more than satisfied, while its political and social aims were extensively thwarted. This supplied an unusually powerful and compensatory force to *bourgeois* economic activity. Powerful economic ambition and political irresponsibility were the result.

In other contexts it has already been noted that the withholding of political competence from the upper middle classes tended to give an exaggerated impetus to action to the cultural and academic striving. This powerful thrust into the universities and technical schools produced a quantitatively extensive scientific and technical body of personnel. These were available to the industrial entrepreneurs for staff and research purposes. A high level of scientific and technical competence was thus present from the beginning, permitting the direct step from a handicraft system to the highest level of industrial development without the tremendous waste of energy in repeating the whole trial and error process by which capitalism arose.

Meanwhile, German industry drew large numbers of routine staff, office, and sales personnel from the middle classes. These had been nurtured on the religious discipline of Protestantism and on the sociopolitical discipline of the absolute state. They were accustomed both to discipline externally imposed and to discipline psychologically sought as a manner of deportment for the control of personal anxiety. The bureaucratic structure of modern large-scale industrial and commercial enterprise was again staffed by a personnel well adapted to its requirements.

Finally at the base of the pyramid of German industry was an industrial proletariat relatively well educated—a product of the self-improvement and educational drives in Protestant countries—and deriving from crafts of high responsibility and skill. Moreover, large numbers of these industrial workers had been drawn from households of Protestant persuasion in which hard work has a quasi-religious meaning. Habits of thrift and hard work tend to persist among these groups, even though the political situation often drove the German laborer to an anti-religious stance. But in any case the observation is made over and again that the German laboring force was more thrifty, hard working, intelligent, and educated than perhaps any other working class in the world.

The cooperation of a number of elements of national character was involved in the phenomenal industrialization of Germany. This industrialization at once tended to confirm and reinforce its characterological trends. Here as elsewhere, German behavior assumes an all-or-none quality. In other areas the results are often absurd. In post-World War I

Germany, for example, as some observers have noted, the cult of Freudianism produced excesses in the German press and theater that would have been prohibited as obscene elsewhere. Sophisticated observers such as Siegfried and Demiashkevich noted that the German carries every fad to extremes, whether it be cubism, abortion of unplanned pregnancies, planned parenthood, scientific method, or whatever. These observers see him as the perfect representative of the *avant-garde* prepared to integrate every upheaval or folly in the framework of discipline. In German economic activity the story is similar, for the German comprehends no limit, and no improvement in technique or efficiency is too slight. Here the industry of which he so often boasts, his *Gründlichkeit*, pays off. The love of the elementary, the pathological devotion to activity, find a proper field. To be sure, the very inflexible force of undeviating activity and the tendency toward monistic thinking may also produce their absurdities as when post-war plans for restoring the economy repeatedly took the form of the search for a single principle that could apply to everything. For a time, for example, in the press and periodicals coal was asserted to be the foundation of Germany. The most advanced nation was defined as the one able to extract the greatest amount of energy from a pound of coal. The German people were advised to think politically in terms of coal. An activity of glacial proportions was set in motion, inspired by a kind of religious intensity. Conceived as devices of national salvation, industrial researches in one area after another were carried out almost with fanaticism, but they led to the splendid gains of German industry. At the same time, the traditions of political irresponsibility could produce the phenomena of an industrial politics of disaster that permitted the merciless sacrifice of the economy and the nation for private gain. In such things German national character was simultaneously expressed and confirmed.

THE STATE

The state represents the set of institutions in the national community which consolidates decision-making, the execution of which is binding on the community as a whole. At times the state is conceived as the institution holding authority in the community. Again it is thought of as that institution which successfully maintains a monopoly on the use of legitimate force. Such definitions all amount to essentially the same thing, though they place the emphasis differently. In any case, the state is clearly distinct from religion (an institution concerned with the collective experience of the unknown) and the economy (as the system of institutions concerned with making a living). To be sure, state, religion, and economy have important inter-relations. The state may, as was often the case for the German state, employ religion as an instrument of political domination. It may, again as did the German state, frequently pursue policies of securing economic self-sufficiency. But despite these and many other possible ties, state, religion, and economy are quite distinct.

As the institution formally changes with coordination and control in the national community, the state is always important to the system of forces which compose a nation. There is infinite argument as to the many obligations of the state, but in any list of its duties the maintenance of the national system in a state of equilibrium always appears. This is so universally understood that when mechanical systems are designed, the mechanism receiving effects of the operation and turning them back into the scheme for control purposes is, by analogy to the state in its playback functions, called a "governor." When any set of forces external or internal threaten to grow too large and tend to destroy the national community, it is a function of the state to activate the opposite forces to repel the threat. This is the justification for the army, navy, and diplomatic corps (in external affairs) on the one hand and the police force and judicial system (in internal affairs) on the other. These are the system-maintaining mechanisms of the state.

Anyone able to seize control in the state is in the best of all positions to "work the controls" to personal advantage. To achieve power over one's fellows, there is no better mechanism in the national community. Moreover, there is no greater national irresponsibility than the use of the controls to wreck the system itself. Even ruthless persons or groups will rarely go this far, however, since it also destroys the basis of their own continued power. Furthermore, in exercise of the controls, the nearer the approach to the point of destruction of the system itself, the greater the opposition created. It is possible to reach a stage where individuals and groups decide that death itself is better than life continued under current conditions. On the other hand, every sub-force in the national community tends to defend itself; if it does not, it soon ceases to be a force. Specifically, this means that within the national system every sub-structure, unless otherwise prevented, tends to assume a political form. To the degree that the forces of the nation are permitted to participate in the political institutions, the tendency is to reduce the various coercive mechanisms to a minimum. To the degree that the variety of actual forces of the nation are prevented from having a political voice, there must be a corresponding development of coercive institutions, in part for use against the nation itself. These contrasts appear constantly between nineteenth-century Britain and Germany, where in the first case the tendency was to reduce the army to the minimum necessary to keep peace, while in the latter case the whole resources of the nation were made to converge on the development of the army and national military potential.

Again and again sensitive observers inside and outside Germany have found one of the major clues to German national character in the relation of the state to the nation. Sometimes this is rather mystically expressed as, for example, when it is argued that everything inspiring and great is a product of the German "spirit," while everything ignoble and vicious is a product of the "state," and all German virtues and vices are derived from the tension between the state and the spirit. But this establishes a tension between artificial entities, for spirit in down-to-earth language can only refer to collective attitudes or collective psychology, and the state is a system of institutions which distribute authoritative behavior. The tension must be located between one attitude and another or between some institution and others.

Qualified in this manner, one of the major clues to German political history is the lack of accord between the state and other institutions of the nation. The first stage of political development in German lands was marked by the integration of tribal society in the Holy Roman Empire. The problem of national integration in German lands was later to be repeatedly frustrated by political activities intended to restore the Holy Roman Empire. Still further energies that might otherwise have integrated the nation were exhausted in conflicts between the Empire and the Papacy.

In a sense German political development presents the precisely opposite situation to her economic development. Economically great efficiencies were promoted by the possibility of stepping, so to speak, straight from feudalism into an advanced stage of industrial capitalism. Politically, achievement of national organization was delayed by the presence in German lands of an obsolete political plant, too powerful to be dislodged and too outmoded to permit the new political efficiencies. All sorts of events of unusually destructive import had to occur before German areas were free to evolve into a modern nation.

The second stage of political development in part picked up at this point. When in 1520 Luther was excommunicated from the Catholic Church, Charles V attempted to bring an end to the revolt, for he hoped to maintain the support of the church for Habsburg power. The desire for social, economic, and religious reform, on the other hand, was an expression of forces seeking recognition in German lands. The people split into divided camps. The Protestant princes seized ecclesiastical lands. Conflicts between the rulers, knights, and peasants led to the Knights' War (1522) and Peasant Revolt (1525). The Peace of Augsburg (1555) as a temporary truce between the Catholic and Protestant leagues reflected the presence of local interests, for according to it the princes, imperial cities, and knights were free to choose their own faith.

There was, clearly, pressure among local forces to consolidate and develop into integrated national life. But once the Catholic and Protestant leagues were reformed, the Thirty Years' War was inevitable. The war opened in Protestant Bohemia, where the Habsburgs broke the arrangement for religious toleration. The next phase was marked by the entry of Danish forces. The third phase opened with the intervention of Swedish forces under Gustavus Adolphus. Finally, under the leadership of the Catholic Cardinal, Richelieu, the French entered the war in 1635. The effects of the war and the Treaty of Westphalia were immense in their implications for the possibility of a nation and of an integrated national life. The powerful leagues of cities were abandoned. The destruction of civic strata eliminated in Germany precisely those groups who, in considerable measure, led the way in European society toward broad participation by the nation in government. Germany was divided into about three hundred sovereign states and fifteen hundred quasi-sovereign principalities and imperial cities. The electors continued to vote the imperial crown to the Habsburgs, but their position as emperors was hopeless. Dominance in German affairs was pasing into the hands of the Hohenzollerns of Brandenburg, the Wettins of Saxony, the Wittelbachs of Bavaria, and the rulers of Hanover. The most significant political event was the development of North German states, where in the seventeenth and early eighteenth centuries administration was centralized, cities were brought under national administration, and numerous paternalistic social reforms were carried through, all of which led to road improvements, agrarian development, and canal construction, as well as the introduction of common school systems and compulsory education.

These events had complex meaning for the nation. Protestantism, by forming a point of integration for local powers, was a factor in breaking up the Holy Roman Empire. At the same time, in strengthening the princes, it promoted a highly particularistic and local subdivision. However, the new religious intensities achieved in the course of the religious conflict served to heighten awareness of national identities. The destruction of civic life occurring in the course of the religious wars liquidated strata which in other lands had served as a counterbalance to tribalism and the peasant village as well as supplying a considerable amount of the liquid wealth that the rising state powers needed for their operations. Although they may for a time travel the same road, sooner or later the national community and the city community come into conflict. Finally, it is a considerable significance that it appears to have been necessary first to shatter Germany into over three hundred variably sovereign principalities before the process of reintegration into the nation-state could begin. The Napoleonic occupation was to have a two-fold effect: the destruction of the final remnants of the Holy Roman Empire and a considerable reconsolidation of local units into workable political structures.

As has already been observed, the Napoleonic wars brought a sweeping destruction of the old order in Germany. These actually initiated the modern movement. Prussia took the lead in the struggle against the French. Internally a series of reforms were introduced, as noted, by Freiherr von Stein and Prince Hardenberg. Self-government was granted to the cities, permitting a resumption of civic development. Germany came out of the wars as a loose confederation of thirty-four sovereign principalities and four free cities. Prussia got the lion's share of the spoils. The Confederation was pledged to the maintenance of internal and external security and independence of the member states. Its weakness, however, was notorious and from the beginning movements for closer unity appear. Prussia led the way in the Customs Union (1818) which eliminated internal tariffs and permitted commercial growth at heightened tempo. By 1834 two thirds of the German area were included in the Prussian organization.

The revolutionary activities of 1848 spread throughout Europe. Metternich was swept out of office in Austria. There were demonstrations in Berlin which, however, were quickly suppressed. The liberals called for a national constituent assembly, which met at Frankfurt in 1848, but before anything could be accomplished, Prussia gained control. The Prussian conservatives were set on a policy of unification, and in 1862 Bismarck became prime minister. He introduced a program of militarization, and discredited the liberals and parliamentary institutions. He diplomatically isolated Austria, and reorganized the Confederation. The Franco-Prussian War (1870–1871) in part grew out of Napoleon III's attempt to block the final unification of Germany and from Bismarck's search for an occasion to perform such unification. Bavaria, Baden, Württemberg, and Hesse-Darmstadt joined the Confederation.

The Prussian king was ex-officio German emperor. Moreover, Prussia held the presidency and chairmanship of all standing committees. Sovereignty was vested in the Federal Council, composed of representatives of the state governments. Prussia possessed seventeen of the sixty-one votes. Executive function was vested in the emperor, who could convoke the Federal Council and Reichstag. Also, he appointed the chancellor and other high government officials. The unification of the German state under the Empire led to the gradual establishment of a uniform legal and judicial system. But at all times popular control was minimized. The Reichstag served as a kind of national parliament, but it was very limited. It did not control the chancellor. Its financial control was minimum, restricted to powers in the budget with none over national debt. Legislative activity was limited by the Federal Council, which initiated all legislation. The Reichstag never represented the people. Meanwhile, the states were governed by hereditary and constitutional monarchs, princes, and dukes. The imperial free cities were practically independent constitutional republics. The sovereign rulers possessed almost absolute power as heads of the state governments, the army, and the church.

Thus, when a unified state emerged in the nineteenth century, it was not as a representative of all Germany (a more genial spirit, for example, was to be found in the south than that displayed by the community of Junkers) but of Prussia. Also for this reason, as has been frequently observed, the German fatherland could hardly display any other connective ties than those of blood and iron, and hardly any ideals other than the dynastic. The political traditions of Prussia had taken form in the conquest of the Wendish, Lithuanian, and Esthonian people by the Teutonic order in the thirteenth century and the forceful imposition on them of Christianity. Its political forms were fixed, as Veblen had phrased it, in the ensuing period of exploitation, terror, revolt, reprisal, servitude, and gradual habituation to irresponsible personal domination and repression. The state was the instrument of the

Hohenzollerns and their followers. It was the "best preserved remnant of medievalism in Europe," and it had sufficient resources to make it a factor in international politics. Prussia's cultural contributions to the German world were medieval militarism and feudal agrarianism. Its ideal of the state was to make it a more effective instrument in service of the Hohenzollerns. Parliamentarism was fought. In the *Kulturkampf* the attempt was made to annihilate the Catholics (in part because the Center Party represented the southern liberals). The Social Democratic party was outlawed, and war was waged on the trade union movement. A cameralistic policy of political economy was advocated. The march of events was moving unfalteringly into World War I.

The Weimar Republic was a brief interval of parliamentary democracy set in a historical frame of centuries of despotism. When one takes into account the fact that the Reich had suffered the loss of a disastrous war and faced both local and world economic crisis; when one takes into account the fact that practically all the groups on which the hopes of parliamentarism could rest had been systematically deprived of political competence and experience under the Empire; when one considers the fact that all the older political formations had operated on the basis of extremely narrow personal advantage and without responsibility for the nation; when one further recognizes the universally negative role played by the imperial groups in the new government, one could hardly have expected great things from the Weimar Republic. To do so was indeed utopian.

At the end of the war Germany was in revolution. Versailles was ratified in June, 1919, and was a source of universal indignation and despair: Alsace-Lorraine was lost to France, Eupen and Malmede to Belgium, Posen and West Prussia to Poland; all colonies and special economic rights were lost; parts of Upper Silesia went to Poland and Czechoslovakia under treaty plebiscites; another brought concession of northern Schleswig to Denmark; Danzig was organized as a free city under the League of Nations; the Saar was placed under international control for fifteen years; the army and navy were reduced to insignificance; Germany was required to pay reparations for the loss and damage suffered by the Allies. The war left Germany economically disorganized, with shortages of food and fuel, with transportation broken down.

Such are the ironies of history. When the nation was defeated, exhausted, broken, facing economic disaster, and pervaded by despair, democracy had its chance. The contribution of Versailles to the situation was to make the task of those groups assigned responsibility for reconstruction of the situation almost impossible. The contribution of those sections of German society that had brought the nation to defeat was to retreat to their estates and their business offices, from which vantage points they growled savagely at every restorative move. They liquidated their debts and consolidated their estates and business combines as a by-product of inflation, thus recouping their private situations at the expense of other segments of German society. They fomented revolt, organized vigilante armies, and carried out programs of political assassination. The new government, meanwhile, responsible for a situation it did not create and implemented by a lack of political experience, was hardly in a position to do anything other than try to stabilize the situation it found. To have expected anything else is to ask for more than human wisdom. Such stabilization could only benefit the very groups that had brought the situation about. It was a foregone conclusion that every difficulty of restoration would be laid at the very door of the republic including, in the long run, responsibility for the total disaster. Recovery would inevitably mean the return to power of those groups which had brought about the situation in the first place. Typically, one of the first steps of the republic was the creation of a number of official and industrial combines, almost from its first act strengthening the traditionally anti-democratic groups. Reactionary armies under Wolfgang Kapp and General Ludendorff attempted a *coup d' état* March 1920, only to be defeated by a general strike of German workers. Counter-revolutionary movements were sponsored by conservative civil service and army elements. These were responsible for the assassination of the Minister of Foreign Affairs, Rathenau, in 1922. Moreover, the conservatives soon obtained control over Bavaria. A right wing coalition headed by Cuno took the lead in delaying the reparations payments, the occupation of the Ruhr, and the printing of paper money. By 1920 the mark had been devalued to 8.5 to the dollar; by 1922 it reached 8,000 to a dollar; and by November, 1923, 3.6 trillion to the dollar.

A coalition of the German People's party, Catholic Center, Democrats, and Social Democrats led by Stresemann stabilized the situation somewhat. The currency was stabilized in 1923, and marked recovery followed. Under the Dawes Plan (1924) steadied reasonable schedules of reparations were set up, and foreign loans for modernization and rationalization of Germany industry were secured. But in the economic depression of 1929 the Weimar Republic collapsed. In May, 1930, Dr. Heinrich Brüning of the Catholic Center party became

Chancellor. He attempted to save the situation by means of emergency financial decrees, but the reactionaries were already preparing for counter-revolution. The conservative Junkers, capitalistic industrialists, and dispossessed middle classes could all be counted on. Political intrigues engineered by General von Schleicher and von Papen brought about Brüning's downfall in June, 1932. On November 16 von Schleicher became Chancellor of Germany. He was almost immediately opposed by the Junkers. His resignation on January 28, 1933, led to the rise of Hitler, who was asked to form a cabinet.

Throughout the period of the Weimar Republic the only groups that had come to the situation with political experience played a politics of disaster. Inflation was used by the Junkers and big industrialists as a device for liquidating their debts, consolidating their monopolies, and beating their opponents into submission. Reactionary formations were utilized in policies of terror and murder. For example, the murderers and accomplices in the murder of Karl Liebknecht were treated as follows: one received a three months' imprisonment, a small fine was imposed on another, and one went free. One of Rosa Luxemburg's murderers was sentenced to two years' imprisonment, the rest went free. The murderers of Jogisches and Dorrenback were never tried. E. G. Gumbel in *Vier Jahre Politischer Mord* published the following figures for January, 1919, to June, 1922.

Political Murders Committed by Persons Belonging to Right and Left

	Right	Left
Number of political murders committed	354	22
Number of persons sentenced	24	38
Death sentences	0	10
Confessed assassins found not guilty	23	0
Political assassins later promoted in Army	3	0
Average length of prison term	4 months	15 years
Average fine per murder	2 marks	0

When it came about, economic improvement was utilized by the same groups to consolidate most of the values to themselves, while economic reverses were employed to depress and consolidate their hold over the industrial proletariat and the peasantry. Meanwhile, a savage inflation had reduced the older middle class and major sections of the new middle class to the situation of a white collar proletariat. Deprived of political power, these groups had nothing left but the shabby pride that lifted them above the industrial worker. It was among these groups that the Nazis made their first major gains. When the final economic crises (before the rise of Nazism) arrived, the big industrialists and Junkers turned eagerly to the Nazis as one further political agency to do their bidding.

It is difficult to escape the impression that Nazism was the ultimate fulfillment in this time of the political aspects of German national character. It was certainly no violation of it, and all the critical traits of national character were present. The deprivation of the mass of the population of political voice was one of the oldest themes of German politics. It was on this traditional note that the essential continuity of the Nazis with the politics of the past was sounded. The emergency decree of February 6, 1933, placed restriction on Freedom of Assembly and the Press. With Germanic thoroughness the Nazis set about to do what was necessary to consolidate power. The Reichstag fire was set February 27 (symbolically locating the place of parliamentarism in the new order) to give an excuse for drastic action against Socialists and Communists. Emergency decrees of February 28, 1933, swept away civil liberties. On July 14, 1933, all parties except the Nazi were abolished. In December, 1933, a law united the Party and the State, and all unreliable elements were purged from public service. In the summer of 1934 a budding Storm Troop rebellion provided Hitler with the opportunity to purge the Party. From 1933 on, there were repeated waves of terror, mass arrests, and trials. From this time to the outbreak of war in September, 1939, there were no less than half a million arrests. Totalitarianism was all-embracing with the function of *Gleichschaltung* as the first principle of political action closely correlated with the isolation of every individual from the social, political, and spiritual aspects of the community to which he would normally belong. The oneness of the nation was to be achieved by the atomization of all natural structures. It has been observed that after the Röhm crisis, the party seemed to have demonstrated itself to be "crisis-proof." The terror apparatus of the Gestapo and SS was ruthlessly employed to prevent mass defeatism from turning into rebellion. From the first, methods of cultural control were extended to a thoroughgoing censorship of teaching and research in institutions of higher learning. Dr. Julius Rosenberg, who provided the rationale for cultural control, denied the existence of purely objective science. The Führer's and Rosenberg's ideas on art were extended by Professor Paul Schultze-Naumburg, Director of the Art School at Weimar (author of *Die Kunst der Deutschen, Die Kunst und die Rasse*). Theater, music, and literature were "purged" almost immediately. By the fall of 1937, the time had come for the purge of the plastic and pictorial arts in the course of a campaign against what was viewed as anti-German disease-ridden tendencies in the arts: cubism, futurism, expressionism, and dadaism. This was under the supervision of Hermann Göring and Dr. Bernhard Rust. As Erasmus had long ago observed, when one begins by burning books, one ends by burning people. Accompanying these activities, with the Germanic capacity for thoroughness, was the ever-increasing activity of the gas chamber and crematoria in the concentration camps as documented in Eugen Kogon's *Theory and Practice of Hell.*

Much of the compulsive inclination toward extremes and the lack of balance in German national character seems to trace back to the place occupied by the state in German experience. Except for the short interval of the Weimar Republic—when it hardly had a respectable chance —or for occasional periods in the "urban" periods of German history, the forces of German society have not generally been permitted to assume responsible political form. A form pressed out of its natural course tends to take its revenge in a course outside its normal sphere. When Bismarck, for example, outlawed social democracy and trade unionism, he did not eliminate their existence; he transformed their shape. If one is prevented from working within the framework of the state, one can only work outside of it. Socialism was automatically given a revolutionary-utopian form, locating its goals outside and beyond the existing state. The moment gains became possible within the framework of Germany society, the trade union movement in Germany quickly lost it more extreme forms of revolutionary ardor. Utopian revolutionism is the romanticism of socialism; it is the response of a balked social force pressed outside the sphere of its normal self-realization and thereby assuming an intemperate form. This again may be taken as a major clue to the ties of German national character with social structure, for this is a paradigm of the career of one social force after another. In German experience the state has functioned to block one area of expression after another. Frustrated and depressed from its normal course, expression then assumes extreme forms, for it is made manifest under conditions where its natural controls are lacking. Meanwhile, the state must assume a doubly coercive form in order to control the abnormal forms that its policies generate. When carried to its ultimate conclusions, this can only lead to the dissolution of the state into the community or the community into the state. The latter carried out with unbelievable savagery was the program of Nazism.

8

THE STATUS OF
AMERICAN GOALS
AND VALUES[1]

THE PRESENT ESSAY WAS WRITTEN
for a conference on Goals and Values in Agricultural Policy sponsored
by the Center for Agricultural and Economic Adujustment of Iowa
State University. In their invitations to the participants, the sponsors
of the conference posed a number of questions, such as: Does America
have a unique set of goals or values? How much discrepancy between
ideal and real goals is permissible?

In a general way these questions may be answered very quickly
and easily. First: Does America have a unique set of goals and values?
Yes. In fact, it has a number of them. Second: How much discrepancy
between ideal and real goals is permissible? If ideal goals differ from
the goals that are actually pursued, there is no reason why the discrepancy between the two should not be infinite. The amount of difference
that is tolerable is measured only by the limits of tolerance itself. Third:
How may conflicts be resolved? If the conflict is between ideal and
real goals, it is most conveniently solved by dropping the ideal; that is,
if there is any reason to solve this sort of conflict in the first place. If,
however, the conflict is between discrepant actual goals of different
people, the solution found in fact will usually express the precise ratio
of strength of the interested parties. It is seriously doubtful whether any
other solution will prove to be stable.

THE NATURE OF GOALS
AND VALUES

Since the present discussion is phrased in terms of "goals" and
"values," it is well to sharpen the distinction between them. By "goals"

let us mean the qualities men attempt to secure in the course of their activities: money, power, esteem, etc. Like all people before them, Americans have goals. They have a unique set of goals so far as they pursue specialized ways of becoming healthy, wealthy, and wise.

By "values" let us mean those principles in terms of which men arrange their goals in axiological systems and fix the relations between means and ends. All people distinguish between trivial and important goals as well as between legitimate and illegitimate goals. The value of a good meal is trivial compared to the value of a good life. The psychological state of well-being secured by employment of drugs is *evaluated* negatively, while the psychological state of well-being achieved by performance of a selfless act of mercy is evaluated positively.

Values not only fix the importance and legitimacy of goals, but the appropriateness of means. Attainment of material success by hard work and devotion to business is evaluated as most praiseworthy, while an equivalent degree of material success achieved by criminal activities is not. Values are, in part, embodied in customary, moral, conventional, and legal codes.[2]

In summary, by "goals" are meant the qualities it is desired to bring about by social action; by "values" are meant the principles which determine the ordering of goals into systems and the legitimate means of their attainment.

LIMITING CONDITIONS
ON THE FORMATION
OF GOAL-VALUE SYSTEMS

There is no people without goals. There is no people without the values which organize the pursuit and implementation of their goals. However, no two goal-value systems are exactly alike. It is not unfair to view any given people's goal-value system as that people's unique life strategy. Since we hope eventually to characterize the goal-value system of America, it will be useful to examine some of the general constants and variables in every goal-value system.

One limit to the variability of a goal-value system is established by individual biology. Some objectives must be achieved in the course of individual and collective activity to permit life itself to go on. The goal-value system of any people can not permanently supply less than the minimum food, protection, and conditions for reproduction. A society that imposed absolute sexual restraint on all its members could continue to exist only so long as it recruited new members from the outside. The moment it stopped recruiting members from the outside, it would begin to shrink away (like the Shakers and some monastic orders). Individual biology thus supplies a lower limit to the variability possible to a goal-value system.

On the other hand, man's behavior is less determined by instinct than is the animal's. Human conduct is a product of learning which, in turn, occurs in a social environment. Goal-value systems are learned in social environments where they constitute established social practices. If the lower limits on the variations in a goal-value system are set by the requirements of individual biology, the upper limits are supplied by the current state of social practice.

EMPIRICAL GOAL-VALUE SYSTEMS AND COMMUNITY TYPES

Individuals endowed with certain minimum biological requirements and very comprehensive potentials for learning are born and reared in environments dominated by other men. In the teeth of some current shibboleths which assign creativity to the community, the present discussion assumes that individuals are innovating, the community is controlling and conserving. *Every community tends to achieve its stability in part by striving to establish a single legitimate goal-value system binding on all its members.*

In communities individuals are no more able to eat their cake and have it too than they are outside them. Moreover, some stability in what individuals expect of one another is necessary for social life. Hence, inseparable from collective action are commitments about objectives and the means for achieving them. If one man obtains money by hard work while another counterfeits it, an unavoidable clash over the proper means of "making money" is in prospect, for one system must destroy the other. Furthermore, whenever any major objective and the means to achieve it are fixed, they become a primary factor in other behavior. In order that conflicts may be avoided, there is a tendency step by step to form the goals and values pursued within a community into one single and exclusive (legitimate) system. *The empirical sociology of value rests unshakably on the assumption that goal-value systems are never absolute, but are relative to community type.*

While almost infinitely varied in detail, the goal-value systems developed by man are restricted to a relatively few general kinds. There have been as many kinds of goal-value systems as there are kinds of communities. A community is a total, autonomous way of life and the complement of groups and institutions that make it possible. Every goal-value system actually effective in conduct acquires its effectiveness only by anchorage in a specific community to which it belongs and to which it gives direction.

While usage is not altogether consistent on the point, most of the time when the suffix *-ism* is added to a concept, it signifies the goal-value system appropriate to the idea. The major types of human community created by men in the last twenty thousand years have each in their time sustained their unique goal-value schemes. The tribes of hunters and gatherers, rural villages, cities, and nations have each in turn developed goals for their members, values which established their principled pursuits, and a complex of loyalties which sustained them against competing forms. Each of these communities developed an appropriate *-ism:* the communities of hunters and gatherers sustained *tribalism;* the various rural communities sustained special *agrarianisms;* the city community supported its unique goal-value system in *cosmopolitanism;* and finally, in our time, there has been increasing coherence of the goal-value system appropriate to the nation, *nationalism.*

There are, to be sure, smaller complexes of loyalties appropriate to single institutions, such as to religion (e.g. religiosity), the family (familism), or even economic institutions (e.g. commercialism), but the more comprehensive goal-value systems are identified by the *-ism* referring to entire communities.

THE CONFLICT BETWEEN IDEALS
AND REALITIES AND THE AMBIGUITY
OF LIBERALISM AND CONSERVATISM

To understand the relation between community and goal-value system is important for clarifying the possible meanings of a conflict between ideals and realities. Conflict may exist between behavior which is in accord with a given community's goal-value system and behavior which is not. The failure of behavior in a rural community to accord with its *agrarianism* may be described as a discrepancy between ideals and realities. However, conflict may also exist between the goal-value systems of two or more communities. The conflict which may occur between behaviors anchored in a rural and urban community with their respective agrarianism and cosmopolitanism is also at times described as a discrepancy between ideals and realities.

It is the confusion between these possible meanings of a conflict between ideals and realities that has, in part, given the contemporary concepts of *liberalism* and *conservatism* some of the properties of a shibboleth.

Let us examine, first of all, the possible meanings of *liberalism* and *conservatism* within the framework of a single community regardless of community type. It was noted earlier that in any given community the man as an individual tends to be innovating, while in his inter-relations with others he is a restraining force. Every community offers values and opportunities to its individual members and various kinds of security for them collectively. Whatever the community, every goal-value system expresses some ratio of individuality to collectivity. Every community has individuals who would, if they could, expand the ratio of individuality to collectivity; others would expand the ratio of collectivity to individuality. Every community, in short, comprises both a liberal and conservative point of view. There is no inconsistency in speaking of a liberal and a conservative *tribalism, agrarianism, cosmopolitanism,* and *nationalism.* Within the framework of any single community, "liberalism" may be equated with "individualism" and "conservatism" with "collectivism."

In the eighteenth century, when the business groups for which Adam Smith spoke agitated against mercantilistic monopolies and for the shift of opportunity and responsibility for economic conduct to the hands of private businessmen, they were advocating a liberal position within the nation: an expansion of the ratio of individuality to collectivity within the community form. However, when the values of the society for the circles of which Adam Smith spoke were counterposed to those of traditional society, on the one hand, and to those of the backward peoples brought within the sphere of European Imperialism as liberal in contrast to non-liberal forms, the reference was no longer to inner-community orientations but to extra-community conflicts. Liberalism and conservatism have repeatedly tended to lose their significance as inner community strategies, acquiring more ambiguous standing in extra-community conflicts.

THE AUTONOMY
OF GOAL-VALUE SYSTEMS

It follows from the previous reflections that whenever a community is stable for any length of time, it tends to develop a single goal-value system. Such a system is often perceived by the members of the community as its single most significant property. Since it contains the community's objectives and shared principles for their pursuit, *the goal-value system is often seen as the very reason for the community's existence—as the thing which gives it meaning.*

Specialists in the community's goal-value system arise (medicine men, priests, wise men, shamans, mediums, prophets, ethical counselors, professors—indeed, sometimes the participants in conferences on values) who at times find it in their interest to treat the goal-value system as autonomous, self-sufficient, and somehow elevated above ordinary concerns. However, these lilies of the human pond are rooted in its muck, and slimy things often crawl about their roots and stems. If this is remembered, there is nothing at all wrong with the view that any goal-value system is the flowering symbol of a given community. When men die in the name of their values, it is because the very meaning of their social existence and the integrity of their community is threatened. The struggle is not for the lilies alone, but for the pond.

THE MAJOR AMERICAN
GOAL-VALUE SYSTEMS

The preceding distinctions have been sketched because they are needed to answer the questions posed in this paper.

If one asks what is *the* American system as if there were only one, the issue has already been pre-judged. If there are in fact a number of goal-value systems, it may be assumed that each will have its wizard or soothsayer as the case may be. The most immediate consequence of the question, what is *the* American value system, is to open the battle ot the soothsayers, as each seeks to monopolize the microphones as the one authoritative "voice of America."

If there is not one American value system, but a number, the question becomes: How are they to be distinguished? The present paper flatly maintains the proposition that there are a number of goal-value systems competing for domination of the American scene. The preceding remarks were intended to set down the basis for distinguishing between them. The community is here taken to be the natural basis for a given goal-value system; hence, if there is more than one value system it is because there is more than one community.

Moreover, if there are numerous communities struggling for ascendancy, this will in part assume the form of a battle of words—dialectical duels by the respective prophets. However, it must not be assumed that real difference between communities will be settled by summit conferences or even by fervent prayers for peace.

The Tribal Communities of the American Indian

Not all the communities that have taken part in the formation of American society have played equivalent or equally enduring roles. To the Europeans who came to the North American continent, the tribal communities of the American Indians existed only as obstacles to be overcome. These were displaced, partly destroyed, and eventually their fragments were removed to reservation lands where, at times, the communities have continued to survive in distorted forms into the present. However, the goal-value systems of the American Indian tribes have not penetrated the goal-value systems of American society.

American Rural Communities

The Europeans who established the communities of the North American colonies took as their starting point the communal forms they had known in Europe. In the seventeenth century Europe was still dominated by feudal communities and by cities. Some European nations were in the course of formation at the time, but the process had advanced so little that the despots of the period were still able to view the national states as their private property. The early American rural communities were formed in some measure according to European feudal models.

This is no place to examine the details of the agrarian communities of feudal Europe. It is sufficient to note that they represented a series of formations ranging from more or less autonomous peasant communities to manorial communities in which legal, administrative, and military competence was consolidated in the hands of hereditary, castle-dwelling families. Both peasant village and manorial community operated almost exclusively on a subsistence basis. The ordinary individual varied in status from that of free peasant to that of serf.

While there were some attempts to introduce feudal communities in the new world (such as the Dutch patroonship and the various experiments in that direction in the southern colonies), there were a number of factors working against them: (1) the new world was opened up by capitalistically inclined adventurers and by profit-sharing companies which intended, not to establish new world subsistence communities, but to make profits through the export of raw materials and agricultural products; and (2) the new world did not present a panorama of peasant communities which could form the foundation of a manorial system, as in Europe. Hence, in colonial America, where such capitalistically motivated adventures proved to be profitable, a course of development was set in motion, not toward manorial communities operating on a subsistence basis, but toward market-oriented plantation agriculture in a system of colonial capitalism. The structures that emerged in the southern colonies of North America bear more similarities to the colonial capitalism of ancient Rome or Carthage than to the manors of medieval Europe.

Southern Plantation Communities. The plantation system of colonial capitalism of the southern colonies could not count, as did European manors, on the labor sources of peasant villages. Labor sources were sought by attempts to enslave the American Indians (which, for cultural reasons, did not work), by the use of indentured servants (which was costly, and at best temporary), and finally by Negro slavery. The production of the plantations was not for subsistence purposes but for European export, indigo, tobacco, and later, cotton being the most important items. The planters strengthened their ties with upper class European circles by importing their luxury goods and imitating their styles, often securing continental educations for their sons, remaining in touch with upper class political trends. At home the growth of the plantation system created tension with the yeoman farmer. Moreover, whenever the plantation system reached such a density as to affect the economy of an area as a whole, it set a characteristic trend in motion. The non-slave owning farmer was depressed into cultural and technological backwardness by the competition of the slave plantation. The yeoman farmer either migrated from the plantation-dominated area or was depressed into a cycle of cultural and economic backwardness, becoming, in the language of the area, "poor white trash." Moreover, plantation society began to evolve into the unique goal-value system romanticized in ante-bellum literature and castigated in abolitionist literature.

From the late eighteenth century to the Civil War, the tidewater planter continued to cherish those qualities for which he gained early renown—social grace, urbanity, a nodding acquaintance with Horace and Blackstone, a dash of hot temper which sometimes led to the duelling field, and a reckless hospitality—though all the while he was losing money through the suicidal economics of the plantation system. The Civil War merely dealt him an heroic *coup de grace.* Yet while it lasted, it had been an attractive life.[3]

Though the main structure of plantation society was shattered by the Civil War and its aftermath, fragments of it continue to create problems into the present: the plantation system was not destroyed; it merely assumed somewhat different form (for example, lawyers, speculators, and former townsmen purchased the plantations of former southern families for prestige or investment reasons), and cotton and tobacco continued to be the main cash crops. Though slavery had been eliminated, segregation and various devices to reduce the Negro to second-class citizenship took its place, while various economic substitutes for the slave system were found (gang-labor systems, tenancy, the crop lien system, etc.); and the tensions between the plantation and the non-plantation farmer continued to operate against the social and economic improvement of the latter. Further, fragments of the goal-value system developed in ante-bellum days continued to give a regional shaping to the goals and values of the South.

One of the goal-value systems still operating with some power within the framework of American society and influencing its farm policy was formed on the basis of the plantation system of colonial capitalism, and is still anchored in the fragments of this system that remain in the South.

Northern Village Communities. In the northern colonies of colonial North America, the trading companies which organized colonization adventures did not usually succeed in making a profit for their backers. This, together with the fact that some of the colonists entered upon these adventures to escape religious persecution, inclined the members of the northern colonies to buy out their financial backers and take the affairs of their communities into their own hands, while their sponsors were happy to liquidate unprofitable investments. The compact, autonomous, self-governing farm community that resulted, as Henry Sumner Maine noted in his study of *Village Communities of the East and West,* reproduced all the main elements of the primitive European village community. They were formed of a nucleus of houses around a village common. They possessed village wood lots. With great frequency the village church served also as a town hall, and village affairs were decided in a town meeting. The villages often turned into little theocracies. Their officials and institutions, and the functions of both, were not essentially different from those of the medieval village community.

They were able to generate a degree of religious bigotry and political inflexibility that forced the experiments in religious tolerance by Anne Hutchinson and Roger Williams and also the experiments in political democracy by Thomas Hooker. *The village community provided the environment for the formation of one of the most powerful goal-value systems still effective in American society, a goal-value system centering in the town meeting democracy, religious toleration, civic consciousness, and a readiness to take community action to meet social requirements.*

The village community system dominated the development of the northern colonies, and provided the primary pattern for settlement of the Old Northwest (the basic Land Ordinance of 1885). In the Old Northwest elements of the northern village community fused easily with elements of the yeoman farmers forced to migrate by the growth of the plantation system in the South. Hence, in the Old Northwest the plantation system never gained a strong foothold.

Meanwhile, from colonial days throughout the nineteenth century the village community was rapidly ceasing to be essentially a subsistence community of peasants, and was being transformed into a community of market-oriented farmers. A number of factors played a role in this change. The new world had an abundance of land. There was every reason for the sons of an agricultural husbandman to aspire to farms of their own. However, to start a farm on virgin land required, even at the time, considerable capital: tools, equipment, farm animals, and supplies. Besides, the purchase price of land had to be found. From colonial days onward there was a powerful tendency for young men to go into debt for the capital to start farms of their own. This immediately meant that they looked upon their agricultural activities, not merely for subsistence, but for market possibilities with which to pay off their indebtedness. They were quick to explore every chance for cash crops.

Moreover, wherever this process was going on, there was a chronic shortage of workers, for about the time a man's sons reached their full utility as workers, they went out to establish farms of their own. There was thus a constant tendency to substitute machinery for human labor. When machinery had to be purchased and paid for, market orientation was reinforced. As a chronic debtor class, farmers supported all political devices for supplying cheap money, and they advocated public policies for the development of transportation facilities which aided access to markets. *Almost from the beginning, the rural husbandman on the American scene was transformed from a peasant working on a subsistence basis into a farmer producing for the market. He was drawn step by step into activity extending beyond his village concerns toward the wider markets for the sale of his goods and toward the wider political system which bore upon his financial and market problems.* The planter evolving from the system of colonial capitalism had operated in national and international markets and politics from the beginning; the northern farmer was drawn out of his village community by his own market and political concerns to confront the planter in the national and international markets with a different set of interests. The one carried with him the goal-value systems developed in plantation communities, the other carried with him the goal-value system developed in village communities of peasants evolving into farmers.

Peasant, Theocratic, and Utopian Farm Communities in America. From time to time various peasant, theocratic, and experimental utopian rural communities have either been transported to America or have been formed in American society. Such, for example, have been the various Amish, Mennonite, and Hutterite communities, from colonial days through the nineteenth century. During the nineteenth century a number of utopian and theocratic rural communities came into being. The most important of these were the Mormon communities which formed from fragments of New England village communities and the religious experiences and organizational abilities of Joseph Smith and Brigham Young. The Mormons occupied the inter-mountain area, originally establishing theocratically-dominated village communities very similar to the original New England forms. However, under the influence of the wider economic and political environment, all such American rural communities tended to follow the same general course toward increasingly national market and political orientation, as did the early New England forms. The Mormons are particularly interesting in that they have tended to emerge under the Eisenhower administration as a belated but powerful reinforcement of that part of the goal-value system of the Republican Party which derives originally from the goal-value system of the New England village community.

American Urban Communities

If we conceive of an urban community as a complete, autonomous way of life and not simply as an aggregation of people, there is no irony in the idea that while the modern world has enormously increased urban aggregations, it has simultaneously destroyed the urban community. Max Weber was of the opinion that the high point of the Western city was attained in the sixteenth century. At that time European cities were still, with some variations, autonomous, self-governing communities, pursuing their urban economic policies, even largely controlling their own tax destinies, and operating under their own elected officials in terms of their own legal and administrative institutions. They constructed and kept in repair their own fortifications, and maintained their own civic armies.[4]

By the seventeenth century the growing national states had developed sufficient power to make serious inroads into the autonomy of the cities. The monarchs increasingly took into their own hands powers that had formerly belonged to the cities: tax powers, military powers, control of economic policies affecting the urban economy, and the like. However, in the seventeenth century the European city was still very much a going concern. In so far as urban traditions made their appearance in the North American colonies, they were a reproduction of current, primarily English, urban traditions.

However, there were a number of reasons why European urban traditions were not reproduced in the new world with any degree of completeness: (1) The new world was a frontier, colonial area and even at the termination of the Revolution was only about 8 per cent urban, and (2) the cities on the North American continent were being founded precisely at a time when the autonomy of the city was declining in Europe. While the older European cities had thousand-year-old traditions and the complete complement of institutions which would operate to slow the corrosion of the urban community, this was com-

pletely lacking in the new world. In the colonial period mercantilistic
Tory elements had no reason to strengthen the cities and form them
into strong, integral unities; it would only have created a force with
which they would have to contend. After the Revolution, the cities
were largely left to their own devices to grow in whatever manner they
would. When nineteenth-century developments led to the founding
and expansion of cities, they were usually modeled after the federal
government. They were overrun by graft and civic corruption to a
point where Lord Bryce described them as the single most conspicuous
failure of government in America.

The result of all this is the apparent paradox that despite the
enormous urban aggregations in America, the urban community has
little reality in the United States. The goal-value systems peculiar to
the city *cosmopolitanism* have developed only slightly. While in their
village communities and small towns Americans display a civic consciousness and responsibility, in their cities this is too often replaced by
apathy. Americans simply have not lived in integrated urban communities long enough to bear the imprint of distinctive civic traditions.[5]

In an ancient land of cities such as Italy, its cities have left an imprint on their inhabitants. The individual is above all a citizen of a
city and will instantly, for example, perceive the difference between,
say, a Neapolitan and a Florentine. His city places its stamp in-
delibly on the Italian urbanite, and this is manifest not only in the
variations of his dialect, but in his attitudes, outlook, tastes, preferences
in literature, and even the form of his humor.

Cosmopolitanism, the goal-value system of the city, finds its point
of gravity in the color, variety, excitement, and contrasts of the urban
milieu. Its love of the exotic is counterbalanced by its discrimination.
It thrives in the salon, the coffee house, the drawing room, and the
café. Its insight dwells in the sparkle of wit, and its thought assumes
the form of rational argument. It is adept in the interplay of social
surfaces, and it transforms judgments of morality into judgments of
taste. The comedy of manners and psychological drama are the natural
art forms of the self-conscious urbanism.

There are, of course, cosmopolites in America, and the various cities
differ somewhat in the comprehensiveness of the circles in which
genuine cosmopolitanism thrives. However, our cities do not leave their
imprint with any depth on their members. After a season or two goes
by, it is almost impossible to tell, without asking him, whether an individual originally came from Los Angeles or Pittsburgh, Chicago or

New Orleans. Though there are fragments of a cosmopolitan goal-value system, they are neither deeply rooted nor well developed among the American value systems.

What at times passes for cosmopolitanism in America is something very different: the *ethnocentrism* of some of the many ethnic communities which form in American cities. Many of the ethnic ghettos of American cities leave deeper and more distinctive marks upon their members than do the cities at large. The lack of cosmopolitanism could not be more dramatically revealed than in mistaking for it the goal-value systems of ethnic ghettos. The parochialism of an ethnic ghetto is the contradiction of cosmopolitanism; if anything, it approximates *tribalism*.

The American National Community

American history falls almost completely within the time period of the modern nation. For many years, in the course of the rise of the modern state, it was possible for the monarchs and their royal families to view the state as their private property. In Europe, the rising states for a time promoted the growth of the cities as sources of taxable wealth. However, once they grew strong enough, the states took over functions that had been permitted earlier to be consolidated in civic hands. The rising states, when it suited their purposes, also promoted various extra-feudal and extra-civic economic forms. At times they took positions in the religious controversies and for the same reason. In all such activities the rulers of the states and their ministers had only their own private interests in mind. As late as the eighteenth century, the enlightened despots of Europe could still view their states as private property.

However, all these activities including the promotion of national economies, national religions, national languages, and the formation of national traditions led increasing numbers of individuals to re-orient their activities around the national state. The revolutions of the eighteenth century (including the American) merely confirmed re-orientation of institutions that the nation represented. Tocqueville observed that the French Revolution carried out a greater consolidation of national power in a decade than the previous monarchy had managed in centuries. The observation holds for all the national revolutions.

In America, too, the Revolution left the national state in the hands of former subjects. The United States was set upon a course which would involve the continual consolidation of federal power at the expense of local forms. The three great nationally shared experiences that have shaped the nation into a unit are the frontier experience which came to a close in 1890, the massive immigrations of the nineteenth century which did not cease until World War I, and the dramatic rise of the mass society in the twentieth century.

As the American nation began to take shape in the nineteenth century, the complex of sentiment it represented took the form of national territorial aspirations, a national policy on immigration and population, and the formation of typical national attitudes on religion, politics, and economics. A national goal-value system began to form, and it continues to evolve partly in accord with, partly in competition with, the goal-value systems of its many sub-communities.

THE CONFLICT AND ACCOMMODATION OF AMERICAN COMMUNITY FORMS

There may be some differences in the way these various American communities are conceived, but there is, I believe, no dispute about their existence. Who would deny that the forms of American life are distributed in rural villages, small provincial towns, great impersonal metropolitan aggregations, defiant ethnic ghettos, supercilious and exclusive status circles, sluggish regional formations, and patriotic national complexes? There may be some dispute about the forms and seriousness of the conflicts that arise between these many communities and their respective goal-value systems, but there is no dispute about the existence of such conflicts. Need such conflicts exist? Why in our democratic menagerie of community forms should they not happily co-exist?

One of the current stereotyped methods of dodging the potential embarrassments contained in acknowledging the existence of community conflict is to shrug them off patriotically as "the American way." The institutional device for handling such conflicts is to refer them to a congressional committee, trusting in its capacity to dodge the issue and postpone action on it for a time. However, it is not possible to avoid permanently the conflict of community forms. One is inclined to laugh it off only when it seems unimportant. If the appropriate attitude toward conflicts between community forms is amusement, the American Civil War was one of the biggest jokes in history.

The unavoidability of community conflicts arises out of the nature of the community and the fact that the various American communities are competing for the lives of the same people. Any single community represents a movement toward a total way of life. When permitted to develop without interference, it integrates all the activities that make up a complete life into a single unity. It will comprise all the activities in the cycle of a normal year and all the institutions in the cycle of a normal life.

A person whose life is simultaneously subject to the claims of two communities may hope to make the best of both worlds, but he is also certain to experience repeated occasions when his loyalties are divided and when he sees himself destined to lose, no matter what he does. Long ago in their study of *The Polish Peasant in Europe and America,* Thomas and Znaniecki[6] typed the kinds of life adjustment of the individual caught between an ethnic community and a wider urban community as tenacious traditionalism (Philistinism), as an unstable wavering between the requirements of both communities (Bohemianism), and as purely personal adjustment that synthesizes the best of both worlds (creative adjustment). Such a person, described by Park and Stonequist as a "marginal man" moving in the area between two worlds, is also, at times, tempted to play in-group, out-group with each side as it best suits his purposes, thus turning into a kind of professional double agent.

The members of an ethnic community trying to survive within the confines of a large American city have little doubt as to what is necessary if they are to maintain their ethnic identity. As far as possible they must provide a complete set of institutions, enough to occupy the whole of the individual's life. The elders particularly dream of establishing a parochial school, for they know that otherwise, day by day, the young will quietly drift away; while alien traditions are learned, their own are not.

However, it is impossible for an ethnic community to supply to its members out of its own resources all of the richness that is offered by a surrounding world. For one thing, the members of an ethnic group, precisely because they are an ethnic group, are in an inferior economic and political situation. (The early Irish worked on the canals and railroads, the Italians on road and sewer projects, the Poles as unskilled workers in the steel mills, eastern European Jews as garment workers, the Chinese coolies as unskilled workers on the Southern Pacific Railroad, the Filipinos as bus boys, dish washers, and unskilled farm hands, the Mexicans as migrant farm hands). A young man growing up in an ethnic ghetto would have to be comparatively deficient in normal impulses not to envy the economic and political opportunities offered by the world outside his ghetto. Under ordinary circumstances the majority of persons remained inside the ghetto only when they were met by powerful prejudice from the outside. At times external prejudice has been powerful enough to keep a young Chinese college graduate at work in a hand laundry, a young Jewish political scientist in the family's clothing store or delicatessen, or a young Negro lawyer in the situation of marginal ambulance chasing. But even under such circumstances it remains difficult to maintain the ethnic community unchanged. It is even possible under conditions of powerful external prejudice on the one hand, and a coherent set of ethnic institutions operating from within on the other, to create the situation where the ethnic community undergoes a series of changes, each approximating the majority community more closely and each stage being accompanied by the loss of some of its members to the outside.

The conflict between the ethnic community, its goal-value system, and the majority community is unavoidable. In the first place, the ethnic community forms because aliens facing an impersonal, if not hostile, surrounding world tend automatically to seek out persons who speak their own language and share the same problems and to enter into a common life with them. Gradually they create the institutions of a sub-community, forming a church of their own, forming mutual benefit insurance societies and labor unions (to avoid exploitation by members of the surrounding world and by unscrupulous members of their own ethnic group), forming specialty stores which stock their favorite or traditional foods, patronizing restaurants which prepare traditional foods, establishing a foreign language newspaper, undertaking the construction and support of a parochial school—or in lieu of such a school, offering special classes, in connection with the church or some other going association, in the native language, literature, history, and culture —establishing literary, dramatic, and musical societies, forming patriotic societies to celebrate and commemorate traditional cultural and political occasions, and perhaps to raise funds and bring pressures to change the original homeland. In short, the ethnic community arises in the course of the attempt by pluralities of aliens, like all men, to live a fuller and more abundant life within the happy circle of their kind.

However, the success of an ethnic community in forming a protective communal shell around its members is no guarantee that the community as a whole or its members will either be permitted or even universally want to continue in that condition. Members of minority communities often develop marginal industries into profitable form only to have members of the majority community cast envious eyes upon these very industries once they have been transformed into profitable undertakings. When the west coast Japanese, for example, took up marginal, unproductive land and developed highly profitable specialty market-garden crops upon it, they suddenly found the big guns of prejudice turned on them in the course of the expropriation of their rights. No complete study has ever been made of all the hundreds of marginal industries turned into profitable businesses which have then been pre-empted by members of the majority.

However, this is by no means the whole of the story. The tendency of an ethnic minority to develop into a complete community gives some of its members the opportunity to learn many skills that majority communities also require: leadership skills, dramatic skills, writing skills (in service of the foreign language press), and legal skills (by lawyers of the minority group). Whenever he shows real talent, the ethnic actor, lawyer, journalist, musician, or labor leader may suddenly find that opportunities in the wider world open to him. Meanwhile, economically and politically successful members of the minority find it increasingly easy to marry into the outside world, adding "social success" to their other achievements. Furthermore, some members of the ethnic group act as leaders of the ethnic community and as its representatives to the outside. They are often especially tempted to enter into social arrangements with the outside world and to introduce its patterns to the insiders they represent. Finally, the ethnic community forms a protective shell around its members, acting to some extent like a hot house, where its internal forms can flourish until the time is ripe for transplanting them outside.

By the time, however, that members at all levels of an ethnic community begin to depart into the outside world, there is already a complex investment in institutions, in money, and in individuals with a stake in the continuation of the ethnic community. The ethnic community may respond to the threat of breakdown by organizing new social forms to counteract it. Still new societies are formed to "meet the needs of the new generation." It is not impossible that research students may be hired and that "scientific studies" may be made of the problems of the group. Active campaigns may be carried through to "modernize" the institutions and to reenlist the active support of those tending to slip away.

Thus, with time, and with great difficulty, and often with tragic and always exciting drama, a great richness of social experience is unfolded to accomplish, in the end, what the reformers had tried to achieve directly—*assimilation*. The assimilation program was well meaning and essentially correct, but it was destined to be hated and misunderstood by the very groups it proposed to help. When millions of ethnic aliens were crowded into unstructured metropolitan environments in the growth period of rising mass industry, they created an almost unprecedented opportunity for exploitation, corruption, disorganization, and reorganization into underworld forms. One cynical response to the often terrifying conditions of urban environments was to blame the alien himself. This placed the blame for the disaster on its victims. But well-meaning social workers and reformers resisted this cynicism, which seemed to them only to abet the very human corrosion that existed. They saw, quite correctly, that if there were no cultural differences between the alien and his environment, the exploitation would not be so easy. Hence, they worked hard to establish Americanization classes and to provide instruction in the knowledge and skills which would increase the efficiency of the aliens. However, to many aliens in the process of forming into ethnic communities, the work of the reformers could only appear as the last straw—a force against the formation of the ethnic ghetto. Therefore the forces of the ethnic community were often brought into opposition to the Americanization plans of the reformers. Programs formulated by persons with high ideals and often at great time, trouble, and expense sometimes failed sadly. Classes were unattended, teachers were scorned, and programs were feared. Assimilation became—and for many groups it still is—one of the most hated forms of the ethnic communities.

Assimilation is one of the many names for the process of establishing one community and one goal-value system—perhaps with differences of internal emphasis and outlook—where two existed before. The thousands of ethnic groups in the United States which have been assimilated or which continue in the process of assimilation are all illustrations of the conflict and accommodation of American sub-communities. Not the least interesting phenomenon to appear, as an ethnic group undergoes the last stages of assimilation, is the emergence of individuals who set up little stands and sell American flags on all patriotic occasions. The current reputations of some notable social scientists rest on such enterprise. The ardent flag-waving of the newly assimilated—as a sort of patriotic *nouveau riche*—seems to exorcise the last vestige of guilt associated with desertion of the ruins of an ethnic community. In fact, at this stage the fragments of the ethnic community can even be tenderly preserved in museums, histories, and the like, as the mausoleums of a defunct culture.

Parallel to the excessively vocal patriotism of the more articulate members of the ethnic ghetto in the process of being dismantled, is an excessive conformity of the average member to the norms of the majority. It is as if the once-forced conformity to the ethnic group had to be paid for by a stronger than usual new conformity. Around this new conformity a number of additional traits tend to be arranged, the most important of which are the expectations of individual and social progress. The world of the parents is rejected; the individual expects—and his parents usually share the expectation—that he will occupy a higher social station than they. It has been argued by Margaret Mead in *Keep Your Powder Dry* that this so-called third generation complex is the central phenomenon of the American mind, the most distinctive of all its properties.

This third generation American, always moving on, always in his hopes moving up, leaving behind him all that was his past and greeting with enthusiasm any echo of that past when he meets it in the life of another, represents one typical theme of the American character structure.[7]

When I say that we are most of us—whatever our origins—third generation in character structure, I mean that we have been reared in an atmosphere which is most like that . . . for the third generation. Father is to be outdistanced and outmoded . . . he is out of date.[8]

While there is no doubt that this is an important product of the transformation of American communities and value systems, it is only one of many processes. There is some distortion in visualizing all Americans as originating in ethnic ghettos or of relating all patterns to this one. It is even logically inconsistent, for in the first place the formation of an ethnic ghetto presupposes the prior existence of a non-ghettoized world. To treat the third generation mentally as the only typical one is to visualize a caste system without any Brahmins. Besides, factually, the conflict and accommodation of ethnic and majority communities is only one form of community interrelation. In addition, America has displayed rural communities in conflict with small towns,

towns with large cities; regional communities have contested with one another; and all sub-communities have come into conflict and accommodation with the national community.

THE FIRST NATIONAL SYNTHESIS
OF AN AMERICAN
GOAL-VALUE SYSTEM—
THE RISE OF THE YANKEE
AS THE DISTINCTIVE AMERICAN TYPE

In the conflict of the many sub-communities with one another, as exemplified by the ethnic and majority communities, there is a tendency for the more powerful, which is usually also the more comprehensive community, to win. The town grows at the expense of the village, the city at the expense of the town, and the nation at the expense of the city. Moreover, sometimes the arena for the conflict between two different sub-communities is shifted to a community more comprehensive than both. For example, the conflict between Negro and white communities of the American South after the Civil War took place within the framework of the region. The conflict between the farm communities of the Old Northwest and the eastern industrial-financial centers prior to the Civil War shifted to the framework of the growing nation. So, too, did the conflict between the plantation-dominated South (technologically backward and resting on slave labor) and the industrial and farm-village communities of the North (resting on a progressive technology and free labor). This is no place to trace in detail all the forms that community conflict may assume. However, it should perhaps be noted that not all forms of such community conflict have the components of alienness and prejudice peculiar to ethnic and majority communities.

However, with the tendency for each conflict to shift to the arena of most comprehensive power, a transvaluation of goals occurs. When former rural communities are replaced by the city, there is a simultaneous redefinition of goals. Though their private preferences were at opposite ends of the scale, the agrarian mystic Oswald Spengler[9] and the cosmopolitan sophisticate Georg Simmel[10] were agreed that the European peasant rural communities and the city differed in characteristic ways: the core of economic life shifted from agricultural to non-agricultural pursuits; a subsistence economy was replaced by a money and market economy; property in land ceased to be the main type of wealth; the organic rhythms of the natural year were replaced by artificial clock and calendar schedules; the family and age grades declined in importance as the clique and social class arose; and even the very modes of thought were changed as a traditional outlook was thrust aside in place of a logical and rational point of view.

The city needs the food and raw materials produced in the country, but when an urban environment takes the place of the formerly autonomous countryside, rural pursuits are not abandoned but reorganized, by degrees, to correspond to a new set of social needs. If he is to produce for an urban market, the countryman must take over the urban money economy. The countryman's needs, in turn, become a market for urban production. The countryman may find it advisable to specialize in new ways, for urban aggregations often make it profitable to concentrate production on highly specialized items. The countryman looks to the city for a more exotic variety of entertainment than he could ever supply himself. The standards of the urbanite increasingly become his standards. Between rural communities and the city, a process of accommodation generally similar to that of ethnic and majority communities occurs.

The transfer of the arena of community conflict to the next higher level of power[11] is an aspect of a process which in the community at large directly parallels the formation of economic consolidations and mergers and the increasing domination of an area of economic life by a few giant concerns. These two kinds of consolidation are merely a specific and general form of the same process. In fact, the community framework within which the giant economic concerns of contemporary North America operate is provided not by the rural community, the ethnic community, or even the city, but by the nation. *The social historical phenomenon of greatest importance on the American social scene—more important than any of the conflicts of American subcommunities—is the growth of the nation at the expense of all local forms.*[12]

The growth of the American nation, the most comprehensive and powerful community of American society, has been accomplished by the destruction of sub-communities and the reincorporation of their fragments into a new system. To a considerable extent the integration of the nation and the predominance of its goal-value system are to be measured by their capacity to create new and special social types. The long-standing dominant communities of the past in their time created their own special social types. This was inevitable, since people are molded to the forms of their societies; and societies, in turn, are the structures which arise in the social behaviors of their members. A social type is an individual whose behavior epitomizes the goal-value system of his community. The communities of hunter and gatherer created the *tribesman;* rural subsistence communities sustained the *peasant;*[13] the urban community supplied the social foundation for the *citizen;* and the new community of the nation-state has created the *national.*

Their preoccupation with sub-communities, unfortunately, has led many American sociologists not only to ignore the rise of the national community but to thrust aside the study of the *national* as an unscientific problem existing only in the unreliable intuitions of persons untrained in the methods of exact science. While political scientists, journalists, anthropologists, and some historians have seen the problem of *national character* as a distinctive issue of our time, it is rare to find the term in the average sociological work. This situation is changing, however, and C. Wright Mills, David Riesman, and the political sociologists are implicitly and explicitly raising the problems of the national community and the social types it sustains.

In other contexts, on the basis of a review of much of the literature on American character, the following formulations were made:

A European, observing an individual who chews gum constantly on the streets, in the museum, restaurant, or café, or at the theatre, will recognize him as an American. If one asks the European for other American traits, he will often say that the American drinks too much; that, in fact, he seems to have a Germanic tendency to identify hard drinking as "he-man" but is without other aspects of the German. He bows instantly to the cultural superiority of his womenfolk and, indeed, seems to identify all higher culture as feminine. His imagination seems to run naturally to exaggeration, and his humor inclines always toward the tall tale. Yet he seems most marked by his practical efficiency. A European, observing a man with any—or particularly with some combination of these traits—will instantly recognize him as an American. A list of additional traits arranged around this core would only emphasize the fact that some traits and trait combinations are typically American. While they typify the American, they distinguish him from the Englishman, the German, the Frenchman, and the Russian.[14]

In this context a more compact summary of American traits was offered:

All major observers agree that American character tends to manifest great practicality, considerable anti-intellectualism, a genius for organization, a strong materialism, a tendency to conceptualize social and political affairs in moralistic terms, a manifestation of great faith in individual initiative, and a sense of civic responsibility. These are the major clues to American character, and the Yankee emerges as the central and unique American type.[15]

The study in which these formulations were made was dominated by objectives different from that of the present paper. While the present paper is concerned with the status of American goals and values, the quoted study was guided by the attempt to examine not the unity of the nation but the variety of its sub-communities. The formulations on American character were designed to supply a general rational reference point from which the variations in America's sub-communities could be evaluated. However, these formulations can serve as an equally valid reference point for the present discussion, but attention is focused not on the spokes and rim of the wheel but on the hub.

This list of traits and trait-combinations is about as near to a general characterization of the uniqueness of the American national as it is possible to formulate. Moreover, the general historical process by which these American traits arose out of American sub-communities can be traced.

The social composition of the eastern seaboard of colonial North America was initially fixed by the fact that the majority of its inhabitants were north European (predominantly English) middle and lower-middle class townsmen of a variety of Protestant faiths. There was no extensive peasant contingent among them; there was only a comparatively thin stratum of upper middle class and royalist elements. Though the primitiveness of frontier traditions forced a rural way of life on the majority of the colonial Americans, their "natural" community was the town rather than the rural village, and they were dominated by a "civic" rather than by a traditional "agrarian" mentality.

The pioneer farmer in America did not have a peasant's attitude toward the land. His orientation to the wilderness was more that of the miner or extractor. With great frequency he was derived not from peasant but from middle class urban stock. Paxson's description of the American frontiersman does not create the picture of a peasant who knows how to handle natural conditions and materials, but of a person comparatively unprepared for situations of extensive primitivism. The pioneer's situation, incidentally, was structured by the influence of speculative motives more natural to an urban than to a rural situation.

The rough and winding paths through the mountain gaps forced the average migrant to abandon hope of quick return. The separation that induced self-reliance in government forced the pioneer to make his own furniture, build his own house out of local materials, and get along with what his environment could supply him . . . . Where there were deep streams, private speculators conducted private ferries at extortional rates.

The typical home was the cabin built of logs and limited by the shape of the material to small rooms, low ceilings, and single stories. In the cabin attic, reached by a ladder of saplings and restricted by the slope of a leaky roof, were pallets and rough beds of log frames with rope or rawhide bottoms. What the axe, maul, and wedge could not produce was lacking from the ordinary home. Nails were too rare for common use, and wooden pegs did service for them. Mortar and plaster were beyond the domestic architect, but mud could and did stop the chinks between the logs.

The housewife came to her new home young and raw, and found for neighbors other girls as inexperienced. She bore many children, and buried a staggering number of them, for medicine and sanitation, inadequate everywhere, were out of reach for the cabin on the border. She fed her man and raised her children, cooked their food and laid it by for the winter. She was at once butcher, packer, and baker. The family clothes showed her craftsmanship, with skins playing a large part, and homespun or knitting revealed a luxury established.[16]

When he studied conditions in America in the 1830's, Tocqueville was struck by the frequency of the derivation of the American frontiersmen from urban middle class situations.

The greater part of the adventurers who migrate every year to people the Western wilds belong . . . to the old Anglo-American race of the Northern States. Many of these men, who rush so boldly onward in pursuit of wealth, were already in the enjoyment of a competency in their own part of the country. They take their wives along with them, and make them share the countless perils and privations which always attend the commencement of these expeditions.[17]

However, this gets ahead of the story. The dominant element in the colonial mind was supplied by middle class Protestant townsmen. Even when peasant settlements were made in the colonies, as in the case of the Mennonites and Amish of Pennsylvania, they tended to remain locked in their self-sufficient peasant communities and did not become a general influence upon the colonial outlook. The early Swedish settlements were composed of urban middle class elements like their Anglo-Saxon neighbors. The French Huguenots were also the counterpart of the urban middle class elements from England. Both the Swedes and the Huguenots were easily assimilated into the colonial population, accenting its central traits.

The major colonial class division existed between the average colonist and the thin stratum of upper class Tories—mercantilistic business

men, governors, and administrators. The average colonist was, in outlook if not in fact, a townsman with a townsman's loyalties. He was
somewhat suspicious of the upper class Tory elements which were
bearers of British nationalism and loyal to the Crown. In England, too,
in this period, a similar tension was manifest between the House of
Commons and the Crown. In the revolutionary period, the colonies had
much moral support in the Commons. From the standpoint of class-
based loyalties, the American Revolution can be visualized as a struggle
between colonial townsmen and upper class Tory elements loyal to
the Crown. Thus, the victory of the American Revolution left the
middle class Protestant townsmen in unquestioned control of the destinies of the United States.

The particularism of townsmen (which would raise loyalties to the
local community above all loyalties to inter-local combinations) was
strong in the days following the Revolution. In the teeth of the obvious
fact that the national government was in their own hands, the colonists
retained a powerful suspicion of central government. The Bill of Rights
is a monument to this attitude. The world was, after all, entering a
period of national consolidations of economic, political, and social life.
Economic, financial, and political concerns were in considerable measure national and international. Hamilton represented those economic
and financial interests in the new state that seized the economic and
financial opportunities that had been forcefully vacated by the British.
Second, the threat of a reinvasion of the state by the British made it
militarily advisable to strengthen the central government. Finally, a
newly-rising society on the frontier was raising problems which it was
unable to solve by its own resources, and was pressing the state and
central governments for assistance. The chief of the frontier problems
requiring federal help were transportation and the Indians. Hence,
while the mentality of townsmen remained dominant, a new national
mentality was rising. The townsman was the clearest voice within the
latter.

Between the period of the forming of the new state and the Civil
War, the evolving community structures of the United States were
shaping into three regional groupings—the Northeast, the South, and
the Old Northwest. The contrast between the northern village communities and the southern plantation communities has already been
sketched. In both North and South the agricultural husbandman was
evolving into a farmer, though in different ways. However, of greater
importance for the moment was the existence of two sets of class

tensions, the resolution of which eventually tended to strengthen the national community as against all of the regions.

The lesser of the class tensions in the early state period were between the eastern capitalist, banker, businessman, and western frontiersman. It is a mistake to view this as a rural *versus* urban conflict, for as noted earlier, the frontiersman was often rural only from necessity. He was often motivated by the desire for speculative profits. He mined the land for its superficial resources, and often left a semi-ruined farm behind him. Only gradually during the course of the nineteenth century, when genuine peasant types (such as the Germans and Scandinavians) settled on the land abandoned by the pioneer farmers, was the same land improved and brought under intensive cultivation. Meanwhile, the original "Old Yankee" pioneer farmer had often cannily moved into the newly forming towns, organized the banks, businesses, and enterprises. The pioneer farmer of the Old Northwest was derived from middle class elements of the eastern seaboard, even as his forefathers on the coast had been derived from middle class elements from north European countries. Between the Old Northwest and the Northeast a drama was played out somewhat similar to the previous drama between the colonists and England. This time, however, the western banker and business man played the role parallel to the Tories of the colonial period. However, between the eastern and midwestern groups there was a more fundamental kinship than in their colonial counterparts. The psychology of both groups was essentially middle class, for they represented the upper and lower sections of the middle classes; they were creditor and debtor regions respectively. The mentality of both east and midwest was essentially that of middle class townsmen. The easterners were Episcopalians, Congregationalists, and Unitarians; the midwesterners were Presbyterians, Baptists, and Methodists. The moment their situation improved and their indebtedness declined, the midwesterners behaved precisely like their Eastern cousins. In fact, as soon as their fortunes improved they liked nothing better than to send their daughters to Boston finishing schools and their sons to Harvard.

The dominant social classes of the Northeast and the Old Northwest carried their problems to a national level. The easterners sought federal support of tariff policies which would protect their new businesses, and they also wanted to establish a national banking system. The midwesterners sought federal support to bring the Indians under control, to finance the building of roads and canals, and later, the railroads. They also sought federal support of liberal land policies and cheap money schemes. As Northeast and Old Northwest carried their contests to a national level, each helped strengthen those aspects of the federal government which would take care of its particular needs.

The major class tension joined the Northeast and Old Northwest in opposition to the South. The plantation communities were tied to the other regions in a number of ways. The northeast manufacturing area was one of the primary markets for southern cotton. Whenever the slave plantation system began to dominate an area, it either drove the non-slave owner to migrate or to retreat to marginal lands, particularly to the Old Northwest. The South was a traditional low tariff area, which put it in tension with the North. The protective tariffs resorted to by the North for the benefit of budding industries guaranteed the high price of southern imports. As an area resting on a wasteful system of agricultural practices, the South contested with the West in the attempt to extend the plantation system. This ran counter to the Western drive from liberal, small, individualized land holdings. Eventually the advanced technology and free labor system of the North clashed with the unprogressive technology and slave labor system of the South. However, the South had rich political traditions and skills carried over from colonial days to bring national support to its interests. The manner in which the southern plantation system tended to channelize political skills has been recounted by Page:

Government was the passion of the Southerner. Trained from his earliest youth by the care and mastery of slaves, and the charge of affairs which demanded the qualities of mastership, the control of men became habitual with him, and domination became an instinct. Consequently, the only fields which he regarded as desirable were those which afforded him the opportunity for its exercise.

Thus every young Southerner of good social connection who was too poor to live without work, or too ambitious to be contented with his plantation, devoted himself to the learned professions—the law being the most desirable as offering the best opportunity for forensic display, and being the surest stepping-stone to political preferment.[18]

Here, too, the contest was shifted to the national scene. The Civil War tremendously strengthened the national community, and led to a reconstitution and simplification of an emerging national character. The war greatly reduced the role of the goal-value system of the South in the emerging national scheme. The war also forced a fusion with many mutual compromises between Northeast and West. In the newly constituted Republican Party the mentality of the middle class Protestant townsman was lifted above the regional formations that contributed most to it and placed in a dominant position on a national scale. The concessions made by the East to the West in the course of this development were notable, including the Homestead Act, the Morrill Act, and the formation of the Department of Agriculture. Meanwhile, the Civil War not only represented a great shared national experience but created fabulous markets for both manufactured and agricultural products. It accelerated the movement toward mass production in industry and toward mechanization and commercial orientation in agriculture.

From the Civil War period to World War I, the South was occupied with the problems of reconstruction and race. The region was too riddled by internal tensions to enter very deeply into other events sweeping the country forward. Between the reorganized Northeast and Midwest, which had been fused by war and industrialization, and the areas farther west, a new drama developed somewhat similar to that which had earlier split the Northeast and Old Northwest asunder. The West was still the debtor region, still in need of transportation facilities, still inclined to take political action to promote its economic interests (in Populism, the Free Silver Movement, and the Greenback Movement). However, the West as a whole presented new problems. The Southwest had a special major set of problems in its Spanish components. The arid western section presented special problems for agricultural and social technology. Among other things, it not only rendered irrelevant the farm techniques successful in the East and Midwest sections, but also many of its social and political arrangements. The Homestead Act, for example, promoted a fragmentation of holdings which was extremely uneconomic in many areas of the arid West. The settlement of the West first leaped over the arid western sections to the coast, where the Oregon territory to some degree enacted a drama similar to the settlement of the Old Northwest. Major events on the Great Plains included the destruction of the buffalo and the brief flowering for two decades of the heroic period of the cattle industry before the windmill, barbed wire, dry farming, winter wheat, and irrigation began to convert the area to agriculture. By 1890 a frontier line had ceased to exist, and all the free land had been taken up.

Though new elements that did not fit the main pattern were beginning to appear on the national scene, there is little doubt that the last two decades of the nineteenth century and the first ten years of the twentieth were the period of the first inclusive synthesis of the American character. It was even experienced by many Americans as a kind of age of awakened self-consciousness. The first flowering of a native American literature in New England in the 1840's[19] affirmed the unity of a region which had developed so far as to produce a style of its own. It was pressed to full self-consciousness by the differentiation of the South and West from its patterns, as indicated by the anti-slavery writings on the one hand, and its sense of cultural superiority to the West on the other. However, in the 1880's, as Kazin notes, America was ready for a truly national literature.

Our modern literature was rooted in those dark years of the 1880's and 1890's when all America stood suddenly between one moral order and another, and the sense of impending change became oppressive in its vividness. It was rooted in the drift of the new world of factories and cities, with their dissolution of old faiths; in the emergence of the metropolitan culture that was to dominate the literature of the new period; in the Populists who raised their voices against the domineering new plutocracy in the East and gave so much of their bitterness to the literature of protest rising out of the West; in the sense of surprise and shock that led to the crudely expectant Utopian literature of the eighties and the nineties, the largest single body of Utopian writings in modern times, and the most transparent in its nostalgia. But above all it was rooted in the need to learn what the reality of life was in the modern era.[20]

It is in the nature of self-consciousness that this national literature rested upon a distinction between the self and the non-self. As the literature of New England came to full self-consciousness in the differentiation from the other regions, so in the 1880's the "new realism" expressed the differentiation between the newly won national synthesis and the new developments that lay outside it. This was evident from the time of the origins of literary realism in the works of William Dean Howells and of Hamlin Garland who, with other midwesterners, gave voice to the complaints of the farmers against the eastern plutocracy. However, it was in the 1890's that this realism reached full expression. As Parkes has summarized the development:

The decade of the 1890's saw the advent of the first fully realistic novelists (Stephen Crane, Frank Norris, and Theodore Dreiser), the beginning of a more realistic painting (in the work of Robert Henri, Johan Sloan, and the so-called Philadelphia Group), and the growth of a more realistic trend in poetry (exemplified by Edwin Arlington Robinson).[21]

In Kazin's opinion, American literature from the new realism to the present is characterized precisely by a painful self-consciousness:

It was this . . . conviction that American "modernism" grew principally out of its surprise before the forces making a new world that led me to understand a little better what is for me the greatest single fact about our modern American writing—our writers' absorption in every last detail of their American world together with their deep and subtle alienation from it.[22]

However, it was not alone in its literature that America was coming to a new self-consciousness. In the pragmatism of Charles Peirce, William James, and John Dewey, American thought for the first time produced a distinctive philosophy of its own. With the skyscraper Americans were making a unique contribution to the architecture of the world. In the prairie style of Sullivan and Wright, America was developing its own style of domestic architecture. In this period, a national self-consciousness was even manifest in the attempt to regulate population through immigration control designed to conform to an emerging concept of an ideal population composition.

The set of characteristics listed earlier as typifying the American character represent its first synthesis. They were more true during the period 1880–1910 than they have been since that time. While they still hold in considerable degree, they seem to hold less true as time goes by. The American character is changing, and it is not yet clear where the change will end.

THE DECLINE OF THE YANKEE AS THE DISTINCTIVE AMERICAN TYPE

At the very time when American character came to its first full synthesis (around 1890) and elevated the Yankee into its distinctive national type, major events were in process which seriously upset the trial balance of the American national community.

By the 1890 the frontier line had come to an end. America was a land of small towns. The Yankee with his Puritanism, his capacity for hard work, his mechanical ingenuity, his strong self-reliance and moral confidence (which permitted him to view success as the natural reward of virtue), his civic consciousness, his town-meeting democracy, was the epitome of the individual in the small Protestant town. Intuitively, he viewed the country as a whole as a sort of federalism in which his small town was the one solid and dependable unit.

For a decade the great mass immigrations of southern and western European peasant and proletarian multitudes, of non-English-speaking, non-Protestant peoples, had been under way. However, these great multitudes were crowded into the great cities, and were initially so disorganized and so completely absorbed with the problem of survival that they were in no position to bring concerted pressure upon the citadels of Yankee strength; besides, in the cities, where the immigrants were massed, the highest positions in business, government, and finance were still occupied by "Old Americans." Many of these very "Old Americans" had taken the lead in importing immigrants as a supply of cheap labor.

To be sure, some cognizance was taken of these urban immigrant masses. There was a revival of the nativistic reaction which had produced the Know-Nothing Party earlier; the nativism of the South turned naturally against these groups, and the program of the Ku Klux Klan was broadened to include the alien and the Roman Catholic; old-line American labor responded to the deterioration of its economic situation under the onslaught of cheap alien labor, and formed the first enduring labor unions and supported nativistic political policies; nativism achieved political expression in a series of immigration control acts beginning with those directed against the Chinese in the 1880's and continuing to the McCarran-Walter Immigration Act of 1952.

It was going to take some time before the immigrant would have sufficient acclimatization, organization, and knowledge to bring his presence to bear upon the national scene. Meanwhile, other factors would delay his influence somewhat. When an immigrant boy "made good," he did so in considerable measure by adopting the attitudes and behaviors of the surrounding world and by taking advantage—of course as a patriotic duty—of the opportunities available to him. The *nouveau riche* may initially have carried out an economic revolution, but once it had arrived, the group tended to be socially conservative. The *nouveau riche* often become the mouthpiece of a jingoistic Americanism.

Even in the act of taking over the dominant ethos, however, the immigrant changed it somewhat. Siegfried pointedly characterized the outlook of the second and third generation immigrant:

What is the moral value of this second generation? As a rule the first has given no trouble, for the immigrant is submissive; he respects the law and brings with him a discipline ripened by centuries. As for his children, we soon see what they have learned—the manners of the New World, a passion for material independence, and a standard of living that leads them utterly to despise worn out old Europe. The danger lies in the fact that they have absorbed the boundless ambition of the Americans, without **acquiring at the same time the traditional stolid restraint of the Puritan** conscience.

The third generation, they will tell you, is thoroughly Americanized, and as a matter of fact it is scarcely distinguishable. Yes, but its Americanism is morally shrunk in comparison with the vigor of the pioneers and is sadly lacking in tradition.[23]

In the very act of taking over the dominant ethos, the immigrant will tend to bring about a transformation in it from the inside. When the immigrant masses feel compelled to turn into Yankees, the results are something slightly different, perhaps best describable as "Yankee Doodle Dandies."

However, in 1890 the masses of immigrants and their ethnic communities were not yet integrated with the American character. The immigrants were largely concentrated in the cities, which were themselves outside the small town complex and hence the location of Yankee strength. How the city and the phenomena concentrated in it could appear to a spokesman for nativism is illustrated by Josiah Strong's volume, *Our Country,* which appeared in 1885.[24] The volume carried the following prefatory note:

This volume was prepared for the American Home Missionary Society by Rev. Josiah Strong, D.D., then its representative for the work of Home Missions in Ohio. As will be seen at a glance, its main purpose is to lay before the intelligent Christian people of our country facts and arguments showing the imperative need of Home Missionary work for the evangelization of the land, the encouragement to such effort, and the danger of neglecting it.[25]

The good doctor had no doubt as to the major perils to American civilization. In his opinion, these were immigration, Romanism, Mormonism, intemperance, socialism, wealth, and the city. It all started with immigration and ended with the city.

Immigration furnishes most of the victims of Mormonism; and there is a Mormon vote. Immigration is the strength of the Catholic church; and there is a Catholic vote. Immigration is the mother and nurse of American socialism; and there is to be a socialist vote. Immigration tends strongly to the cities and gives them their political complexion. And there is no more serious menace to our civilization than our rabble-ruled cities.[26]

When he comes to the city itself, Strong's eloquence is unbounded:

Here is heaped the social dynamite; here roughs, gamblers, thieves, robbers, lawless and desperate men of all sorts, congregate; men who are ready on any pretext to raise riots for the purpose of destruction and plunder; here gather foreigners and wage-workers; here skepticism and irreligion abound; here inequality is the greatest and most obvious, and the contrast between opulence and penury the most striking; here is suffering the sorest.[27]

As a rule, our largest cities are the worst governed. It is natural, therefore, to infer that, as our cities grow larger and more dangerous, the
government will become more and more corrupt, and control will pass more
completely into the hands of those who themselves most need to be controlled.[28]

When he examined the city in detail twenty years later, Strong's
opinions had grown more firm. The "two roots of moral life"—the home
and religion—in his opinion were both weakened in the city. The city
was becoming a menace to the state and to the nation. As it grew more
powerful, the city was less capable of self-government. At one time or
other, he argued, most of our great cities were in the hands of a mob,
and the saloon had become an institution of power within them.
Foreigners and criminals were concentrated in the metropolitan areas.[29]

While many persons, like Strong, were convinced that the cities
were un-American, the conviction grew that they were here to stay.
When, around the turn of the century, the Muckrakers turned their
attention to the cities, however, they were not long in laying responsibility for the corruption of the cities more closely to home. Lincoln
Steffens, for example, shifted responsibility for civic corruption away
from immigration and Roman Catholicism to the shoulders of the
American businessman.

The typical American citizen is the business man. The typical business
man is a bad citizen; he is busy. If he is a "big business man" and very
busy, he does not neglect, he is busy with politics, O, very busy and very
business-like. I found him buying boodlers in St. Louis, defending grafters
in Minneapolis, originating corruption in Pittsburgh, sharing with bosses in
Philadelphia, deploring reform in Chicago, and beating good government
with corruption funds in New York. He is a self-righteous fraud, this big
business man. He is the chief source of corruption.[30]

In the sixty years since the Muckrakers began to dramatize the
problem of city corruption, there have been major attempts to bring
about a genuine incorporation of the American city in the framework
of American society. In their study of the metropolis, the editors of
Fortune Magazine reported a dramatic change in the situation described
by Steffens.

There has been a change in City Hall because there has been a change
in the city itself. For the better part of a century, the core of big city life
was its immigrants—waves and waves of them, many illiterate, few English-
speaking, all poor. Their grinding misery kept the machine in power at
the hall.[31]

The reasons for this change were thought to be many: The 1924 Immigration Act in slowing immigration gave the city time to absorb its earlier immigrants, reduce cultural differences, and permit many people to rise into the middle class. Federal social security and unemployment insurance reduced the dependence of big-city masses on political machines; the National Municipal League and the Institute of Public Administration and other government research groups brought about important changes and political reforms; better qualified people came into government during the unemployment period of the 1930's; the public began to demand better administered services, including fire protection, water, sewerage; new services were developed, including psychiatric clinics and youth boards.

The profile of today's big-city mayor—with one difference—is quite similar to that of the chief executive of a large corporation. Typically, the mayor is a college graduate, usually with a legal or business background, and is now in his late fifties. He puts in hard, grinding hours at his desk, sometimes six or seven days a week, and his wife suffers as much as his golf game.[32]

However, while the incorporation of city into the framework of American society is under way, this objective is so far from being accomplished that William H. Whyte, Jr., opened one of his contributions to The Exploding Metropolis with the question: "Are Cities Un-American?"[33] The norm of American aspiration, Whyte observes, is not the city but suburbs. The happy family of the commercials is a land of bluejeans, shopping centers, new schools, barbecue pits, garden clubs, and do-it-yourself clubs. "Heterogeneity, concentration, specialization, tension, drive—the characteristics of the city have often been deprecated, but rarely have they been deprecated with such unwonted vigor."[34] Even the city planners and architects are designing, according to Whyte, anti-cities. Either they are busy constructing monuments to themselves or garden cities. The garden city, Whyte believes, is not a city, but a design sanctified by utopians.[35] Moreover:

The rebuilding of the down town is not enough; a city deserted at night by its leading citizens is only half a city. If it is to continue as the dominant cultural force in American life, the city must have a core of people to support its theatres and museums, its shops and its restaurants—even a Bohemia of sorts can be of help. For it is the people who like living in the city who make it an attraction to the visitors who won't. It is the city dwellers who support its style; without them there is nothing to come down town to.[36]

However, as the *Fortune* study shows, while the city has moved closer to incorporation within the national community, the nostalgia in Whyte's plea for a genuine cosmopolitanism merely accents more completely the lack thereof. It is highly doubtful whether the city can ever achieve autonomy under modern conditions. Moreover, a case could be made for the thesis that a genuine cosmopolitanism is not truly possible under circumstances in which the city itself cannot achieve full community form. If one may be permitted to offer a wild guess, *suburbia derives its tremendous significance for the American popular mind from the fact that it is the manner in which mid-century America is trying to assimilate the city to the image of the small town which still functions as its criteria of a true community.*

The third major complex besides the ethnic community and the city, which was developing in 1890 outside the national synthesis, was the economy developing on a national scale. The background for the rise of mass industry in Europe and America was varied as well as long in the making; it included the rise of the modern state and the mercantilistic policies which created national and international markets, the capitalistic revolutions which encouraged social, political, and legal conditions favorable to mass business, and the industrial revolution with the application of science to almost every phase of industrial processes. In America, big business of a contemporary type began to take shape during the Civil War. From 1859 to 1889 the number of wage workers in industry increased three fold, while the value added by manufacturing increased five fold without a rise in the general price level.[37] This increasing production tended to be consolidated in the hands of large new industrial formations. After the Standard Oil Company of Ohio adopted the legal trust form (1879) to bring this about, and was imitated by a number of other new combinations like sugar and whiskey, the name "trust" came to be generally applied even to consolidations in which the stockholders did not surrender their shares and voting power to trustee managers.[38]

From 1890 to 1897, 84 new combinations appeared with a combined authorized capital stock of around one million dollars. However, it was only the beginning. In 1898 the merger movement began in earnest, and by 1902 there were 189 new combinations with a capital of 4 billion.[39] The merger movement slowed down after 1904, according to Whitney, only for lack of new fields to conquer or the discovery of new sources of financing.

The size of the funds involved in the economic activities of major contemporary American industries may be shown by a few examples. The net value of the final shipments of meat packing in 1954 was 6.2 billion dollars, and of prepared meats, 1.4 billion.[40]

Petroleum is a major mining and manufacturing product. In 1955 the crude oil produced in the United States was worth 7 billion dollars. Oil refining added 1.9 billion to the value of the petroleum produced in 1954.[41]

Chemicals and allied products had a sales value of 23 billion dollars in 1955.[42] Producing 40 per cent of the world's steel in 1955, the United States iron and steel industry represented an industry with 658,000 employees and sales of 13.9 billion dollars.[43]

Sales of paper in 1955 were estimated at 10 billion dollars in an industry employing 453,000 persons.[44] Bituminous coal employed 210,-000 laborers in 1955, and its output was valued at 2.3 billion dollars.[45] Motor vehicles and parts ranked first among the industries in value added by manufacture. The industry averaged 921,000 persons employed in 1955, and turned out a product valued at 6.1 billion dollars.

From the Civil War to the present, these gigantic industries have been developing outside the framework of the countryside and city alike; their framework is supplied by the nation. In considerable measure these new giant industrial combinations were developed by bold unscrupulous men who operated as often as not in semi-legal if not illegal ways. The story of these "robber barons," as they came conventionally to be described, has been told many times over. The immigrant millions in considerable measure came to work in the industries which the robber barons were creating; the cities with their fabulous human waste were a byproduct of their operations. However, despite the cry raised against them, in almost every area of economic life the formation of larger and larger combinations was brought about. Usually, by the time one device for industrial combination had been declared illegal, new and more effective devices were already in operation. A few illustrations may be given.

Meat packing is important, because more than 90 per cent of the meat animals raised on six million farms are sold. While two thirds of the livestock are raised west of the Mississippi, around two thirds of the consumers live east of it. Since the late nineteenth century Swift and Armour have been the two giants of the industry. For thirty years Wilson and Cudahy were coupled with them as "the big four" meat packers, but in 1955 Cudahy dropped to seventh place, while some independents were expanding their scale of operations. In 1955 the ten largest producers had 64 per cent of the sales.[46]

In petroleum in 1950, fifty-four companies operated in producing, transporting, refining, and marketing, with a few hundred more integrated in two or three fields. At the end of 1955 the thirty-four leading oil companies had a gross investment of 18 billion dollars in production facilities, 3.4 billion in transportation, 7.3 billion in refining, 3.9 billion in marketing, and 0.5 billion in other interests.[47]

The giant of the chemical industry is E. I. du Pont de Nemours. Union Carbide and Carbon is second. In 1955, fifteen big chemical corporations had sales and operating revenues of 150 million dollars or more a year. Du Pont had 10 per cent of the chemical industry sales of 20 billion dollars in 1944; the four largest chemical companies had 22 per cent.[48]

The great bulk of iron and steel output is in the hands of so-called integrated companies. In 1955 twenty-four were in operation. Fifteen of the largest had 89 per cent of the country's pig iron capacity, 76 per cent of its ingot capacity, and 84 per cent of its hot rolled steel capacity. The United States Steel Corporation had 30.6 per cent of its ingot capacity.[49]

In paper, integrated companies producing both pulp and paper numbered 102 in 1949, and their 179 pulp mills used four fifths of the nation's supply of pulp. The International Paper Company is the largest unit in the industry with twenty-one pulp and paper mills and thirty-one converting factories. In 1955 it accounted for 8 per cent of the industry's sales. The four largest producers had 17 per cent of the 1955 sales; the fifteen largest, 34 per cent.[50]

Bituminous coal had a relatively low degree of concentration compared to most industries. In 1955 there were 7,500 to 8,000 mines. The largest single company with twenty-four mines accounted for only 6 per cent of the output; the four largest for 18.3 per cent; and the fifteen largest for 35 per cent.[51]

The automobile industry is centered in a small group of companies. The General Motors Corporation accounted for 50.8 per cent of the new passenger car registrations in 1955, the Ford Motor Company for 27.6 per cent, and the Chrysler Corporation for 16.8 per cent. The only independents that survived into 1956 were the Studebaker-Packard Corporation and American Motors. The gross income from all products ranged from 441 million dollars for American Motors to 12,443,000 dollars for General Motors.[52]

In 1890, almost precisely at the time American society had arrived at its first national synthesis as a nation representing a kind of federalism of small towns and with a national character of its own (the Yankee), with contributions to world architecture (the skyscraper), a genuinely original domestic architecture (the prairie style), and a brilliant first fully self-conscious national literature—almost at this very time immigrant ethnic communities began to form by the hundreds, the cities were beginning to look like a sinister menace to everyone, and the great new industrial combinations entered a new period of consolidation.

The bearers of the newly won national consciousness quite correctly sensed a threat in these new industrial combinations. The response was typical—a wave of anti-trust activity. There have been periodic waves of anti-trust legislation and sentiment ever since. At the end of each period, though an occasional industrial combination is broken up, concentration has usually increased. On the basis of his careful study of twenty industries, Whitney insists that the major trend has always been toward concentration.

The majority of industries studied conform to the typical American picture —production of well over half the output by a handful of large corporations and of the rest by a number of small firms. Bituminous coal and cotton textiles were exceptions, with their largest corporations controlling a much smaller percentage of the output; but even here the merger movement is in process of creating the typical structure. At the other extreme, one company makes 80 to 90 per cent of shoe machinery of different types; one makes half the passenger cars and has only four competitors; and one makes 40 per cent of the primary aluminum and has only three competitors.[53]

This is despite the fact that in the first forty-eight years of the Sherman Anti-Trust Act 433 suits were filed at an average of nine a year. After July, 1938, the rate was stepped up, and 347 suits were filed between July, 1938, and June, 1943 (about 69 a year). As recently as 1950, the anti-trust laws were buttressed by the Celler-Kefauver amendment to Section 7, the anti-merger measure of the Clayton Act.[54]

The fundamental idea continues to be entertained by many American liberals that these great industrial combinations are contrary to "true" American interests. So long as "true" American interests are taken to be those of the small town complex which sustained the image of the American as Yankee, this indubitably true. The repeated consolidations of industry in the face of these periodic attempts to halt it indicate the need for Americans to develop a new self-image more in accord with the facts of their actual community life.[55]

THE NATIONAL
VERSUS THE LOCAL COMMUNITY
AND SOME DILEMMAS
OF LIBERALISM AND CONSERVATISM

One consequence of the presence of masses of immigrants to be assimilated, cities to be controlled and integrated into the national framework, and great industrial concerns to be accommodated, is an unusually rich growth of government to deal with the problems they represent. All these developments, in turn, signify the emergence of a new and more integrated national community. To this new national community the concept of national society as a sort of federation of small towns is quite inappropriate.

It was pointed out earlier that liberalism and conservatism make sense when they are applied within the framework of a single community. Every community offers its members some combination of stability and individuality. The liberal point of view, whatever the community, would maximize its individuality; the conservative point of view would maximize its stability. However, when liberalism and conservatism are applied in the same way to different communities, they often make little sense.

American conservatism and liberalism became fixed largely with respect to the first synthesis of national social life. The majority of the spokesmen for both positions assume that the "true" America is a nation of federated small towns. Of course the proposition is not formulated explicitly, for this would be a description which is challenged by the facts. However, this assumption is a major component of what Galbraith describes as the "conventional" wisdom which he correctly asserts is accepted by American conservatives and liberals alike.

The conventional wisdom is not the property of any political group. On a great many modern social issues, . . . the consensus is exceedingly broad. Nothing much divides those who are liberals by common political designation from those who are conservatives. The test of what is acceptable is much the same for both.[56]

The conservative point of view is marked by general suspicion of big government. The point of stability which it seeks in local society, however, is not extended to the ethnic community and city which, it suspects, are still more than a little un-American. Its *laissez-faire* attitude toward all aspects of central government activity accounts for its resistance, in the time of their rise, to social security, unemployment insurance, and similar programs. It continues to manifest these attitudes in resistance to federal aid to education and fear of socialized medicine. It treats American business as a component in local society, and it rather admires the authoritarian structure which business assumes as it is consolidated into larger combinations. Its solution to the problems of American society generally seems to be to a strengthening of the authoritarian patterns of local forms. So far as the federal government is concerned, its budget ought to be balanced, its functions—which interfere with local society—should be curtailed as much as possible. The much curtailed central government should then be "run on a business basis."

Galbraith's books are filled with illustrations of the kind of contradictory situations to which this leads.

The scientist or engineer or advertising man who devotes himself to developing a new carburetor, cleaner, or depilatory for which the public recognizes no need and will feel none until an advertising campaign arouses it, is one of the most valued members of our society. A politician or a public servant who dreams up a new public service is a wastrel. Few public offenses are more reprehensible.[57]

A feature of the years immediately following World War II was a remarkable attack on the notion of expanding and improving public services.

A certain mystique was attributed to the satisfaction of privately supplied wants. A community decision to have a new school means that the individual surrenders the necessary amount, willy-nilly, in his taxes. But if he is left with that income, he is a free man. He can decide between a better car or a television set . . . . The difficulty is that this argument leaves the community with no way of preferring the school.[58]

The "conventional wisdom" of American liberalism has tended to rest on the same notion of society as American conservatism. The chief difference between the two is that while conservatism has feared big government and looked to the authoritative structure of business as a source of stability, liberalism has feared big business and has promoted political programs designed to curtail it in the name of securing greater freedom and opportunity for the individual. Galbraith has not been the only major American scholar to feel it necessary to take issue with the "conventional wisdom" of American liberalism as with the "conventional wisdom" of American conservatism if one is to think freshly about major issues. In his attempt to free analysis from pre-suppositions in order to look clearly at the continued evolution of the national economy, Berle found it necessary, in *Power Without Property,* to write a special preface for liberals:

Whenever American business, especially American big business, and American corporations are mentioned, your American liberal almost instinctively snaps his thinking into a stereotype. Big business is the "enemy." Its interests are opposed to "the people." You are on one side or the other. If recognition is paid to the solid achievements of big business, including the substantial advance it has made toward meeting a social point of view, you have sold out to the enemy.[59]

It was, Berle urges, absurd for the individuals to accept the fiction that all virtue lies in smallness and that vice inheres in size. Moreover,

liberals have to recognize a solid fact. Business is, in the main, the economic service-of-supply of the United States. In some fields, possibly electric power for one example, government organisms can do better than private business, as the Tennessee Valley Authority and Columbia River projects have shown. But there is danger in merging political government with the economic system—perhaps as great as that inhering in concentrated economic power not tied up with the political system. Now a government cannot be perpetually at war with its service-of-supply.[60]

Berle here touches an extremely sensitive point in the structure of American liberalism. The point is, American liberals have not faced the fact that they may be promoting political progress that could terminate in concentrations of political power which would dwarf the economic concentrations of power they oppose. When American liberals are invited to develop their desired political system, they almost always conjure up an idealized Jeffersonian democracy. When they develop their notion of the "true" American social system, they dwell at length upon the "authentic" picture of America contained in the works of Alexis de Tocqueville. Nothing could more clearly signalize the persistence of the idea at the core of American liberalism that America is at bottom a federation of small towns, for Jefferson promoted the liberal position appropriate to precisely that kind of society in the early days of the nineteenth century, and the brilliant and somewhat opinionated Frenchman provided the most skillful description available of the ethos of the small town in the United States of the 1830's.

Contemporary liberalism and conservatism, thus, are split across the lines of local *versus* national communities. Americans tend, in thought, to retain the local community as the inviolate sphere of individuality. Yet both liberals and conservatives pursue strategies in the national community which destroy the traditional values of the local community. Meanwhile, precisely because the local community is the implicit reference point, the national community evolves new forms which tend to pass unnoticed. Perhaps Galbraith is right:

The enemy of the conventional wisdom is not ideas but the march of events . . . the fatal blow to the conventional wisdom comes when the conventional ideas fail signally to deal with some contingency to which obsolescence has made them palpably inapplicable.[61]

One of the interesting features of the thought of the decade of the 1950's was the marked break-through of long standing stereotypes and the capture of the popular imagination by a dramatic group of unorthodox social scientists. The most notable of these were John Kenneth Galbraith, C. Wright Mills, David Riesman, and William H. Whyte, Jr.

The works which simultaneously aroused the opposition of many of the conventional exponents of their disciplines and attracted the popular mind as authentic voices of long disregarded facts of every American's experience were Galbraith's *American Capitalism* and *The Affluent Society*, Mills' *White Collar* and *The Power Elite*, Riesman's *The Lonely Crowd*, and Whyte's *The Organization Man*.

These works are not all equally original or scholarly or "even" in their formulations. However, all of them have one significant property in common—they sketch events in the national community which defy the stereotyped conceptions of that community.

Galbraith carried out a direct assault on the stereotypes of conventional wisdom in order to create the free space to develop his theory of countervailing power which takes the national community as its unquestioned foundation and thrusts aside the old dichotomy of national *versus* local community. While adhering more closely to the presuppositions of old-fashioned radicalism than does Galbraith, Mills traces the formation of middle and upper classes which have the national rather than local society (including the city) as their foundation. Riesman traced the rise and diffusion to all areas of modern life of a new ethos, or as he calls it, "other-directedness," which contrasts with the "inner-directedness" of the American Yankee past. Whyte visualized the new "organization man" as the bearer of attitudes and values which are beginning to typify contemporaries. A new ethic of togetherness, the social ethic, is thought to replace the traditional individualistic Protestant ethic. Other traditional attitude consolidations are also being replaced, such as the traditional attitudes toward saving which are being replaced by the debt entrapment represented by Budgetism.

If these social scientists, who cause dismay among so many of their colleagues, are correct, a new and more comprehensive goal-value system is taking shape on the American scene and a new kind of American social type is replacing the Yankee.

A POSTSCRIPT
FOR THOSE WHO HATE ESSAYS
WHICH END NEGATIVELY
OR INCONCLUSIVELY

Around 1890 American society achieved its first community synthesis as a federation of local societies. Within these local societies the dominant social type represented middle class Puritans of North European cultural derivation as modified by the American frontier. The epitome of American character was the Yankee. At this time the forces destined to modify this structure were already in operation; they have continued to operate ever since.

The best guess at present as to nature of the synthesis of community and character of America, 1990, suggests similarities and differences with the 1890 picture. In America, 1990, the packaged suburbs will have taken the place of the small town as the norm of community correctness. These packaged suburbs will be peopled by happy—or at least smiling—Yankee Doodle Dandies. Individuality will be carefully provided for in the new society; in fact, it will be almost illegal not to have one's own prefabricated dream house, painted in a different combination of pastels than one's neighbor's. Around these dream houses will blossom the latest hybrids from plastic pots and boxes of preplanted seeds which have been scientifically potted in specially fertilized soil.

Inside one of these dream houses a young mother will smile with that badge of true happiness—the grimace of a person who has just said "cheese" for the cameras—as she uses an electrically operated mechanism to open scientifically pre-cooked and vitamin-fortified baby food. Meanwhile, in its crib the baby sleeps beatifically under the influence of a special baby-sized tranquilizer administered because of a touch of colic the day before. And in the utility room the young husband works carefully in the midst of a couple of thousand dollars worth of do-it-yourself equipment, patiently assembling, according to instructions, an item of do-it-yourself furniture. As he works, he whistles the happy jingle of an ad which cheerfully announces the development of a new cancer-suppressing cigarette.

9

THE AMERICAN

PEOPLE

BY ORIGIN THE AMERICAN PEOPLE ARE Europeans with significant non-European components, formed into a new unity by distinctive collective experiences. The American people have established the oldest and most conservative democracy, the most radical technology, and the most exclusively middle-class society of the contemporary nationalities. Though composed of more heterogeneous ethnic groups than any other contemporary nation, the American people have been homogeneously integrated by four major events: the frontier, immigration, the rise of mass society, and a unique pattern of national crises On the foundation of these collective experiences the structure of a distinctive American civilization is arising.

Practices appearing in the collective experiences of a people belong to all who adopt them, for they reflect cultural, not biological continuities. All Americans, not simply the biological descendants of the pioneers, share the heritage of the frontier, even though their parents arrived only a generation ago. Similarly, the one-time powerful everyday ethic born in early American Protestant circles is a common heritage of all Americans, and at times is more strictly observed among second generation American Catholics or Jews than among the actual descendants of the early Protestants. This diffusion of the experience of some to the whole is no different, to chose a famous historical example, from the manner in which the Exodus from Egypt under Moses by one section of the people became a common symbol for the entire ancient Jewish nation. The great distinctive experiences of a people in first instance only affect a segment, but when they send out waves from this center they become bonds of unity in the whole.

THE FRONTIER EXPERIENCE

The frontier experience of Americans codetermined (1) its class structure, (2) its sectionalism, (3) the character of its agriculture, (4) the form of its industrial revolution, (5) the nature of its religion, and (6) the distinctiveness of its popular culture.

Social Class and the American Frontier

Quite different social structures have emerged in the northern and southern hemispheres of the New World, for in the latter, colonization was pressed by military adventurers and peasants from Portugal and Spain, while in the former colonization was accomplished by middle class townsmen from northern Europe, particularly from England.

Originally the voyage across the Atlantic was long, expensive, and hazardous. The primary motive for undertaking it among north Europeans was the opportunity for wealth from New World resources. When individuals (rather than politically sponsored military adventurers) came, they represented persons who could afford the trip (which ruled out the peasants) and who were motivated by the prospect of commercial profits (which largely ruled out the aristocrats). At times commercial companies organized to exploit New World resources and in need of labor to do so presented the opportunity of immigration to poor persons, many of whom were seeking to avoid religious or political persecution. The fate of colonial North America lay primarily in the hands of well-to-do, middle class entrepreneurs from northern Europe. In the New World they established a social structure in which the middle classes served as a norm for all later development.

After America became a state, its frontiersmen were recruited from middle class groups along the seaboard in much the same manner that colonial America had derived from middle class north Europeans. The poorest elements of the seaboard were left behind, for capital was required to make penetration of the frontier effective. The richest elements also stayed behind, for they had more to gain by remaining in the East, from which vantage point they supplied capital and manufactured items needed on the frontier. Successive waves of middle class recruits opened the frontiers: the Old Northwest (Midwest), the Southwest, the Far West (spurred on by the discovery of gold), the Oregon Territory, and finally, the Northwest.

The formation of the American territory and of an Indian policy were by-products of the frontier. Again, as one frontier after another was pierced, the spearhead of expansion was supplied by the middle classes. Jefferson, who was personally oriented toward the frontier, took the lead in consummating the Louisiana Purchase (1803), which doubled the territory of the Union by adding to it one million square miles. Similar middle class pressures were urging an often reluctant government to the acquisition of Florida from Spain (1819), the annexation of Texas (1845), the acquisition of California (1848), the Gadsden Purchase (1853), and the settlement of the Oregon territory (1848). The aggregate territory of the United States at present is 3,628,130 square miles.

Each frontier brought new conflicts with the Indians, from the days of the Pequot War (1637) led by John Endicott to the final submission, through superior numbers and technology, of the Indians who resisted both the frontier advance and federal reservation policies. The last great Indian wars were the Cheyenne-Arapaho War (1861–1862), the Red River War (1874), the Sioux Wars (1865–1867), the Apache War (1871–1887), and the Ghost Dance Uprising (1890). Indian troubles of the Old Northwest led President Monroe to sponsor (in 1825) the policy of transferring eastern Indians to trans-Mississippi regions. This reservation policy got under way with the transfer of the Cherokees to a strip of land in Kansas and Oklahoma.

The Frontier and Sectionalism

A somewhat different organization of middle class colonial enterprise occurred in the northern and southern colonies, laying the foundations for its first regional sectionalism. In the North, where commercial companies, in part for climatic and geographic reasons, did not enjoy commercial success, the companies were succeeded by the colonists, who then took social and economic affairs into their own hands and formed self-governing village communities.

In the South, the large-scale plantation producing for European export proved profitable. However, it was faced with the perennial problem of a labor shortage. Since he had no tradition of disciplined agricultural work, the male American Indian proved to be an unreliable labor source. Indentured servants also proved to be unsatisfactory, for their ship passage was costly and once they arrived in the New World they set about to become independent farmers as rapidly as possible. Negro slavery, first introduced by Portuguese traders, solved the labor problems of the plantations, only to spawn a devastating series of other social and economic problems later, some of which the country wrestles with to this day.

In the expansion of groups of Americans into areas outside the original sphere of colonial setlement, the social forms of the northern colonies with their small, self-sufficient village communities resting on free labor and those of the large agrarian plantations resting on slave labor came into conflict. As the slave population increased from 697,000 (1780) to nearly 4,000,000 (1860), sectional tensions mounted. In the first clash of northern and southern institutions in the Old Northwest, institutional arrangements of the northern colonies won and supplied the social and political forms by means of which the frontier was organized and formed into new states. The Basic Land Ordinance (1786), modeled after the New England village, provided for the rectangular survey of territorial lands and the division of them into townships six miles square with 36 lots of 640 acres each, one of which was set aside for support of a public school. The Northwest Ordinance (1787) provided for the division of the western domain into states and for a procedure by which they could enter the Union on terms of equality with the original members. These ordinances served as a basis for incorporating new territories, such as the statehood of Alaska and Hawaii, into the Union.

The Frontier and Agriculture

The class derivation of colonist and frontiersman and the unique conditions of the hemisphere sent American agriculture on a course distinct from that of Europe. American agriculture fused Old World crops and farming techniques with those of the American Indians. New World crops destined to become of world importance included corn, tobacco, white potatoes, and sweet potatoes. Some twenty-seven other crops were also taken over from the Indians.

In colonial times agriculture in Europe was largely in the hands of peasants engaged in subsistence farming for home consumption. The New World colonist and frontiersman were townsmen by vocation; rural husbandmen were so only by necessity. They applied a townsman's standards to their rural activities, and moved from the land into the evolving businesses and industries of the frontier towns as soon as possible. From the beginning, the New World rural husbandman was a farmer selling his agricultural products for a profit and in turn purchasing manufactured articles he himself could not make.

The southern planter was as different from the medieval lord as the northern farmer was from the European peasant. He was not an hereditary aristocrat living from the income of his estates but an entrepreneur or rural businessman. He produced for the market, particularly the overseas market. Thus from colonial days the South has been a low tariff area. The labor on his plantation was performed by slaves, not by peasants. The southern plantation was not a medieval estate, but a form of agrarian capitalism.

Meanwhile, the abundance of new land lured the young men into the West. However, if one went into debt for the capital to establish a farm or estate, the tie between agrarian activity and the market tightened, for one now had to sell enough produce to pay one's debts. In the course of western expansion, American farmers became a perennial debtor group at odds with their fellow businessman, the eastern capitalists. Since the farmers needed access to markets, which they were unable to provide out of their own resources, they petitioned the state and federal governments for aid in developing roads, turnpikes, canals, and railroads.

Frontier farmers also sought government assistance in securing better settlement conditions (resulting in the Homestead Act of 1862), and for assistance in securing higher education for their children (resulting in the Morrill Act of 1862 granting each loyal state thirty thousand acres of land for each senator and representative with which to provide for one agricultural college, and sixty-nine land grant colleges were established). The market orientation of the farmer was an important component in the formation of the Department of Agriculture in 1862 and its continuous expansion. Attempts to control their markets and the political conditions bearing on them provided the impetus for the formation of the great farm organizations: The Grange (1867), the Farmers' Alliance (1880), the Farmers' Union (1902), and the American Farm Bureau Federation (1915).

The Frontier and the Industrial Revolution

The frontier shaped participation in the industrial revolution. From the earliest colonial days it was so costly to import manufactured items from Europe that only the southern planters could afford them. The northern colonists immediately entered into the production of things they needed. Raw materials were cheap, human labor was expensive, markets were expanding. America became the home of labor-saving inventions. America's industrial innovations are illustrated by the automatic milling sequence of Oliver Evans (1783) who employed a conveyor belt and other labor saving devices in flour milling and loading, by the "dis-assembly lines" introduced by the hog butchers of Chicago, and by the assembly lines of the early Ford factories which supplied the model for those of American industry at large.

In the wake of the frontier, supplied by its wealth of raw materials and answering to its needs, a great series of commercial and industrial cities came into being. The five major cities of the United States— New York, Chicago, Philadelphia, Los Angeles, and Detroit—vary from two million to eight million in population, and in size from 127 square miles (Philadelphia) to 315 square miles (New York). On the northeast seaboard there are areas with a density of population of more than three thousand persons per square mile.

The Frontier and Religion

The middle class north Europeans who dominated the American colonial population were predominantly Protestant. In their isolated village communities they were free to work out their religious destinies. At times they formed intense little theocracies such as John Cotton's (1584–1652) Boston. In reaction to the religious bigotry generated by such theocracies, they formed new communities in which religious toleration was practiced, such as Thomas Hooker's (1586–1647) Hartford and Roger Williams' (1603–1683) and Anne Hutchinson's Narraganset Bay (1613–1662). On the frontier, religion developed local, intense, self-sufficient forms. Religious fragmentation on a local scale has characterized America to the present.

In the face of religious splintering, the only possibility of collective action avoiding explosive sect differences was political neutralization of religion by the separation of Church and State. This, too, has characterized American religion from colonial days and throughout the years.

Finally, in shifting responsibility for religion into the hands of a local community, the frontier brought about periods of religious dilution alternating with intense revivalism. In predominantly Protestant America the leading Protestant groups became the frontier sects—the Baptist and Methodist. These, too, have been a focal point for waves of evangelicalism. These have periodically shaken America from the days of George Whitefield (1715–1770), the associate of the Methodist Wesleys who, more than anyone else, preached the first great evangelical movement, the Great Awakening of 1739, to the later religious crusades including those of Billy Sunday following World War I and Billy Graham after World War II.

The Frontier and Popular Culture

From the days of Cooper's Leatherstocking through the tall tales of Paul Bunyan and his Blue Ox to the latest TV horse operas, the frontier experience has directly and indirectly through literary elaboration entered the forms of popular culture. Many actual frontiersmen have gradually acquired a semi-mythical status as folk heroes: Daniel Boone, Kit Carson, Jim Bridger, and Buffalo Bill are typical. Folk heroes, legendary tales, and a store of popular lore remain as a residue of the frontier.

IMMIGRATION

As a shaping influence on the American people, immigration is comparable to the frontier. Such observers as Margaret Mead and Geoffrey Gorer have even taken a third-generation psychology to be America's most distinctive feature. Immigration has (1) helped fix the character of the American economy, (2) helped determine the character of its labor, (3) added distinctive properties to its religion, (4) established the American language, and (5) added lustrous names to its pantheon of fame.

The Volume and Periods of American Immigration

Into the vast land opened by the frontiersman surged the populations of the Old World. In 1610 there were 210 persons from Europe in North America; by 1790 there were 3,929,214. By 1950 the American population was over 151,000,000, and by 1990 there will be an estimated 230,000,000 to 272,000,000 people in the United States. Historically, the American population was largely formed through immigration, though it has been increasingly self-recruited (by birth) in the twentieth century. From 1820, when the first statistics on immigration were drawn up by the United States Census, more than 40,000,000 persons have immigrated. Of these more than 34,000,000 came from

Europe, more than 5,000,000 from the Americas, more than 1,000,000 from Asia, and a few hundred thousand from Africa, Australia, New Zealand, and the Pacific Islands. (This does not include the millions of Africans brought over as slaves.) Throughout its history America has faced a continuous problem of absorbing varied immigrant groups.

American immigration may be differentiated into four periods: (1) the colonial, ending with the Revolutionary War, (2) the period from the Revolutionary War to the Civil War, (3) the period from the Civil War to World War I, and (4) the period from World War I to the present.

Immigration and America's Socio-Economic Requirements

Colonial immigration (1610–1790) occurred in response to New World opportunities for commercial exploitation. The great storehouse of New World raw materials was ready for persons with capital to venture and entrepreneurial skills. The predominant immigrant was an upper-middle-class North European. Although occasional groups did not fit this pattern, such as the German-Swiss peasant Mennonites (1683) led by Daniel Pastorius (1651–1720) who formed into hermetically sealed ethnic communities in a manner which later was to occur frequently, the great majority of immigrants were so similar in socio-economic background that they mingled freely. In 1790 more than 60 per cent of the population was English and the remaining groups were of closely related stock: 8 per cent Scotch, 9 per cent Irish, 8 per cent German, and so forth.

From the Revolution to the Civil War the economic requirements surrounding immigration changed. There was no longer so great a need for entrepreneurial types, for America was beginning to supply them out of her own resources. There was, however, a strong demand for skilled laborers in the emerging American industries. Moreover, since the pioneer was leaving the farm and taking up the commercial and industrial pursuits of the towns, a vacuum was being created on the land. America had a need for better and more stable farmers.

Immigrants were needed from socio-economic classes somewhat lower than those required in the colonial period: artisans, skilled workers, and well-to-do farmers. The cost of immigration still had to be borne by the immigrant; hence this operated as a screen, for though transportation was more rapid and less costly than it had been in the colonial period, it was still beyond the means of the very poor. While revolutionary ferment in Europe, such as existed in 1830 and 1848, brought some highly educated and wealthy professional and business-men to America, and while some disasters, like the Irish potato famine, bought some very poor peasants to American shores, the bulk of the migration prior to the Civil War consisted of lower-middle-class trades-men, artisans, skilled workers, and well-to-do farmers. The first large contingents of well-to-do German, Irish, and Scandinavian peasants came to the New World at this time and formed the core of the most stable farm groups of the United States.

From the time of the Civil War to World War I American industry left the household and the artisan's shop for the great factories. The need for skilled workers declined. For the first time America began to dip deeply into the vast labor pool represented by the poor peasant masses of eastern and southern Europe. Since these could not pay their own passage, they were recruited by agents sent out by land companies interested in sales, railroads and steamship companies interested in fares, and budding industries interested in workers. Masses of immi-grants had their fares paid in return for contracts to work out their debts in the new mass industries. On the West Coast a similar importation of coolie labor from China and Japan was under way.

This type of immigration accelerated early in the twentieth century. Twice as many Austrians, Italians, and Russians, for example, came to America between 1901 and 1910 as had come in the entire period from 1820 to 1900. From Europe as a whole, half as many immigrants came in the first decade of the twentieth century as had come in all previous history.

Traditional middle class America soon began to respond in alarm to what, from its perspective, it could only view as an invasion of bar-barians. Sporadic rejection of the new immigration began with the Chi-nese Exclusion Act of 1882. In 1903 the inspection of immigrants was instituted. The Bureau of Immigration was established in 1906. Liter-acy tests and various bans on types of immigrants deemed undesirable were introduced between 1917 and 1920. Finally the first quota law on immigrants was passed in 1921. Thereafter immigration control was dominated by the concept of reducing the number of immigrants from any group to a fixed percentage of numbers of that group present in the country at some previous date. The quota law was revised in 1924, and again in the McCarren-Walter Act of 1952.

Immigration and the Labor Movement

Economic requirements steered the New World immigration from its inception, leading from the beginning to a linkage of ethnic group and occupation: the English and Scotch businessman, the Dutch trader, the French chef, the Welsh miner, the German musician, the German and Scandinavian farmer, the Irish railroad worker and politician, the Italian road worker, the Polish steel worker, the Japanese abalone fisherman and market gardener.

As one ethnic group followed another, tensions often developed between them when they were forced into competition for the same jobs. Other tensions developed between employers and workers, intensified by unscrupulous employers who played one ethnic group against another. These conflicts rose to fever pitch with the rise of large-scale industry after the Civil War, when the older skilled laborers were facing displacement by the new unskilled workers.

When the middle class derivation of the traditional American laborer is taken into account, the failure of enduring union activity to appear in the pre-Civil War period becomes comprehensible. The traditional American laborer was an individualist who dreamed of some day setting up a business of his own—rather than of forming into unions for collective action on the assumption that his laboring status was permanent and that his only recourse toward bettering his lot was through collective action. However, when these traditional, conservatively inclined, skilled laborers found their level of living menaced by mass importations of unskilled workers, they responded by organizing the first enduring national labor unions of America. Between 1864 and 1873 twenty-six major unions formed, with a membership of more than 300,000. The first semi-successful national union, the Knights of Labor, was organized in 1871; it declined after the Haymarket Massacre of 1886. More enduring was the American Federation of Labor (AF of L), organized in 1914 with a backbone of skilled laborers. The AF of L, in accord with the middle class inclinations of its members, shunned radical movements and avoided political involvement.

Sporadically the new unskilled workers were swept into union activity. These organizations, however, often undertook radical political or revolutionary activities. Their fate is typified by the revolutionary Industrial Workers of the World (IWW), which survived only from 1905 to 1918, when its leaders were jailed as subversives. American labor came fully into its own only after 1933, when organized labor largely divided into two great camps: the AF of L and the powerful group led by the Committee for Industrial Organization (CIO), formed in 1938 by leaders expelled from the AF of L.

Thus American labor acquired its first stable national forms when its point of gravity was located in conservative craft groups threatened by the unskilled immigrants. All politically radical or revolutionary labor groups, such as the IWW, were short lived. However, in the course of time and accompanying the stabilization of mass industry, the descendants of the same immigrants against whom the conservative unions had been formed, quietly moved into position in the great unions, where today they form the bulk of organized labor in America. By the time these new groups had become integrated into organized labor, their psychology had also become middle class in orientation.

Immigration and Religion in America

As the *milieu* in which immigration occurred changed, new kinds of immigrants began arriving in numbers. In place of the north European Protestant townsman, there came the south European Roman Catholic peasant. Among the Jews a similar change was evident: in place of the sophisticated, secularized Spanish Jews who composed the first Jewish immigration and the educated professional German Jews who formed the second, there came the intensely religious, culturally backward Russian Jews. As masses of such aliens with their strange language, customs, and religion moved into predominantly middle class Protestant America, they were often met with intense prejudice, usually from nearby ethnic groups. The German Jews, for example, were of all groups most immediately threatened with a loss of status when the Russian Jews appeared on the scene. German immigrants spearheaded resistance to the Irish; the Irish sharpened the lances of prejudice against the Italians and Poles. Time has modified or eliminated all of these forms of prejudice.

Two religious principles developed under frontier conditions came into play to ease ethnic tensions: particularism and the separation of Church and State. The acceptance of religious particularism left every ethnic group free to form withdrawn communities around its own church. In the heart of the cities, church-centered ethnic ghettos formed by the hundreds. A variety of other specialized institutions developed around their churches: labor unions, foreign language presses, parochial schools, nationalistic societies, burial societies, insurance associations. The principle of separation of Church and State then came into play, permitting these formations to develop without official interference. Within the ghetto it was possible for the alien to pursue a semi-protected life apart: to speak his native language, eat his national food, participate in specialized cultural activities, and perhaps send his children to a parochial school. This could continue until institutions of the wider world, such as the factory and public school, gradually dissolved the walls of his sub-community and began to absorb its members. The thousands of ethnic communities served as decompression chambers in which the transition from ethnically alien status could be accomplished by stages. Furthermore, the withdrawn ethnic communities sealed off the worst of the potential tensions between American religious groups. Ironically, closely related sects and ethnic communities, made accessible to one another by their very similarity, often despised one another whole-heartedly, while major religious differences serenely co-existed. And when evangelical movements shook the sects of the wider society, they usually stirred the adherents of the ethnic religions as well.

The American Language

The form of American immigration played a significant role in establishing English as a national language without the slightest need for political pressure. The language of the first inhabitants of a region has considerable advantage over its later-arriving rivals. When the Normans conquered England, they imposed French on the English nation from the top, but the language of the Anglo-Saxons carried out a cultural reconquest of the Normans. People coming to a new area are usually compelled to adopt the place designations of the inhabitants. In the United States one often encounters a basic layer of Indian place names, on which is imposed a stratum of French names, above which flows the current English. Place names often represent a cryptic history of the cultural tides which washed over a region.

English moved without contest to unquestioned dominance over colonial speech, and then, as the language of the first predominant American group, to become the speech of the country. The original non-English immigrations were small, usually less than one per cent of the existing population in any given year. Non-English immigrants usually took up the language of the majority as fast as possible. Without the slightest need for external pressure, by the third generation, the language of the non-English immigrant had vanished without a trace. Although larger groups of immigrants arrived, American English was often enriched by the incorporation of many terms from the various non-English groups, by this time it was too strongly entrenched to be shaken.

The only exception to the dominance of a region by the English language is found in the Spanish-speaking Southwest. There, Spanish was the resident language over which English swept as an incoming tide. Among the states, only New Mexico is bilingual and many of its citizens still speak only Spanish. There are also a few language islands: some Indians retain their native languages, and French is spoke in parts of Louisiana. Otherwise, non-English languages are used only in parochial schools.

The ethnic ghettos in which the immigrants usually assembled promoted the smooth transition to English. For a time in the confines of the ethnic ghetto, the alien could depend on his national language. From this vantage point, when he was ready, the immigrant learned English as easily and naturally as he learned to practice the everyday ethic which early Protestantism bestowed on the nation—as cultural equipment essential for success in the wider society.

Immigrant Contributions to the American Pantheon of Fame

The varied immigrations have placed at America's disposal highly diversified cultural resources and offered the possibility for each ethnic group to find the niche where it could make its best contribution to the whole. The French have played a unique role in molding American etiquette and elaborating its most refined cuisine. The Germans have made contributions to the development of its agriculture and its musical tastes. The Irish have contributed a genius for organization. The Japanese developed its West Coast fishing and market gardening. These are mere illustrations of an endlessly varied drama.

Each immigrant group has also supplied candidates for the American pantheon of famous persons. Some 10 per cent of the entries in the *Dictionary of American Biography* are wholly or partly of French descent, including the Deweys, La Follettes, and Du Ponts. The Du Ponts are not only one of America's top industrial families, but they have produced famous soldiers, naval officers, and diplomats. Prominent Americans of German stock include politicians like Robert F. Wagner, artists like Emil Ludwig, scientists like Albert Einstein, industrialists like Henry G. Kaiser, inventors like Steinmetz, and scholars like H. L. Mencken. Again, these are mere illustrations, for every ethnic group has made its contributions to America's hall of fame.

THE RISE OF MASS SOCIETY

While the frontier and immigration were great shared experiences of the American people, they bore within themselves a powerful impetus toward particularism and the atomization of society into tiny hermetically sealed independent groups. Every frontier community developed its own peculiar solution to its local problems, and every ethnic group intensified its linguistic, institutional, and historical peculiarities. By themselves the frontier and immigration experiences terminated in thousands of specialized local communities which differed endlessly in detail.

The Homogenization of Taste

At the very time when the frontier and immigration were particularizing the American people, the Industrial Revolution was reversing the process. The Industrial Revolution was one of the most significant offspring of the Old World that migrated to the American frontier. In contrast to its parental forms in England, the New England version of the Industrial Revolution did not have to contend with the vested customs of a traditional society.

In the Old World the products of the mechanically powered machine industry were forced to appeal to the tastes of a people adjusted to the refinements of ancient traditions of craftsmanship. In the New World the machine product was presented to tastes modified by the makeshift necessities of frontier and immigration. The New World buyer was more inclined to accept a standardized machine-made item, so long as it was better or cheaper than his make-do home product, than the European immersed in the traditions of craftsmanship which had been evolving toward perfection since the Middle Ages. In the New World the Industrial Revolution offered to the American people a crude, practical, and cheap product during the period when the struggle with the frontier and with immigration prevented them from supplying qualitatively superior items out of their own resources. While the frontier and immigration were tending to crystallize the customs of the American people into infinitely varied local forms, the Industrial Revolution, like a giant cement mixer, was homogenizing their tastes.

The Destruction and Reconstruction of the Mass Society

A shortage of labor and an eagerness to substitute machine for hand labor, a vast reservoir of cheap raw materials, and expanding markets provided the conditions in which the North American branch of the Industrial Revolution could experiment with its potentials and gradually achieve its own unique perfections. To the present day the crafted quality product is characteristic of European industry; the reliable standardized item is characteristic of American industry. To the industry of the world, America bestowed the assembly line and interchangeable parts.

A vast liquidation of traditional culture was necessary for machine productivity to realize its potentials. Production was transferred from the home and the small artisan's shop to the great industrial plant. Women and children who had operated the home industries moved to the factory, and returned home as equals of the men. The patriarchal family became a thing of the past. Small industries collapsed under competition with the machine product. The old middle classes of independent small businessmen, artisans, and professionals melted away, and a new tide of white collar workers in giant industrial and commercial bureaucracies replaced them. To acquire the new skills and knowledge of the industrial society, pressure for professional education developed. To transform consumption into the forms needed by giant industry, a new army of experts appeared.

Thus, accompanying the destruction of traditional ways of life was a reconstruction of life to fit it to the needs of a mass world: production was consolidated in giant concerns; labor was organized; the arts of advertising which mobilized taste and adjusted it to the standardized product were consolidated in the hands of advertising shock troops. Great bureaucracies of business and government appeared; white collar persons, the salaried employees, and bureaucratically organized professionals replaced the old self-employed professional and small businessmen; and a development of higher and professional education was carried out.

The Effects on the Level of Living

In the United States mass production and distribution have lifted income and consumption to the highest in the world. The *per capita* income in the United States is twice as high as that of its nearest rival, Great Britain; it is three times higher than that of France; it is seven times higher than that of the rest of the world. Three fourths of the world's automobiles are owned by people of the United States. In the United States in 1950, one passenger automobile was registered for every four persons, as compared to one for every twenty-one in Great Britain, one for twenty-six in France, and one for one hundred and ninety in Italy. With 6 per cent of the world's population and 7 per cent of its land area, America produces and consumes more than one third of the total goods and services of the world. It produces nearly one half of the world's factory goods.

NATIONAL CRISES

Along with the Industrial Revolution, national crises have been a major counterinfluence to particularism. National crises cut the lines of locality and sect and sharpen the realization that there are times when a people must either hang together or they will hang separately. National crises strengthen political institutions and create shared experiences and loyalties that rise above the divisions of party, color, and creed. The American people have been shaken to national self-consciousness and faced with the task of creating new institutions by five major crises: the Revolutionary War (1775–1781), the Civil War (1861–1865), World War I (1917–1918), the Great Depression (1930–1938), and World War II (1941–1945).

The Revolutionary War

The Revolutionary War lifted the United States out of colonial status and sent it on the route toward nationhood. It broke down the internal differences between aristocratic strata loyal to England and the average colonial American, and it relocated the point of gravity of New World development in itself. It was associated with the creation of America's democratic political institutions—the oldest and most conservative of the world's democracies. It tightened the market orientation of the American farmer who was called upon to provision Washington's armies. It created a body of common experience and America's oldest galaxy of national heroes.

The Civil War

The Civil War melted down many powerful internal differences, and reversed a trend toward sectionalism which had threatened to tear the new society to bits. The focal point of the struggle was the institution of slavery central to the southern plantation system. The slave plantation of the early nineteenth century was cross-tied to the industrial revolution. The application of an invention to agriculture, Eli Whitney's (1765–1825) cotton gin (1793) had made the slave-operated plantation profitable at the very time it was tending to disappear. The produce of the cotton plantations in turn fed the emerging factory systems of England and New England which composed their markets.

However, in the long run no economy can tolerate the coexistence of free and slave labor. The highly paid, technologically progressive free labor system must either eliminate the lowly paid, technologically unprogressive slave labor system or be eliminated in turn. Moreover, associated with the contrasting economic systems of North and South were other contradictory institutions and antagonistic class systems. These differences, sustained by powerful forces for states' rights, threatened to destroy the Union.

In eliminating the more extreme of these regional differences, the Civil War solidified the Union, brought about political, economic, and social changes which worked toward synthesis, and bestowed on the nation the spawn of slavery. The contemporary problem of segregation is the final phase of the integration by the American people of the 10 per cent of its population descended from the original slaves.

The Civil War also served as a military proving ground for the twentieth-century world wars. The great markets it created promoted the growth of mass industry and transportation. In simultaneously creating a great demand for agricultural products and putting millions of farm boys under arms, the Civil War tightened the national market orientation of agriculture and encouraged the mechanization of farms. The Department of Agriculture was established as a Civil War measure. The national farm organizations formed soon thereafter, in part to control the national agricultural markets and in part to control the political forces affecting agriculture.

World Wars I and II

In the course of total mobilization of men and materials, the great twentieth century wars have retooled American industry at public expense; they have accelerated the expansion of giant industry, speeded the mechanization of the farm, promoted the application of science to industry, fixed the national market orientation of both industry and agriculture, provided vast collective experiences which cut through all lines of race, religion, creed, and locality, and hardened the American people into a unit conscious of itself in contrast to other nationalities.

The Great Depression

While it was only one of a long series of panics and depressions, the Great Depression was the most profound of all the periodic collapses which accompanied the wave-like progress and relapse of the developing mass economy at the expense of local forms. In bringing internal problems to a head, it was comparable only to the Civil War. It resulted in the impetus to create new institutional expedients which have permanently changed the structure of American life. The Great Depression lifted the American labor movement to its contemporary form; it provided the occasion for instituting present-day agricultural policies; and it started America on the road toward its contemporary welfare and social security systems. All of these new institutional arrangements have shifted activities, formerly operated locally, to a national level.

AMERICAN CIVILIZATION

As the synthesis of a people's culture, a civilization rests on two major elements: the richness of its stock of cultural forms and the perfection of its synthesis of them into a whole. High civilizations develop refined manners which enrich daily life; they create artistic forms and styles in which the ideal image—not to mention the tensions —of a people are explored; they sustain distinctive theologies and philosophies in which the conceptions of a people are integrated and its peculiar viewpoint is expressed. In its play and in its arts a people reveals its civilizational synthesis, for at these moments it lives for its own sake and not for some exterior reason, such as making money or acquiring power.

The emergence of distinctive forms of play and of arts is facilitated by some stability of life permitting cultural forms to be fixed and perfected; by sufficient leisure for the emergence of standards of discrimination between cultural forms; by the appearance of cultural specialists such as artists and critics whose object it is to perfect cultural forms; and by sufficient clarity on the part of artists and their publics to encourage spirals of development and synthesis of cultural forms.

Until recently these conditions so necessary for the rise of a civilization were only erratically realized by the American people. The events of the frontier (which closed in the 1890's) and immigration (which was slowed to a moderate pace in World War I), while providing a vast storehouse of Old World cultural forms and New World experiences, were too fluid to permit the fixing of forms so necessary for development of a civilization. Nor was there the leisure so necessary for the reflective recasting of social and cultural forms into integrated styles. Finally, while experience was casting up an enormous volume of new forms, national crises and mass industry were simultaneously liquidating these same forms.

Prior to the Civil War the elements of a genteel civilizational synthesis were arising in the South and a flowering of culture occurred in New England, but there was not, as yet, a synthesis of culture for America as a whole. However, the dominant social stratum of middle class Protestant townsmen as modified by the frontier was establishing a style of deportment for the country as a whole. When they "made good" and moved out of their ethnic communities, immigrants and their descendants usually took over the culture of these middle class Protestant townsmen, even though they had originally differed in language, culture, and religion.

The Yankee was emerging as the distinctive American type. All major observers agreed on his characteristics: practicality, anti-intellectualism, a genius for organization, strong materialism, the tendency (a residue of the Protestant ethic) to conceptualize social and political affairs in moralistic terms, the possession of great faith in individual initiative, and a well developed sense of civic responsibility. The

Yankee was to serve as the foundation for a distinctive American civilization.

In shattering a major impulse toward sectionalism and the acceleration of mass industrialization shortly thereafter, the Civil War brought America by the 1880's and 1890's to a new self-consciousness. In his study of American literature, Alfred Kazin noted that the rapid drift of the New World into factories and cities and the consequent dislocation of old faiths were closely associated with the first appearance of a genuinely national literature. Out of the West arose a literature of protest against the plutocracy of the East; a theme that had been part of American life since colonial days was brought to national expression. The threat of the new forces of industrialism evoked an expectant Utopian literature. A new realism emerged: in literature (Stephen Crane, Frank Norris, and Theodore Dreiser); in painting (Robert Henri, John Sloan, and the Philadelphia Group); and in poetry (Edwin Arlington Robinson).

The new national self-consciousness was also expressed in the first distinctive contribution made by America to the philosophy of the West: in the pragmatism of Charles Peirce, William James, and John Dewey. In the skyscraper, America made a unique contribution to the architecture of the world. In the prairie style of Louis Sullivan and Frank Lloyd Wright, America developed a domestic architecture of its own. The new national self-consciousness, negatively manifested in the attempts to manage its population composition by immigration control, was positively expressed in these first movements toward a distinct civilization.

These events jettisoned into the world the American of today: fabulously endowed with material riches, suddenly invested with leisure that might evoke the envy of an ancient king, yet somewhat bewildered as to what to do with his free time, for his old social forms are being cast aside, and there has not yet been time to work out an effective synthesis of the cultural form of the mass world. At the mid-century the American people were spending on the average of 10 billion dollars a year on recreational goods and services alone. Vacations and travel expenses were consuming 12 billion dollars. Around a billion dollars a year were being spent on liquor, 4.4 billion dollars a year on tobacco, 5 billion dollars a year on sports clothes, candy, and soft drinks. Total expenditures for all types of recreation today may be close to 40 billion dollars a year.

At the very time when American civilization was approaching

synthesis, the powerful forces of the twentieth-century world began to render it obsolete. The full expansion of mass industry was yet to occur; the cities were exploding into megalopolitan agglomerations which would have to assimilate their thousands of ethnic ghettos before they could be integrated fully into American life; the major world wars and a great depression with significant consequences for all aspects of institutional life remained to be experienced. Nevertheless, never has a society been so affluent on all levels nor had such vast opportunities for creating a civilization of its own.

PART FIVE

STUDIES
in the SOCIOLOGY
of CULTURE

Among the exciting areas of contemporary sociology primarily established by the Formalists is the sociology of culture. Unfortunately the area has been developed only by fits and starts. While sporadic volumes have appeared in specific sub-areas of the sociology of culture (the sociology of art, of science, of law, and of knowledge), no integrated theory has been constructed to account for its properties as a whole. Moreover, no methodology acceptable to the majority of sociologists has been developed for dealing with the major problems of the sociology of culture.

The subject matter of the sociology of culture consists in *the socially learned forms of inter-human life*. All social activities have cultural components.

The Cultural Components of Social Activities

Forms of Interhuman Activity	Cultural Component
Social Act	Social Relation
Groups	Institutions
Communities	Social Structure

The forms that arise in the course of human social behavior must either be invented or learned from others. There are forms in the social behavior of nonhuman creatures, even though they have few, if any, cultural components. When the biological conditions are ready and the proper stimulus is experienced, the robin builds a special kind of nest. The form of the bird's nest-building is neither invented by or taught to the bird; nest-building is an instinct genetically transmitted; it is not a cultural form.

The plasticity of human instincts makes it necessary for men to invent or learn from others the forms of their social life; this necessity is rarely exhausted by the invention of any one single form. In contrast to the social insects which always construct their hives or nests in the same manner, or the beaver which always solves the same engineering problems in the same way, or the bird which builds the type of nest fixed in its species, human creativity continually wells up around the forms it creates, improving old ones and developing new ones. Forms which were developed to serve one area of life may be pressed into multiple uses in others. In any case, although cultural forms of varying degrees of complexity arise directly in connection with inter-human activities, a variety of additional forms arise as well. Thus, the sociology of culture comprises more than the array of forms arising directly in connection with social activities.

Ethnologists have long called attention to the fact that culture is not a great seamless web, but is capable of being analyzed into units. In one terminology the ultimate units of culture are "traits." The use of tobacco, for example, was a trait widely distributed among the American Indians at the time of Columbus. Moreover, a number of traits may be closely integrated and the related groups may diffuse together. The notion of a "culture complex" has been utilized for such closely related sets. Tobacco smoking was only a single trait, for example, in the "tobacco-growing-complex." While there is nothing intrinsically wrong with the use of "complex" for this purpose, the anchorage of the term in psychiatry makes it inadvisable in the area of culture: it is too easy to carry with it the connotation that there is some sort of group mind. Rather, a series of closely related cultural forms (or traits) integrated in terms of some concept of fitness is more appropriately described as a *style*. When the forms in a number of life areas are submitted to integrating formula, one often speaks of a "style of life." It is quite possible, for example, that the mode of behavior in a group's commercial life should be utilized in a number of related spheres. It is quite appropriate, at such times, to speak of the commercialization of life. Or, again, attitudes and practices originally found only in the military may be imposed on a variety of surrounding life spheres. The style of life that results is describable as militarism.

Not only is it possible for social forms to be integrated into styles (not only styles of life, but styles of thought and of art), but at times great integrating movements may, in turn, be set in motion. Such large integrations of cultural forms and styles are civilizations.

Social and General Cultural Institutions

Interhuman Activity	Cultural Components of Interhuman Activity	General Cultural Forms
Social Acts	Social Relations	Cultural Traits or Forms
Groups	Institutions	Styles
Communities	Social Structures	Civilizations

The sociology of culture must ultimately explain three kinds of problems: the multiplication of social forms beyond those socially required; the integration of social forms into styles; and the formation of civilizations.

Tentatively, three principles of civilization formation have been advanced to solve these problems: *playfulness,* which operates throughout the range of human life to multiply cultural forms beyond those required for daily social needs; *aesthetic receptivity,* or a sense of form which inclines men to see a fitness between cultural traits and to derive an enjoyment from their rearrangement to realize this fitness; and *sublimation,* the transformation of problems unsolved in the course of man's social life to an ideal plane.[1]

The two studies in the present section examine special aspects of the sociology of culture. Max Weber's imaginative study of *The Rational and Social Foundations of Music* examined the hypothesis that the unique course of Western music is in part accounted for by the transformation of this art under the forces of rationalization. This would construe Western musical development as a special case of the sublimation of social phenomena (rationalization processes in science and technology) in the sphere of culture. The other essay on "Sociology and Aesthetics" explores some of the differences between aesthetics as a normative discipline and the sociology of art as an empirical or scientific study.

10

MAX WEBER'S SOCIOLOGY
OF MUSIC*

THE STUDY OF THE INTERRELATIONS
between society and music is not to be undertaken carelessly nor is it
one affording easy solutions. Since the patterns of music production
and appreciation may change while the society remains constant and
the same music may be received and loved by the people of quite
different societies, there is no one-to-one casual interdetermination of
society and music. One must reject as vulgar errors the Nazi idea that
there is a true Aryan music and the Communist idea that Western
music is of a decadent bourgeois type. The sociology of music could
not mean this, for it would need be rejected out of hand.

However, it is a matter of familiar observation that there are close
ties between various social elements and music. The musician is a
member of society like anyone else. His requirement for making a living
may be bound up with his artistic role. If he earns a livelihood independently of his art, his music has the form of a hobby or leisure-
time pursuit. The manner in which he cultivates his talents will tend
to differ from that of the musician who makes a living by means of his
art. The musician requires an audience. His product is molded by the
demand or lack of demand for his art. In his art the musician employs
instruments related to the level of technology of his civilization. His
finest performances may be attended for status rather than aesthetic
reasons as occasions for the better elements of society to see and be
seen by each other in appropriate dress, jewelry, furs. The artist may
be a free agent producing his wares in open competition with others.
He may be a kept and pampered object, as much a part of an elegant
household as a combed and brushed poodle. It is a matter of familiar
observation that all such factors enter as encouragements and dis-
couragements in the production and consumption of music.

Thus, there is a kind of common sense sociology of music familiar
to us all. We know that, generally, fine art is for fine people and vulgar

* With Johannes Riedel.

art is for the not so fine. We know that status factors affect the change in artistic styles. We know that artistic performances have extra-musical functions. The sociology of music takes its point of departure from such familiar observations. It explores the boundaries between the sciences of sociology and musicology, attempting to explain those links between society and music that common observation reveals.

Max Weber's pioneering essay, "The Rational and Social Foundations of Music,"[1] has special interest to both sociologists and musicians, for it cuts below the surface of a common sense sociology of music to fundamental issues. Weber attempted to trace the influence of social factors on the very creative core and technical basis of music. In its broadest sense, Weber's thesis was that Western music has peculiar rational properties produced by social factors in Occidental development. Right or wrong, Weber's thesis assumes a relevance for the deepest levels of musical theory. It also forms a test case as to the values of sociological and musicological sciences for each other.

As one of the great sociologists in modern times, Max Weber is universally known among social scientists. Inasmuch as he is much less widely known in musical circles, it will be useful for some of our readers briefly to review those aspects of his thought relevant to his sociology of music.

BASIC SOCIOLOGICAL IDEAS

Max Weber (1864–1920) was born in Berlin of an upper middle class family. His father was a prominent figure in the National Liberal Party of the Bismarckian era, serving for some years in the Reichstag. Weber was entered upon the study of law, his father's profession. His first academic appointment was that of *Privatdozent* at the University of Berlin. Very early in his career he accepted an appointment as Professor of Economics at Freiburg, becoming successor to the great economist Karl Knies. Not long after this he suffered a severe nervous breakdown which required his retirement from academic life. For the greater part of his productive career he lived as a private scholar in Heidelberg. During World War I he accepted an appointment at the University of Vienna, and later—in 1919—he was appointed to the chair of Economics at Munich. During this period he was an active member of the delegation to the League of Nations. He died of pneumonia in 1920 at the height of his scholarly powers.[2]

The full stature of Weber as an original scholar became fully clear with the publication in 1904 of *The Protestant Ethic and the Spirit of Capitalism*.[3] In an atmosphere largely created by Marxist intellectuals, all spheres of life, including the artistic, were being explained more or less exclusively in terms of economics. Political, religious, social, ethical, and aesthetic concerns were interpreted as extensions of economic interests. *The Protestant Ethic and the Spirit of Capitalism* was a dramatic essay in which Weber corrected the simplism of an exclusively economic interpretation of cultural life. Other areas of life were treated as semiautonomous with effects of their own. The thesis that religion is necessarily or only the opiate of the masses was implicitly rejected. Causal influences were traced from religious experience to economics. Many of the distinctive features of Western capitalism were traced from the central attitudes and characteristic modes of deportment generated in the circles of the Protestant sects.

The essay set off one of the great intellectual debates in modern times. From the days of *The Protestant Ethic* to the collected works in the sociology of religion left unfinished at his death, Weber's work ranges over an amazing compass of the modern social sciences. He made original contributions to such different fields as economics, politics and administration, the sociology of religion, the sociology of law, the sociology of authority, leadership, and knowledge.[4]

Weber developed a rich array of concepts which he applied to every area of social life he brought under review, from the sociology of authority to the sociology of music.[5] At bottom sociology studies social action. When the sociologist examines an institution, a group, a community, or a society, he is only studying ways in which people act toward one another, for all things social reduce to interhuman behavior.[6] Social behavior is not only interhuman but meaningful as well. If in a crowd waiting in line before a theatre one person steps on another's toe, there has been a physical contact of individuals but no social action. When one offers an apology which the other accepts, the physical act has initiated a temporary social act. The meanings present in social action are assumed to exercise a causal influence upon the course that action takes. A scientist is interested in regularities in the phenomena he studies. For the social scientist, taking meaningful social actions as his object matter, interest attaches to the kinds of recurrences they display. Accepting the usual analysis of action into means and ends, Weber isolates certain fundamental ways in which social actions may be stabilized: through the rational efficiency of means to achieve the ends desired; through the establishment of ends as fixed; through acting out of an excess of emotion; through acting habitually, or if the habit is socially shared, traditionally.[7] In these various types of action (rational, evaluative, emotional, and traditional) the properties of action are determined by the relation of means to ends. In the first (rational) the action is determined by the complete freedom of the choice of ends and by the choice of means purely in terms of their efficiency. The actions of a scientist are the very epitome of rationality. A housewife choosing freely among food values and shopping where she gets the highest quality of food values at the lowest price is behaving rationally. An action is evaluative when the ends toward which it is directed are assumed to be absolutely valid. Religion presents many examples. One may take salvation to be the unquestioned ultimate value of human conduct and order all other aspects of life as means to achieve it. One is acting evaluatively when he takes as absolute some value such as honesty and tells the truth on all occasions regardless of the consequences. An artist might take some ideal of beauty as an absolute end and sacrifice fame, fortune, and perhaps even his family and health to it. An action is affective when it is determined by the presence of strong emotion: actions in rage or terror, grief or despair are typical. An action is traditional when determined by long familiarity and habit: when one votes for one party because his family has always done so. Many hundreds of little actions in everyday life are traditional.

There are three primary ways in which action may be regularized: rationally, evaluatively, and traditionally. Most affective or emotional actions are highly unstable and variable. Most societies spend much time controlling unstable affectively determined actions. Collective emotional behaviors, like those of the actions of mobs, are ordinarily avoided when possible.

Since sociologists are interested in recurrent patterns of conduct, an important economy of thought is represented by a concept which permits reference to the pattern without the need to refer to every single act in which the pattern is displayed. For Weber a social relation consists in the existence of a probability that there will be in some meaningfully understandable sense, a course of social action.[8] A social relation is an arrangement of persons present in any social action. If two persons interact in such a way that A always gives orders and B carries them out, one may say that whenever A and B act a social relation of superiority-subordination holds between A and B. The concept of social relation substitutes for the need to refer to a whole multiplicity of specific actions, concentrating on the common pattern.

A social structure is an organized system of social relations. A state, for example, is an extensive system of social relations between officials and citizens. Such social relations when organized into structures are often very specifically defined such that very definite rights and obligations adhere to any single person. A citizen of the state, for example, may be obligated to pay taxes, to fight in its armies, to refrain from certain kinds of actions defined as treasonable. The president of the state receives a specific salary and has a whole series of definite powers and responsibilities, perhaps even with specified punishments (such as impeachment and loss of office).

The stabilities of social action due to rational, evaluative, and traditional forces also apply to social relations and social structures. A scientific laboratory, for example, may represent a stabilized social structure the relations of which are predominantly of a rational type. A religious sect may be primarily characterized by relations of an evaluative nature. A family may display a fundamental system of traditional patterns.

Social actions are the units of interhuman life also in the collective aesthetic life of man. Here, too, social relations are stabilized and social structures appear. The musical life of men also may be organized into a variety of forms. It is evident that to some degree the musical life of men is susceptible to analysis in terms of the same sociological categories as are other areas of life.

RATIONAL SOCIAL ACTION
IN OCCIDENTAL DEVELOPMENT
AND SOCIAL STRUCTURE

One of the most fundamental theses running through Max Weber's many studies is that an ever-growing preponderance of rational social action runs through the development of the Western world. Ultimately this thesis was applied by Weber to the Occidental arts, particularly its music.

The term "rational" does not have a single meaning in ordinary discourse. It has a range of meanings from "reasonable," "representing good judgment," to "conducted in terms of logical or scientific principles." At times ideas, actions, persons, and even social structures are said to be "rational." Modern psychologists, particularly the Freudians, have familiarized us with the concept of rationalization as the psychological process of giving pseudo-reasons for the real ones in conduct, concealing one's true motives from others and often from oneself. The term "rationalism" has been employed to refer to a kind of philosophic outlook such as that current in the eighteenth century.

In applying the term "rational" to social action, Weber was concerned to isolate one kind of relation between the means and ends of action. A social action is rational when the means utilized in the course of action are chosen because of their efficiency or adequacy to the attainment of the ends in view. We can be most certain of the rationality of the choice of means to ends to the degree to which logical or scientific standards have been established permitting judgments of adequacy or appropriateness. To a lesser extent ordinary experience supplies us with many standards of adequacy. A person who tried to cross a stream by flapping his arms and flying over like a bird would hardly be considered to possess an average knowledge of appropriate or adequate means. Modern science has tremendously expanded our knowledge of relations between things of the world; it has enormously widened the sphere of man's rationality.

The term "rational" does not apply to the ends of action or to the values to which action is addressed. This separates the technical from the ordinary usage. A youth who argues with his parents or teachers may be told that he is irrational or unreasonable when often what is actually meant is that he is taking some unusual stand or making some unconventional demand. Such identifications of "rational" with "conventional" blur its meaning by referring it partly to the ends of action. The "rationalism" of the eighteenth-century philosophers was of this type. The rationalistic philosophers believed that every man has a faculty of reason and men share the same universal set of values. Weber's usage has nothing to do with the ends of action, only with the choice of means in terms of their appropriateness to ends. An act of thought conducted in terms of the rules of logic is rational. An act of inquiry conducted in terms of the norms and criteria of science is also rational, for rationality means precisely the conduct of the thought process in terms of such norms and criteria. The technical conception of rational social action as developed by Max Weber is a direct extension of these meanings.

A social relation is an arrangement present in social action; social structure is a complex, organized pattern of social relations. By simple extension one may describe a social relation or social structure as rational. So far as the actions of a young man and girl in love are determined by the presence of powerful emotion they are, in Weber's terminology, affective. When the stirrings of adolescence send the young boys of America into the trees in the girl's front yard to behave in ways leading sager minds to think that perhaps Darwin had a point, such irrationalities are not atypical of affectively determined actions. By contrast, the same girl's elder sisters may employ every artifice with a deliberately calculated rationality. Thus rational social actions may appear even in areas where the most powerful emotions normally appear, such as erotic spheres.

A social structure is rational to the degree to which the system of social relationships rests on an organization of ends to means in terms of efficiency, adequacy, and appropriateness of means to ends. It has already been observed that rationality may even appear in a courtship. Rational strategies may be observed by the staff officers in war. A business corporation may be rationally organized: computing all actions in terms of their effect in increasing profits; basing hiring and firing policies on judgments of efficiency; calculating all assets and expenditures; continually adjusting behavior to cut costs and increase earnings. Not all groups are equally susceptible to rational organization. A business corporation is ordinarily more rationally organized than a love affair; a scientific laboratory is usually more rationally organized than a family; the experiment conducted by a group of atomic scientists is ordinarily more rationally conducted than a blind date. But while differentially susceptible to rational organization, rational structuring of action may appear anywhere.

It was Weber's view that one of the ground trends in Western civilization is the movement toward rationalization. In every institutional area, in the rise of business, in political parties, in government, in religion, calculation in terms of efficiency and the appropriateness of means to ends tends to be the rule. Old mythologies are exposed, taboos are exploded, magical forms are destroyed, and the colorful and varied forms of old mysteries are clarified in the cold light of scientific day. In Friedrich Schiller's phrase, a "disenchantment of the world" is carried out.

Thought itself tends to find its norm in science, the most rational of all thought forms. The economic historians have familiarized us with the idea that our economics is characterized by the development of rational business enterprise for the pursuit of profit. In political administration the Western world has experienced the most complete growth of bureaucracy, the most rational of all administrative forms. Philosophy and theology are driven on to new forms under its impulse.

This process in Occidental culture of disenchantment or, as it is often called, "progress," to which science belongs as a link and motive force, has, according to Weber, gone beyond merely practical and technical spheres to touch the very problem of the meaning of the world. As time went by Weber found himself increasingly turning to the works of Leo Tolstoi, where, he believed, the problem posed by rationalization reaches a critical intensity. As Tolstoi saw it, for civilized man death itself has no meaning. When the life of a civilized man is placed in a scheme of infinite progress according to its immanent meaning, it should never come to an end. While for the present, like the patriarchs of old, life and death were linked in an organic cycle such that a sense of the completion of life in death was possible, this sense of completion has vanished for civilized man. The process of disenchantment has extended to the very meaning of life and death.[9]

RATIONALITY IN THE ARTS

Weber did not develop his theories as to the relation between the arts and the rest of life. But there is an unexpressed assumption of continuity. Western man does not change his nature when he turns to his arts. The same thematic tendencies apparent in other spheres of his life are apparent here.

The drive toward rationality, that is, the submitting of an area of experience to calculable rules, is present here. Only in Western architecture had the pointed arch and cross-arched vault been rationally used as a device for distributing pressure and roofing spaces of all forms. Only here had these been turned into the constructive principle of great monumental buildings and utilized as the foundation of an architectural style.

Only in Western painting does the rational use of lines and perspectives come into central focus manifesting a parallel drive toward rational calculability equivalent to the employment of the Gothic arch in architecture.

Printing was invented in China, but only in the West was the rationalization of literature carried through on the basis of printing. Only here does a literature designed only for print make its appearance.

This drive to reduce artistic creativity to the form of a calculable procedure based on comprehensible principles appears above all in music. Western tone intervals were known and calculated elsewhere. But rational harmonic music, both counterpoint and harmony and the formation of tone materials on the basis of three triads with the harmonic third are peculiar to the West. So too, is a chromatics and an enharmonics interpreted in terms of harmony. Peculiar, too, is the orchestra with its nucleus in the string quartet and organization of ensembles of wind instruments. In the West appears a system of notation making possible the composition of modern musical works in a manner impossible otherwise.[10]

In all these areas the experience of Western man is assumed to display a basic continuity of theme from its practical and technical to its artistic spheres. By itself this is no new idea, for the continuity of art and the rest of social life was widely held throughout the nineteenth century and dramatically formulated by Hegel. Many times the judgment has been expressed that music is the most modern of the arts. Or, again, it has been asserted that music is the most spiritual of the arts. It has also been called the most mystic and most emotional of the arts.

Weber's study, *The Rational and Social Foundations of Music*, undercuts all such relatively superficial estimates by raising the equivalent questions in more specific form. The issue is not simply left with the rhetorical question, To what extent does the structure of Western music display a rationality paralleling that found in other areas of Occidental social, institutional, and technological life? Rather the concrete investigation is carried out in one feature of Western music after another. One may, for example, ask to what extent has our basic musical scale been reduced to an ordered system of rules? By comparison with the scales developed elsewhere it is possible to determine whether greater rationality has been achieved elsewhere—and, incidentally, to establish what is peculiarly Western in our musical scales. Equivalent types of investigation are possible for many other features of Western music.

The remainder of the present essay is concerned with a quick review of Weber's study. For this purpose, it may be presented in four basic divisions: the examination of harmony in its relation to melody; the study of the scale system of Western music in contrast to others; the review of the kinds of solutions possible to polyvocality and polysonority in musical schemes; and an examination of the role of instruments as vehicles of musical rationalization.

HARMONY IN RELATION
TO MELODY

Harmonic chord music is a great and practically unique achievement of Western man. As an aesthetic adventure into the world of simultaneous sound, harmonic chord music is peculiarly dependent on the rationalization of tone relations and progressions. Only on the basis of an ordered structure of sound intervals could one expect to conjoin tones with the anticipation of regular results. If one wishes to achieve pleasant or interesting effects with some combination of tones, if one wishes to reproduce it and create others like it, one is moved in the direction of formulating a comprehensive system of rules for establishing acceptable tone relationships.

The human ear is capable of an enormous range of sound discriminations. The precondition of aesthetic enjoyment of artistically created sound patterns is the fixing of some fundamental pattern of sounds as an acknowledged instrument for the creation of such patterns. Scales have made their appearance in every known society from the most primitive to the most civilized. But harmonic chord music depending upon the exploration of changing patterns of simultaneously sounded tone combinations is hardly capable of equal development with all scales. Weber believed that the diatonic scale resting upon the sound interval of the octave (1:2) represented the scale of maximum effectiveness for this purpose. Its primary structure rested on the interval 1:2; through successive divisions of the intervals within the octave, the fifth, fourth, the major and minor thirds, and the whole and half tones were obtained (with the exception of the sixth and seventh). Weber called attention to the fact that harmonic chord music resting on a scale permitting a maximum of ordered relations does not in the diatonic scale have a closed logical system. From the very beginning a nonsymmetric division of sounds is evident. The octave is unequally divided into the fourth and the fifth. Harmonic division of the fourth is omitted and the interval of the seventh is left aside.

When one ascends or descends in rows or circles of octaves, followed by rows of fifths or other intervals, these divisions can never meet on the same note. The fifth fifth approaches the third octave by forty-five cents; the seventh fifth surpasses the fifth octave by fifty-seven cents; the twelfth fifth reaches beyond the seventh octave by only twelve cents. So far everything is in order. All this changes, however, when in accord with harmonic rules one forms the seventh, and the entire logical structure tends to come apart at the seams. A suppressed sense of excitement attaches to Weber's discussion of this problem that transcends any mere passing curiosity over the fact that there is an uneliminatable logical looseness which appears at the heart of harmonic chord music. It cannot be dismissed, apparently, with the question, What's the difference?

There is almost a sense that one has touched one of the ultimate boundaries of human reason itself. In the West a great drama is under way in the extension of man's reason. In one area after another, colorful old mysteries dissipate like morning mist in the cold light of reason and the process of disenchantment of the world is irreversible. One area after another of human experience is transformed into a problem of arithmetic. Who would abandon the formidable gains of the logic and science of Western man? At the same time, in all honesty who would deny that it is more than nostalgic to look with regret at the disappearance of one colorful old mystery after another. We are like children who are told that there is no Santa Claus, nor Easter Bunny, and later, no stork. The room for free flight of the imagination is circumscribed by the rules of logic. The spheres to which the attitudes of humility, astonishment, and awe are appropriate vanish. The attitudes around which the psychology of Western man are built are matter-of-factness and unemotional logical perception. The world of Western man belongs not to his heart but to his head. No day goes by without some new area becoming inappropriate to his emotional apprehension as it is clarified in his intellectual perception.

There is, of course, no absolute antithesis between reason and emotion, rationality and irrationality, logic and love. This, however, should not blind one's perception of the fact that they may and, in Western man, repeatedly have come into tension. This may be seen when the most ultimately evocative emotional area of all, Death itself, may be rendered meaningless by the peculiar development of the rationality of Western man.

In Western music the drama of the experience of Western man is reenacted. Practically his music is addressed to the simultaneous requirements of expression and reason. The history of tuning and temperament, according to Weber, reflects the contradictions between theoretical and practical needs. Harmonic chord music does not from the onset rest on a rationally closed system. It is based on triads obtained through intervals which are the result of the first two successive divisions of the octave: the fifth and third. If both intervals are used in ascending and descending fashion, the complete tone material of the diatonic scale, both major and minor, is covered. By obtaining fifths and thirds, up and down, from any given tone, an intervallic discrepancy known as a diesis will result.

Thus, harmonic chord music rests on a rationally divided system of basic tone relationships, but basic to the system is a residual irrational division whose consequences form a primary object of theoretical reflection for Occidental musical theorists.

The intervals of the diatonic scale have been decided by tonality and harmony. While sounds may be perfect according to the phythagorean theory of acoustical laws, when sounded together they may produce unpleasant effects. The introduction of harmony led to a change in the intervals established by the Greeks. That between the D and E and between G and A were lessened and that between E and F and A and C were increased. The diatonic scale with C as a keynote already had two semi-tones. The addition of the black keys of the piano or organ suggests a continuous succession of semitones. However, the semitones do not represent a continuous succession of regular tone distances. A given tone like A when counted downward from the tone above A, which is B, is not identical with the first. A-sharp will be a little below the second, B-flat. This difference is a pythagorean comma. The differences of opinion between physicists and musicians have been a central point of theoretical discussion. These problems emerged as harmony because pursued as an objective separate from melody. The tonic and the keynote became the two terminal points within which the attempt was made to fix the intervallic system of the diatonic scale.

In connection with tonality, modulations, inversions, and cadences become important. Tonality remains undisturbed as long as dissonances can be resolved into consonances, *i.e.*, triads. But precisely the most important dissonance of all, the seventh chord is built on the upper fifth of a tone, the dominant seventh chord. It emerges not as a product of arithmetic division but as an extension of the diatonic scale progression. Another third is added to the triad. But the seventh cannot be included in triadic calculation.

The irrational nature of the seventh chord is emphasized, furthermore, by the fact that whenever its root is omitted, a diminished chord is present; whenever the minor seventh is altered to the major, an augmented chord arises. Diminished and augmented chords form fragments of altered scales which differ considerably from the diatonic scale.

Seventh chords are not derived harmonically, and they cannot be established on purely harmonic grounds. Since they are the result of the transposition of a third, the result of a change of pitch level, they should be accounted for through melodic needs. Harmonic chord music, thus, is not only made up from tone relations which are the result of arithmetic divisions manifest in the organization of the diatonic scale, and its intervals, in triads and their respective tonality; it is also influenced by melodic devices of tone proximity. Harmonic chord music is no mere sequence of triads, of harmonic disonances and their resolutions, but an exchange between the latter and chords which do not stand for a key, a tonality, a fixed function within a tonality, tones whose melodic function has been explained as "passing, sustained, anticipated tones," and "appoggiaturas" or "suspensions."

Harmonic chord music, thus, consists of a fluctuating tense interpenetration of the harmonic principle by another, that of tone proximity. These chord alien tones are considered by Weber as the most effective means of the dynamics of chord progressions. Without their irrational tensions, no modern music could exist. The irrationality in modern music is given through its melodic-dynamic harmony.

A great many of these nonchord tones have been treated by Hindemith in his *Craft of Musical Composition* as offshoots of chords. What Weber described as dynamics of chord progression Hindemith described as follows: "But there are many such tones which do not produce independent chords, chord splinters, or offshoots, they might be called. Such tones enrich chords without essentially changing them." And again: "The rigid chordal structure thus has to give up portions of itself bit by bit to melody, the reaction of which in these scrimmages is comparable to that of an acid upon metal. A tiny bit of a mighty force gnaws and bites at the material under attack, not strongly enough to destroy it, and yet affecting the surface enough by etching scratches and grooves into it, to roughen its smooth finish."[11]

This phase of Weber's essay brings into central focus the relations between the harmonic and melodic elements of nineteenth-century music and locates many of the most interesting features of it in the tension between rational and expressive requirements involved. The protagonists of the aesthetic adventure of Western man are seen as driven to attain a maximum of logical order, rationality, on the one hand, and the intensified, lyric, free, creative expression, affectivity, on the other. This is the aesthetic counterpart of the drama of Western man in other areas of his life.

The question could be proposed: Has Western music achieved the maximum rationality within the limits of expressive possibility? Has one, here, finally located one of the ultimate limits of rationality itself? Could one have simultaneously achieved greater rationality and more full expressive flexibility with some other scale system?

Having posed the problem of harmonic rationality and melodic expressiveness in a characteristic manner, Weber deepens the level of his analysis by raising the question of the limits of the rationality of the Western scale system through comparison with prediatonic and Eastern-Asiatic musical systems.

PREDIATONIC IN RELATION
TO WESTERN SCALE SYSTEMS

Weber reviewed the literature of his day on Eastern-Asiatic musical systems in connection with the controversial role of the seventh in nineteenth-century European harmonic chord music. In the course of this review Weber came to a number of conclusions: (1) The state of rationalization of the scale system cannot be improved through the utilization of the integral 7 or by still higher prime numbers. This is revealed by numerous examples of scales in the Eastern-Asiatic area resting on the seventh upper partial and the tritone. (2) In contrast to the use of the integral 7 as a basis for rationalization, the musical system of the Greeks and the early Christian church eliminated the number 5 and thereby the diatonic scale, the differentiation between major and minor, tonality and triads. It is an old story that modern harmonic music was only possible by changing all this. (3) In systems such as the Greek and the modal system of the early church, devices playing the role of tonality are of interest. In these systems the harmonic third was supplanted by the ditone, the semitone by the limma. In lieu of the harmonic division of a fifth and a conjunct fourth, the division into two equal fourths each consisting of equal whole tones is introduced. The instrumental division with its tone relationships is replaced by an intervallic division in which modulations, the principle of tone proximity, is of constructive importance.

In the course of this review of the musical systems of the Eastern-Asiatic area, of the Greeks, and of the early church, Weber appears to suggest that a maximum of rationality, within the limits of a range of expressive possibilities, has been achieved in Occidental music. Presumably any further rationality could only be secured by the sacrifice of expressive plasticity.

Weber turned next to the problem of expressiveness bound up with the principle of tone proximity and intervallic distance. This was the motivating interest in his review of prediatonic scale systems. Numerous examples of pentatonicism were reviewed to determine the full nature of the contrast between harmonic and melodic music, between music with and without triads.

Pentatonicism is characterized by the utilization of the frame of two equal tetrachords into which an additional tone is added. The fact that two equal tetrachords are used presupposes the subdivision of the octave. The acceptance of the octave as a basic point of departure shows partial rationalization (in the sense of harmonic chord music).

Since pentatonic music is partly rationalized, as found, for example, in the systems of the Chinese and slendro scales of the Javanese, it must be distinguished from primitive music. The same would hold for the pentatonicism of the Jewish synagogue and of the Roman Catholic Church as well as the music of the Indians, Mongols, Papuans, and Fulah Negroes.

Innumerable studies in comparative and ethnomusicology have confirmed the wide distribution of pentatonicism. Although pentatonicism is to be distinguished from primitive music, it had some things in common with it. Moreover, the music of many primitive tribes, such as the ceremonial music of the Chippewa Indians, was of a pentatonic nature. Chromaticism or semitone music, for instance was used by primitive tribes as well as by representatives of the Eastern-Asiatic cultures. It appears in Negro melodies as well as in Japanese music. The avoidance of the expressive half-tone devices can also be found in the music of many North American tribes and in the musical systems of the Chinese and Cambodians. In both primitive and pentatonic music the major third or its harmonically measured equivalent is extremely rare. However, a great variety of imperfect thirds is to be found.

In both primitive and pentatonic musical culture we often find pentatonic scales in addition to other scale devices. The Hindu Râga system had seventy-two in all.[12]

It is not possible to determine the extent to which the seven-tone or octave scales originated out of alterations and corruptions of pentatonic scales. There is no doubt, however, as to the importance of the pentatonic scale for the history of scale development toward the seven-tone and twelve-tone scales, nor is there any doubt as to the rationalistic organization of a tetrachordal tonality in contrast to authentically primitive scales which consist of unorganized conglomerations of non-rational tone successions.

The complexity of prepentatonic, pentatonic, prediatonic, and diatonic development of scale formations in many primitive societies, a problem, partially, of the reciprocal influence between tonality, scale formation, and society is brilliantly described by Weber in terms of the insertion of auxiliary and filler tones within the rationalized frame organization of the fourth. Driven by melodic requirements such filler tones may range from a quarter-tone to a third. Tetrachordal scales using these melodic forces for the selection of intertetrachord intervals are far more free for scale formation than any harmonically designed scale.

Eastern-Asiatic theorists experimented with a great many scales consisting of such novel intervallic combinations within the diazeutic fourth. Residues of these theoretic scales can be seen in the division of the Greek tetrachords into the chromatic and enharmonic genders, giving the specific role of affective and expressive meaning.

Similar evidences of melodic microtonal formations are present in the seventeen Arabian third tones,[13] the śruti system[14] of Hindu music with its twenty-two equal tone steps to the octave. Survivals from equivalent theoretic scales can be seen in certain local scales of Greek origin which refer to specific filler tones of the corresponding tetrachords (Dorian, Phrygian, Lydian).

It may be noted that in the passages where Weber raises these issues he has touched an important social factor affecting the basic scales and the possibility of their rationalization. Such theoretic systematization and ingenious experimentation with microtonal intervals has often been the work of professional musicians interested in two artistic values: increasing expressiveness on the one hand, and codifying procedure on the other.

Another kind of general sociotechnical influence is apparent so far as the requirements of instrumental timing may affect melodic intervals. If they are to be used together, one instrument has to be tuned to the other. The tuning of wind instruments, for example, may be adapted to that of string instruments, as seems to be the case in the semitone and microtone tetrachord tuning of the aulos and kithara.

A kaleidoscopic picture of the intervals as established within the tetrachords is presented in the tuning of the five-string Arabic lute with its twelve chromatic tones, in pythagorean tuning, and five additional and irrational intervals which increase the number of chromatic tones to seventeen, due to the fact that some intervals were used in an ascending, others in a descending fashion. In general, however, the effect of instrumental tuning is toward the fixing of rational intervals.

Another possible rationalizing influence in the early development of music is language. Linguistic practice sometimes moves in the direction of creating a tone language based on shifting pitch levels and changing tone volumes. Idiomatic melodicism, by producing clear intervals, may have helped in the fixing of rational intervals as well as in the establishment of the musical motive and its repetition. In the latter case, one rationalizing element such as language is substituted for another, *i.e.*, the repetition of a musical motive on a different pitch level makes the equalization of the motivic intervals necessary. The latter can be achieved only through the rationalization of melodic intervals. Thus a chain reaction of rationalization may already occur at the level of pentatonic music.

However, too much must not be made of the relation between music and language, for it has been proved by Stumpf,[15] Revesz, and others that speech does not know fixed intervals. The movement of speech tones depends exclusively on the prevailing mood of the person at the time of speaking. Nevertheless, an interdetermination of language and music is evident in the range of the melody. In ceremonial formulae of magical or sacred character small intervallic range and stepwise melodic progressions are preferred.

While language and instruments both contribute important rationalizing influences to musical culture, special interest attaches to the effects of the use of instruments in connection with the secular music accompanying dance songs. Curt Sachs proves convincingly that instrumental music, as seen primarily through the history of the drum and flute, derived from magical rationalization.[16]

Secular music and dance forms of instrumental music break through the small, litany-like range of intervals of vocal and sacred music. The range is extended. Tone steps become tone skips. Through instrumental performance, large intervals such as the octave, fifth, and fourth are recognized, established, rationalized, and utilized as consonances. The clear recognizability of these larger intervals permits development of an elementary prediatonic feeling for tonality. Instrumental activities in these secularized contexts have been of paramount importance in the rationalizing of tone intervals.

MAGICIANS, VIRTUOSI, AND THE RATIONALIZATION OF MUSIC

Max Weber's discussion of magicians and virtuosi form a part of his general review of prediatonic scale systems and the music of the immediately premodern period. It has rather special sociological interest, since it contains the question of the influence upon musical culture of social roles.

Weber believed that at relatively early cultural levels of human civilization, alongside purely personal, emotional, or aesthetic enjoyment of music there appears music designed for socially important and practical requirements. Music may be present as a magical device designed to serve cultic (apotropaic) or medicinal (exorcistic) ends. Weber maintains that whenever music is used in the service of such magical practices it tends to assume the form of rigidly stereotyped magical formulae. The intervals of such magically effective musical formulae are canonized: classified rigidly into right and wrong, perfect or imperfect. The same applies to the accompanying instruments. Such magical mottoes were identified as highly arbitrary and incomplete scales.

A magical fixing of forms serves rationalization indirectly. For in music as in other areas of life magic may be a powerfully antirational force. But the fixing of intervals serves the purpose of establishing a set of forms against which others are to be tested. In this it may serve as the basis for a uniform musical culture. The people who realized this anonymous rationalization of invocatory formulae were priests and magicians, probably the world's first professional musicians. Unquestionably melodic formulae serving various deities were the source of rationalized scale formations such as the Dorian, Phrygian, and Lydian. Weber attributes to the magician a role in musical development equivalent to that attributed to him by other thinkers in intellectual development.

Special interest attaches to the role of magic in musical development from a sociological point of view for still another reason. Weber, it has been noted, analyzed behavior into rational, evaluative, traditional, and affective types. Magical actions are of an evaluative or traditional type, operating in terms of fixed means and ends and traditional stereotyping. They are thus able to promote rationalization only to a limited degree, for when magical requirements lead to the stereotyped fixing of instrumental use and intervallic pattern, experimentation is discouraged. In extreme cases the slightest deviation from a magico-musical formula is punished by instantaneous death. Moreover, so long as the musical scale is restricted to special occasions for magical reasons, it is withheld from free development.

On the other hand, a professional stratum has been created. It has become the bearer of a uniform musical development. The very magical fixing of musical formula trains both the musician and the audience in the exact perception and rendition of the musical intervals involved.

The reverse situation to the influence upon musical rationalization played by the magical musician is presented by the musical virtuoso. He appears when sacred tones are transplanted into nonreligious contexts and adapted to aesthetic needs. Here experimentation rather than stereotyping may be the rule. Accompaniment by instruments is sought rather than impeded, and it in turn forces an interpenetration of musical and technical requirements. Music addressed to aesthetic and expressive needs may deliberately savor the bizarre. Progressive alteration of intervals in the interest of greater expressiveness may occur, even leading at times to experiment with the most irrational microtones. Purposeful rationalization becomes apparent when tones lying close together are not permitted simultaneous use. This is made possible by the organization of typical tone series such as the Greek, Arabic, Persian, and Hindu scales permitting the tuning of instruments. The full chromatic scale was available on both the aulos and the kithara. The

Arabic lute contained all rational and irrational intervals. The dissolving influence of musical virtuosi upon fixed musical structures under the impulse of sheer expressive needs is not confined to premodern stages of musical culture. Weber saw the musical virtuosi as one of the forces eating away the structure of tonality itself.

Early stages of melodic rationalization in the field of sacerdotal music is further exemplified by Weber through three characteristic elements of the later church modes: the concluding formula, the *tonus currens*, and the *tropus*. Illustrations from Vedda music demonstrate the priority of the concluding formula and outline reverse procedure in musical composition. Starting with a fixed concluding formula, musical development may lead to the fixing of the prefinal cadence and, in time, the remainder, and eventually the beginning of the piece.

In Western development musical rationalization appears to have been determined by two factors: the concluding formula and *tonus currens*. Primitive musical systems have fixed rules for concluding formulae. The *tonus currens* forms the melodic center and is usually situated in the middle of the tonal system. It is the *mese* of the Greek greater perfect system, the *finalis* of the plagal church modes, the initial tone for ascending and descending motion, for tuning, transposition, and modulation. The combination of the concluding formula and the *tonus currens* establish melodic tonality. However, when music develops into an art of virtuosi, the predisposition for fixed concluding formulae, cadences, or principal tones is abandoned.

Principal tones within purely melodic musical systems are the so-called "up tones" appearing in descending concluding formulae. Their function should not be confused with that of harmonic leading tones. The final note may consist of the frame tones of the fourth, but in systems which do not posses tetrachordic structure, it may be made up of tones from any other interval. The initial tone may be equivalent to the final tone or related to it as in the case of the church modes. On the other hand, in Greek music the initial tone is not related at all to the final tone.

Throughout this discussion, it may be seen, Weber assigns complementary roles to the magician-musician and virtuosi in the rationalization of music. Under the influence of magic, fixed musical forms are established and a class of priest musicians appears. Under the influence of magic rigid upper limits on rationalization are established. When such formulae are released from magico-religious contexts and when the professional musician is free to employ such musical formulae in secular contexts, actions cease to be evaluative and traditionalistic and may become rationalistic and affective. Often for expressive reasons the virtuoso explores musical effects gained precisely from violation of fixed final formulae and the *tonus currens* of the melodic system.

The frame tones of concluding formulae, most often the fourth and fifth, are, thus, in the course of the histories of their migration from magical-religious to secular contexts, freed by the virtuosi to serve as the basis for rationalizations of the systems in which they occur.

Weber discusses at length the importance of the fourth and fifth for the rationalization of music, their occurrence in modulations both of private and art music (Javanese and Ewe Negro). The fourth is a fundamental melodic interval. The fifth arose to importance in instrumental tuning. While in Greek and Byzantine music systems the fourth was predominant, its role fluctuated in the church modes. It became a dissonance in the Middle Ages through applications of the successive divisions of the fifth into the thirds of many-voiced art music.

There were many reasons why the interval of the fourth gained the upper hand over the fifth in ancient music. Weber observes that it is the smallest unambiguously consonance-making interval. It tends to come to be relied upon for rational division in musical systems resting on the principle of intervallic distance. Moreover, in polyphonic singing the higher of two voices tends to monopolize the melody, forcing the lower to adjust melodically to it on the fourth.

Cooperation and competition of both fourths and fifths is illustrated in the unsymmetrical organization of the double octave of the Greek greater perfect system. The two octaves are built upon diazeutic and conjunct tetrachords and an additional lower tone (proslambanomenos) respectively. The lowest tetrachord is in fourth relationship with the next lowest tetrachord, while the latter is in fifth relationship with the next higher tetrachord.

The frame tones of the tetrachords were considered immovable and fixed. Modulations could only occur through these frame tones. An additional B♭ string was added for modulatory purposes. A new middle tetrachord was obtained which was not in fifth but in fourth relationship. The shift from the fifth to the fourth was considered to be a modulation. Further examples of the combination of disjunct and conjunct tetrachords are found in the octave organization in Arabic and Javanese systems.

Weber's study of prediatonic scale systems and of the problems presented by premodern musical forms is not by any means simply one more history of music. It is a comparative and analytical study of prediatonic musical systems to determine the degree to which they were rationalized, the forces operating for and against rationalization, and the probable directions that rationalization could assume. Only in this way could the full peculiarities of Occidental musical development be established. It would make little sense to characterize Western music as the most rational if more rational models were available than are represented by it. If there actually was a movement within musical development such that steps toward more rational structure tended always to prevail over their opposites, it should be possible to establish the stages by which the rational forms emerge. As one is able to trace the stages in the emergence of more rational thought models, or more rational forms of administration, or business, it should be possible to trace the stages by which the rational elements of premodern music anticipate modern music. It should be possible to clarify the forces bringing this about.

Weber found premodern music to be far less rationalized than our own. When it was rationalized it tended to be on different principles: melodic rather than harmonic. Premodern music with its often baroque multiplication of rational and irrational microtones was often as expressively subtle as it was harmonically crude.

Within this music various factors were operative for and against a harmonic type of rationalization: the magical fixing of musical motives; the rationalizing influences of language and instrumental tuning; the expressive experimentalism by virtuosi in secular contexts. Of very particular importance were those developments which began to occur in early church music with the adaptation of the musical tradition to the requirements of singing choruses. Most of these forces for musical rationalization were present in the music of other cultural areas. But in the West the trend demonstrable in other spheres of life also appears in its music and the more rational forms always tend to prevail.

POLYVOCALITY AND
POLYSONORITY
IN RELATION TO
MUSICAL RATIONALIZATION

The rationalizing process that emerges and guides the development of Western musical culture reaches a kind of definitive stage with the mastery of problems of poly-voiced music. It forms the point of no return, the point beyond which something quite new appears.

Polyvoiced music is not confined to the Occident. While it appeared also in Oriental cultures, it followed a peculiar course of development in the West. It developed through contrapuntalism to diatonicism.

In Greek, Eastern-Asiatic, and various primitive cultures, polyvoiced music appeared in the form of heterophony, the simultaneous sounding of a given melody and its motivic variation, extension, and improvisation. Weber excludes from his concept of polyvoiced music the many-voiced singing in unisons or octaves, anticipating the viewpoint of Curt Sachs and other musicologists who maintain that parallel octaves are the unavoidable result of any vocal cooperation of the two sexes and therefore practised by people on the lowest level of civilization.[17]

Three basic types of polyvocality are distinguished: the modern chordal harmony or "polysonority" (to use Weber's term) in which the fullness of chordal sound effects is of primary importance; contrapuntal polyphony in which all participating voices have equal rank, their progression being submitted to specific rules or prohibitions (heterophony is a preparatory stage of this polyphonic type of coordinated music) and harmonic homophonic music, in which the entire tone setting is subordinated to one voice, it being the melodic vehicle.

Weber reviews the parallels of chordal harmonic and polysonorous music found in Oriental and Eastern-Asiatic systems. He maintains that though musicians in these areas were familiar with the simultaneous sounding of intervals, they did not perceive triads as such, but as combinations of other intervals. In his examination of contrapuntal polyphony, his discussion of such techniques as canon, fugue, and imitation is followed by the presentation of rules, the tritone problem, dissonance to contrapuntal polyphony and in chordal harmony, and the prohibition of parallelism. These discussions serve to reveal, often in fascinating manner, the complexities that surround the stages in the emergence of rational harmonic forms.

Weber tried both to characterize precisely the three types of polyvocality and to develop the reasons why they appear in some parts of the world but not in others. He explores the bearing of various factors on the local emergence of polyvocal forms: the different tempo adequate for the use of instruments by themselves in contrast to that required when they are used in relation to a vocal part; the significance of the sustained tones of instruments in relation to the plucked ones of the strings, the role played in antiphonal singing of the sustaining of one voice during the entrance of others; the importance of the sonority of the repercussion tones of the harp at the arpeggio; the role of simultaneous chance tone-production while tuning instruments. Any one or any combination of these phenomena could lead to the perception of the aesthetic effects to be achieved through one or another form of polyvocality.

In Western music practically all the conditions that could bring the aesthetic effects of polyvocality to attention were present. If the effects to be achieved through polyvocality are once accepted as a primary musical objective, an extraordinary powerful stimulus for further rationalization is present. The rationalization process plays a considerable role in bringing polyvocality to the fore; polyvocality plays back upon musical development as a tremendous incentive to further rationalization. This spiral of rationalization can gives rise to others.

Western musical notation is in considerable measure a product of the movement in Western music toward polyvocality. The acceptance of polyvocality in the monastic chant in the ninth century intensified the need to develop a more adequate musical notation than was offered by the neumes. The first important step, the insertion of the neumes into a system of staff lines appeared as an aid to sight reading of music in singing. The notational improvement of the neumes was secured by transforming them into dots, squares, and oblongs—a product of the requirements of musical pedagogy. Mensural notation of the twelfth century made the establishment of relative time value of tone symbols possible. It became easy to survey the unambiguous determination of relations of progression of individual voices. A true polyvocal composition had become possible.

Notation always retained its character as a compromise between theory and practice, the harmonic and intervallic, the rational and irrational. In the case of the neumes there was no differentiation of whole and semitone steps. This very ambiguity favored the penetration of popular vocal traditions into musical development. The *daseia* notation of the *Musica Enchiriadis,* most emphatically through the *daseia* sign, attempted to establish an order in the arbitrary melodic patterns. Even with the complexly regulated mensural notation, free space was left to the *contrapunta amente* of the descant part. The figured bass part of the baroque era did not put an end to improvised irrationalities. It did not abandon its right of *musica ficta* in order to balance melodic harshnes by chromatic tone alterations. The nature of the compromise also becomes apparent in the chord writing of the nineteenth and twentieth centuries. Notation has to ignore the fact that the chord d-f-a according to provenience is either a genuine minor triad or a musically irrational construction.

In the Western world the extent to which melodious alterations should be included in the notation was continuously discussed. Weber calls attention to the fact that several chorales with purely diatonic intonation were known since the fifteenth century and are sung today with a chromatic alteration. One need only mention, for example, the three original monodic versions of *Christ ist erstanden* and the chromatic alterations of its first phrase in the settings of the Schott *Gesangbuch* by Gesius and in the *Christ lag in Todesbanden* variation of Johann Sebastian Bach.

Weber was fully aware of the fact that chromaticism and all irrational intervals are not necessarily the product of a specifically primitive musical development. In fact the *musica ficta* grew precisely within a musical system which already possessed a rationally regulated polyvocality. On the other hand, music systems which once permanently appropriate one irrational interval are particularly inclined to accept further intervals. The discussion of Arabic music which experiences a twofold enrichment with increasingly irrational intervals, restricted any development toward harmony, diatonicism, and finally, polyvocality.

The most striking general theme running through this phase of Weber's essay is that polyvoiced music soon reaches a point where its further development can only occur in terms of more efficient notation. Notation in turn makes the achievement of quite new polyvoiced musical effects. The problem of musical notation, thus, is lifted to a position in musical development parallel to the invention of writing for literature or of notation for mathematics.

If one considers the differences in literary efficiency made possible by writing resting on an alphabet in contrast to that of a pictographic writing, or the differences in mathematical efficiency made possible by the use of Arabic rather than Roman numbers, one gets some idea of the importance for polyvoiced music of the development of Occidental systems of musical notation. The mutual rationalizing tendencies of polyvocal music and notation supplies one of the dramatic spiral developments in the musical culture of the West.

INSTRUMENTS AND THE RATIONALIZATION OF NONHARMONIC TONES THROUGH EQUALIZATION AND TEMPERING

In the course of his discussion of prediatonic scale formations, Weber had raised a question as to the extent to which premodern music was rationalized. He had also inquired into the factors that had apparently played a role in the partial rationalization of pentatonic systems. He had come to the conclusion that one of the major factors in establishing such rationalization as premodern systems display is found in instruments and their tuning.

One of the unique features of Western music is its unprecedented development of instrumental music. Nowhere else has it been possible to bring to bear the techniques of science to the problem of instrument construction to the same degree. The problems of tuning and temperament are brought to a new quantitatively determined level of problems. A spiral of rationalization appears also here comparable to the one between polyvocal music and notation.

When instruments are the vehicle, rationalization may occur in a partly extramusical manner. There are two basic types of tuning: instrumental tuning according to heard tones, fixed tones, and fixed intervals; instrumental tuning which establishes tones and intervals according to purely visual, symmetrical, and ornamental requirements of instrumental construction. This second type of tuning is illustrated by some Central American wind instruments. The tuning of the main instrument of the Chinese orchestra, the shun,[18] was not determined by musical considerations but by aesthetic requirements for mechanical symmetry. Chinese music demonstrates that intervals created mechanically can be embodied in musical systems, influencing development in a manner making it unavailable for harmonic and tonal relations.

One type of rationalistic alteration of the tone system from within is found in distance tempering. Javanese and Siamese musical systems supply examples of an octave simply divided into equally large tone distances. Purely intervallic tempering is designed to permit the transposition of melodies into any pitch without retuning the instrument.

The most important type of rationalistic equalization from within the tone system is tempering with regard to the requirements of chordal and harmonic music. In the West partial tempering existed for the keyboard instruments since the sixteenth century. The range of these instruments was little more than that of the human voice, the accompaniment of which was one of their functions. Under such circumstances tempering depended upon the balance with the four middle fifths of our present piano (C-c′) and the purity of the interval of the third.

With the extension in range of the piano and organ and the rise of an independent instrumental music, the division of the octave into twelve equal distances of twelve equivalent semitones became necessary. The peculiarity of this modern temperament is found in the fact that the practical execution of the principle of distance is treated and is effective on our keyboard instruments as a tempering of tones which are gained harmonically. Besides the distance-wise measurement of the intervals is found chordal and harmonic interpretation of the intervals.

The keyboard instruments and the strings have been central to development of music in the West so far as instruments have played a role. Through these instruments the using social strata, on the one hand, and the technical traditions available for instrument construction, on the other, had a bearing upon the development of musical culture. This may be seen with regard to the violin.

Organizations of instrumentalists played a role in shaping the development of the modern violin. The playing of the crwth[19] was subject to regulations established by the Congress of Bards in 1176. Practice, thus, is fixed by organization requirements which create a common musical culture, on the one hand, and provide a market for standardized instruments on the other. Toward the end of the Middle Ages the building of stringed instruments was influenced by the guild organizations which appeared in the thirteenth century. These provided a fixed market for manufactured instruments, helping establish the types.

The gradual acceptance of the instrumentalist alongside the singer in the *Kapellen* of kings, princes, and communities fixed their social role. When this fixing of social roles occurred, it gave the production of instruments an even more productive economic foundation.

Since the fifteenth century in close conection with humanistic music theorists, the attempt has been made to provide instruments ready to be played in orchestras. The separation of high and low viols was accomplished with the French *ménétriers*. A standardization of instruments and markets goes on continually.

Uninterrupted experimentation in combination with the different traditional practices of the leading orchestras led to the final separation of the violin, viola, and cello. The supremacy of the violin was secured by the persistent experiments of manufacturers of instruments from Brescia and Cremona. The urge for expressive sonorous beauty and elegance of the instrument were the driving forces in Italy for the continuous technical development of the instrument. Once the violin had reached it final form, its possibilities far surpassed the musical potential that had been demanded of it. The capacity of the Amati instruments was not fully exploited for decades. The products of the great violin builders rested on skills gradually acquired in empirical experience.

Similar circumstances appeared in the development of the keyboard instruments. Piano virtuosity developed hand in hand with a heavy harpsichord industry which was based in turn on the demands of orchestras and amateurs. Between the combined force of social requirements and the development of technical skills great changes were brought about in the instrument which was typified. The great builder of harpsichords (the Ruckers family in Belgium) created individual instruments commissioned by their consumers (orchestras and particians). At this stage manifold adaptation to all possible concrete needs of communities and individuals was possible.

The fixing of the piano occurred in the nineteenth century, when it became the instrument typical of the culture of the middle-class home. Interesting social factors played a role in this. This piano was not a product of Italian culture, which did not have the indoor character of the Nordic north. The center of gravity of the production and further technical improvement of the piano lay in Saxony, where middle-class home comfort developed for climatic and historical reasons played the critical role.

SUMMARY

Weber's sociology of music rests on his typology of action, though this is not made explicit. Musical culture is analyzed in terms of the rational and nonrational patterns it displays. The peculiarity of Western music was found in the unusual development of rational structures. The intrinsic property of this musical rationality was explored analytically and comparatively. The social and technical forces that shaped it were examined. The influence of various sorts of technical and rational, evaluative and magical, traditional and affective forces were reviewed.

In the dynamics of Western musical development lie many tensions between rational and affective motives. The value of musical rationalization is the transformation of the process of musical production into a calculable affair operating with known means, effective instruments, and understandable rules. Constantly running counter to this is the drive for expressive flexibility.

One of the fascinating aspects of Weber's discussion is the patience with which he seeks out every irrational residue, every musical element that escapes or seems to escape the rules. It is difficult not to suspect that it is almost with relief that Weber finds that even at the basis of the most fundamental scale formation lack of symmetry appears. There is more than curiosity in the discovery that melodic and harmonic principles appear in tension which is precisely where Western music assumes its most dramatically effective form.

Here, as in other areas of his sociological analysis, Weber touches his moving theme of the disenchantment of the world. As science banishes the colorful mysteries of old magic, as rational thinking converts all things into calculable relations, Weber suspects that the drive was powerfully present at the heart of Western man's musical culture to transform the highest of his musical expressions into an equation in mathematics.

11

SOCIOLOGY

AND AESTHETICS

Then the first thing will be to establish a censorship of the writers of fiction, and let the censors receive any tale of fiction which is good, and reject the bad; and we will desire mothers and nurses to tell their children the authorized ones only. Let them fashion the mind with such tales, even more fondly than they would the body with their hands, but most of those which are now in use must be discarded.[1]

THIS PASSAGE FROM *The Republic* raises issues that lend significance to the kind of analysis we designate as the "sociology of art." It was Plato's view that art and society bear a most intimate relation to one another. He viewed art as an "instrument" of education, something which could "transform" society. He believed that art has the obligation of portraying the "good," that it has what we now call a "truth function." In much the same spirit he labeled many works of art "dangerous" even though they were considered invaluable by the society of his day. He urged that all musical instruments be banned other than the lyre, the flute, and the shepherd's pipe.[2] Only simple music should be permitted, music which cultivates simplicity and nobility of the soul.[3] Tragedy and comedy, being mere "imitations," should be excluded.[4] And as for the actor:

When any one of these pantomimic gentlemen, who are so clever that they can imitate anything, comes to us and makes a proposal to exhibit himself and his poetry, we will fall down and worship him as a sweet and holy and wonderful being; but we must also inform him that in our State such as he are not permitted to exist; the law will not allow them.[5]

Many religions of the world, while at times fostering certain forms of art, like Plato, have viewed the artist with suspicion and his product with ambivalence. A few familiar examples from our religious history illustrate this. In the fundamental sections of ancient Hebraic law we find the prescription:

You shall not carve any idols for yourselves, the shape of anything in heaven above or on the earth below or in the sea; you shall not bow down to them or worship them, for I the Eternal, your God, am a jealous God.[6]

Granting that this prescription was aimed primarily at the cultic objects of competitive religions, the attitude expressed included all plastic and pictorial representations whatsoever. This injunction severely restricted the development of plastic and pictorial art forms in ancient Palestine. This constituted, furthermore, a heritage not only for Judaism but for Islam and Christianity as well. The church itself was never completely indiscriminate in its reception of the arts, and during periods of intense religiosity it was swept with radical iconoclasm and ascetic renunciation of worldly temptations of art. Suspicion of the arts on the part of the Protestant sects is well known and requires no reiteration here. At times they have even forbidden multicolored clothing. Fundamentalist religious groups still retain a strong suspicion of aesthetic experience. It is often considered "sensuous" and sinful, and the artist himself is viewed as the epitome of Godlessness.

Nor is this peculiar to the "religious attitude." There are echoes of Plato in the suspicions of art held by totalitarians of today. The Nazis violently condemned what they called "decadent Jewish art" and encouraged, as an element of state policy, a "truly German," "truly Aryan" art. Similarly, Russia has developed its own definitions of permissible art. "True" Russian art is distinguished from "decadent capitalist" and "decadent democratic" art. The aesthetic is viewed in both the German and Russian situations as a social force, potentially dangerous, but a potent instrument in the hands of the state.

The problems raised by Plato have significance beyond the reach of political or religious institutions. Are the movies and other popular arts morally degenerative influences? Is training in the classical arts a morally elevating influence? Are developments in modern painting socially destructive? Is the artist a moral pervert, a political radical? These and similar questions indicate that the Platonic formulations are by no means out of date.

THE AESTHETIC
AND THE SOCIAL

The more or less continuous discussion from the days of classical Greece to the present, of the relation of art to the social order is, clearly, eminently worthy of study. It is not in any way a purely "academic" issue. The artist has been alternately praised and damned, lavished with the highest honors and rewards of society, persecuted and ostracized.

Fortunes have been made from the works of artists who died in poverty and disgrace.

In the very act of posing the problem we acknowledge a difference between "aesthetic" phenomena and those we call "social." When we speak of the tension that may develop between what is customary and what is artistic, between art and religion, or between art and political institutions, we indicate that "aesthetic" phenomena must be in some way unique. In fact, all arguments as to the dangers of art presuppose that the aesthetic experience is not a purely secondary or derivative phenomenon.

Let us refer, provisionally, to the "social" as the collective, interactional life of men. By social behavior we mean what men do in response to each other.[7] Social behavior is not simply "sociable" behavior, however, for it includes all things men do with respect to one another. It includes fighting and making love, working together for common ends, or competing for the same prize.[8] And human social behavior is made immeasurably more subtle, plastic, and complex than animal behavior, of course, by the presence of language.[9] Aesthetic behavior is a subcategory of what we have called social behavior.

Since the time of the ancient Greeks, behavior has been analyzed into four or five elements which, taken together, constitute its "structure." Behavior—action, relating one individual to another (or to a thing)—is analyzable into four elements: (1) the disposition of the creature to act—a purpose, impulse, motive, instinct, etc.; (2) a means —the instrument of action; (3) an end, or value; and sometimes, (4) its consequences—which may or may not represent achievement of the value involved. Let us examine each of these.

For a time, social scientists envisioned the possibility of identifying the aesthetic as a "disposition to act" based on emotions such as hate, love, ambition, greed, and generosity. Had they succeeded in classifying behavior in terms of a fixed set of such instincts, attitudes or wishes, we would, indeed, have an invaluable method for analysis of the aesthetic. It would be an "impulse" of some sort or a secondary consequence of a primary impulse in action.[10]

But is there something which may be designated an "aesthetic" impulse or an "aesthetic need"? Presumably, there are two methods of answering this question. The first is experimental analysis of individuals displaying such an impulse,[11] while the alternative method is to make a comparative analysis to demonstrate the general presence of some "aesthetic" tendency. So far, among all peoples, as soon as conditions of life have risen above the survival level, artistic embellishment and decorations of elements of daily life have appeared. However, there is no automatic or instinctive choice of a particular "aesthetic" evaluation, and one people's judgment may be wholly disagreeable to another.

The attempt to account for the aesthetic in terms of the "consequences" of behavior does not take us any further towards solution than the attempt to explain it in terms of some peculiar "impulse." Perhaps the most famous representation of this kind of the "aesthetic" is the identification, in Greek classical times, of the beautiful and the good. This approach often assumes that the aesthetic and the pleasant are identical and suggests that the pleasant is also the good. The difficulty inherent in all such views is apparent when the aesthetic is forced into a propagandistic role. Under such circumstances the aesthetic evaporates because neither the beautiful and good, nor the beautiful and the pleasant, can be satisfactorily equated with one another.

More rewarding than either of the above approaches to the aesthetic are attempts to account for it in terms of "means" and "ends." An extreme form of the attempt to define the aesthetic in terms of "means" is the interpretation of art as technique. That this by itself is unsatisfactory, however, is clear from the fact that mechanical perfection of technique itself is not enough. The technician is clearly not always aesthetically superior to the artist. Furthermore, the aesthetic cannot be exclusively conceived in terms of ends peculiar to it, even though some objects—poetry, musical compositions, painting, and the like—are specifically produced for aesthetic purposes. The utilitarian object, spoon, vase, garment, or building may have significance in both aesthetic and nonaesthetic contexts. Nevertheless, interpretation of the aesthetic in terms of means and ends (or both) remains one of the more satisfactory analyses of the problem.

There are, however, aesthetic pleasures that lie beyond simple "means." A workman often takes pride in his skill, and spectators will gather to watch the rhythmic grace of a proletarian virtuoso in the execution of his tasks. The mechanical shovel tearing up the earth, a bulldozer leveling a hill, the erection of a steel skeleton for a new building, each attract and hold our interest. We take interest in the drama of a crisis or an accident. We respond to sunsets, springtime, rainbows, and ocean surf. In all of these we see, not something different from the arts, but the essence of the arts themselves. For art is the elevation and refinement of these very kinds of experience. The aesthetic represents a range of phenomena extending over a wide range of human experience and includes both natural and artificial objects. It includes the delight in the trill of a frog and the appreciation of a Bach fugue. It may include incidental delight in the affairs of everyday life, as well as the pleasure in contemplating an artistic masterpiece representing half a lifetime of labor.

THE AESTHETIC
AND NONAESTHETIC

Our general understanding of the problem of the aesthetic can be advanced by turning aside for a moment to some related distinctions. How is the aesthetic to be differentiated from what we call "good," "useful," "pleasurable," or "true"?

The "good" is a conception we apply to certain orders of preference found in human behavior. Theories concerning an absolute good are based on the assumption that there is one such order of preference. Relativistic theories of good, on the other hand, assume that there are multiple and alternative orders of preference.[12] Theories of good which claim to rest on a theological basis, or those based on intuition (direct apprehension of the good) are attempts to legitimize one or another such system of preferences. Although a system of preferences may include the true, the pleasant, the useful, in its hierarchy, the useful, pleasant, and true are not alway considered "good." This indicates that they are in some measure quite distinct.[13]

It is useful to distinguish the "customary good" (systems of preference traditionally transmitted) from the "ideal good" (systems of good which serve to modify practice even though never fully realized). But our present aim is merely to distinguish the good from the aesthetic. This is important in view of the argument we frequently encounter which says that the good is beautiful, and the beautiful is good.

Aesthetic experiences, like ethical experiences, form systems of preference. If they did not, no meaning could be assigned to such concepts as "taste," "discrimination," and "judgment." It is precisely such terminology that invariably appears in aesthetic discussions. Moreover, it would be meaningless to award prizes in an art if there were no aesthetic "better" or "worse." Some such ordered arrangement of aesthetic value is implied in the very notion of "preference" itself.

A preference system, then by its very nature, consists of an ordered arrangement of "better," "worse," "more," or "less." The core of the aesthetic lies in such comparative judgments. And such an ordered arrangement of our judgments presupposes principles or laws which form the basis for judgment, standards of taste, principles of a criticism, and the like. In a general way, we may say with respect to the values to which we apply these standards, that in a purely external fashion the "best" is that value which we will surrender last if we are forced to make a choice. The same general propositions hold for ethical as for aesthetic systems. We establish systems of reward and punishment as hierarchies of ethical preference, *e.g.*, murder by "degrees."

Ethical and aesthetic systems are different types of preference systems. They differ in both the kind of values involved and in the principles for their realization. Most ethical systems fall into two general groups: those forming a hierarchy of "community" values, and those constituting a hierarchy of "individual" values. "Community" and "individual" are correlative concepts although they differ a great deal, as we readily see if we examine ethical systems which subordinate the individual to the community. On the other hand, aesthetic systems are hierarchies of values which are enjoyed for themselves. While the same event may involve both moral and aesthetic considerations, they are by no means identical. A beautiful woman, need we say, is not necessarily a good one. An immoral painting may be aesthetically far superior to one with a moral message. The attempt to subordinate the aesthetic to the moral arises from moral rather than aesthetic interests. Not infrequently does it lead to a degeneration of the aesthetic. Even though the moral activity of a community may produce phenomena upon which the aesthetic judgment operates, this in no way guarantees superior aesthetic character.

Elevation of the "practical" to primary significance does not in any way simplify the problem of the ethical and aesthetic. For the "practical" presupposes some system of values itself. They are simply taken for granted. In a simply homogeneous folk community, for instance, a system of ends is usually accepted without question by everyone. The "ethical" problem in such a situation is simply how to attain them practically. But where alternative ends appear, as in a complex society such as our own, "practicality" no longer provides a foolproof criterion for choice between them. In all complex communities, customary evaluations are constantly in conflict. For example, to anyone who accepts individual salvation as an ultimate aspiration, nothing is more "practical" than the organization of life around that goal. But to someone who does not accept individual salvation as a final value, nothing could be less "practical." In short, we cannot eliminate the problem of alternative ethics by ignoring it.

Should we, on the other hand, reject questions of the useful and the practical as merely secondary issues to the "good"? While the problem of "good" (either ethical or aesthetic) concerns primarily the ends of action, and the ordering of such ends in systems, the problem of "practicality" applies primarily to the means of action. Judgments of practicality may be made both with respect to moral and aesthetic values. Granted that a given aesthetic or moral value is capable of realization, there is a very real question as to the most expedient technical manner of achieving it.

However, the significance of technical considerations is more complex than this. The development of new technical procedures and instruments may make possible the realization of values previously impossible to attain. In the history of the human race technical invention has played a decisive role. Perhaps the most amazing illustration is language itself. Without it, organized social life is scarcely possible. Now the structure of modern life is inseparable from the complex technical procedures we call science. But it is a confusion of the moral and technical to conclude that science can be "responsible" for anything. To hold science at fault for its abuses, as some anti-scientific viewpoints do, is like holding plumbing responsible for leaky faucets. Of course, the development of science can be controlled, or directed in the interests of social groups or pressures, and there are types of social *milieu* which are more favorable to its development than others. But science, itself, is a pure instrument. It is the highest development of the "practical" thus far on our planet.

The practical and useful, including science, are instrumental values. They are essential to the realization of various aesthetic and ethical values. But the practical and useful, however closely related to given ends, derive their significance from the ends to which they are instrumental.

The relation between the aesthetic and the practical is easier to grasp than the relation between the aesthetic and the "pleasant," both of which are sometimes considered modalities. When "pleasantness" is conceived to be a primary value, it gives rise to a number of social and psychological problems. Only two of these, however, are of immediate concern here. If happiness is the essence of value, it would seem reasonable to assume that such happiness is that of an individual person. But the question then becomes: Is the happiness of the individual an absolute criterion of value even though it may involve the unhappiness of others? The utilitarians sought to reply to this question by their formula which said that the greatest happiness of the greatest number ought to be the absolute criterion of value. Unfortunately, when the individual person pursues his own happiness, the greatest happiness of the greatest number does not automatically ensue, and the issue is decided by the interests of the stronger.

The value of hedonism, another important view, presumably lies in the fact that it gives a firm psychological (or physiological) basis to the problem of value. Fundamental difficulties crop up here, too, however, when the specific conditions under which pleasure occurs are analyzed. How is one to weigh the pleasure of a good meal against the pleasure of a good book? An attempt to supply formulas which quantify the amount of pleasure either by its time or intensity, are meaningless unless such questions can be answered. Furthermore, the intensity of pleasure afforded by a given experience is often related, paradoxically, to the amount of pain that preceded it. The most exquisitely prepared meal can be distinctly unappealing when one has just eaten. And, roughly, the hungrier one is the more intense the pleasure of eating. So, presumably, the appreciation of pleasures is best achieved by the systematic cultivation of obstacles, difficulties, and even pain of various sorts.

When even so simple a delight as that offered by a steak will vary in the amount of pleasure it makes possible, pleasure is, clearly, a rather shaky foundation upon which to build the claims of ethics or aesthetics. Indeed, there is a view which we might mention, too, that pleasure is not a primary value at all but a secondary and derived phenomenon. Pleasure, according to this view, emerges with the successful achievement of a goal.

All this, of course, does not say that aesthetic activities are not a source of enduring forms of happiness and satisfaction. An argument can be made for the position that the "highest" and most subtle of all satisfactions are aesthetic. But it is also clear that intense pleasure is at times found in immoral and unaesthetic experiences. That, of course, is why moralists have frequently looked upon all pleasure with suspicion.

While we are not concerned with the technical problems in the concept of "truth," two views of it are relevant. The pragmatist sees truth in terms of the solution of human problems. Truth from this standpoint is identical with the overcoming of a difficulty. And since there are degrees of success, the highest degree of truth is the best solution. This notion is most compatible with the idea that the "true" and the aesthetic are one and the same. The construction of an art object is considered a solution to a problem. The aesthetic appreciation of a natural object is seen as a construction of a suitable "solution" from the materials of experience. Perception of a sunset, for instance, represents a selection of perceptual data so that it is "seen" as a whole.

The other point of view which is related to "truth" is the idea that "truth" is a quality of propositions rather than experiences. In this analysis, widely used by modern philosophical analysts, the term "truth" is applied to the logical consistency of propositions within a set of propositions. It contrasts with empirical "truth" which is considered the relation of propositions to actual events. A map, for example, contains symbols such as hatcher marks or contour lines to represent geographical features such as elevation or bodies of water. Such a map is "true" if it corresponds to actual natural conditions. The "truth" of the map is tested by such verifying procedures as surveying, to confirm the height of a mountain indicated on the map. Such empirical truths are, of course, hazardous assertions about events which, strictly speaking, cannot be proved in advance. They are always subject to correction. They are, in short, probably statements about the real world.

What, then, is the relation between "truth" and the "aesthetic"? In the first place, the problem of truth is crucial to any representational theory of aesthetics. The beauty of a sunset is "true" in that its perception corresponds to the real sunset which exists apart from the perceiver. The "truth" of art, therefore, lies in the fact that it is a correct portrayal of reality. In all such cases the aesthetic becomes a sort of inferior science. For a scientific description is of much greater value than the experience of the "beauty" of the sunset. We might, then, be glad we can replace art with representational photography. The arts of music and dance are in analogous positions. An advanced psychology would, then, provide a more adequate account of man's emotional life than art. Needless to say, few of us will accept a fully representational theory of aesthetics.

An empirical approach to aesthetics does not rule out the possibility of a logic of the aesthetic. If we grant that an art involves some sort of structure, various principles for its production and appreciation, and that it is not completely accidental, certain rules might be applied to its consistency or inconsistency. We might so judge the logic of aesthetic production. Even though the application of such rules were wholly unconscious and automatic in us, they could constitute a logic of aesthetics. In literary arts, the lyric, the poem, the narrative relies on the grammatical structure imposed by the language. Variations in their use may take place (poetic license is often considerable), but they still operate within relatively narrow limitations. Even though we can come at the problem of "truth" and aesthetics from all these various positions, it remains clear that the two are quite distinct.

We may summarize the previous discussion. We approached the aesthetic from two standpoints. First, we approached it from the standpoint of the elements into which human behavior may be analyzed: impulses, means, values, consequences of action, etc. Secondly, we drew distinctions between the aesthetic and other areas of experience often confused with it. Although the two overlap, we noted that the aesthetic cannot be reduced to impulse or simple need. We observed, too, that it is distinct from the moral, the pleasant, the useful, and the true. We established the fact that the aesthetic may be viewed as a sphere of experience consisting of things "enjoyed for themselves" and that this sphere may be analyzed in terms of means and ends. We likewise noted that aesthetics involve preference systems, and that these preference systems are hierarchies of values.

THE UNITY OF THE AESTHETIC

Is there a single aesthetic preference system? This question is, of course, thoroughly empirical in nature. It can be answered only in terms of an examination of aesthetic phenomena themselves. Certainly, on the basis of general experience the answer appears to be that there are multiple aesthetic systems: between societies, between groups, within a given social group, and within the experience of an individual.

The aesthetic of one society, or of one group in it, may be quite repugnant to another. And no method has yet been devised to bring the possible differences of the aesthetic within the experience of a single individual into an inclusive system. How is one to compare, for instance, the song of a thrush and a Beethoven sonata? Or, if one were to isolate "spring sounds" as an aesthetic category, how is one to estimate the value of the croak of a frog compared to the scream of a loon or the drumming of a bittern? Or, how are we to compare a Buddhist Tori and a painting by Van Gogh? The aesthetic experience of the individual form a multiple system of preferences which is only partially organized.

As we move from group to group and from society to society, the attempt to view aesthetic preferences within an inclusive system becomes more untenable still. How is one to estimate the relation between oriental and occidental music, even though they both are treated as "music"? What is the relation between the realistic wall painting in paleolithic caves and the geometrical painting on rawhide boxes of the American Plains Indians? Can a single scheme be used to examine impressionist, expressionist, or Dadaist painting of the last half-century?

The cautious thing to do is to take the position that aesthetic systems are multiple, alternative, and often only partially ordered. If all aesthetic forms do, in fact, constitute a grand harmony, it is something yet to be proved. So obvious, in fact, is the diversity of aesthetic phenomena that some theoreticians conclude that there is no such thing as an aesthetic order. In fact, some conclude that between different aesthetic orders there can be no rational grounds of choice: "In matters of taste there can be no dispute." But this position seems as extreme and unwarranted as one which says that there is one and only one system of preference in aesthetics.

One of the appealing features of the aesthetic "impulse" theory is that it gives a naturalistic basic to an activity which, from some standpoints, is devoid of "practical" value. The search for a psychological or physiological basis for the aesthetic is at times carred back into the animal world. A "proto-aesthetic" is seen at times, for example, in the love call of a bird or the resplendent coloring of a baboon's posterior. Even insects, often bright as sparks and lustrous as gems, seem more colorful than required for protective coloration. Among the activities in the animal world that seem to preview the aesthetic are the love dances of the salamander and certain snakes, and the pirouetting of courting fish and birds. Rats and magpies, too, are known to hoard bright objects like marbles and silverware. The penguin collects bright and unusual stones for his nest. Indeed, Steffanson found that stones painted red were stolen back and forth from nest to nest. Chimpanzees have been observed to drape themselves with colored scraps of cloth and strut about in crude slue-footed dances.

The frequent relation of such phenomena with sex has led some to view the aesthetic as a by-product of sexual behavior. But the difficulty with efforts such as this to locate the exact basis of the aesthetic is that they break down precisely when we need them most. If the aesthetic were instinctive, we would expect its display to be the same everywhere. It would at least take the same general form under the same conditions. Although there may be some variations in it, the song of a robin is much the same in New York or the Dakotas. As far as humans are concerned, however, there is no guarantee that the arts developed in New York will resemble those of the Dakotas. Nor is there any guarantee that standards of taste will be at all similar.

But there is not the slightest doubt that the aesthetic rests upon aspects of our biological and physical nature. We take our values from the world around us, and the techniques we press into the service of the aesthetic are products of areas of our lives which have nothing to do with the arts. We find subject matter in people, the natural, world, human misery and degradation, aspiration and sacrifice. A precondition of the aesthetic is the human capacity for enjoyment and the ingenuity it takes to transform the material world around us. But a vital characteristic of the aesthetic is its variety, range, diversity, and plasticity.

The basis for the aesthetic, in the fully human sense, is social. It is human cultivation; it is largely learned. We learn to appreciate nature, to value classical music, Renaissance portraiture, Gothic architecture, and Greek sculpture. Learning may be largely unconscious, a continuous process of conditioning within a society, but the fruits of the aesthetic are the product of effort and long experience. Whatever the biological preconditions of the aesthetic, the forms of most concern to us are products of human association.

PART SIX

PURE and

APPLIED SOCIOLOGY

At the time sociology arose, it was the dream of its founders to bring the powers of science, which had proved to be so significant in dealing with the physical world, to bear on society. In a sense, the early sociologists did not need to worry about the application of their formulations to society. The ideological atmosphere in which their reflections arose was so powerful as to embed deep-seated biases in their formulations In its aspiration to be a science, the fundamental problem of sociology has not been to make its formulation relevant to society, but to prevent some set of special social preferences from depressing it from a scientific course.

At least three kinds of factors have prevented the consistent pursuit of objectivity in sociology. Some sociologists have been unwilling or unable to pursue an objective, value-free sociology. Thus the late C. Wright Mills, after turning his rhetoric against both what he called "Grand Theory" and "Abstracted Empiricism," rejected, in principle, all sociological attempts to "formulate invariant laws of society,"[1] reducing all generalizations to statements about particular structures of particular times and places. "Other 'laws' turn out to be empty abstractions or quite confused tautologies."[2]

The degree to which Mills departed from the concept of an objective social science is shown by his readiness to assign a political task to the social scientist.

It is . . . the political task of the social scientist to address himself to . . . three types of men. . . .

To those in power and with awareness of it, he imputes varying measures of responsibility. . . .

Those whose actions have such consequences, but who do not seem to be aware of them, he . . . attempts to educate and then, again, he imputes responsibility. . . .

To those . . . without . . . power . . . he reveals by his work . . . the ways in which personal troubles are connected with public issues; in the course of these efforts, he states what he has found out concerning the actions of the more powerful.[3]

In short, it is, Mills argued, the task of the social scientist to needle those in power and permit those without power to stand around and watch and learn something.

Mills' formulations are at the opposite pole from the requirements of an objective social science. The only political task of the social scientist *as a scientist* is to stay out of politics, be it of a left- or right-wing sort. Formulations such as those of Mills can only prevent the emergence of an objective scientific sociology. This, of course, does not mean that the individual social scientist in his nonscientific activities should not pursue whatever values he finds most significant.

However, it is not alone from the ranks of persons unable or unwilling to separate social science from ethics and politics that the difficulty for scientific sociology has come. Some of those who were seriously devoted to the task of constructing an objective sociology free from bias, followed the accepted scientific practice of reducing their problems wherever possible to small compass, permitting quantitative or, if possible, laboratory study. This is in the best tradition of science. However, when scientific specialism is carried on too long in separation from the more general developments of a field, it may be accompanied by a loss of perspective on the whole. The result may be to erase the lines between the significant and the insignificant, for the significance of a study always derives from its place in the wider context of which it is a part. As the lines between significant and insignificant are blurred, myths can grow up that one is being scientific if only the study gives the appearance of quantitative exactness. Even worse, there is a tendency to set up studies because they seem, in advance, to fit one's tools. The grotesque impracticality of this is evident if one considers what type of plumbing system a plumber would set up if the controlling principle was to employ his tools. It is quite easy to sympathize with those who, in the face of such distortion, denounce this as pseudoscience. Mills was not wrong in damning this. His mistake was to be trapped by the blurring of significant and insignificant into the notion that all empirical study is insignificant.

The third thing that has prevented the consistent pursuit of an objective sociology has arisen from the persistence within sociology of the original attitude that sociology should have a constructive application to ongoing society. For a long time in one form or other and under various names, sociology has been asked to bring its analysis to social issues. The various names for such studies are "social disorganization," "social pathology," or simply "social problems." Whatever their name, such enterprises have also blurred the lines between ideology and social science.

The blurring of the lines between ideology and social science, which occurs with deadly regularity in problems texts and in the courses as ordinarily taught, arises from the best of motives—the pursuit of legitimate but contradictory objectives. The attempt is made to be scientific and "socially" significant at the same time. The entire enterprise usually begins with an attempt to define social problems—of course, in a purely objective, scientific manner. The issue is usually lost before the task is completed. What constitutes a "social" problem as that concept is used in the ordinary problems course, depends on one's values. "Social" significance is the location of a value in a context of values. The first step in a problems course ought to be the formulation of the system of evaluations on which the argument rests. However, to admit this is to invite trouble, for a complex contemporary society possesses many groups with a variety of interests. When the teacher of social problems takes an explicit stand on one of the many political or ethical platforms available to him from the social groups of the society, he opens himself to the charge of bias. In the name of fairness at this point, those of his students who have a different set of values ought to demand "equal time." Hence, he prefers to make his stand upon a presumed objective, scientific ground. He is placed in a position where his task is to disguise various value suppositions as scientific propositions. Sometimes, in fact, what passes for objectivity in the texts and courses on social problems is the tendency for the "expert" indiscriminately to slip from one set of value premises to another from case to case, taking contradictory positions on the same issue. Even when there is no other major source of confusion between ideology and social science, social problems texts and courses are continuously at work keeping the mud stirred up.

The object of theory is not to abandon the task of achieving an objective social science in the manner of the late C. Wright Mills, nor to seek some middle road which compromises both scientific sociology and the social use of sociology, but to clarify them and keep separate those elements which combined would destroy one another. Perhaps we should sharpen once again the old distinction between pure and applied sociology. The following essay reviews the materials of the usual problems course from the standpoint of the distinction between an empirical social theory and normative social theory. Only when this distinction is kept clear can the blurring of the distinction between ideology and social science be avoided.

12

SOCIAL DISORGANIZATION:

THE CONFLICT

OF NORMATIVE AND

EMPIRICAL APPROACHES

THE THEORIES THAT HAVE SO FAR been advanced in the area of social problems have for thousands of years been judgmentally normative (hereinafter referred to simply as "normative"). Indeed, the great confusion in this area has resulted from the tendency to disguise normative social theories as empirical types. It is important to distinguish between normative and empirical theory, since the only type appropriate to the study of social problems is normative social theory.

In science, a developed theory consists of a logically interrelated body of laws. Although such laws are crucial to scientific explanations, they are not the sole requirement for making scientific predictions; a knowledge of particular properties and circumstances is also required. Description consists in establishing the "facts" of the event or events under study. Two vital phases of description are: (1) the identification of properties of the events, and (2) the establishment of relevant quantitative aspects of these properties. *Explanation,* so far as it is distinguishable from descriptions, consists in discovering relations between the various properties described. There are two important types of explanation: (1) those that seek to *generalize* the relations between the facts—that is, to establish the existence of laws; and (2) those that apply established laws to sets of observed facts—in the process of prediction. Both forms of explanation are frequently present in a given scientific study.

In a recent study, these distinctions have been clarified by Feigl, who has treated explanation as essentially an inferential procedure. One may distinguish, according to Feigl, among various levels of explanation in terms of their generality. Reading from the bottom up they are:

Theories, 2nd order	Still more penetrating interpretation (still higher constructs).
Theories, 1st order	Sets of assumptions using higher-order constructs (results of abstraction and inference). (Deeper interpretation of the facts as rendered on the Empirical-Law Level.)
Empirical Laws	Functional relationships between relatively directly observable (or measurable) magnitudes.
Description	Simple account of individual facts or events (data) as more or less immediately observable.[1]

In Feigl's presentation a "law" is a relatively low-order explanation. It simply states a regularity in a number of specific facts. The number of deductions that can be made from it is relatively limited. A theory is a higher-order explanation that states regularities abstracted from a number of laws; the total case of descriptive material which it encompasses is thus tremendously greater. By the same reasoning, the higher the order of theory, the greater its eventual empirical power.

The Essentials of Empirical Theory

The results of this process of exposing degrees of regularity in facts may be called empirical theory. It has no object other than explanation, and in the pursuit of this object the only ultimate criteria of acceptability are (1) the highest possible generality that gives (2) the maximum explanatory power. Typically, such theory develops in complete disregard of what *ought to be*. It is not anti-ethical but non-ethical.[2]

The Nature of Normative Theory

If theory making is broadly considered as the construction of concepts into systems from which deductions can be logically made, only one kind of theory making serves scientific explanation. Scientific explanation is concerned with facts and relations, and theory construction has also been addressed to objectives and aids in reaching them. There is no reason why the conceptualization of such action desirabilities should not be given theoretical form. When it is, the result may be called *normative theory* in contrast to empirical theory.

The contrasts between empirical and normative theory are important. The ultimate materials of empirical theory are facts; the ultimate materials of normative theory are value-*imperatives*. As noted above, empirical theory is formed out of a system of laws. Normative theory converts facts and laws into requisite means and conditions and is unique in being addressed to a system of objectives desired by the formulator or by those in whose service he stands.

SOCIAL CHANGE AS A MAJOR APPROACH TO SOCIAL PROBLEMS

Normative (dogmatic) and empirical theory are never parallel. The values to be *achieved* determine the content of a normative theory, and anything that clarifies the conditions affecting the values becomes relevant. It is not inconceivable that the findings of a half-dozen empirical disciplines can be drawn upon. However, some branches of empirical theory will normally be closer than others to any given normative position. In terms of our analysis, the closest empirical counterpart to the theory of social problems is the theory of social change.

The theory of social change attempts to explain such things as the formation and dissolution of institutions, social orders, societies, social strata, social roles, etc. It is occupied with those structures and situations in which human social values are anchored. No other field continuously raises so many questions relevant for a normative theory of social problems. However, these theories should be kept distinct: an empirical theory of social change does not prescribe goals; nor does a normative theory of social action ever make complete or exclusive use of the theory of social change. This, of course, is not to say that in the literature these two kinds of theory are always kept distinct.

Theories of Social Evolution: Comte and Spencer

The works of Auguste Comte and Herbert Spencer were to sociologists the most important sources of theories of social problems prior to World War I. These works may also serve to illustrate the relation between normative and empirical theories.

Despite considerable differences in the manner in which they worked it out, Comte and Spencer held the same general theory of social change—a conception of large-scale societal evolution. To be sure, Comte was idealistic, Spencer materialistic. Comte developed only broad outlines; Spencer conceived a theory of evolution of single institutions as well. But in spite of numerous differences, some essential similarities remain: evolution is a transformation of the forms of life of all mankind; century-long changes form the only proper unit for comparison; all societies develop from simple to complex forms; the general form of change is from military to industrial types; and, finally, developments can occur only through a specific series of basic steps.[3]

Social Evolution and the Emergence of Social Problems

The question of how social problems arise is interesting for a social evolutionist. Since the development of society is envisaged as a natural process with certain fixed stages, problems must in some sense also be natural. The stages of development for Comte were three: from a Military-Theological form, society developed through a Critical-Metaphysical, to an Industrial-Scientific stage. Each stage was necessary and although each was the most perfect form possible, each had typical limitations. Indeed, the limitations of any given stage of social evolution are its social problems.

But what are the limitations of any given stage of social evolution? One can scarcely read a line of Comte without sensing the presence of basic valuations. The values dearest to Comte were order, stability—and, above all, peace of mind. Human progress was viewed as the increasing control of the intelligence over feeling. Problems are failures of control. The first great advance of the human mind was found in the control of the physical environment. The task for the future is securing control over human nature. (Even war had its value insofar as it established order; industry, through its discipline in abject obedience, had even more. The family is essential as a source of stability in private affairs; only religion can provide ultimate stability in public affairs.) Comte's thought tended in later years to be addressed to the designing of a "scientific community" in which everyone was to have his proper place. Women's place was in the home, where they should rule supreme over domestic morality. Society was to be under the tutelage of sociologist-priests of the religion of Humanity—Humanity being conceived as the Great Being, predecessor of Durkheim's "Society *sui generis*." They were to function as educators, conciliators, arbiters of disputes, as the conscience of the people, recommending to them their stations and classes, the formulators of public opinion and the censors of thought and action.

Herbert Spencer gave the doctrines of social evolution a more materialistic twist. Society still moves from Military-Theological to Industrial-Peaceable types. The notable contrasts between Spencer and Comte appear, however, (1) at the level of their values and (2) in their programs to implement these values. Comte desired order, stability, and peace of mind, but he feared to leave the pursuit of these values to individuals. Spencer, by contrast, wanted to be let alone and given freedom to act; he therefore became a passionate opponent of reform and state activity.

The important point to note is that the same general theory of social change (evolutionism) was for both Comte and Spencer the anchorage point of the sanctions of desirable goals and a concept of social reform. Thus, it is not the theory of social change that makes the programs of Comte and Spencer different; it is the set of values each brings to bear on the concept of change. The very thing Comte held most dear—the fixation of individuals in a caste-like order—was conceived by Spencer as the bitterest of all fates.

Evolutionism in American Sociology: Ward, Sumner, and Giddings

Prior to World War I, the positions of Comte and Spencer represented the most important alternative points of view offered by sociology regarding social problems. However, the only major follower of Comte in America was Lester Ward.[4] In a sense, Ward is far more orthodox than either Comte or Spencer. To the extent to which he accepted Spencer's goals and Comte's program, he realigned a radicalism of method with a liberalism of values. But sociology has never been noted as a hive of radicalism, and Ward was without heirs. Spencer fared better; such major academic and intellectual figures as William Graham Sumner and Franklin H. Giddings manned the battalions against the reformers in the name of the forgotten man[5] and vigorously ferreted out evidences of suspected tendencies toward socialism.

The "Conflict School" of Social Problems

A possible rival to evolutionism in interpretation of social problems during these years was Social Darwinism, as represented by Bagehot and Gumplowicz[6] in Europe and Small[7] in America. The novelty of the approach was the conception of conflict as a fundamental social process. Gumplowicz, for example, saw society as a product of conquest of groups and its more developed structural forms as the product of military subordination. However, the conflict point of view did not appear favorable to the conceptualization of ideal social states, perhaps because moral formulas approached from this perspective often appeared to be the will of the conqueror or the uneasy compromise formulas accepted to preserve peace. In any case, something in the approach was sobering, tending to suppress the elaboration of normative theories. Spencer's formula, moreover, was too attractive to be denied—it permitted one to be a thoroughgoing conservative in every act and thereby to achieve the liberal goals. Who could ask for more?

THE RISE OF THE CONCEPT
OF SOCIAL DISORGANIZATION

Urbanization and the Decline of Optimism

An number of things combined to bring the easy optimism of the past century to an end. The most significant general process of the period was the rise of urbanism. In the period after the Civil War the prevailing atmosphere had been characterized by the excitement of the boom town. Everything tended, to be sure, to be slipshod and jerry-built. But everyone knew this to be temporary. Almost every major city of the period saw a crowding of people it was not prepared to receive. Service lanes were converted into shantytowns; streets too narrow and crooked and inefficient for new volumes of traffic disintegrated completely; methods of garbage and waste disposal were so badly understood that streams and waterways were polluted; a series of dramatic fires revealed the general failure to think in terms of a new level of risks. Even in a physical sense, the new urban complex was beginning to force thinking people to take stock. If industrialism and urbanism are the highest product of social evolutionism, change is not an unmixed blessing.[8]

The event most significant in helping transform the easy optimism of sociologists into a more sober type of reflection was World War I. Spencer, among others, had assumed that society had grown so complex and interdependent in its industrial stage that as a natural result of the evolutionary process war had become virtually impossible. If evolution was to be retained as a basis for a conception of social problems, a radical change of emphasis from the Spencerian point of view was therefore indicated. However, the theory of evolution was itself being brought under critical review. In time social problems came to be conceptualized on a new base which was found, not in a theory of social change, but in a theory of social structure. Social problems were increasingly viewed as the negative or contradictory aspects of social organization. Subsequently, new approaches to social problems have been organized around the concept of *social disorganization*.

Durkheim's Theory of Disorganization and Anomie

Although he accepted the evolutionary framework that prevailed in his time, Durkheim was primarily interested in it as a base for understanding social facts and societies.[9] Social facts are collective representations (including such things as ideas, sentiments, habits, norms, etc.), identifiable by their general acceptance and by the constraint exercised in their name over the actions of individuals. Societies are not mere aggregates of people; they are shared ways of life characterized by social solidarity. Whereas the social solidarity of mankind in the past was merely *mechanical* (based on such things as kinship, friendship, etc.), in the modern world social solidarity is increasingly *organic* (based on a division of labor).

Yet the division of labor sometimes creates the very negation of solidarity. Division of labor makes criminal organizations more elaborate and effective. Moreover, the various social and industrial crises, such as class disturbances, labor struggles, etc., indicate how things may go awry. But Durkheim tended to locate the source of all such difficulties in the collective sentiments—the rules, regulations, and norms—which were the essence of society and social solidarity.

If the division of labor does not produce solidarity . . . it is because the relations of the organism are not regulated, because they are in a state of *anomie* . . . . Since a body of rules is the definite form which spontaneously established relations between social functions have taken in the course of time, we can say, *a priori*, that the state of *anomie* is impossible wherever solidary organs are in contact or sufficiently prolonged.[10]

One of the most interesting things about Durkheim's development is the tendency for his formulations to grow less optimistic. The concept of *anomie* ("normlessness") is expanded in the course of his studies and given ever broader formulation.[11]

Cooley and the Dissipation of Primary Groups

A second form of social-disorganization theory appears in the writings of Charles Horton Cooley, who attacked the central issues of sociology from the standpoint of the relation of the individual to the group. In general, Cooley's ideas bear a close resemblance to Durkheim's concepts of collective representations, social solidarity, and the central importance of regulation norms. The novelty of his work lies mainly in the location of the source of norms in primary groups, which are characterized by close association and cooperation, play a primary role in the formation of the social nature (the ideas) of the individual, and are typified by the family, the play group, the neighborhood community, and the community of elders. They are the source of primary ideals.

Larger society is, at least in its more acceptable phases, a construction out of primary ideals. Democracy and Christianity are, for Cooley, simple primary ideals writ large on the scale of world history. However, the presentation of the primary-group ideals at the level of society at large leads to mechanization, formalism, and the draining away of the energies of human nature. Religion becomes intolerant, deadening routine appears in the schools, the universities become filled with cant, the cheap press and habits of hasty reading are fostered. In his later work the view is further extended as Cooley calls attention to the conflict of group standards within the larger society.[12]

Personal and Social Disorganization: The Theories of Thomas and Znaniecki

Thomas and Znaniecki were led to their concept of social disorganization from a starting point quite different from that of either Durkheim or Cooley. For some years Thomas had been interested in a phenomenon particularly characteristic of American cities after the Civil War and through the first decade of the twentieth century: the pool of cheap labor. Pursuing this interest, Thomas had begun assembling masses of facts on the Polish immigrant in America, and in the course of his work came in touch with the brilliant young Polish philosopher-sociologist, Florian Znaniecki.

The process Thomas and Znaniecki were trying to understand was the reception of the immigrant Polish peasant into the American community. In the course of their study, they were led to introduce: (1) a typology of motivational categories; (2) the concepts of life-organization and social organization; (3) a typology of individual life-organizations; and (4) special concepts of personal and social disorganization. Only the last two of these contributions are directly relevant to our purposes.

The typology of individual life-organization introduced by the authors represented a characterization of formal differences in the adjustment of life to social organization. The *Bohemian* is the person who finds no point of stability in himself, but flows into the social mold of the moment. He is all things to all people because he is nothing to himself. He pursues no consistent career because he cannot. He drifts and eventually tends to fill the ranks of the hobo. The *Philistine* represents an inelastic adjustment to the social order. He, too, finds no point of order in himself; he can only cling fanatically to *tradition*. The *Creative Man* finds a stable basis for development within himself and is capable of a dynamic adjustment of personality.

Anyone of average intelligence reading Thomas and Znaniecki's work would hardly regard either Bohemianism or Philistinism as particularly desirable. Bohemianism is, in a sense, the epitome of individual disorganization. The difficulty with Philistinism is that the individual who finds no stability in himself can hardly rebel without falling into Bohemianism.

Applying these distinctions, Thomas and Znaniecki defined social disorganization as the decrease in the influence of social rules over the behavior of group members. They understood this decrease in influence as existing in varying degrees, from the breaking of a particular rule by a particular individual to a general decay of institutions. They recognized the fact that an individual may break rules because he is losing the capacity for life-organization required by his society, or because he rejects rules as hindrances to his attainment of a more inclusive life-organization. But the assumption that individual and social organization are directly related is not necessarily warranted; individual demoralization is not equivalent to social disorganization. Social disorganization is thought of as a universal process. During eras of social stability, *incipient* disorganization is neutralized by actions that re-enforce the social rules and norms. It is only during periods of change that it tends to become important.[13]

Criticism of Disorganization Theories

The entire theory of social disorganization was brought under vigorous attack by Mills,[14] who found it to be a facile display of "a paste-pot eclectic psychology," demonstrating an "occupationally trained incapacity to rise above a series of 'cases.'" If social-disorganization theorists were really capable of examining the norms, Mills suggests, they would perhaps have been led to see the "total structure of norms" and to "relate these to distributions of power."

Unfortunately, dispassionate analysis of social disorganization *has* generally been lacking. Wirth quite rightly pointed out that there are elements of evaluation in the conceptualization of both social organization and social disorganization.[15] And Lemert made a responsible and suggestive analysis of some aspects of both.[16] But these analyses leave many significant problems untouched.

The one thing that all the critics—from Mills to Lemert, and many others in addition—are agreed upon is the presence of valuations in the theory of social disorganization. There is no question whatsoever about the fact that they are correct. The criticism is frequently marred, however, by the fact that the critic objects to *particular* evaluation rather than to the confusion of values with facts.

The type of analysis suggested by the critics of social-disorganization theory is a comparative analysis of the different value-presuppositions of its advocates. It is quite correctly pointed out that Cooley's values seem to be those of the small town—friendly feeling, neighborliness, etc. There seems, however, to be a strong unwillingness to admit that social-disorganization theorists ever preferred anything else. But Thomas and Znaniecki seem not to have grieved at the decline of the small town. Their highest value clearly appears embodied in their Creative Man. Throughout their work, the assumption is that the natural environment of the Creative Man is the larger urban center. Moreover, Thomas and Znaniecki are no more remote from the criticism of provincialism than is Durkheim, although Durkheim does not commit himself to a "creative man" as an ideal. Durkheim everywhere prefers what he called "organic" to "mechanical" solidarity, indicating a preference for an urban, industrial, and scientifically minded social order.

These examples certainly demonstrate that the distinction between normative and empirical social theory still remains when the concept of social problems is generalized into a concept of social disorganization. However, in part because this distinction was not drawn, the evaluative aspects of the issue were not sharply separated from the empirical. It is evident, moreover, that the highest values of the chief authors of the concept of social disorganization were not identical.

THE RISE OF THE CONCEPT
OF CULTURAL LAG

Although the concept of cultural lag is frequently treated as a form of the concept of social disorganization, in the present discussion it is examined separately. Social disorganization is here taken to refer to those approaches to social problems that involve a concept of social *organization* as an empirical base. Cultural lag, on the other hand, entails an analysis of social problems projected on the foundation of a conception of social *change*.

In the new edition of *Social Change*, Ogburn observes that at the time of the first edition, social evolution had been a lode temporarily worked out. On reflection, nearly thirty years later, it seemed to him that social evolution—modified, to be sure, and identified with cultural evolution—provided the best account of social change after all. Four fundamental processes are seen to compose social evolution: (1) *invention*, including both material and social innovations, as the product of mental ability working on a material base addressed to wants; (2) *accumulation*, which generally adds more to culture at any given time than is lost—a process that tends to accelerate; (3) *diffusion*, the spread of inventions and the process by which people profit from innovations they have not made themselves; and (4) *adjustment* of one part of society to another, such as the economy of the family, the family to education, and so on.[17]

The Theory of Cultural Lag

Ogburn observed that cultural elements persist for at least two reasons: they may have a practical utility; or they may satisfy a psychological need. These two kinds of things can, of course, coincide; but if they were not distinguishable, it would be difficult to account for "survivals" having no apparent utility. Magical practices of all types are an excellent example; they satisfy psychological needs and at the same time tend to suppress the development of genuine utilities. Similarly, change occurs in response to material and psychological needs through the processes of innovation and diffusion.

Yet a number of conditions may obstruct change. It may be resisted by vested interests, which tend to preserve the *status quo* at all costs. Resistance to change may also be due to traditional hostility to the new, to habit, to pressure toward conformity, the tendency to forget the unpleasant, and fear. Curiosity, restlessness, pain, and ambition are among the psychological forces making for change.[18]

It is in these terms that Ogburn laid the basis for his theories of social problems. The position taken here is that Ogburn presented not one but two theories of social problems. The first of these may be considered under its usual designation, "cultural lag." Ogburn argued that the accumulation of culture is occurring at an ever-accelerating rate.

The thesis is that the various parts of modern culture are not changing at the same rate, some parts are changing much more rapidly than others; and that since there is a correlation and interdependence of parts, a rapid change in one part of our culture requires readjustments through other changes in the various correlated parts of culture.[19]

The general argument is that material culture tends to develop relatively rapidly, "adaptive" culture much more slowly. The lag between the two, then, is the source of tensions. This is illustrated by forestry and conservation. In the early history of our culture there were vast forests, a tremendous need for wood for fuel and building, and men with an eye to the main chance. The forests were slashed in the quickest but most wasteful manner possible. This, together with the growth of population and industry, led to the approaching exhaustion of the forests. Consequently, the new "adaptive" culture of the "conservation" movement arose to meet changed material conditions.

Among the reasons for cultural lag are: (1) the scarcity of invention in the adaptive culture;[20] (2) mechanical obstacles to adaptive changes —for instance, legislatures meet at infrequent intervals and for too short times, whereas needs continue without intermission or holidays; (3) closeness of contact with material culture—sometimes the relation between adaptive and material culture is indirect and hence takes much longer to be brought into correspondence; (4) the connection of adaptive culture with other parts of culture—for instance, the mores of exploitation serve to increase resistance to forest conservation; and finally, (5) group evaluations, the emotionalism of groups, love of the past, etc., may lead to resistance to adaptation.

The Implicit Theory of Biological Lag

The theory of cultural lag seems to have been viewed by Ogburn as capable of accounting for only a limited range of social problems, for after advancing it, he went on to introduce another theory that, for want of a better name, may be called a theory of *biological lag*. Indeed, he wrote:

It was shown that a number of social problems arise because the different parts of culture change at unequal rates. In the present chapter we wish to consider some of the problems that arise, not from the lack of adjustment of the various parts of culture, but from the lack of adjustment between human nature and culture.[21]

Summing up the facts known about the physical evolution of man, Ogburn observed that man has been on earth for several hundred thousand years or so, and that skeletal remains indicate that his evolution has been slow. Generally, there is agreement that there has been no significant evolution, biologically, in man since the last glacial age. Man's psychological nature is quite similar to that of the anthropoids. Man's nature would thus seem to be "much more like that of the cave men than the appearance of cultural differences would lead one to think."

Ogburn thus suggests that, although man is the same biologically as in the ice age, his culture has profoundly changed. He further suggests that we may be like a group of Cro-Magnon children in a modern city. And he considers the hypothetical possibility that modern man suffers from indigestion because he does not eat the food of cave men and does not experience primitive hunger. He also suggests that adjustment to marriage and to rigid sex codes may be difficult for the same reason.

It is claimed that a great many social problems such as war, crime, sexual phenomena and disease arise because of the inability or difficulty of the original nature of man to adapt itself to modern conditions and cultural standards. So also it is claimed that much of our unhappiness, nervousness, and insanity is traceable to the same general causes.[22]

Our biological nature, Ogburn argues, has not been adapted to civilization because of the short time available for such adjustment. We cannot be absolutely sure where the greatest discrepancies lie. However, at the present time there is probably far more demand for intellectual concentration, sustained thought, and attention than ever in the past. There is at present probably far less opportunity for an equivalent range of emotional experience. Modern man undoubtedly has the same instinctive equipment as his ancestors, just as he has the same musculature. He must therefore suffer at least as severely for lack of proper exercise of his instinctive nature as he does from the failure to act physically according to the needs of his apelike body.

To the tensions born of discrepancies between modern civilization and the nature of the old ape—to biological lag—Ogburn attributes much nervousness and insanity. He observes that some nervous troubles are due to accidents, injuries, or hereditary defects; but over and beyond these are such things as hysteria, morbid compulsions, anxiety-neuroses, paranoia, melancholia, and manic-depression, in which the difficulty lies in the *functioning* of structure and which are hence occasioned or modified by the cultural environment rather than by physical or organic factors.

Further examples of problems due to discrepancies between human nature and culture are found in crime. "In periods of economic depression there is more temptation to violate laws regarding property. The amount of crime fluctuates with economic conditions." Thus "crime is clearly evidence of lack of adjustment between human nature and culture." In the field of sex, such things as adultery, prostitution, and illicit sexual intercourse are seen as social problems. These, together with divorce and family breakdown, indicate that the "conflict of sex codes and human nature" is a frequent "cause of unhappiness." Moreover, human nature seems to be basically self-seeking. Given half a chance, it creates an "inequality in the distribution of wealth." This, in turn, is a factor in "poverty, disease, taxation, labor, government, war, and many other problems."[23]

Cultural Lag vs. Biological Lag

Not the least interesting feature of Ogburn's two theories of social problems is the fact that they are in some measure contradictory. Cultural lag attributes problems to tensions between material and nonmaterial culture. Biological lag attributes problems to tensions between man's original nature and his acquired nature (culture). It could perhaps be argued—and it is rather surprising that no one ever confronted Ogburn on this point—that these are complementary approaches applying to different spheres. But if this is the case, it is not immediately evident. The lag between the exploitation of the forests and conservation was utilized to illustrate the first kind of theory. However, orgies of unrestrained selfishness were also thought to be characteristic of the second type of problem explanation. Forest exploitation could as easily be fitted into the second as into the first scheme. This is true for almost every illustration of either type of problem; with slight changes of emphasis each one can be fitted into either mold.

It is impossible to escape the conclusion that the same old valuative points of view are present. The most striking feature of Ogburn's discussion is that he presents both in turn. If one accepts the culture-lag theory, the solution to problems seems to be an extension of scientific intelligence. If one accepts the biological-lag theory, presumably one must either adjust human nature to culture or culture to human nature. In the first approach, problems appear because man is rather stupid; following the second approach, man is still a savage and civilization a thin veneer. The cultural lag theory inclines toward liberal perspectives, the biological-lag theory toward conservative orientation.

Critique of "Lag" Theories

Moreover, important theoretical and methodological problems are raised by both theories. Cultural-lag analysis, for example, presupposes a distinction between material and adaptive culture, but neither of these has been adequately defined conceptually or specified operationally. The examples were developed so vaguely that the ideas are unclear. Presumably, for example, there is a lag between forest exploitation and forest conservation. But why is forest exploitation any more "material culture" than forest conservation? Ideas seem to be nonmaterial whereas things are material. But science is thought of as material culture; yet it is not a thing. It hardly makes sense to think of science as a set of material facts without ideas, intentions, enterprise. In none of the examples is the distinction between material and nonmaterial culture made clear and unambiguous. Why should a general property tax be material, whereas some other type of tax is not? Is an instrument material? The least interesting properties of an instrument are its purely material properties; it is significant for the ideas and activities for which it is designed. But these latter seem more properly to belong to non-material culture.

The Evaluative Basis of "Lag" Theories

The failure to draw the distinctions between normative and empirical theory adds to the confusion. The very notion of "lag" seems to imply that something is "ahead." The only way to answer the question of what is lagging is to state the aims, goals, and values—the basis of judgment. The old saw holds in this area as well as in others: what is one man's meat is another's poison. What is viewed as a lag or even a positive regression by one person may represent an advance or gain to another.

Clarity in cultural-lag theory depends upon a formulation of culture goals. And these are only implied in the theory. It is clear that Ogburn was "for" the following: conservation, the more adequate compensation of victims of industrial accidents, a revision of the tax laws, and organizations to promote international peace. Stated in this way the theory of cultural lag takes on some of the properties of the program of a political party—which, at bottom, it is.

The theory of biological lag also presents problems. The most important theoretical and methodological problems consist in the necessity of adequately conceptualizing and empirically verifying "original human nature." An interesting but risky series of assumptions appears to be made in the concept of biological lag. The two most important are: (1) that there is an original human nature, and (2) that there is a culture appropriate to it. But what is the solution to a set of simultaneous equations made up completely of unknowns?

The kinds of goals presupposed by this second approach seem to be the direct opposite of those suggested by the first. The cultural-lag approach seems to suggest that the general body of social life be brought into accordance as fast as possible with the latest gadget or combination tool. The biological lag theory, however, seems to suggest either that human nature be adjusted to culture or that culture be adjusted to human nature. The ideal here seems to be stability and peace of mind and thereby the elimination of most psychoneurosis, crime, and suicide.

FROM CONFLICT TO ECOLOGY

It has been observed that the analysis of social life from the point of view in which conflict is accepted as the basic process had its most important American representative in Albion Small who, at the University of Chicago, became the primary representative of this view in America. As he developed the theory, interests conceived as unsatisfied capacities corresponding to unrealized conditions were held to be the simplest modes of motion in human beings. The basic interests were health, wealth, sociability, knowledge, beauty, and rightness. All action occurring in society consisted of movements of persons compelled by various interests. Society was the resultant at any given moment of all the efforts of particular persons to achieve particular satisfaction. *"All social problems are problems of the relations of personal units that have in themselves distinct initiative and choice and force. This personal equation must be assigned its real value, in order to reach a true formula of the social reaction."*[24]

The Role of Interests in Social Problems

The incidents in the life of a person are contacts with the physical world or with other individuals. In the process of making social contacts, a constant differentiation of interests occurs from which follow differentiation of structure and function. Numbers of people whose relation to each other is sufficiently important to require attention constitute a group. People are continuously in associative combinations, and human social life is primarily group life. The social process is thus a perpetual action and reaction of interests lodged in individuals who are in contact. In spite of disguised or open struggle, people fuse into groups. Conflict then goes on at the new level, between group and group. Although conflict (following Ratzenhofer) is primary and universal, it tends to resolve itself into cooperation. In brief, socialization is the transforming of conflict into cooperation.[25]

At first glance, this conception of conflict would seem to recommend itself as the most direct of all possible positions for analyzing social problems. It is difficult to conceive of a simpler model of trouble: two hungry dogs, one bone. The more nearly equal in size, strength, and ability the dogs are, the more interesting the events.

Yet the character of the ordinary type of analysis of social problems is nowhere more completely shown than in the reluctance of some thinkers to approach social problems from the standpoint of conflict. Such a standpoint makes assignment of praise and blame strangely inappropriate. This is not to say that conflict itself is viewed as desirable —reluctance to rush into the middle of human affairs with a mouthful of moral condemnations is not equivalent to making perverted value-judgments. However, when people are seen as acting on a plurality of interests that lead them in pursuit of limited values and into encounters in which both cannot win; when cooperation is seen, as it so often is, as a combination to achieve more effective group conflict; when a peaceable social state is seen as a slow compromise of diverse interests—such perceptions tend to dampen an over-enthusiastic reforming zeal. This is particularly true when reforming zeal is observed to be often itself an instrument in conflict. For these reasons, it is interesting to trace those shifts of emphasis that lead from an empirical examination of conflict processes back to a normative consideration of social problems.

The Ecological Approach to Social Problems

The concept *social process* (with conflict at its core), which was being moved into central position by Small, was adopted by Park and Burgess.[26] When it was brought under closer analysis, social process was subdivided into four major types of interaction: competition, conflict, accommodation, and assimilation. Competition was thought of as the human form of that struggle to survive which is characteristic of all life. It was not social; it was *sub-social*. It was constant, largely unconscious and impersonal. In the economic order, it was ecological in nature. It was the force that creates the territorial and vocational distribution of the population basic to the division of labor and organized economic interdependence.

Conflict, on the other hand, was thought to be more social in nature, as competition became conscious, with other persons taken into account. The political process shows *par excellence* how competition may become conscious and take the form of conflict.

Accommodation is the attempt by individuals and groups to make the internal adjustments to the situations created by competition and conflict. When they are made, conflict subsides. Assimilation completes the process with a thoroughgoing transformation of personality under the influence of intimate social contacts.

But it was the concept of *competition* as the human form of the universal struggle to survive that served as the bridge from a theory of social process in which conflict was central, to the conceptualization of the city. The modern city was thought of as a system of interactive life produced in the course of modern man's commercial activity. Economic activity is the primary field of competition; economic competition tends to produce the kind of order known as *ecological*. Just as in the plant world the biological competition of diverse forms tends to produce an order in which various habitats are natural to a given plant form, in which one form may invade the area of another, and in which the plant "community" is seen as an integrated balance of vegetative types, so the human city, constructed out of competition, has its natural habitats for social groups, its potentials for invasion of areas by different groups, and typical successions of groups through an area.[27]

The Urban Matrix of Social Problems

Burgess centered attention on the order that was, theoretically, produced by the operation of the urban ecological processes and presented an idealized picture of the characteristic zones produced. Zone 1 was the central business district; in Chicago it was the Loop.

Encircling the downtown area there is normally an area in transition, which is being invaded by business and light manufacture (II). A third area (III) is inhabited by the workers in industries who have escaped from the area of deterioration (II) but who desire to live within easy access of their work. Beyond this zone is the "residential area" (IV) of high-class apartment buildings or of exclusive "restricted" districts of single family dwellings. Still further, out beyond the city limits, is the commuter's zone—suburban areas, or satellite cities—within a thirty-to-sixty minute ride of the central business district.[28]

This conception of the competitive processes of the city producing a characteristic ecological order made possible a unique investigation of social problems. One was able to examine them, not from the standpoint of the basic character of human social conflict, but from the standpoint of their physical location in the physical structure of the city. At the time Park and Burgess were developing these formulations, Burgess reported the following projects under his direction. "Nels Anderson, *The Slum: An Area of Deterioration in the Growth of the City;* Ernest R. Mowrer, *Family Disorganization in Chicago;* Walter C. Reckless, *The Natural History of Vice Areas in Chicago;* E. H. Shideler, *The*

Retail Business Organization as an Index of Business Organization;
F. M. Thrasher, *One Thousand Boy's Gangs in Chicago: A Study of
Their Organization and Habitat;* H. W. Zorbaugh, *The Lower North
Side: A Study in Community Organization."*[29] Almost all the studies
in progress at that time resulted in familiar publications. They were
the first of a flood of similar studies: of the physical location of areas of
high incidence of crime, juvenile delinquency, suicide, disease, etc.; of
variations and differences in incidence of almost everything in one area
after another of the city.

The Conversion to Environmentalism

As studies of the location by areas of various types of ills and
socially disapproved behavior become more frequent, the theoretical
origins of the research—conflict theory—are eclipsed. Appeal to this
theoretical core disappears. With increasing frequency the observation
is made that a specific area of a city tends to show a uniform problem-
incidence regardless of who occupies it. More implicitly than explicitly,
the idea that human problems are a function of environmental location
rises to the surface. The formula, thus, tends to be reversed. The properties of a neighborhood, rather than conflicting interests, become important.

The inevitable result was a new program of reform, and this was not
long in coming. By 1930 the conception had already developed that a
program of neighborhood reform was the proper way of meeting these
issues. In one of the more recent reports on developments in one of
the projects, it is observed:

Since its inception in 1930, the Chicago Area Project, with a small staff of
competent, zealous workers had introduced its distinctive philosophy and
program of neighborhood betterment into thirteen different areas in the
metropolitan district, areas of varied racial and national strains, but all of
them definitely underprivileged and with comparatively high rates of
juvenile delinquency.[30]

Thus, the conflict point of view was gradually transformed into an environmental account of social problems, making a place after all, for the
reformer.

In a fairly short period, during and immediately after World War I,
an array of new ideas was addressed to social problems. With some
simplification they have been reduced to three groups: (a) social disorganization concepts, (b) concepts of cultural and biological lag, and

(c) neighborhood-situational explanations of social problems. By 1925 the main outlines of these approaches were complete.

Social Problems on the Textbook Front, 1925–1945

It would be quite inappropriate to single out any particular work for either theoretical blessing or blame during the next fairly long period. The typical social-pathology or social-problems text tended to have generally the following format: There was either a chapter or a series of chapters on "social problems," "social disorganization," "social change," or "social pathology." This was normally followed by a series of chapters on particular social problems ranging from homosexuality and suicide to war and revolution. And there was usually a concluding chapter expressing hope for a better future.

The so-called theoretical phase of the ordinary study usually—and in most cases fortunately—has been confined to the opening sections of the book as a kind of ceremony that must be observed before settling down to business. Some preferences are shown for given theories or approaches: one prefers the social-disorganization terminology, another cultural-lag theory, a third a situational approach. Not infrequently, all three types of approach are confused. The divergent implications of locating problems in the framework of social structure rather than of change, or by means of the situational approach, are ignored. But these approaches, although stirred together vigorously, cannot be made to mix.

The social situation in which these works were written was one of world-wide depression and war. What was needed at the time was the application of any available body of thought to social issues. When any given work made a serious contribution to the field, it was usually in the form of an addition to the knowledge of concrete isues or an organization of empirical data rather than addition to theory. One must in fairness conclude that these are works by men of good will trying to measure up to their social responsibilities.

The Dominance of Social Disorganization and the Normative Approach

Quite apart from the fact that ideas with different derivations were usually stirred together in one pot, the concept of social disorganization tended to be central. There was even some tendency to simplify and codify it. Organization was increasingly thought of as a system of actions in a state of equilibrium, disorganization as a system in a state of disequilibrium. But when this is utilized as a criterion for analyzing particular problems, it quickly proves to be inadequate. Crime rings, for example, are treated as examples of disorganization. Yet they are often more "organized" than the society in which they appear and in which they are assumed to represent "disorganization." Clearly, normative judgments, in these instances, are being disguised as factual judgments. Crime rings are not objected to because they are examples of disequilibrium but because they are normatively objectionable.

Perhaps the most misleading aspect of the whole field is the reluctance to examine just what is and what is not in equilibrium. At times a given author appears to assume that society as a whole is one great system. Its equilibrium states are good; its disequilibrium states are bad. But this would assume (1) the existence of social wholes of enormous size and (2) the uncritical identification of the *status quo* as good. Yet almost all the writers on social problems would reject the first idea on theoretical grounds and the second on value grounds.

RECENT DEVELOPMENTS

Old Wine in New Bottles

Since World War II, there has been a renewed interest in social disorganization with the reissue of old books in revised form and the appearance of many new studies. A brief review of a few of these books may indicate some of the trends. In the foreword to Brown's *Social Pathology*,[31] Mowrer, who had himself contributed much to the study of personal and family problems, observes that the study of social disorganization has gone through two stages and is entering a third. In the first stage, the student of society, confronted with social problems, was motivated by reform. In the second, a scientific spirit was introduced and social maladjustments were treated as pathologies. In the third, the need to harmonize scientific knowledge about both individuals and societies is being recognized and approached.

Brown himself treats social organization as the result of social processes. Social process is in itself neither normal nor abnormal. Social disorganization is in principle not different from social organization;

it is, in fact, that kind of social organization that is not culturally approved.[32] With these basic statements there can hardly be any quarrel. The key question is: what is culturally approved? Presumably in answer to this, Brown develops the notion of the place of ideologies in social disorganization. Ideologies rise in human nature and social order, and any ideology may be manifested in war, religion, or education, even in vice and crime. The operation of social forces produces many diffuse elements, each with its own ideology.[33] Apparently one's conception of social problems depends on which ideology one holds. Since Brown designated some things as problems, he presumably made a choice among ideologies. Unfortunately, however, he did not specify which "ideology" underlay his treatment.

Robert E. L. Faris' study is somewhat closer to the strict social-disorganization schema. A successful society is conceived as one that achieves a fairly stable system adapted to its surroundings and permitting its members to carry on their generally accepted tasks. Social disorganization is thought of as the disruption of the functional relations to the point that the performance of accepted group tasks is made difficult. There are then many symptoms of disorganization. Among the more important are: formalism, decline of the sacred, individualism, hedonism, mutual distrust, etc.[34]

It may be noted that in the studies of Brown and Faris society is implicitly thought of as a kind of organic whole. Value-judgments are not clearly specified but are buried under such notions as "accepted" group behavior.

Back to Cultural Lag

A. P. Herman makes a serious attempt in his *Approach to Social Problems* to review alternate approaches to social problems and to isolate his own. He wishes to relocate social problems against the concept of social change. "Social problems arise, and existing problems are aggravated, when a society creates or accepts instruments of change, yet fails to understand, anticipate, or deal with the consequences of such action." Among the kinds of issues which either create new issues or aggravate old ones are: mechanical inventions (radio, industrial machines, drug therapy, X-ray, soil analysis, etc.); population movements (decline in rate of growth, migrations, age trends); changes in natural resources (changes in the supply of raw materials that can be exploited); natural occurrences (floods, tornadoes, earthquakes, insect

pests); physiological changes (disease and the other organic pathologies).[35] Herman's work is an attempt to revise and bring up to date an
approach similar to that of Ogburn.

The Value-Conflict Approach

In 1950 two books on social problems were reissued: the third
edition of Elliott and Merrill's *Social Disorganization* and the second
edition of Barnes and Ruedi's *The American Way of Life.*[36] The point
of view of Elliott and Merrill was roughly that of the earlier social-
disorganization theories, a view which has been sufficently commented
on above. Barnes and Ruedi dealt with social problems wholly in terms
of cultural lag: "In the case of nearly every problem, we shall find the
underlying cause to be culture lag—the failure to adapt our institutions
to new material conditions of life."[37]

In Weaver's *Social Problems,* which appeared in 1951, social problems are treated as conditions that involve strain, tension, conflict,
frustration, and interference with the fulfillment of a need. The theory
is, and was apparently intended to be, rather cursory. Cultural lag and
social disorganization are treated as identical or at least complementary.[38]

Of the major volumes appearing in 1952, Phelps and Henderson
avoided as far as possible any theoretical commitments. Reinhardt *et al.*
developed a form of disorganization approach under the new terminology of disadjustments, and Herbert Bloch reintroduced a new
version of the fused cultural-lag and social-disorganization approaches,
performing, by all odds, the most serious theoretical job of the year.[39]

Like Herman's study, Jessie Bernard's *American Community Behavior* appeared in 1949. Bernard sees the basic problem of American
society as the result of "the gap between our professed, official, documented ideals—sometimes called overt ideals—and our unprofessed,
unofficial, even repudiated, but nevertheless actually sought goals. . . ."
But more than this, she goes on to state that there is no genuine consensus and we want a multiplicity of conflicting things.

A genuine conflict approach is thus presented; in fact, even reform
is treated as a special case of conflict. "Because the goals sought by
reform are usually controversial, reform activity is simply a special
case of conflict in general." The parties to the conflict are those who try
to correct the evils and those who profit from the evils. The conflict
nature of planning is recognized in the formula of "freedom under

planning," which represents either a much higher degree of consensus than was present earlier or an ironing out of some of the basic differences of interests. Social engineering is conceived as the highest level of planning implemented by science. "Science . . . can be a powerful weapon for the control of community welfare. But it is not omnipotent. It can give us data on which to make decisions, but it cannot make our choices for us."[40]

Cuber, working from the general description of a social problem as an undesirable social condition, indicates that this assumption presupposes the existence of value-premises, which may be the value-judgments either of an expert or of the public. However, since a man is an expert only if the public so recognizes him, all value-judgments are ultimately made by the public. Value conflicts are treated as the *source* of social problems and the disorganization point of view is rejected.[41]

An Empirical Approach to Social Disorganization

Lemert's discussion contains one of the beter analyses of current theories of social disorganization, though it differs in a number of respects from the present one. Lemert proposes positive criteria for a systematic theory of social problems. This, he believes, should include clear delimitation of the field and its conceptualization in terms of a limited number of postulates that are both logically interrelated and empirically adequate to the facts to which they are addressed. Moreover, the hypotheses should follow as logical consequences from this conceptual structure.[42]

Lemert's proposal has particular interest, since for the theory of social problems he advances criteria of *empirical* theory. His specific proposals for such a theory include the following ideas: (1) that behavior varies; (2) that deviant behavior arises from culture conflict; (3) that social reactions to deviant behavior vary; (4) that sociopathic behavior is effectively disavowed; (5) that a deviant person is one who has been basically influenced by deviant behavior and its consequences; (6) that the restrictions on deviant behavior are more completely social than biological; and (7) that deviates differ with respect to their susceptibility to influence by the social reaction.[43]

This general formulation is in all key essentials so close to that of Thomas and Znaniecki that it may be best viewed as a modern version of the same general view. The most important—and most hazardous—

idea is contained in point (4), that sociopathic behavior is behavior that is effectively disavowed. The danger is that in practice this tends to mean that behavior is a problem only when it is no longer a problem, or that the *status quo* exhausts what is legitimately to be considered good.

Homans and the Group Variables of Social Disorganization

Not all of the interesting recent developments in the study of social problems are to be found in textbooks. One important step was taken by Homans. In his study, *The Human Group,* Homans proposed to analyze the group in terms of such variables or clusters of variables as sentiment, activity, norm, and value. The group was conceived essentially as a system of action in equilibrium. Actually, it was thought of as composed of two systems: (1) the *external* system, consisting in part of its formal structure, in part of its relations to the external environment; and (2) the *internal* system, or the system of activities of members toward each other. In Homans' framework, changes taking place in one system tend to work themselves out in the companion system as well.

After completing an analysis of a number of groups in terms of this schema, Homans raised the problem of social disorganization, giving a new accent to its conceptualization. Taking the case of Hilltown, a New England town that underwent serious decline toward the end of the nineteenth century and into the present, Homans introduced a special version of disorganization theory. Following Durkheim, Homans describes a situation in which the group is losing control over its members as an example of "normlessness" or *anomie,* in which the organization is going to pieces and which should not be confused with conflict, where there is no difficulty in the control of the group over its members.[44] This distinction is proposed as clearing up one primary confusion in social-disorganization theory.

Homans' analysis of the steps in the social disintegration of Hilltown takes the following form. The difficulty started in the external system: (1) the sentiments that led group members to collaborate declined in number and power; (2) the number of activities the members carried on together declined; (3) the frequency of interaction between members decreased. These changes in the external system reacted on the internal system; (4) as interaction in the external system decreased, so it declined in the internal system; (5) decrease in the frequency of interaction brought a decrease in inter-personal sentiments; (6) decrease in interpersonal sentiments led to a decline of the norms; (7) leadership became less firm; and (8) social control thereby weakened.[45]

The extent to which Homans' analysis can be generalized to social problems is a question. It depends, among other things, on the adequacy of this analysis of the forms and variables of the group and the extent to which all social life has essentially this form. There are reasons, which cannot be examined here, for seriously questioning both. It cannot be denied, however, that Homans took a step long needed in the area. Social disorganization has suffered from the failure to be spelled out in terms of particular variables and brought down to concrete cases. Homans therefore took an important forward step.

Social Problems and Structural Sources of Deviation

Robert Merton's increasing interest in social problems is shown in his analysis of "social structure and *anomie*." The general problem he wishes to examine is the manner in which social structure itself may be a source of deviant behavior. Normally, Merton argues, social structures tend to do two fundamental things: (1) to define goals and (2) to enforce ways of achieving them. However, in a society where there is tremendous emphasis on the goals without emphasis on institutional procedures, Durkheim's state of *anomie* is produced. Contemporary American culture is in Merton's mind a peculiar type tending to emphasize success-goals without emphasizing institutional means.

The culture enjoins the acceptance of three cultural axioms: First, all should strive for the same lofty goals since these are open to all; second, present seeming failure is but a halfway station to ultimate success; and third, genuine failure consists only in the lessening or withdrawal of ambition.[46]

The effect of this is to deflect criticism of the social structure onto the persons in society who do not have full access to opportunities. It forces persons to judge themselves not by their peers but in terms of those they hope to join and threatens those who do not accept such ambitions.

The result of this, as Merton sees it, is the emergence of a variety of typical individual adaptations: (1) the *conformist* accepts both the cultural goals and the institutional means; (2) the *innovator* accepts the cultural goals but not the institutional means; (3) the *ritualist* accepts the means but not the goals; (4) the *isolate* withdraws from both the goals and means; and (5) the *rebel* cannot make up his mind on either.

Like Homans, Merton has presented a challenging new approach to social problems based on Durkheim's *anomie.* The rather startling novelty of Merton's approach is the notion of laying the responsibility for *anomie* on the very doorstep of social structure itself!

A second innovation in Merton's approach to social problems appears in his proposed development of functionalist theory. Functionalism is that modern version of sociological organicism assuming that cultural items can be properly analysed only if conceived as parts of organic or even organismic wholes. Merton proposes to change the fundamental postulates he ascribes to the prevailing type of functionalism. These postulates are: (1) that social activities are functional for the entire social system; (2) that all such activities fulfill sociological functions and are indispensable. Merton, by contrast, seems to be convinced that functionalism must operate with functional wholes smaller than the entire social system and hence with limited numbers of items. Thus he distinguishes between functional prerequisites and functionally necessary items and advances a concept of functional alternatives.

But the point in Merton's analysis that is of interest to us is his introduction of the distinction between manifest and latent functions, and hence his transition to the theory of social disorganization.

Numerous . . . sociological observers have . . . from time to time distinguished between categories of subjective disposition ("needs, interests, purposes") and categories of generally unrecognized but objective functional consequences ("unique advantages," "never conscious" consequences, "unintended service to society," "function not limited to conscious and explicit purpose").

Merton urges that functional deficiencies in the official structure tend to generate unofficial structures to fulfill the needs. These fulfill functions for groups not otherwise provided for and demonstrate that eliminating an existing structure without providing for the requirements abolished makes failure certain. Hence, "To seek social change, without due recognition of the manifest and latent functions performed by the social organization undergoing change, is to indulge in social ritual rather than social engineering."[47]

In the course of his analysis, Merton not only introduced the concept of manifest and latent function as providing the basis for a conception of conflict and reinforcement between different aspects of a given system, but insisted as well that a conception of dysfunctions was also required.

A theory of functional analysis must call for specification of social units subserved by given social functions and . . . items of culture must be recognized to have multiple consequences, some of them functional and others, perhaps, dysfunctional.[48]

As far as one can tell, the concept of dysfunction has a role in Merton's theory comparable to that of the concept of disorganization in a theory of social problems. *It, too, raises issues that can only be settled on normative grounds.*

The Attack against "Scientism"

A general spirit of good will pervades almost all the thinking about social problems. However, it should be no surprise, perhaps, that ill will and misrepresentation do appear in this area. A. H. Hobbs has recently launched a slashing attack on all persons who have suggested that science may be of some help in the solution of social problems. If Hobbs had held to his own definition of what he calls scientism ("a belief that science can furnish answers to all human problems," a view which he says "makes science a substitute for philosophy, religion, manners, and morals"), he would have had fewer people to attack. For example, Hobbs has accused Professor Monachesi and me of "scientism" on the basis of the following quotation:

In spite of the many obstacles that curb social planning in the various spheres of social behavior, planning has come to be regarded as the most effective way to anticipate and to solve social-problem situations. This view is unavoidable, since planning is an efficient way of creating a solution to an anticipated problem before the problem actually occurs.[49]

From the suggestion that science might help people solve their problems, Hobbs reasons: "Since scientism attempts to regulate the lives of people, it must begin by making puppets of them." He argues further that there are many professors and Ph.D's. among the scientists who, technically not Socialists or Communists, are joiners of front organizations. Hence, they are not Communists only in the sense that they are not members of the Communist Party.

Failure of scientistic liberals to accept the communism or socialism implied in the extension of their principles may be due, not to convictions about the evils of such regimentation, but because . . . [they] lack the character for communist faith because they lack the character for any faith.[50]

PERSPECTIVES

At the beginning of this chapter, two sets of distinctions were introduced. The first contrasted general value-perspectives. An interplay can be discerned between different approaches to social problems at any one time and between the elements constituting a given position over a period of time. The two perspectives were groupings of values into liberal and conservative types respectively. Perhaps the most novel approaches were those of Comte and Spencer: Comte presented a radicalism of method in the interest of conservative values; Spencer presented a conservatism of method in the interest of liberal values. In disorganization theory, Durkheim advocated a conservative type, Thomas and Znaniecki a liberal type; Cooley presented an old-fashioned (Jeffersonian) liberal form. In his field analyses, Ogburn advanced first a semi-liberal and later a semi-conservative approach to social problems. In general, the uniformity of value-judgments so often imputed to the social-problem thinkers is a myth, although by and large the so-called liberal type of orientation tends to prevail.

The second set of distinctions introduced in the early pages of this chapter was the contrast between a normative and an empirical theory. Empirical social theory was defined as a system of hypotheses developed in the interest of explanation. Normative social theory was defined as the systematic exploration by means of empirical theory of the procedures for achieving a given program of action. The general theses of this study were: (1) only normative social theory is appropriate to social problems, and (2) whenever a set of normative formulations is disguised as empirical, only confusion results. This study has repeatedly verified both these theses. Time after time, in one form or other, value-premises have been discovered in the positions reviewed. The presence of these value-premises is not in itself bad; it was to be expected. What is bad is to have value-judgments disguised as judgments of fact.

If these theses are accepted, and if they are felt to be at least in some measure verified, then the most important question of all may be posed. What is the student of social problems to do?

Fundamentally, he appears to be in a dilemma. The theory of social problems cannot assume efficient form unless it is recognized for what it is—a judgmentally normative social theory. Moreover, so long as we admit the legitimacy of alternative value structures, we must recognize that there is no *single* theory of social problems, but many *theories* of social problems. Meanwhile, insofar as the theories of social problems are of a normative rather than an empirical type, they are outside the province of the scientist as scientist. As a scientist, one can apply one's knowledge to any given set of goals, demonstrating (1) whether they are attainable; (2) if so, how they can be most efficiently attained; and (3) what the consequences of attaining them may be. However, as a scientist one cannot prescribe goals.

Thus the peculiar adolescence of this particular field, its tendency to blow hot and cold by turns, its sudden embarrassments and hollow pretensions—these, it is maintained, are due to the attempts to cast contradictory role requirements in a single mold. It has been the peculiar destiny of thinkers in this field to search for a single solution to social problems—as if there were only one—and to seek scientific objectivity under conditions where it was in principle impossible.

NOTES

Chapter 1

1. Walter Bagehot, *Physics and Politics* (New York: Alfred A. Knopf, 1948), quoted by Jacques Barzun in his Introduction, pp. xiv–xv.

2. *Ibid.*, pp. xv–xvi.

3. *Ibid.*, p. 63.

4. Paul Radin, *Primitive Man as Philosopher* (New York: D. Appleton & Co., 1927), p. 5.

5. *Ibid.*, pp. 23–24.

6. *Ibid.*, p. 37.

7. *Ibid.*, pp. 166–168.

8. *Ibid.*, p. 169.

9. St. Augustine, *The City of God* (New York: Hafner, 1948), p. 437.

10. *Ibid.*, p. 437.

11. *Ibid.*, pp. 519–520.

12. *Ibid.*, p. 520.

13. *Ibid.*, p. 557.

14. Plato's *The Republic*, trans. by B. Jowett (New York: Modern Library, n.d.), p. 60.

15. *Ibid.*, p. 64.

16. *Ibid.*, pp. 65–67.

17. *Ibid.*, p. 68.

18. *Ibid.*, pp. 182–183.

19. Leon Bramson, *The Political Context of Sociology* (Princeton: Princeton University Press, 1961), p. 16.

20. Karl Jaspers, *Man in the Modern Age*, trans. by Eden and Cedar Paul (New York: Doubleday, 1957), pp. 144–145.

21. *Ibid.*, p. 146.

22. *Ibid.*, p. 147.

23. C. Wright Mills, *The Sociological Imagination* (New York: Oxford University Press, 1959), p. 50.

24. *Ibid.*, p. 51.

25. *Ibid.*, p. 52.

26. *Ibid.*, pp. 71–72.

27. *Ibid.*, pp. 149–150.

28. Robert K. Merton, *Social Theory and Social Structure* (Glencoe, Ill.: The Free Press, 1957), pp. 5–6.

29. *Ibid.*, p. 5.

30. See Don Martindale, *The Nature and Types of Sociological Theory* (Boston: Houghton Mifflin, 1960).

31. Karl Marx, *The Communist Manifesto*, trans. by Samuel Moore (Chicago: Henry Regnery Co., 1954), pp. 13, 14, 15.

32. Richard Hofstadter, *Social Darwinism in American Thought* (Boston: The Beacon Press, 1955), p. 6.

33. *Ibid.*, p. 9.

34. *Ibid.*, p. 201.

35. See Don Martindale, *Social Life and Cultural Change* (Princeton: D. Van Nostrand, 1962), pp. 642 ff.

36. See Don Martindale, *The Nature and Types of Sociological Theory, op. cit.*, pp. 211 ff.

37. See Merton, *op. cit.*, pp. 5 ff.

38. Martindale, *The Nature and Types of Sociological Theory, op. cit.*, pp. 267 ff.

39. Sherman Krupp, *Pattern in Organization Analysis: A Critical Examination* (Philadelphia: Chilton Co., 1961), pp. ix–x.

INTRODUCTION TO PART TWO

1. Robert K. Merton, *Social Theory and Social Structure* (Glencoe, Ill.: The Free Press, 1957), p. 3.

2. *Ibid.*, p. 19.

3. *Ibid.*, pp. 102–103.

4. *Ibid.*, p. 3.

5. *Ibid.*, p. 117.

6. Gabriel Tarde, *The Laws of Imitation*, trans. by Elsie Clews Parsons (New York: Henry Holt, 1903), pp. 102–105.

7. Charles P. Loomis and Zona K. Loomis, *Modern Social Theories* (Princeton: D. Van Nostrand, 1961), pp. 327–328.

8. *Ibid.*, p. 430.

9. Don Martindale, *The Nature and Types of Sociological Theory* (Boston: Houghton Mifflin, 1960), pp. 421–425, 484–490.

10. Max Black, ed., *The Social Theories of Talcott Parsons* (Englewood Cliffs, N.J.: Prentice-Hall, 1961). See particularly the article by Edward C. Devereux, Jr., pp. 1 ff.

11. *Ibid.*, pp. 250–252, 321–324.

12. *Ibid.*, pp. 349–350, 418–421, 467–471, 499–500.

13. *Ibid.*, pp. 425–427, 471–476.

Chapter 2

1. John C. McKinney, "Methodology, Procedures, and Techniques in Sociology," pp. 186–235 in Howard Becker and Alvin Boskoff, eds., *Modern Sociological Theory* (New York: Holt, Rinehart and Winston, 1957), p. 226.

2. Auguste Comte, *Positive Philosophy*, trans. by Harriet Martineau, (London: J. Chapman, 1853), Vol. 2, pp. 103–105.

3. The works of Herbert Spencer, Lewis H. Morgan, and Emile Durkheim illustrate this.

4. Wilhelm Dilthey's *Gesammelte Schriften* (Leipzig and Berlin: B. B. Tuebner, 1936) particularly *Einleitung in die Geisteswissenschaften: Versuch einer Grundlegung für das Studium der Gesellschaft und der Geschichte*, 1, and "*Der Aufbau der geschichtlichen Welt in den Geisteswissenschaften*," *Gesammelte Schriften*, III. Reviews of Dilthey's position for social science and for history may be found in Maurice Mandelbaum, *The Problem of Historical Knowledge* (New York: Liveright Publishing Corporation, 1938), pp. 59 ff., and Alexander Goldenweiser, "The Relation of the Natural Sciences to the Social Sciences," in *Contemporary Social Theory*, Harry Elmer Barnes, Howard Becker, and Frances Bennett Becker, eds. (New York: D. Appleton Co., 1940), pp. 93–98.

5. Heinrich Rickert, *Die Grenzen der Naturwissenschaftlichen Begriffsbildung* (Tübingen: J. C. B. Mohr, 1920). Summaries are also found in Mandelbaum and Goldenweiser (see note 4 above).

6. *Ibid.*, p. 100.

7. *Ibid.*, pp. 93 ff.

8. *Ibid.*, p. 281.

9. *Ibid.*, p. 272.

10. Max Weber, *The Methodology of the Social Sciences*, trans. by Edward A. Shils and Henry A. Finch (Glencoe, Ill.: The Free Press, 1949), p. 89.

11. *Ibid.*, pp. 91–92.

12. *Ibid.*, p. 90.

13. *Ibid.*, p. 93.

14. *Ibid.*, p. 97.

15. *Ibid.*, p. 100.

16. *Ibid.*, p. 101.

17. *Ibid.*, p. 92.

18. *Ibid.*, p. 187.

19. Ernest Nagel, "The Logic of Historical Analysis" in *Readings in the Philosophy of Science*, Herbert Feigl and May Brodbeck, eds. (New York: Appleton-Century-Crofts, Inc., 1953), pp. 688 ff.

20. R. M. MacIver, *Social Causation* (New York: Ginn & Co., 1942), pp. 258–259.

21. Talcott Parsons, *Essays in Sociological Theory* (Glencoe, Ill.: The Free Press, 1949), p. 76.

22. *Ibid.*, p. 78.

23. Talcott Parsons, *The Social System* (Glencoe, Ill.: The Free Press, 1951), p. 58.

24. *Ibid.*, p. 59.

25. *Ibid.*, p. 60.

26. *Ibid.*, p. 66.

27. *Ibid.*, p. 152.

28. *Ibid.*, p. 152.

29. *Ibid.*, p. 153.

30. Howard Becker, *Through Values to Social Interpretation* (Durham, N.C.: Duke University Press, 1950), p. 90.

31. *Ibid.*, p. 109.

32. *Ibid.*, p. 108.

33. In addition to the statement in *Through Values*, others are contained in "Constructive Typology in the Social Sciences" in *Contemporary Social Theory, op. cit.*, pp. 17–46, and "Interpretive Sociology and Constructive Typology," in *Twentieth Century Sociology* (New York: The Philosophical Library, 1945), pp. 70–95.

34. Robert K. Merton, *Social Theory and Social Structure* (Glencoe, Ill.: The Free Press, 1949), pp. 12–16.

35. *Ibid.*, pp. 49 ff.

36. *Ibid.*, pp. 133 ff.

37. *Ibid.*, p. 132.

38. *Ibid.*, p. 133.

39. John C. McKinney, "Constructive Typology and Social Research," in *An Introduction to Social Research* (Harrisburg: The Stackpole Co., 1954), pp. 144–145.

40. In Howard Becker and Alvin Boskoff, *op. cit.*, pp. 226–227.

41. Joseph R. Schumpeter, "Capitalism," *Encyclopaedia Britannica* (1958), IV, 801–807.

42. Theodore Abel, "The Operation Called Verstehen," *American Journal of Sociology* (Chicago: University of Chicago Press, 1948), reprinted in *Readings in the Philosophy of Science, op. cit* pp. 677 ff.

43. Talcott Parsons, *Essays, op. cit.*, p. 91.

44. J. W. N. Watkins, "Ideal Types and Historical Explanation," *The British Journal for the Philosophy of Science*, 3 (1952), reprinted in an expanded version in Feigl and Brodbeck's *Readings in the Philosophy of Science, op. cit.*, pp. 723 ff.

45. *Ibid.*, p. 729.

46. Talcott Parsons, *Essays, op. cit.*, p. 78.

47. Carl G. Hempel, *Symposium: Problems of Concept and Theory Formation in the Social Sciences, Language and Human Rights* (Philadelphia: University of Pennsylvania Press, 1952), pp. 65–86.

Chapter 3

1. Talcott Parsons, *The Structure of Social Action* (New York: McGraw-Hill, 1937).

2. Emile Durkheim, *The Elementary Forms of the Religious Life*, trans. Joseph Ward Swain (Glencoe, Ill.: The Free Press, 1947), p. 444.

3. Max Weber, *The Theory of Social and Economic Organization*, trans. A. M. Henderson and Talcott Parsons (New York: Oxford University Press, 1947), p. 118.

4. *Ibid.*, pp. 718–719.

5. *Ibid.*, pp. 731–748.

6. Talcott Parsons, "The Present Position and Prospects of Systematic Theory in Sociology," in Georges Gurvitch and Wilbert E. Moore, *Twentieth Century Sociology* (New York: The Philosophical Library, 1945), pp. 42–69.

7. *The Theory of Social and Economic Organization, op. cit.* Introduction, p. 20.

8. *Ibid.*, p. 15.

9. Talcott Parsons, "The Position of Sociological Theory," in *Essays in Sociological Theory* (Glencoe, Ill.: The Free Press, 1949), p. 315.

10. *Ibid.*, p. 7.

11. Talcott Parsons, *The Social System* (Glencoe, Ill.: The Free Press, 1951) and *Working Papers in the Theory of Action*, with Edward Shils and Robert Bales (Glencoe, Ill.: The Free Press, 1953).

12. *The Social System*, p. 66.

13. This caused one of Parsons' imitators in the Midwest so much consternation that he immediately worked out thirty-two types of sacred and secular society.

14. *The Social System*, p. 152.

INTRODUCTION TO PART THREE

1. Talcott Parsons, *Structures and Process in Modern Societies* (Glencoe, Ill.: The Free Press, 1960), pp. 56–57.

Chapter 4

1. Man belongs to the order of *Primates*, which is divided into three suborders: the *Lemuroidea, Tarsoidea,* and *Anthropoidea.* He belongs to the family *Hominidea* of which *Homo sapiens* is the single extant representative. For a sketch of the biological evolution of man, see William Howells, *Mankind So Far* (New York: Doubleday, 1945).
2. Howells, *op. cit.,* Chap. 24.
3. For the utility of "type constructs" in social science, see Howard Becker, "Interpretative Sociology and Constructive Typology," in *Twentieth Century Sociology,* edited by Georges Gurvitch and Wilbert E. Moore (New York: The Philosophical Library, 1945), and also his "Constructive Typology in the Social Sciences," *Contemporary Social Theory,* edited by H. E. Barnes, Howard Becker, and Frances Bennett Becker (New York: Appleton-Century, 1940), pp. 17–46, or his *Through Values to Social Interpretation* (Durham, N.C.: Duke University Press, 1950), Chap. 2 and pp. 189–247.
4. The term "instinct" has been one of the most ambiguous in the literature of psychology and social psychology. Here the term is restricted to behavior that takes a special form about fixed classes of objects. A vague tendency, an undefined drive, a general need or urge is *not* an instinct.
5. H. G. Wells, Julian S. Huxley, and C. P. Wells, *The Science of Life* (New York: Literary Guild, 1929), pp. 1162–1199.
6. *Ibid.,* p. 1225.
7. *Ibid.,* p. 1231.
8. *Ibid.,* pp. 1239–1252.

9. For a complete list of primate characteristics, see Howells, *op. cit.,* pp. 44–93.
10. For a tabulated listing of primate brain measurements, see Robert M. Yerkes and Ada W. Yerkes, *The Great Apes* (New Haven: Yale University Press, 1934), p. 478.
11. For a tabulated listing of primate brain measurements, see *ibid.,* p. 568.
12. S. Zuckerman, *The Social Life of Monkeys and Apes* (New York: Harcourt, Brace, 1932), p. 238.
13. *Ibid.,* p. 238.
14. *Ibid.,* p. 213.
15. C. Ray Carpenter, "A Field Study of the Behavior and Social Relations of Howling Monkeys (*Allouatta palliata*)," *Comparative Psychology Monographs,* 10 (1934), pp. 1–68.
16. Zuckerman, *op. cit.,* p. 227.
17. *Ibid.,* pp. 226–229.
18. C. Ray Carpenter, "A Field Study in Siam of the Behavior and Social Relations of the Gibbon (*Hylobates lar*)" in *Comparative Psychology Monographs,* 16 (1940), pp. 1–212. See also Yerkes and Yerkes, *op. cit.,* pp. 47–110.
19. Robert M. Yerkes, *Chimpanzees* (New Haven: Yale University Press, 1943), p. 40.
20. Yerkes and Yerkes, *op. cit.,* pp. 195–561. See also H. C. Bingham, "Gorillas in a Native Habitat," *Carnegie Institution of Washington Publications,* 426 (1932); also H. W. Nissen, "A Field Study of the Chimpanzee," *Comparative Psychology Monograph,* 8, 1 (1931).
21. Wells, *op. cit.,* p. 1007; Carpenter, however, has done much to demonstrate gibbon territoriality. See (1940), *op. cit.,* pp. 1–212.
22. Yerkes and Yerkes, *op. cit.,* pp. 222–228.
23. *Ibid.,* p. 45.
24. *Ibid.,* pp. 552–561, for a tabular comparison of the great apes.
25. *Ibid.,* p. 236.
26. The concepts "instinctive behavior" and "noninstinctive behavior,"

as used here, are deliberately constructed one-dimensional types. See Howard Becker and Robert C. Myers, "Sacred and Secular Aspects of Human Sociation," *Sociometry*, 4 (August, 1942), 5 (November, 1942), pp. 207–229, 355–370.

27. "Intelligence" is here used in the sense of the capacity of the creature to adapt in behavior to new circumstances. Whenever the new situation is interpreted as a problem and adaptation takes the form of the organization of means to ends, the application of intelligence is indubitable. The apes show a marked capacity for such problem-solving. The only definitive difference between the intelligence of ape and man is the use by man of "significant symbols." See George H. Mead, *Mind, Self and Society* (Chicago: University of Chicago Press, 1934).

28. See Chapter 1 for a full description of the various types of social action. Here we simplify.

29. See Howard Becker and Harry Elmer Barnes, *Social Thought from Lore to Science*, hereafter also cited as *STFLTS* (2d ed., Washington, D.C.: Harren, 1952), Chap. 1 by Becker.

30. Becker and Barnes, *op. cit.*, trace some phases of this general increase of secularization. It should be noted, however, that *new* sacred types may emerge when least expected. Witness Nazi Germany: it had many features of a highly sacred society.

31. Howard Becker sums up the case against this methodology in "Interpretative Sociology and Constructive Typology," *Twentieth Century Sociology*, edited by Georges Gurvitch and Wilbert E. Moore (New York: The Philosophical Library, 1945), p. 93, footnote 39.

32. The ideas of affiliational dominance and kinship are sometimes implied by the use of the terms *matrilineal* and *patrilineal* for the principle of descent, and of *patriarchate* and *matriarchate* for the systems that result. Furthermore, "clan" is often used without qualifying adjectives, and may mean

simply the "relatives." These usages should not confuse the problem of tracing descent in the consanguinal family with the problem of affiliational dominance.

33. For an extended classification of kinship systems, see John Lewis Gillin and John Philip Gillin, *An Introduction to Sociology* (New York: The Macmillan Co., 1942), Chap. 9, pp. 205–245.

34. See Chapter 1 for the extended description of the approach and the bibliography thereto appended for further explanatory studies.

35. See Abram Kardiner, *The Psychological Frontiers of Society* (New York: Columbia University Press, 1945).

36. Under such circumstances there may be a gradual intensification of the problems of a community that paves the way for the sudden dramatic rise of a charismatic leader—that is, not all crisis situations are a result of pressures from outside the community. Change, when it occurs, may be revolutionary, followed by the slow entrenchment of the followers in the categories established by the leader. See Chapter 1.

37. See Gladwyn Murray Childs, *Umbundu Kinship and Character* (London: Oxford University Press, 1949).

38. *Ibid.*, pp. 42–45.

39. Hortense Powdermaker, *Life in Lesu* (New York: W. W. Norton, 1933).

40. An excellent example of matrilocal residence among American Indians is afforded by the pueblo-dwelling Zuñi.

41. Bronislaw Malinowski, *The Sexual Life of Savages* (New York: Halcyon House, 1929).

42. *Ibid.*, p. 35.

43. *Ibid.*, p. 146.

44. Ruth Bunzel, "Economic Organization of Primitive Peoples," in Franz Boas, *General Anthropology* (Boston: D. C. Heath & Co., 1938), p. 335. For a general survey of Eskimo economics, see Alexander Goldenweiser, *Anthro-*

pology (New York: Crofts, 1937), Chaps. 6, 7.

45. Bunzel, *op. cit.*, p. 340.

46. Goldenweiser, *op. cit.*, p. 74.

47. *Ibid.*, p. 376.

48. But see Peter Freuchen, *Eskimo* (New York: Horace Liveright, 1931).

49. Goldenweiser, *op. cit.*, p. 95.

50. Reichard, in Boas, *op. cit.*, pp. 436, 481.

51. See Paul-Emile Victor, *My Eskimo Life*, trans. by Jocelyn Godefrai (New York: Simon & Schuster, 1939), for a day-to-day account of the life of the Greenland Eskimo.

52. Cora Du Bois, *The People of Alor* (Minneapolis: University of Minnesota Press, 1944).

53. For an almost complete antithesis, see Reo Franklin Fortune, *The Social Organization of Dobu* (London: George Routledge & Sons, Ltd., 1931).

54. In Dobu there is said to be such suspicion of male descent that even the children may not be buried in the same cemetery as the father.

55. In general, female ownership of land and dominance of maternal relationships are correlated. This is in process of breaking down the importance of paternal lines and male houses.

56. "Financial" success is not reckoned in terms of subsistence, but with respect to ceremonial exchanges that mediate other ceremonies.

57. Abram Kardiner, *op. cit.*

58. This picture is, of course, oversimplified, but there is much "white-collar" crime which matches it closely.

59. Conrad M. Arensberg, *The Irish Countryman* (London: The Macmillan Co., 1937).

60. Becker and Barnes, *STFLTS*, p. 1170 (by Becker). The discussion by Becker, it should be noted, and the general discussion in this section are based upon pre-Pearl Harbor conditions in Japan. Under American Military Government, large-scale changes took place in post-war Japan, and there is much evidence to show that these changes are regarded as more than temporary.

61. See Inazo Nitobe, *Bushido, The Soul of Japan* (New York: Putnam, 1905).

62. For a general cultural background of contemporary Japan, see G. B. Samson, *Japan: A Short Cultural History* (New York: Century Company, 1932).

63. See Frieda Hauswirth, *Purdah: The Status of Indian Women* (New York: The Vanguard Press, 1932), Chaps. 9–15.

64. S. V. Ketkar, *The History of Caste in India* (Ithaca: Taylor & Carpenter, 1909), Chap. 5.

65. Pandharianath H. Valavalkar, *Hindu Social Institutions* (London: Longmans, Green, 1939), p. 298. The word *Aryan,* is should be noted, derives from the word meaning *honorable.*

66. Ketkar, *op. cit.*, p. 99.

67. *Ibid.*, p. 5.

68. Hauswirth, *op. cit.*, p. 52.

69. *Ibid.*, Chap. 7.

70. *Ibid.*, p. 28.

71. *Ibid.*, Chap. 7.

72. *Ibid.*, Chaps. 9–15.

73. Samuel Guy Inman, *Latin America* (New York: Willett, Clark, 1937), p. 158.

74. *Ibid.*, p. 159.

75. *Ibid.*, p. 160. This is well summarized by Freyre: "But predominant over all these antagonisms was the more general and the deeper one: that between master and slave." Gilberto Freyre, *The Master and the Slave,* trans. by Samuel Putnam (New York: Knopf, 1946), pp. 79–80.

76. Denis de Rougemont, *Love in the Western World*, trans. by Montgomery Belgion (New York: Harcourt, Brace, 1940), p. 25.

77. *Ibid.*, pp. 4–5.

78. For the development of concubinage in Brazil, see Freyre, *op. cit.*, p. 85.

79. De Rougemont, *op. cit.*, p. 299. For a more detailed account of the evolution of romantic love, see Chap. 4, pp. 117–120.

80. Freyre, *op. cit.*, pp. xxv, 107.

81. *Ibid.*, p. 206.

82. Robert Redfield, *The Folk Cul-*

ture of Yucatan (Chicago: University of Chicago Press, 1941).

83. *Ibid.*, p. 6.
84. *Ibid.*
85. Kenneth Scott Latourette, *The Chinese: Their History and Culture* (New York: The Macmillan Co., 1946), p. 685.
86. *Ibid.*, pp. 685–686.
87. *Ibid.*, p. 687.
88. See Latourette, *op. cit.*, pp. 607–646. For a general sociological analysis, see Becker and Barnes, *STFLTS*, Chap. 2.
89. Latourette, *op. cit.*, pp. 648–649.
90. *Ibid.*, p. 669.
91. *Ibid.*, p. 687.
92. Florence Ayscough, *Chinese Women* (Boston: Houghton Mifflin, 1937), p. 35.
93. *Ibid.*, pp. 92–99.
94. Latourette, *op. cit.*, pp. 678–680.
95. *Ibid.*, p. 666.
96. *Ibid.*, p. 685.
97. Both Becker and Redfield were influenced in the use of the terms *sacred* and *secular* by the lectures of Robert E. Park at the University of Chicago. See footnote 3 of Howard Becker and Robert C. Myers, "Sacred and Secular Aspects of Human Sociation," in *Sociometry*, 5 (August, 1942). "To the best of our knowledge, the first sociological use of the terms *sacred* and *secular* was made by Robert E. Park in his lectures at the University of Chicago. Our use of these words is an adaption rather than a strict 'Parkian' interpretation, and stems from Howard Becker, *Ionia and Athens: Studies in Secularization* (unpublished doctoral dissertation supervised by Park, University of Chicago, 1930), and 'Processes of Secularization,' *Sociological Review* (British), 24 (April, July, and October, 1932), pp. 138–154, 266–286."

The terms *sacred* and *secular* as used by Park were in turn based upon the concepts *Gemeinschaft* and *Gesellschaft* of Ferdinand Tönnies. As used by Becker, the terms *sacred* and *secular* are considerably expanded beyond their original employment by Park. For a fuller description, see Becker and Myers, *op. cit.*, and Chapter 1 of this book.

Redfield uses the terms *folk society* and *urban society* instead of *sacred* and *secular*. It should be noted, moreover, that Redfield's terms *folk* and *urban* are far more restricted in application than the terms *sacred* and *secular* as used by Becker and could not be employed, for example, for the analysis of trends in contemporary civilization. By contrast, see Section V of Becker and Myers, *op. cit.*, for the analysis of the forces at work in prewar Germany, or Becker, *German Youth: Bond or Free* (New York: The Grove Press, 1946).

98. Abram Kardiner, *op. cit.*

Chapter 5

1. James Bryce, *American Commonwealth* (London: The Macmillan Co., 1888).
2. A. F. Weber, *The Growth of Cities in the Nineteenth Century* (New York: The Macmillan Co., 1899).
3. *U.S. Eleventh Census*, I, 698–701.
4. Kate H. Claghorn, "The Foreign Immigrant in New York City," *U.S. Industrial Comm., Reports*, XV, 465–492, and J. A. Riis, *How the Other Half Lives* (New York: Scribner's, 1890). For a general summary of the movement, see Arthur M. Schlesinger, *The Rise of the City* (New York: The Macmillan Co., 1933), pp. 53–57.
5. G. W. Tillson, *Street Pavements and Paving Materials* (New York: The Macmillan Co., 1900).
6. J. A. Fairlie, *Municipal Administration* (New York: The Macmillan Co., 1901).
7. H. G. Tyrrell, *History of Bridge Engineering* (Chicago: The Author, 1911).
8. Allan Nevins, *The Emergence of Modern America* (The New York Times, May 24, 1883), p. 90.

9. H. H. Vreeland, "The Street Railways of America," in C. M. Depew, *One Hundred Years of America* (New York: D. O. Haynes, 1895).

10. H. N. Casson, *The History of the Telephone* (Chicago: A. C. McClurg, 1910).

11. J. B. McClure, ed., *Edison and His Inventions* (Chicago, 1879), and Henry Schroeder, *History of the Electric Light* (Smithsonian Miscel. Colls.) LXXVI, no. 2.

12. *World Almanac* for 1929.

13. The literature on the origin and location of towns includes Roscher's *System der Volkswirtschaft*, Vol. III (Stuttgart: J. G. Cotta, 1895), and *Die Nationalökonomie des Handels und Gewerbefleisses* (Stuttgart: J. G. Cotta, 1899). His theory of the location of cities is developed in "Ueber die geographische Lage der grossen Städte" in *Ansichten der Volkswirtschaft, op. cit.*, Vol. I. Also see E. Sax, *Die Verkehrsmittel in der Volkswirtschaft* (Wien: A. Hölder, 1878), and A. de Foville, *De la Transformation des Moyens de Transport et ses Consequences economiques et sociales* (Paris: Guillaumin, 1880). Cooley's *The Theory of Transportation* (Baltimore: Publications of the American Economic Association, 1894).

14. Adna Ferrin Weber, *The Growth of Cities in the Nineteenth Century* (New York: The Macmillan Co., 1899).

15. Georg Hansen's *Die Drei Bevölkerungsstufen* (Munich: J. Lindauer, 1889).

16. Weber, *op. cit.*, p. 370.

17. *Ibid.*, p. 407.

18. Josiah Strong, *The Twentieth Century City* (New York: Baker & Taylor, 1898).

19. *Ibid.*, p. 53.

20. *Ibid.*, p. 61.

21. *Ibid.*, p. 67.

22. *Ibid.*, p. 78.

23. For another expression of the moral reaction to the city, see Jane Addams, *The Spirit of Youth* (New York: The Macmillan Co., 1909).

24. Robert E. Park, Ernest W. Burgess, Roderick D. McKenzie, *The City* (Chicago: The University of Chicago Press, 1925).

25. Robert E. Park, *The City*, "Suggestions for the Investigation of Human Behavior in the Urban Environment," pp. 1–46.

26. *Ibid.*, p. 4.

27. *Ibid.*, p. 40.

28. There were complex ties between these various students. Not a little of the original stimulus for the ecological point of view seems to have come from the study of C. J. Galpin, "The Social Anatomy of an Agricultural Community" Wisconsin Agricultural Experiment Station, Research Bulletin No. 3 (1915). Galpin collected data from families in a county showing where they banked, traded, sent their children to school. He prepared maps showing their spatial locations and the distribution of their activities. This was important for demonstrating that the actual units of living were often quite at variance with the political units. Also, it should be noted, however simple minded this procedure, a sociologist was actually in the field gathering the data he needed himself. This fitted into the plans of R. E. Park who promoted urban research very actively between 1915 and 1921. In 1918 Park borrowed some concepts from the plant ecologist and turned them into a unified explanation. This was soon followed by the first-hand study of various areas of the city —which were often thought of as "habitats" by analogy from plant ecology. R. D. McKenzie published a study of "The Neighborhood," *American Journal of Sociology*, Vol. XXVII (September, 1921; November, 1921; March, 1922; May, 1922). Columbus, Ohio, was studied in terms of the distribution of dependency, delinquency, nationality, and a number of other indices. The concept of "cultural areas" was utilized and maps were employed for delimiting urban areas. Other studies included Nels Anderson's *The Hobo*

(Chicago: University of Chicago Press, 1923). The idea of an over-all spatial organization of the city was systematized by Burgess in "The Growth of the City" reprinted in *The City*, pp. 47–62.

29. Park, *op. cit.*, p. 50.

30. *Ibid.*, p. 62.

31. R. D. McKenzie, "The Ecological Approach to the Study of the Human Community," *American Journal of Sociology*, XXX, 287–301, and "The Scope of Human Ecology," Pub. A.S.S., XX, 141–154, and in E. W. Burgess, *Urban Community*, pp. 167–182. See also *The City, op. cit.*, pp. 63–79.

32. *The City*, p. 71.

33. *Ibid.*, p. 74.

34. Nels Anderson and Eduard C. Lindeman, *Urban Sociology* (New York: Alfred A. Knopf, 1928).

35. Maurice R. Davie, *Problems of City Life* (New York: John Wiley, 1932), and Niles Carpenter, *The Sociology of City Life* (New York: Longmans, Green, 1932).

36. Davie, *op. cit.*, pp. 4–5. The reference is to William Bennett Munroe, *The Government of American Cities* (New York: The Macmillan Co., 1926), pp. 13–16. It should be noted, however, that Munroe's statement is theoretically superior to that of the Chicago school.

37. Rose Hum Lee, *The City* (New York: Lippincott, 1955), and Egon Ernest Bergel, *Urban Sociology* (New York: McGraw-Hill, 1955).

38. Bergel, *op. cit.*, p. 8.

39. Lee, *op. cit.*, p. 7.

40. Louis Wirth, "Urbanism as a Way of Life," *American Journal of Sociology*, XLIV (1938), p. 8.

41. Georg Simmel, *The Sociology of Georg Simmel*, trans. by Kurt Wolff (Glencoe, Ill.: The Free Press, 1950), pp. 409–424.

42. Published in Dresden, 1903.

43. *The City*, p. 1.

44. Oswald Spengler, *The Decline of the West*, trans. by Charles Francis Atkinson (New York: Alfred A. Knopf, 1928), 2 vols.

45. The fullest treatment of *The City* by Spengler is contained in Volume II of *The Decline of the West*, Chapters 4–6, pp. 85–186.

46. Louis Wirth, "Urbanism as a Way of Life," *American Journal of Sociology*, XLIV (July, 1938), 1–24.

47. *Ibid.*, p. 4.

48. Wirth got up the annotated bibliography on the city for the Park, Burgess, McKenzie volume. It is noteworthy that he included Simmel's *Die Grosstädte und das Geistesleben.* He observed that it was "the most important single article on the city from the sociological standpoint." *The City, op. cit.*, p. 219.

49. Josiah Strong, *The Twentieth Century City, op. cit.*, p. 86.

50. Fustel de Coulanges, *The Ancient City* (New York: Doubleday Anchor Books, 1956), pp. 126–127.

51. G. Glotz, *The Greek City*, trans. by N. Mallinson (New York: Alfred A. Knopf, 1930), pp. 4–5.

52. Henry Sumner Maine, *Ancient Law* (London: John Murray, 1894).

53. *Ibid.*, p. 170.

54. Frederick William Maitland, *Township and Borough* (Cambridge: Cambridge University Press, 1898), p. 18.

55. *Ibid.*, p. 24.

56. Henri Pirenne, *Medieval Cities*, trans. by Frank D. Halsey (Princeton: University Press, 1946).

57. *Ibid.*, p. 76.

58. *Ibid.*, p. 102.

59. Delos F. Wilcox, *The American City: A Problem in Democracy* (New York: The Macmillan Co., 1904).

60. *Ibid.*, p. 8.

61. *Ibid.*, p. 9.

62. *Ibid.*, p. 10.

63. *Ibid.*, p. 14.

64. *Ibid.*, p. 15.

65. *Ibid.*, p. 21.

66. *Ibid.*, p. 28.

67. *Ibid.*, p. 29.

68. William Bennett Munroe, *The*

Government of American Cities (New York: The Macmillan Co., 1926).

69. *Ibid.,* p. 13.

INTRODUCTION TO PART FOUR

1. Here and in the discussion following where anthropologist-psychiatrists are discussed, reference is to the special clique that took up the task of explaining national character and not to all anthropologists nor to all psychiatrists. This combination actually represents a minority of the individuals from both fields. In the interpretations of some other members of the same disciplines they are a cult of faddists and not at all representative of either anthropology or psychiatry as a whole. All observations in the following passages concern only this special group of individuals.

2. These arguments are presented as if the studies were made by teams of anthropologists and psychiatrists. There were some, but most of the time the two roles were brought together by single individuals. And in the given case the anthropologist took over the theory of the psychiatrist or a given psychiatrist had recourse to the typical data of the ethnologist as content for his explanations. The argument here is constructed as if one dealt with teams because of its greater analytical clarity.

Chapter 6

1. For a full discussion see Rene Leibowitz, *Schoenberg and His School* (New York: The Philosophical Library, 1949).

2. See Hanna Priebach Closs, "German Painting," in Jethro Bithell, *Germany* (London: Methuen, 1932) for the aesthetic details of these developments. Here concern is with the characterological tendencies they embody.

3. Oscar A. Schmitz, *Die Weltanschaung der Halbgebildeten* (Munich, 1914).

4. Baron de Montesquieu, *The Spirit of the Laws,* trans. by Thomas Nugent (New York: Hafner, 1949), pp. 305–306.

5. Carl Becker, *The Heavenly City* (New Haven: Yale University Press, 1932), p. 47.

6. André Siegfried, *The Character of Peoples,* trans. by Edward Fitzgerald (London: Jonathan Cape, 1952), pp. 79 ff. Published in America as *Nations Have Souls* (New York: G. P. Putnam Sons, 1952).

7. See the sensitive discussion by Salvador de Madariaga, *Englishmen, Frenchmen, Spaniards* (London: Oxford University Press, 1928), p. 14 ff.

8. N. Cardus, *Cricket* (New York: Longmans, Green, 1930), p. 5.

9. G. B. Shaw, *Man and Superman* (New York: Brentano's, 1914), p. 2.

10. Siegfried, *op. cit.,* p. 80.

11. Michael Demiashkevich, *The National Mind* (New York: The American Book Co., 1938).

12. Eyre Crowe, *The Government of Oxford* (New York: Oxford University Press, 1931), p. 63.

13. Siegfried, *op. cit.,* p. 87.

14. A. Maurois, *Aspects of Biography* (New York: D. Appleton, 1929) and H. A. Vachell, *Arising Out of That* (London: Hodder and Stoughton, 1935).

15. The literature on this subject, like the previous, is enormous. Typical studies may be found in Michael Demiashkevich, *op. cit.,* pp. 181–336; Salvador de Madariaga, *op. cit.,* pp. 14 ff.; and André Siegfried, *op. cit.,* pp. 45–70.

16. Paul Morand, *Hiver Caraibe,* quoted by Siegfried, *op. cit.,* p. 64.

17. Quoted by Demiashkevich, *op. cit.,* p. 184.

18. J. A. Spender, *The Public Life* (New York: Frederick A. Stokes, 1925), Vol. I, p. 320.

19. H. Taine, *Les Origines de la*

France Contemporaine (Paris: Hachette, 1876).

20. J. S. Mill, *Autobiography* (New York: Oxford University Press, 1924).

21. N. S. Wilson, "The Literary Cafés of Paris," *The Fortnightly* (London: 1936).

22. Quoted by C. Bougle and P. Castinel, *Qu'est-ce que L'esprit Français?* (Paris: Librairie Marcel Rivière, 1930), pp. 110 ff.

23. A. Lawrence Lowell, *The Governments of France, Italy, and Germany* (Cambridge: Harvard University Press, 1914), pp. 81 ff.

24. For characteristic treatments of Italian national character, see Siegfried, *op. cit.*, pp. 29–44; Count Carlo Sforza, *Italy and Italians* (London: Frederick Muller, 1948), Lenardo Olschki, *The Genius of Italy* (New York: Oxford University Press, 1949).

25. Typical recent explanations of Russian national character are found in Nicholas Berdyaev, *The Russian Idea* (London: Geoffrey Bles, 1947); Dinko Tomasic, *The Impact of Russian Culture on Soviet Communism* (Glencoe, Ill.: The Free Press, 1953); Stuart Ramsay Tompkins, *The Russian Mind* (Norman: University of Oklahoma Press, 1953).

26. Typical studies of German national character appear in Demiashkevich, *op. cit.*, pp. 337–498; J. Ellis Barker, *The Foundations of Germany* (London: John Murray, 1918); Willi Helpach, *Der Deutsche Charakter* (Bonn: Athenäum, 1954); Emil Ludwig, *The Germans*, trans. by Heinz and Ruth Norden (Boston: Little, Brown & Co., 1941).

27. Friedrich Nietzsche, *Beyond Good and Evil*, in *The Philosophy of Nietzsche* (New York: Modern Library, 1954), p. 553.

Chapter 7

1. Friedrich Nietzsche, *Beyond Good and Evil*, in *The Philosophy of Nietzsche* (New York: Modern Library, 1954), p. 555.

2. William James, *The Letters of Wiliam James*, edited by his son Henry James (Boston: The Atlantic Monthly Press, 1920), Vol. I, p. 263.

3. On the role of the city and country in German character, see C. F. C. Hawkes, *The Prehistoric Foundations of Europe* (London: Methuen, 1940); C. Taeuber, *Migration to and from German Cities* (Rome: Instituto poligrafico dello stato, 1932); Kuntz, Cuba, Theissig, *Die Deutsche Gemeindeordung* (Leipzig: Brietkopf und Harte, 1891); Alexander Gershenkron, *Bread and Democracy in Germany* (Berkeley: The University of California Press, 1943); John Bradshaw Holt, *German Agricultural Policy* (Chapel Hill: University of North Carolina Press, 1936); Lothar Meyer, *Die Deutschen Landwirtschaft wärend der Inflation* (Tübingen: Mohr, 1924); Sarah Rebecca Tirrell, *German Agrarian Politics after Bismarck's Fall* (New York: Columbia University Press, 1951).

4. Henri Pirenne, *Medieval Cities*, trans. by Frank D. Halsey (Princeton: Princeton University Press, 1940), and Max Weber, *The City*, trans. by Don Martindale and Gertrud Neuwirth (Glencoe, Ill.: The Free Press, 1958).

5. Emil Ludwig, *The Germans*, trans. by Heinz and Ruth Norden (Boston: Little, Brown, 1941), p. 41.

6. Gerschenkron, *op. cit.*, p. 17.

7. Useful materials on German social stratification are to be found in Robert H. Lowie's *Toward Understanding Germany* (Chicago: The University of Chicago Press, 1954) and *The German People* (New York: Rinehart, 1954); Paul Kosok, *Modern Germany* (Chicago: The University of Chicago Press, 1933); S. Baring-Gould, *Germany* (New York: G. P. Putnam, 1882); Ernst Kohn-Bramsted, *Aristocracy and the Middle Classes in Germany* (London: P. S. King, 1937); Georg Knapp, *Die Bauernbefreiung und der Ursprung der Landarbeiter* (Leipzig: Duncker and Humbolt, 1887); Heinrich Gerdes, *Geschichte des deutschen Bauernstandes* (Leipzig:

Teubner, 1910); Adolf Bartels, *Der Bauer in der deutschen Vergangenheit* (Leipzig: E. Diederichs, 1900).

8. Cleveland Amory, *The Proper Bostonians* (New York: E. P. Dutton, 1957), p. 295.

9. C. Wright Mills, *White Collar* (New York: Oxford University Press, 1953).

10. William H. Whyte, Jr., *The Organization Man* (New York: Doubleday Anchor Books, 1957).

11. C. Beard, *The Reformation in Relation to Modern Thought* (London: Constable, 1927); Dahlmann-Waitz, *Quellenkunde der deutschen Geschichte* (Leipzig: K. F. Koehler, 1912); Martin Rade, *Die Welt des freien Protestantismus* (Stuttgart: E. Klotz, 1952).

12. Clive Day, *Economic Development in Modern Europe* (New York: The Macmillan Co., 1933); Robert Brady, *Rationalization Movement in German Industry* (Berkeley: University of California Press, 1933); Ludwig Pohle, *Die Entwicklung des deutschen Wirtschaftslebens* (Leipzig: G. B. Teubner, 1938); G. Schmoller, *Grundriss der allgemeinen volkswirtschaftslehre* (Leipzig: Duncker and Humbolt, 1900); Werner Sombart, *Die Deutsche Volkswirtschaft* (Berlin: G. Bond, 1927); Thorstein Veblen, *Imperial Germany and the Industrial Revolution* (New York: Viking, 1954).

13. The present review of the factors in German national character important for the nature and shape of German industrialization primarily follows the formulations of Day, Sombart, and Veblen.

Chapter 8

1. A short version of this essay was prepared for the Conference on Goals and Values in Agricultural Policy, Iowa State University, Ames, Iowa, June 27, 28, and 29, 1960. This short version was published in *Goals and Values in Agricultural Policy,*

edited by Earl O. Heady and Lee G. Burchinal (Ames, Iowa: Iowa State University Press, 1961), pp. 66–74.

2. In many discussions "values" are defined in a way which would make them equivalent to "goals" as used above. The term "norms" is often used in the same sense as our term "values."

3. Dixon Wecter, *The Saga of American Society* (New York: Charles Scribner's Sons, 1937), p. 28. For an idealized description of the social life of the Old South prior to the Civil War, see Thomas Nelson Page, *The Old South* (New York: Charles Scribner's Sons, 1892).

4. Max Weber, *The City*, trans. by Don Martindale and Gertrud Neuwirth (Glencoe, Ill.: The Free Press, 1958).

5. A relatively unusual plea for the development of a genuine American cosmopolitanism has been made by William H. Whyte, Jr., in the introduction and first chapter of *The Exploding Metropolis* by the editors of *Fortune* (New York: Doubleday Anchor Books, 1958), pp. vii–31.

6. W. I. Thomas and Florian Znaniecki, *The Polish Peasant in Europe and America* (Chicago: University of Chicago Press, 1918).

7. Margaret Mead, *And Keep Your Powder Dry* (New York: William Morrow, 1942), p. 37.

8. *Ibid.*, p. 52.

9. Oswald Spengler, *The Decline of the West,* trans. by Francis Atkinson (New York: Alfred A. Knopf, 1928), Vol. II, pp. 85 ff.

10. Georg Simmel, *The Sociology of Georg Simmel,* trans. by Kurt H. Wolff (Glencoe, Ill.: The Free Press, 1950), "The Metropolis and Mental Life," pp. 409 ff.

11. This, to be sure, is not always voluntary. The conflict between two communities may be utilized by a third with more power than either to improve its own situation the easy way. It may offer its services as moderator as a part of a long-range program of taking over both.

12. Unfortunately, since the late

1930's, for historical and sociological reasons, American sociologists have tended to study the problems of some sub-communities in endless detail, while the growth of the national community has generally been ignored. There are, to be sure, notable exceptions. The great popularity of the work of C. Wright Mills, David Riesman, and William H. Whyte, Jr. is in considerable measure due to the fact that they have brought sociological attention to bear upon major phenomena in the national community. Economists, political scientists, and historians have displayed somewhat less of the kind of myopia which cannot see the forest for the trees. Many of the political sociologists who have been emerging since World War II are also beginning to change this situation. Hans Speier, Reinhard Bendix, and Seymour Lipset currently seem to be recovering perspective on the broad picture and restoring continuities with the earlier work of Thomas and Znaniecki, Sorokin, Chapin, and MacIver.

13. The *farmer* is rarely a distinctive social type to the same degree as the *peasant*, but an occupational category.

14. Don Martindale, *American Social Structure* (New York: Appleton-Century-Crofts, 1960), p. 3.

15. *Ibid.*, p. ix. For comparative purposes, see Bradford Smith, *Why We Behave Like Americans* (Philadelphia: J. B. Lippincott, 1957), pp. 77–98.

16. Frederick L. Paxson, *History of the American Frontier* (Boston: Houghton Mifflin Co., 1924), pp. 114–115.

17. Alexis de Tocqueville, *Democracy in America*, trans. by Henry Reeve (New York: Oxford University Press, 1947), p. 394.

18. Thomas Nelson Page, *The Old South, op. cit.*, p. 46.

19. See Van Wyck Brooks, *The Flowering of New England* (New York: E. P. Dutton, 1957).

20. Alfred Kazin, *On Native Grounds* (New York: Doubleday & Co., 1956), p. viii.

21. Henry Bramford Parkes, *The American Experience* (New York: Alfred A. Knopf, 1947), p. 271.

22. Kazin, *op. cit.*, p. ix.

23. André Siegfried, *America Comes of Age*, trans. by H. H. Hemming and Doris Hemming (New York: Harcourt, Brace, 1927), p. 30.

24. Josiah Strong, *Our Country: Its Possible Future and Its Present Crisis* (New York: Baker & Taylor, 1885).

25. *Ibid.*, p. ii.

26. *Ibid.*, p. 43.

27. *Ibid.*, p. 132.

28. *Ibid.*, pp. 136–137.

29. Josiah Strong, *The Challenge of the City* (New York: Young People's Missionary Movement, 1907), pp. 41 ff.

30. Lincoln Steffens, *The Shame of the Cities* (New York: Sagamore Press, 1957), p. 3.

31. Seymour Freedgood, "New Strength in City Hall," in *The Exploding Metropolis*, by the editors of *Fortune* (New York: Doubleday Anchor Books, 1958), p. 65.

32. *Ibid.*, p. 67.

33. *Ibid.*, p. 1.

34. *Ibid.*, p. x.

35. *Ibid.*, pp. xi–xii.

36. *Ibid.*, p. 2.

37. U.S. Census Bureau, *Historical Statistics of the U.S., 1789–1945*, pp. 179, 234.

38. Simon N. Whitney, *Anti-Trust Policies* (New York: The Twentieth Century Fund, 1958), p. 4.

39. *Ibid.*, p. 6.

40. *Ibid.*, p. 27.

41. *Ibid.*, p. 95.

42. *Ibid.*, p. 188.

43. *Ibid.*, p. 253.

44. *Ibid.*, p. 330.

45. *Ibid.*, p. 385.

46. *Ibid.*, p. 29.

47. *Ibid.*, p. 95.

48. *Ibid.*, p. 190.

49. *Ibid.*, p. 254.

50. *Ibid.*, p. 331.

51. *Ibid.*, p. 386.

52. *Ibid.*, Vol. I, p. 432.

53. *Ibid.*, Vol. III, p. 403.

54. *Ibid.*, Vol. I, p. 9.

55. Some extremely rich material on aspects of the continuing evolution of American business, in ways that have gone unnoticed because of the prevalence of modes of thought deriving from what has been called above the first national synthesis, has been developed by John Kenneth Galbraith, *The Affluent Society* (Boston: Houghton Mifflin, 1958), and Adolf A. Berle, Jr., *Power Without Property* (New York: Harcourt, Brace, 1959).

56. Galbraith, *op. cit.*, p. 9.

57. *Ibid.*, p. 261.

58. *Ibid.*, pp. 267, 268.

59. Berle, *op. cit.*, p. 11.

60. *Ibid.*, p. 15.

61. Galbraith, *op. cit.*, p. 13.

INTRODUCTION TO PART FIVE

1. For a sketch of the Social Behaviorist theory of Civilization, see Don Martindale, *Social Life and Cultural Change* (Princeton, New Jersey: D. Van Nostrand, 1962), pp. 49 ff.

Chapter 10

1. First published by Drei Masken Verlag (Munich, 1921); republished as an appendix to Volume II of Weber's *Wirtschaft und Gesellschaft* (Tübingen: J. C. B. Mohr, 1921); reprinted in the edition of 1924, and in that of 1956. The 1956 edition has textual corrections by Johnnes Winckelmann.

2. Marianne Weber, *Max Weber: Ein Lebensbild* (Tübingen: J. C. B. Mohr, 1925); for an excellent intellectual biography, see H. H. Gerth and C. Wright Mills, *From Max Weber: Essays in Sociology* (New York: Oxford University Press, 1946).

3. Max Weber, *The Protestant Ethic and Spirit of Capitalism*, trans. by Talcott Parsons (New York: Charles Scribner's Sons, 1930).

4. A bibliography of Weber's writings is contained in Marianne Weber's *Max Weber: Ein Lebensbild, op. cit.*

5. The most complete review of his basic concepts appears in Part I of Max Weber's *Wirtschaft und Gesellschaft,* 4th ed. (Tübingen, 1956), pp. 1–30. This has been translated by A. M. Henderson and Talcott Parsons in *Max Weber: The Theory of Social and Economic Organization* (New York: Oxford University Press, 1947).

6. This type of sociology has been called "social behaviorism." There are other kinds of sociological theory that violently reject this, asserting it to be a kind of social atomism. Contemporary sociological functionalism, for example, assumes that social life is found only in systems.

7. The famous typology of action erected on this foundation described these various kinds of actions as *zweckrational, wertrational,* affective, and tradition. See *The Theory of Social and Economic Organization, op. cit.*, p. 114.

8. See *ibid.*, p. 118.

9. See Weber's formulation in "Science as a Vocation," in Gerth and Mills, *op. cit.*, pp. 139 ff.

10. See the introduction to *The Protestant Ethic* (Parsons' translation, pp. 13 ff.) for a brief summary of Weber's views on these matters.

11. Paul H. Hindemith, *The Craft of Musical Composition* (New York: Associated Musical Publishers, 1945), p. 164.

12. See E. Clements, *Introduction to the Study of Indian Music* (London: Longmans, Green, 1913), pp. 11–14.

13. Henry George Farmer, *A History of Arabian Music* (London: Luzac, 1929), pp. 205 f.

14. Clements, *op. cit.*, Appendix E, pp. 100–101.

15. Carl Stumpf, *Die Anfänge der Musik* (Leipzig: J. A. Barth, 1911).

16. Curt Sachs, *The History of Musical Instruments* (New York: Norton, 1940).

17. Curt Sachs, *The Rise of Music in the Ancient World: East and West* (New York: Norton, 1943).

18. This is the literary appellation of the instrument shaped like the mortar. Its popular name is ch'ing. It is struck with a wooden hammer. When used at religious ceremonies it is placed in a kind of silken purse richly ornamented with rare fish scales.

19. Oldest form of bowed instrument known to England, dating to four hundred years before Christ. Ancestor of the violin and descendant of the Irish cruit.

Chapter 11

1. Plato, *The Republic*, trans. by B. Jowett (New York: Modern Library, n.d.), pp. 72–73.

2. *Ibid.*, p. 102.

3. *Ibid.*, p. 104.

4. *Ibid.*, p. 95.

5. *Ibid.*, pp. 99–100.

6. *Exodus* 20:4. Moffatt translation (New York: Harper & Bros., 1935).

7. Of course, social behavior includes more than human social behavior. Social behavior may be defined generally as the interbehavior of creatures of the same type, or in mutual stimulus and response to one another, whether it be dogs or men or insects. Since we are not concerned with the technical problem involved, we may accept Mead's definition: "A social act may be defined as one in which the occasion or stimulus which sets free an impulse is found in the character or conduct of a living form that belongs to the proper environment of the living form whose impulse it is." George Herbert Mead, *Mind, Self and Society* (Chicago: University of Chicago Press, 1934), p. 7.

8. When we say that they interact as men, we intend simply to exclude behavior toward another individual as a mere object, for example, jostling in a crowd, which may have reciprocal social significance. On the other hand,

social meaning may be extended to nature, as when one curses the hammer that smashes a finger. Mead states, "The physical object is an abstraction which we make from the social response to nature. We talk to nature; we address the clouds, the sea, the tree; we carry over a thinking process into nature, we are making nature rational. It acts as it is expected to act." *Ibid.*, p. 184. Weber urges: "Action is social, insofar as, by virtue of the subjective meaning attached to it by the acting individual (or individuals), it takes account of the behavior of others and is thereby orented in its course." Max Weber, *The Theory of Social and Economic Organization*, trans. by A. M. Henderson and Talcott Parsons (New York: Oxford University Press, 1947), p. 88.

9. Here we take language to mean simply an ordered system of signs, making possible mutual orientation of action. See Mead for one account.

10. Lester Ward, among others, postulated an aesthetic impulse. Ward suggests that it is traceable in the animal organizm at least as far back as the protozoa. It develops through three stages: the receptive, the imaginative, and the creative. Primitive art is conventionalized because of the incompetence and lack of imagination. Lester F. Ward, *Dynamic Sociology*, Vol. I (New York: D. Appleton & Co., 1910), pp. 431–432, 434. Thomas and Znaniecki try to account for it among their four wishes as the wish for new experience. See W. I. Thomas and Florian Znaniecki, *The Polish Peasant in Europe and America* (Boston: Richard G. Gadger, Gorham Press, 1918), introductory notes to Vols. I, III. These, of course, are merely two representative sociological attempts to account for the aesthetic experience in this fashion.

11. The experimental aesthetics of G. T. Fechner, expressed in *Vorschule der Aesthetick*, however, take a different tack. Fechner searches not for an

aesthetic impulse but treats the aesthetic as a branch of the study of pleasure and pain. By having subjects make choices of forms, by getting them to draw geometrical figures, and by measuring the proportions of things in everyday use, Fechner demonstrates that very long rectangles and perfect squares are displeasing. Most pleasing are rectangles constructed in the proportion he describes as the *golden section*.

12. If it be argued that we are equating good and preference, hence constructing a mere tautology, the answer is simply that "preference" is a less emotive term. Judgments of good occur in situations in the form of "I prefer," "I ought to prefer," and the like.

13. *Valuation*, for us, means "placing in a system of preference."

INTRODUCTION TO PART SIX

1. C. Wright Mills, *The Sociological Imagination* (New York: Harcourt, Brace, 1959), p. 149.

2. *Ibid.*, p. 150.

3. *Ibid.*, p. 185.

Chapter 12

1. Herbert Feigl, "Some Remarks on the Meaning of Scientific Explanation," in Herbert Feigl and Wilfrid Sellars (eds.), *Readings in Philosophical Analysis* (New York: Appleton-Century-Crofts, 1949), p. 512.

2. See Howard Becker, *Through Values in Social Interpretation* (Durham, N.C.: Duke University Press, 1950), pp. 281–305.

3. In the discussions of Comte and Spencer, the arguments are not developed in detail but are only outlined,

for they are intended primarily to illustrate the early form of the theory of social problems in sociology. See Auguste Comte, *The Positive Philosophy*, trans. by Harriet Martineau (3d ed.; London: J. Chapman, 1893), 2 vols., and *Système de politique positive* (Paris: Carilion-Goeury, 1851–1854), 4 vols. Also see Henri Gouhier, *La vie d'Auguste Comte* (Paris, 1931); Herbert Spencer, *The Principles of Sociology* (New York: D. Appleton, 1896), 3 vols.; *The Study of Sociology* (New York: D. Appleton, 1897), and *Man vs. the State* (New York: D. Appleton, 1908).

4. See L. F. Ward, *Applied Sociology* (Boston: Ginn, 1906).

5. W. G. Sumner, *The Forgotten Man and Other Essays*, edited by A. G. Keller (New Haven: Yale University Press, 1919). Sumner complained bitterly of the sad lot of the middle class, which was most heavily taxed and benefited least by legislative aids.

6. Ludwig Gumplowicz, *Der Rassenkampf* (Innsbruck: Wagner, 1909), and *Sociologische Essays* (Innsbruck: Wagner, 1899).

7. A. W. Small, *General Sociology* (Chicago: University of Chicago Press, 1905) was influenced not only by Gumplowicz but by Ratzenhofer, among others.

8. See Howard Becker and H. E. Barnes, *Social Thought from Lore to Science*, 2d ed. (New York: Dover, 1952), Vol. I.

9. See Emile Durkheim, *The Division of Labor in Society*, trans. by George Simpson (Glencoe, Ill.: The Free Press, 1947), and *The Rules of Sociological Method*, trans. by Sarah Solovay and J. H. Mueller (Glencoe, Ill.: The Free Press, 1950).

10. Durkheim, *The Division of Labor*, p. 368.

11. See Durkheim, *Le Suicide* (Paris: F. Alcan, 1897).

12. C. H. Cooley, *Human Nature*

and the Social Order (New York: Scribner's, 1902), *Social Organization* (New York: Scribner's, 1909), pp. 5, 7, 9–10, 23–24, 35, 342, 347, and *Social Process* (New York: Scribner's 1919), p. 106.

13. W. I. Thomas and Florian Znaniecki, *The Polish Peasant in Europe and America* (Boston: Little, Brown, 1919), Vol. 2, p. 74.

14. C. Wright Mills, "The Professional Ideology of Social Pathologists," *AJS*, 49 (September, 1943), pp. 165–180.

15. Louis Wirth, "Ideological Aspects of Social Disorganization," *ASR*, 5 (August, 1940), pp. 472–482.

16. E. M. Lemert, *Social Pathology* (New York: McGraw-Hill, 1951), Chap. 1.

17. W. F. Ogburn, *Social Change* (2d ed., New York: Viking, 1950), pp. 369 ff.

18. *Ibid.*, pp. 170, 176, 180, 186, 190–191.

19. *Ibid.*, pp. 200–201.

20. *Ibid.*, p. 257.

21. *Ibid.*, p. 283.

22. *Ibid.*, p. 287.

23. *Ibid.*, pp. 33, 290, 293, 312, 332–334.

24. Small, *General Sociology*, pp. 426, 433, 481.

25. *Ibid.*, pp. 49–491, 495, 499.

26. R. E. Park and E. W. Burgess, *Introduction to the Science of Sociology* (Chicago: University of Chicago Press, 1921).

27. R. E. Park, E. W. Burgess, and R. D. McKenzie (eds.), *The City* (Chicago: University of Chicago Press, 1925). See Park's suggestions, pp. 1–46. The stimulus for the approach is often traced to C. J. Galpin, *The Social Anatomy of an Agricultural Community* (Wisconsin Agricultural Experiment Station Bulletin 34, Madison, 1915). Between 1918 and 1920 Park was promoting the study at the University of Chicago and utilizing the concepts developed by the plant ecologists. See his "The City: Suggestions of the Investigation of Human Behavior in the City Environment," *AJS*, 27 (September and November, 1921; January, March, and May, 1922).

28. Park, Burgess, and McKenzie, *op. cit.*, p. 50.

29. *Ibid.*, p. 62.

30. C. R. Shaw, "The History and Basic Principles of the Chicago Area Project" (mimeographed report, Chicago, 1942), and Celia Stendler (Burns), *Bright Shadows in Bronzetown* (Chicago: University of Chicago Press, 1949), p. 10.

31. L. G. Brown, *Social Pathology* (New York: Crofts, 1946), p. vii.

32. *Ibid.*, pp. 358–359, 365.

33. *Ibid.*, pp. 378 ff.

34. R. E. L. Faris, *Social Disorganization* (New York: Ronald Press, 1948), pp. 4, 19.

35. A. P. Herman, *An Approach to Social Problems* (New York: Ginn, 1949), Chap. 1 and pp. 51, 57.

36. Mabel Elliott and Francis Merrill, *Social Disorganization* (New York: Harper & Bros., 1950); H. E. Barnes and I. O. Reudi, *The American Way of Life* (New York: Prentice-Hall, 1950).

37. Barnes and Reudi, *op. cit.*, p. 13.

38. W. Wallace Weaver, *Social Problems* (New York: 1951), pp. 3, 40 ff.

39. H. A. Phelps and David Henderson, *Contemporary Social Problems* (New York: Prentice-Hall, 1952); J. M. Reinhardt, Paul Meadows, and J. M. Gillette, *Social Problems and Social Policy* (New York: American Book Co., 1952), pp. 2 ff.; H. A. Bloch, *Disorganization: Personal and Social* (New York: Knopf, 1952), pp. 1–130.

40. Jessie Bernard, *American Community Behavior* (New York: Dryden, 1949), pp. 67, 609, 631.

41. J. F. Cuber and R. A. Harper, *Problems of American Society* (New York: Henry Holt, 1951), pp. 25, 27, 446.

42. Lemert, *op. cit.*, pp. 3–27.

43. *Ibid.*, pp. 22–23.

44. G. C. Homans, *The Human Group* (New York: Harcourt, Brace, 1950), pp. 336–337.

45. *Ibid.*, pp. 359–360, 362, 366.

46. R. K. Merton, *Social Theory and Social Structure* (Glencoe, Ill.: The Free Press, 1949), pp. 125, 128, 132–133.

47. *Ibid.*, pp. 27, 35, 63, 73, 79–80.

48. *Ibid.*, pp. 37, 41, 51, 139.

49. A. H. Hobbs, *Social Problems and Scientism* (Harrisburg: The Stackpole Co., 1953), pp. 17, 45.

50. *Ibid.*, pp. 22, 38, 124, 170.

INDEX